MW00461900

8-17

DEMOCRACY IN IRAN

DEMOCRACY IN IRAN

WHY IT FAILED AND HOW IT MIGHT SUCCEED

Misagh Parsa

Harvard University Press

Cambridge, Massachusetts
London, England
2016

First printing

Library of Congress Cataloging-in-Publication Data
Names: Parsa, Misagh, 1945– author.
Title: Democracy in Iran : why it failed and how it might succeed / Misagh Parsa.
Description: Cambridge : Harvard University Press, Massachusetts / 2016. |
Includes bibliographical references and index.
Identifiers: LCCN 2016017883 | ISBN 9780674545045
Subjects: LCSH: Democratization—Iran. | Democratization—Developing countries. |
Islam and politics—Iran. | Iran—Politics and government—1997–
Classification: LCC DS318.825 P38 2016 | DDC 320.955—dc23
LC record available at https://lccn.loc.gov/2016017883

*To the Iranian people who persist in the pursuit of democracy
and all those who support their struggle*

Contents

PART IV: IRRECONCILABLE CONFLICTS

Preface

This book seeks to answer a question that has challenged theories of democratization: what factors determine whether democratization is more likely to be achieved through reform or revolution? It proposes a new framework for analyzing paths to democracy by specifying the relevant structural and process-related variables based on developments in other Asian and Middle Eastern countries. The framework is based on a comparative perspective that explains why South Korea succeeded in democratizing through reform, whereas others—such as the Philippines, Indonesia, Tunisia, and Egypt—could not achieve democracy without ousting their rulers. The work applies the model to the Islamic Republic of Iran and illustrates alternative routes to democratization, with insights from other developing countries.

The Islamic Republic of Iran has certain exceptional ideological features and a unique political system but shares a number of economic and political characteristics and challenges with other developing countries, making it an intriguing case for this analysis. The book examines Iran's political conflicts and democratization struggles during the recent decades, explains the causes of their failure, and proposes the likely route to democracy. The model suggests that the Islamic Republic is highly unlikely to democratize through political reform. The theocracy rescinded the civil liberties Iranians enjoyed before the revolution. The Islamic Republic's rulers failed to fulfill the revolutionary promises and generated multiple, irreconcilable contradictions and conflicts. These conflicts undermined support for the Islamic Republic and produced active and passive resistance among Iranians against the theocracy. Thus far, the Islamic regime has been unable to suppress Iranians' struggles for democratic rights. The Islamic Republic's intransigence and endless repression are highly likely to pave the way for a disruptive, revolutionary path to democracy.

I would like to thank the Nelson A. Rockefeller Center for Public Policy at Dartmouth College for providing the grant that made this research possible. I am grateful to Carol L. Folt, former provost and interim president, at Dartmouth, for her support. My research greatly benefitted from the diligent work of my assistant, Sonia Faruqi.

I would like to thank the following people who granted interviews: Ali Afshari; Hamid Alizadeh; Akbar Atri; former president Abolhassan Bani-Sadr; theologian and former member of the parliament Hassan Yousefi Eshkevari; Rouzbeh Farahanipour; Nazila Fathi, former *New York Times* reporter; former member of the parliament Fatemeh Haghighatjoo; Esmail Jamili; theologian Mohsen Kadivar; Hadi Kahalzadeh; Houshing Keshavarz; Yaddollah Khosrow-Shahi; Abolghasem Lebaschi; Amir Hussein Mahdavi; Reza Mohajerinejad; Manouchehr Mohammad; former member of the parliament Ali-Akbar Mousavi Khoeiniha; Mansour Osanloo; former member of the parliament Ahmad Salamatian; Mohammad Shanehchi; Heshmatollah Tabarzadi; Mohammad Tahavori; Mohammad Tahmasebi-Pour; Reza Toudehrousta. I have privately thanked a number of people who did not want to be mentioned publicly.

I would also like to thank Marc Dixon, Gene Garthwaite, and Ned Lebow for reading parts of the manuscript and suggesting valuable revisions. Susan R. Nelson read the entire manuscript, and her insightful comments enriched the book. I am grateful to colleagues for discussions on various aspects of the work: Ervand Abrahamian, Reza Afshari, Hamid Akbari, Kazem Alamdari, Asef Bayat, Sohrab Behdad, Cyrus Bina, Bruce Cumings, Randy Earnest, Ali Ghaisari, Mohammad Jahan-Parvar, Akbar Mahdi, Mansour Moaddel, Behrooz Moazami, Haideh Moghissi, Majid Mohammadi, Jeffery Paige, Donald Pease, Saeed Rahnama, Ahmad Sadri, Asghar Schirazi, Kamran Talattof, and Charles Tilly. Arlen K. Parsa's intellectual curiosity continues to be an inspiration. I owe a special thanks to my editor, Andrew Kinney, for his invaluable comments and suggestions.

❧ I ❧

INTRODUCTION AND THEORY

CHAPTER ONE

Iran's Dilemma

MARGINALIZED AND EXCLUDED people across the globe rose up in the last quarter of the twentieth century to demand democratic rights. In South Korea, protesters successfully forced the government to agree to constitutional changes and, even as military rulers remained in place, gradually democratized the political system through reform. Contentious movements in the Philippines, Indonesia, Tunisia, and Egypt eventually swept power-holders from office through revolution. Iranians, too, mobilized for democracy in reaction to the 2009 presidential election. The Green Movement persisted for twenty months and shook the foundation of the Islamic Republic. It influenced the Arab Spring, according to some observers.[1] Movement leaders sought to achieve democracy through reform, but street protesters demanded fundamental changes, including forming an Iranian—not an Islamic—republic. Although the movement failed, the unresolved conflicts further polarized the Islamic state and Iranian society. More importantly, the Green Movement placed democratization on Iran's historical agenda, a topic explored in this book.

More broadly, the book attempts to elaborate the conditions under which democratization can be achieved through reform and those conditions under which it can only be attained through a disruptive, revolutionary path. Thus far no comprehensive literature has emerged to specify the complex social, economic, and political variables that influence the route that will prevail in the struggle to achieve democracy. This book will present a new theoretical framework that will allow us a better under-standing of why some developing countries follow a path of reform and others the path of revolution.

This work has two major objectives. The first is to examine Iran's polit-ical conflicts and movements spanning nearly four decades. What were the principal demands of the major collectivities, classes, and the leadership during the revolutionary struggles, 1977–1979? Why did the revolution fail to establish democratic institutions? What were the roots of conflict within the Islamic Republic, beginning with the rise of the reformists, eruption of student protests, and the rise and demise of the Green Movement? Why did the revolutionary struggles succeed in 1979, and why did the Green Movement fail in 2009? The second objective is to identify and analyze those factors that determine which route a country takes as it democratizes. What are the alternative paths to democracy? Why do some countries succeed in democratizing through reform while others require revolution to proceed? Why has democratization in Iran failed despite repeated attempts? The existing literature on democratization has not pro-vided satisfactory or complete answers to these fundamental questions. To understand these issues, we need a comprehensive analysis of the struc-tures and processes. Such an analysis has to focus on the nature of the state, economy, society, and challenging movements.

To explore these issues, the work relies on extensive previously unexam-ined primary data covering a period of more than three decades, dating back to the 1970s. The research also includes Ayatollah Khomeini's own publications, statements, and interviews. Data sources include official and semiofficial reports and documents, national newspapers, publications, as well as international media.[2] In some instances, the research uses opposi-tion websites, but extreme care was used to avoid using their political claims and to verify the veracity of their reports. The work uses national and international sources for data on economic development and distribu-tion of wealth and income. Finally, the research also relies on personal interviews with former political leaders, theologians, former students, merchants, labor leaders, and political activists.

The Green Movement's failure ignited a public debate among Iranian activists and intellectuals over which path—reform or fundamental change, including revolution—would more likely achieve democratization. Prominent reformists—such as Mohammad Reza Khatami, a former deputy in the Majles, Iran's parliament, and brother of former president Mohammad Khatami—asserted that they did not favor revolution, because they believed that it would derail the democratic process and often pro-duced results that were unfavorable to democracy. A revolution, in

Khatami's view, would fail to deliver the promised result. Instead, "after a few years or decades," Iran would still be struggling with the same issues.[3] Similarly, Ali Shakoori Raad, another former Majles deputy, insisted that reformists were not revolutionaries but, in fact, supported an Islamic republic. Shakoori Raad noted a growing divergence between the popular understanding of Islam and the official view, and argued that the Islamic Republic should reflect the people's views, votes, and preferences.[4]

Other activists advocated or predicted radical changes. Hossein Khomeini, Ayatollah Khomeini's oldest grandson, argued that the Islamic Revolution was a failure and that people no longer wanted an Islamic regime. He called for separation of religion and the state and welcomed an American invasion to free Iranians. Hadi Khamenei, former Majles deputy and brother of Iran's supreme leader, declared, "We have not been able to fulfill the goals of the revolution, because of the intervention of military and quasi-military forces, absence of political freedom and freedom of the press, and the house arrest of Mousavi, Rahnavard, and Karroubi."[5] More importantly, he was against a state religion. Without explicitly calling for the separation of the clergy from the state, he argued that it was important to implement Islamic principles and not involve the clergy in the state.

Some academics and politicians pointed to the erosion of social support for the Islamic Republic and predicted the possibility of its collapse. Mohammad Maleki, the first postrevolutionary chancellor of Tehran University, criticized government repression after the 2009 presidential election, declaring, "The spring of freedom of the Iranian people is near." Sadegh Zibakalam, the foremost Iranian political scientist at Tehran University, argued, "The Islamic order is increasingly placed in a minority situation and will experience the fate of the Soviet Union."[6] Ahmad Tavakkoli, conservative Majles deputy, stated, "The most important danger to the Islamic Republic is economic corruption that can result in the demise of the system." He added that it was very difficult to fight against systemic corruption—that is, when managers, executives, and supervisors become corrupt and engage in legalized corruption. "This is a dangerous stage that our country is facing currently," Tavakkoli declared.[7]

Iranian Struggles for Democracy and Failure of the 1979 Revolution

Iranians were among the first in Asia to agitate for democracy. The Constitutional Revolution of 1905–1911 successfully established a democratic constitution and government, but a combination of conservative

internal forces along with Anglo-Russian invasion of the country soon dismantled these achievements. Iranians briefly reestablished democratic
institutions in 1951 through a nationalist movement led by Mohammad
Mosaddegh. A coup d'état organized by the CIA and supported by royal-
ists, conservative segments of the population, and some members of the
Shiite clergy ended Iran's democratic experiment in August 1953. It also
set the stage for subsequent developments and conflicts.

In the decades following the coup d'état, Iranian society experienced
large-scale structural transformations similar to those that produced
democracy movements elsewhere. The state promoted these transformations through significant economic resources from increased oil revenues
and substantial aid from the United States. State intervention in the
economy contributed to the country's impressive economic growth and
development in the 1960s and 1970s, generating new industrial, commercial, and financial classes, and a new educated middle class with expertise
to meet the needs of a rapidly expanding economy and society.

At the same time, structural transformations and economic development
led to urbanization and the rise of an urban working class. Urbanization,
city growth, and the emergence of a workforce engaged in big manufacturing establishments enhanced Iranians' capacity to mobilize and launch
sustained collective action. Together with political repression, economic
inequalities, and corruption, these conditions contributed to contentious
politics and democratization movements in the 1970s.

The overthrow of the monarchy in 1979 constituted one of the great
revolutions in the modern world. Iran's intellectuals, students, merchants,
and working and middle classes engaged in large-scale collective action
and demanded political freedom, independence from Western powers, but
also improvement in their economic conditions and greater equity in the
distribution of wealth and income. All the major actors denounced political repression and dictatorship and the absence of political freedom.
However, no one called for restrictions on cultural freedoms—such as listening to music or drinking alcohol—or imposing dress codes on women
and limiting their rights.

Ayatollah Khomeini became the undisputed leader of the revolution by
condemning dictatorship and promising political freedom, social justice,
and a more egalitarian distribution of wealth and income. Although prior
to the revolution all opposition political organizations were banned and
repressed, Khomeini was able to issue statements against the regime and
even call for the shah's overthrow from the safety of exile. He borrowed
the basic tenets of the liberal-nationalist movement of the early 1950s:
freedom from dictatorship and imperialism, and an end to corruption and

the pillaging of the country's national resources. He also condemned the government's violation of Islamic principles and expressed concern over the clergy's declining status and the erosion of Islam. However, Khomeini never called for the establishment of an Islamic theocracy in his public statements. Instead, he consistently promised that an Islamic government would guarantee national independence and political freedom for all citizens, specifically noting that even Marxists would be free to express themselves.[8]

The Islamic Republic did not fulfill all the promises of the revolution. Despite some republican and democratic features, the new system became, in reality, a theocratic state that denied basic social and political rights to the populace. The new regime quickly elevated the clergy to key positions of power, establishing a theocracy ruled by the *velayat-e faghieh* (literally, the jurist's guardianship), a position commonly known as "supreme leader." Thus, the highest political position in the country was reserved for the clergy, which comprised only a small minority of the population. The supreme leader's immense constitutional powers and privileges violated the basic premises of democracy, despite the argument put forward by Ayatollah Khomeini that the position would prevent dictatorship. Although the new rulers retained preexisting democratic rights and the right to vote for parliament and added a popular referendum for the presidency—a new post created after the revolution—they sharply restricted the nature of these institutions and who could occupy the offices of power. They employed ideological and political criteria to restrict access to positions of power and disqualify opponents and rivals from taking office.

The regime's new rulers, the unelected clergy, together with their civilian and military allies, formed an exclusive state and rejected the promise of democracy. They expelled most of their coalition partners from the polity during successive rounds of conflict and established an exclusive Islamic state that fueled political conflicts. Faced with challenges, Ayatollah Khomeini declared that maintaining the Islamic Republic was one of the most important religious obligations and that it was necessary even to lie and spy to protect Islam and Muslims. Khomeini and the other rulers of the Islamic Republic effectively used the hostage crisis and the Iran-Iraq war to enhance national cohesion and exclude the opposition from the polity. They repressed democratic political forces and rendered them ineffective. In the process, the rulers of the Islamic Republic killed several times more people than had been slain during the revolutionary struggles. The exclusion and repression of reformists following the 2009 presidential election was only the latest example of a long process that began with the formation of the Islamic Republic.

The emergence of an exclusive polity and the continuing erosion of support for the conservative faction of the regime are exemplified in the political fortunes of the twenty-six members of the Revolutionary Council, a body that played an important role after the 1979 revolution. Four council members were assassinated by opponents of the Islamic Republic shortly after the revolution. A fifth, Ayatollah Mahmoud Taleghani, one of the most prominent leaders, boycotted council meetings and repeatedly spoke critically about political repression in the country. He expressed misgivings that the "standard and level of (Islamic) Constitution would be much inferior to the one we had 70 years ago."[9] In his last sermon, less than seven months after the revolution, Taleghani expressed concerns about the dangers of despotism promoted under the guise of religion. He died three days later under mysterious circumstances.[10] His remains were not autopsied because Ayatollah Khomeini declared that such an action would be an insult to the clergy.[11] Eight Revolutionary Council members were either forced from power (including Prime Minister Bazargan, President Bani-Sadr, and Prime Minster Mousavi), imprisoned (Minister of Interior and Minister of Justice Haj Seyyed Javadi, Habibollah Peyman, Yaddollah Sahabi, and Foreign Minister Ebrahim Yazdi), or executed (Foreign Minister Ghotbzadeh). Ten members either joined the opposition or withdrew from politics.[12]

Only three clerical members of the Revolutionary Council remained in the polity by 2009, but one of them took a critical stand against the hardliners after the postelection conflicts. Akbar Hashemi Rafsanjani, a founder, former president, and head of the Expediency Council, as well as one of the most powerful figures of the Islamic Republic, addressed a Friday prayer gathering after the 2009 presidential election to call for the rule of law, freedom of debate and dialogue about the election, release of imprisoned protesters, and reconciliation.[13] Like Ayatollah Taleghani thirty years earlier, Rafsanjani expressed concern about the people's rights and welfare. He subsequently argued that Iran faced the threat of "Islamic fascism" and was in a "dangerous crisis." His comments directly contradicted the supreme leader, who insisted that Iran was a "beacon of freedom" and was making "astonishing leaps of progress."[14] Rafsanjani also criticized the pillars of the Islamic regime. He deplored the emergence of the Revolutionary Guard (a military force founded after the revolution) as a major actor in the economic arena, with massive competitive assets.[15] Rafsanjani also faulted the clergy for supporting Mahmoud Ahmadinejad during his presidency, a period of eight years that he characterized as "rabid disease."[16] In contrast to conservatives who claimed divine support for the regime and sanctified the Islamic Republic, Rafsanjani spoke of diversion from the revolutionary path. He publicly stated, "Unfortunately, the civilization the imam wanted to create with this revolution has now experienced deviation."[17] He declared in an interview that the supreme leader had absolute power in the country and that, at a minimum, the entities under the leader's control should be supervised.[18]

Rafsanjani's power declined after he spoke out against political repression and the country's mismanagement. Some of his children were targeted by state repression and arrested during the postelection protests.[19] His daughter, Faeze Hashemi, was charged with propaganda against the Islamic Republic. She served a prison sentence of six months and was prohibited from political, cultural, and media activities for five years.[20] His son, Mehdi Hashemi, was arrested and sentenced to ten years in prison.[21] At the urging of various reformist organizations, he entered the presidential race in May 2013 but was disqualified by the Guardian Council, which vetted all candidates.[22]

Support for the conservative faction dwindled to the point that only two original Revolutionary Council members fully supported the Islamic regime and remained in the polity three decades after the formation of the Islamic Republic: Ayatollah Ali Khamenei, the supreme leader, and Ayatollah Mahdavi Kani, head of the Assembly of Experts that appoints the supreme leader.

Erosion of support for the dominant conservative faction of the Islamic regime can also be seen in the politics of those who held important elected and appointed positions in the first decade of the Islamic Republic. The vast majority of the occupants of these positions that survived either opposed conservative policies or joined the opposition during the 2009 presidential elections.[23] In fact, only a minority of the prominent elected or appointed elite sided with the conservatives. Besides Ayatollah Khamenei, only three individuals who occupied such powerful positions in the first decade of the revolution continued to support the supreme leader and the conservative faction in the aftermath of 2009 postelection protests. The three were Grand Ayatollah Lotfollah Safi Golpaygani, Mohsen Rezaie, and Ahmad Salek.[24]

A similar fate befell leading members of the Students Following the Imam's Line, a group that played a crucial role in promoting the cause of the Islamic regime in the early stages of the Islamic Republic. None of the masterminds of the American hostage crisis—Mohsen Mir-Damadi, Ebrahim Asgharzadeh, and Habibollah Bitaraf—supported the conservatives, but instead joined the reformist opposition. The two outspoken former student leaders, Mir-Damadi and Asgharzadeh, were sentenced to prison. Abbas Abdi, Saeed Hajjarian, and Mohsen Aminzadeh were also

arrested and imprisoned for joining the reformist opposition and criticizing the Islamic regime. Masoumeh Ebtekar, known as Mary, spokesperson for the students in the U.S. embassy, also joined the reformists and
became critical of the repressive policies. She lamented the situation of the
students, noting, "We have to ask why students who were called national
heroes by the imam are now suffering these circumstances."[25]

The rulers of the Islamic Republic also failed to fulfill their promises in
the economic arena. The new revolutionary elite, composed of the clergy
and their allies in the Revolutionary Guard, monopolized the commanding
heights of Iran's economy. They seized the assets of the royal family and
their wealthy allies who had fled the country during the revolution. As a
result, the new revolutionary leaders failed to fundamentally transform the
distribution of resources and improve the conditions of the downtrodden.
Moreover, a deteriorating economic situation and the concentration of
wealth and income led to the unprecedented expansion of corruption and
cronyism undermining the new rulers' capacity to fulfill their promises to
end these practices after the revolution. Corrupt practices in the Islamic
Republic adversely affected the majority of the population—particularly
the poor and the working classes, (the *mostazafin*), the very constituencies
they had promised to serve.

The Islamic regime failed to improve the economic conditions of the vast
majority of the population as Khomeini had promised. As a result, most
Iranians' standard of living either stagnated or deteriorated due to economic mismanagement, widespread unemployment, and inflation. Iran's
prerevolutionary GDP per capita was fifty-fourth in the world in 1976,
higher than that of South Korea and many Asian countries. The per capita
GDP of Iran and South Korea were roughly equal in 1980, but by 2009,
Iran's was less than a third of South Korea's (see Chapter 4). It had dropped
to ninety-fifth (UN data) even before international sanctions intensified.
Iran's real per capita GDP (in 2005 US$) peaked in 1976 at $13,329 and
plummeted to $9,644 in 1978. It was mired at $9,421 in 2009. Such was
the extent of the Islamic Republic's economic failure that even highly educated Iranians were forced to work in menial jobs. In 2015, the mayor of
Khorramabad, capital of Lorestan, announced that 23 of the 150 people
hired to sweep the streets had bachelor's or master's degrees, according to
Iran's official news agency.[26]

Once in control of the state and the economy, the revolutionary elite
introduced traditional Islamic practices, which none of the major collectivities had expected or demanded during the revolutionary struggles. As a
result, they politicized the cultural sphere and placed cultural transformation at the center of their revolutionary agenda. The Islamic regime

restricted and prohibited a number of social and cultural activities that were part of the popular culture before the revolution—ones that the government had not supervised. By doing so, the new rulers abrogated personal freedoms Iranians had enjoyed prior to 1979. For example, the state banned drinking alcohol. First- and second-time offenders were given eighty lashes; third-time offenders could be executed.[27] The Revolutionary Guard confiscated and "destroyed the rich wine cellar of the Tehran Intercontinental Hotel, pouring down the drain an estimated $1.2 million worth of wines and spirits including a stream of the proudest French champagnes, according to the Associated Press."[28]

The Islamic state prohibited other social and cultural activities. It severely curtailed gender relations and interactions, segregating men and women in public spaces such as beaches, pools, and buses.[29] Iran's revolutionary regime invoked Islamic tradition and harshly punished those involved in sexual transgressions; adultery was punishable by stoning.[30] Also, the new rulers prescribed death for homosexuality. The first stonings—of two female prostitutes and two gay men—were carried out in 1980.[31] Music and concerts were discouraged, and Ayatollah Khomeini demanded a ban on all music: "Music should not be broadcast over the radio and television. Music is something that everybody is attracted to naturally, but it takes them out of reality to a futile and lowly livelihood. Like opium, music also stupefies persons listening to it and makes their brain inactive and frivolous," he declared.[32] Except for revolutionary songs, music was banned from radio and television, and the Majles subsequently outlawed popular songs regarded as "immoral."[33] The regime also prohibited people from walking dogs in public parks, and police often confiscated the pets.[34] In 2013, the police declared that dogs could not ride in vehicles that also carried humans.[35] Earlier, in 1994, the interior minister had banned foreign satellite television to prevent the spread of Western culture. The minister ordered the police to confiscate satellite dishes within two months.[36] Several months later, the Majles instituted the ban and gave people thirty days to remove the dishes,[37] imposing a fine of about $1,700, which was raised to more than $5,000 in 2006.[38]

More importantly, the regime discouraged traditional Persian celebrations such as the fire festival, observed for thousands of years. Islamic leaders, including Ayatollah Khomeini, disapproved of and discouraged the practice because the highest religious leaders maintained that it had pagan origins and was un-Islamic.[39] Khamenei had criticized the practice over the years and called upon the people to avoid it.[40] A number of grand ayatollahs—including Fazel Lankarani, Mohammad-Taghi Behjat, Safi Golpaygani, and Makarem Shirazi—consistently disapproved of the practice and maintained that it had no religious basis.[41] The prohibitions sometimes led to arrests, and even attacks against the celebrants that resulted in casualties and loss of life. For example, paramilitary forces killed Behnoud Ramazani, a 19-year-old university student, during a fire festival in Tehran in March 2010.[42]

Most importantly, the Islamic rulers quickly relegated women to second-class citizenship, violating promises made during the revolutionary struggles. While in Paris, Khomeini assured equality and freedom for women: "In Islamic society women will be free to choose their own destiny and own activity. God created us equal."[43] He also declared that the chador (traditional female dress) was not obligatory, and that women were free to make their own choices.[44] After the monarchy's ouster, the Islamic Republic imposed inequality and gender discrimination in many spheres, including family relations, inheritance, divorce, and child custody.[45] The new constitution barred women from becoming the head of state and removed female judges from their positions. Polygamy, which had been legally restricted in the 1960s and 1970s, was decriminalized and no longer prohibited.[46] Islamic law required married women to obtain permission from their husbands to travel abroad,[47] work, or further their education.[48]

The Islamic Republic also restricted women's participation in social and cultural spheres. Performances by lone women singers were banned on state media, including radio and television. The state subjected violators to fines, jail terms, and even flogging. Women were discouraged from wearing makeup, considered a symbol of Western decadence, and the regime insisted that they observe Islamic tradition by covering their hair in public. Female government employees were told to cover their hair or lose their jobs.[49] Mandatory observance of Islamic covering was later extended to all women. During Ahmadinejad's presidency, thousands of women were arrested for wearing improper veils and sometimes fined up to $800 for immodest dress.[50] The police were authorized to issue fines to female drivers and passengers who did not observe Islamic covering and to confiscate the drivers' licenses of repeat offenders.[51]

Attacks against women sometimes took violent forms. Islamic fundamentalists, encouraged by the clergy's repeated condemnation of improperly or inadequately covered women, occasionally physically attacked women. Over a matter of a few months, extremists poured acid on women's faces on seven or eight occasions.[52] One woman in Tehran died in such an attack.[53]

State policies exacerbated gender inequality. From 2006 to 2015, Iran's gender gap was one of the highest among the countries surveyed by the World Economic Forum.[54] Despite considerable educational achievements, the labor force participation of women remained at 32.5 percent in 2008, compared with men's participation of 73.3 percent. Only seventy-eight women were elected to parliament between the revolution and the ninth Majles elected in 2012. [55] Iranian women held the second fewest parliamentary seats in the world in 2008, ahead only of Papua New Guinea.[56] The changes in the polygamy laws widened gender inequality within the family. By 2008, at least sixty-five members of the parliament, or 22 percent, had more than one wife.[57]

But popular resistance disrupted state attempts to fully enforce the social and cultural changes. The rulers of the Islamic Republic still have not succeeded in fully implementing the cornerstone of the theocratic system and enforcing their cultural agenda, despite relentless efforts. More than three decades after the revolution, Supreme Leader Ayatollah Khamenei expressed deep concerns about the country's "cultural problems" in a meeting with members of the Assembly of Experts: "The cultural problem is important because the persistence and functioning of the Islamic system is dependent on the preservation of Islamic culture."[58]

As people increasingly resisted imposition of strict Islamic social and cultural codes of behavior, some leaders of the Islamic Republic called for a heightened state intervention to enforce Islamic practices. Ayatollah Ahmad Khatami, Friday prayer leader of Tehran, advocated use of state power to enforce God's laws. He opposed giving people the freedom to do anything they wanted in the areas of morality, economy, and culture, saying, "It is the government's duty to take the people to heaven even by force or whip."[59] Similarly, Ayatollah Ahmad Alamolhoda also called upon the state to intervene in spreading Islamic culture. Noting that "whipping is easy," he declared that "we will use all our powers to stand against those who intend to prevent people from going to heaven."[60]

Other members of the elite went further and expressed concerns about the future of the revolution. Gholamali Haddad Adel, a member of the Expediency Council and former speaker of the Majles—also a close relative of the supreme leader—publicly called into question the new generation's commitment to the revolution. He opened his public address about what he called "the anxieties that we all have." Adel noted that the generation that had carried out the revolution would gradually give way to future generations. He asked, "Will this revolution, with all its goals, be secured by the future generation?" Adel continued: "It is not at all certain that if the parents were revolutionaries, the children will also become revolutionaries. Even in our own families, we see that our children do not have the perceptions that we have of the revolution." Adel noted that "if we let go, we cannot expect that they will stand committed to the revolution." He argued that the same amount of effort should be made to transfer the experience of the revolution as was made in making the revolution. Adel maintained that the enemy was mobilized at every stage with full force against the revolution: "Wherever and whatever sphere we touch, we see that some enemies are busy working."[61] Ali Akbar Nategh Nouri, a conservative cleric and head of the supreme leader's inspection office, acknowledged in a sermon that the Islamic Republic had regressed in the past 37 years and could not claim to be a model for others.[62]

Ayatollah Mahmoud Amjad publicly lamented conditions in the Islamic Republic and questioned the nature of the regime and people's loyalty to it, according to *jamaran.ir*, a site maintained by Ayatollah Khomeini's grandson Hassan Khomeini. In a gathering of mourning commemorating the Prophet Mohammad's death, Amjad stated, "A great revolution occurred in the name of the Islamic Republic; unfortunately, it is neither a republic nor Islamic . . . alas, and with thousands of regrets, we, with our worldliness and selfishness, have wasted everything and disgraced our honor and valuable prestige . . . we let the wind take away all the people's sacrifices, the martyrdom, people's loyalty, and the sacrifices of those who gave everything for the system."[63]

Active and Passive Challenges to the Islamic Republic

The failure of the Islamic Republic to fulfill the revolution's promises, the imposition of social and cultural restrictions, and the denial of political rights and civil liberties set the stage for contentious politics in Iran. While regime supporters claimed legitimacy, many Iranians resisted the Islamic Republic, both actively and passively. The initial challengers, who emerged shortly after the revolution, were those moderates and radical revolutionaries who favored a different outcome. Although the regime succeeded in repressing these challengers in the first decade of the revolution, a reformist movement emerged in its second decade, the 1990s. Pressing for measures to modify the system, the reformists gained and held power from the latter part of the 1990s through the first five years of the twenty-first century. The reformist faction made a concerted effort to change some aspects of the Islamic Republic and provide greater freedom and civil liberties but could not substantially alter the system in the face of a powerful conservative faction backed by security forces.

Nevertheless, reformists' promises of greater freedom and civil liberties provided an opportunity for students to push for democratic transformation.

Students had opposed the formation of the Islamic Republic shortly after the monarchy's ouster but were repressed by the regime, which closed all universities for some thirty-two months and purged dissident students and faculty. With the reformists' rise to power, students mobilized and produced two large-scale protests in 1999 and 2003, attacking the very economic, political, and ideological foundations of the Islamic Republic. When students demonstrated against the closure of a reformist newspaper in July 1999, their protests quickly became radicalized. They shouted, "The people are miserable! The clerics are acting like gods!"[64]

It is useful to compare the response to student protests in Iran in the 1990s with those in South Korea in the 1980s. South Korean police and security forces regularly brought mattresses and trampolines to protect protesting students who threatened to jump to their deaths. For example, the Korean police placed nets and mattresses on the ground in June 1985 in preparation for students attempting to avoid capture by jumping from windows. "In the case of students jumping from the office in their possible desperate escape, police prepared net and mattresses on the ground," one report noted.[65] On another occasion, security forces placed mattresses around a building at Konkuk University in Seoul to prevent students from carrying out self-immolation. "Before launching the operation, police had placed mattresses in case of suicidal jumps and put 30 fire engines on standby to prepare for the possibility that students would set the building on fire."[66] In contrast, the Islamic regime used harsh repression to kill protesting students. Agents of the Islamic Republic did not hesitate to throw students from dormitory windows and balconies, causing serious injuries during 1999 and 2009 protests. Several of the protesting students are still missing (see Chapter 6). Hassan Rouhani, deputy speaker of the Majles at the time and member of the Supreme Security Council, warned that protesters could be executed. "Those involved in the last days' riots, destruction of public property and attacks against the system will be punished as *mohareb* [fighters against God] and *mosfed* [people spreading corruption]," said Rouhani at a rally.[67]

Iranians mobilized again for democratic rights following the 2009 presidential election. The Green Movement truly shook the foundation of the Islamic Republic, as Supreme Leader Ayatollah Ali Khamenei and other leading officials publicly admitted. While the movement's leaders were disputing the election results, the popular protesters quickly became radicalized and demanded fundamental change. In Tehran they shouted, "Independence, Freedom, Iranian Republic" (June 20, 2009) and "We didn't give our lives to compromise and won't praise the murderous leader"

(February 11, 2010). In the religious center of Qom, protesters chanted, "This is the month of blood. Seyyed Ali [Khamenei] will be overthrown" (see Chapter 7).

To counter severe state repression, Green Movement protesters also developed a slogan new in Iran's political history to encourage resistance: "Don't be afraid, don't be afraid. We are all together." Although resistance ultimately failed, the movement played an important role in Iran's democratization struggles. First, it revealed the extent to which the Islamic Republic's rulers were isolated and vulnerable. Second, it eroded the elite's social base of support even among parts of the Revolutionary Guard and for months hampered the rulers' efforts to demobilize the protesters. Third, the conflicts and protests further polarized Iran's political arena, radicalizing segments of the population and also those of the factions of the Islamic Republic. Finally, the movement revealed the existence of irreconcilable ideologies and conflicts in Iranian society and politics—conflicts that could be contained only by endless state repression.

The regime's failure to fulfill the revolution's principal promises produced not only political protests but also daily, passive resistance. As regime supporters claimed legitimacy, substantial numbers of Iranians refused to observe many of the Islamic social and cultural practices imposed by the theocracy because they had not demanded such changes during the revolutionary struggles. Many Iranians defied the Islamic regime's imposition of practices that became the cornerstone of the theocracy. Passive resistance centered around mosque attendance, eschewing alcohol, dress, and other fundamental obligations in Islam. Some religious practices, such as mosque attendance, had been a source of cohesion during the revolutionary struggles, but they became a source of contention and division after the establishment of the Islamic Republic. Iranians, in other words, refused to be coerced into heaven.

Therefore, passive resistance affected mosque attendance. Despite the unifying and mobilizing function of mosques during the revolution, shortly after the revolution, some Iranians—particularly intellectuals and students—refused to attend. When mosques came under state control and lost their autonomy, they no longer played their historic role, and Iranian intellectuals avoided participating. Decline in participation was noted by the leader of the revolution. Less than four months after the establishment of the Islamic Republic, on June 6, 1979, Ayatollah Khomeini lectured Shiraz University students, saying, "People, protect your mosques. Intellectuals, protect your mosques. Intellectuals should attend the mosques. They are not going to the mosques; they should attend the mosques so that this movement succeeds and the country is saved."[68] As attendance continued to decline, a year later, on June 4, 1980, Khomeini again criticized those who had left the mosques: "The lewd ones have emptied the mosques," he lamented.[69] People continued passive resistance in the following decades. More than half the country's mosques were inactive in 2009, government officials acknowledged, despite receiving increased budgetary allocations.[70] A Revolutionary Guard commander, Zia Eddin Hozni, recently announced that about 3,000 of the country's 57,000 Shiite mosques, or only 5 percent, were fully operational during the year. He also noted that some mosques were operational only during the religious months of Ramadan and Muharram.[71]

Once clerics assumed important positions in the government and state institutions, religiosity declined among the populace. Masoud Adib, a cleric and seminary faculty member in Qom, noted that people's commitment to Islamic laws had been greater in the past: "At present, public behavior does not have an Islamic character." He argued that people's unfulfilled expectations gave rise to demands and that they blamed religion. Adib also claimed that repressive measures and attempts to impose religious behavior on those who did not follow Islamic laws resulted in rejection of religion.[72] Declining religious observance, along with the movement of many clerics to the state sector, led to a shortage of clergy. Nearly one-half of the country's mosques, some thirty thousand, lacked clerics and prayer leaders in 2012, according to Morteza Moghtedaie, director of Iran's seminaries.[73] Mohsen Gharaati, a cleric and head of the Headquarters of Prayer Adduction, asked families to devote a child to the Imam of the Age and to send him to the seminary because the country needed more Islamic experts to preach Islam.[74]

As with mosque attendance, passive resistance also impaired the fundamental practice of daily prayer and other obligations. The revolution's leaders repeatedly underscored the importance of daily prayers: "In Islam, no obligation is above prayer," declared Ayatollah Khomeini after the revolution.[75] The state controlled the media, mosques, and educational institutions, and regularly attempted to promote Islamic values and culture. It also allocated substantial sums annually to promote Islamic culture and religious practices. For example, the state allocated more than $2 billion in 2015 to thirty-six organizations, including a few government agencies but mostly independent religious groups dedicated to promoting Islamic culture.[76] Even so, passive resistance severely undermined the practice of praying daily. An official survey in 2000 found that 75 percent of the populace and 86 percent of young students failed to say their obligatory prayers.[77] In response to widespread defiance, authorities decided that students in all schools should organize thirty minutes of daily collective prayers.[78] The vast majority of Iranians failed to pay Zakat, a contribution made to religious authorities for the poor and needy. Mohsen Gharaati, a Shiite clergy, complained that the practice of paying Zakat was weak. "Unfortunately, only five percent of the people in various provinces pay Zakat," Gharaati noted.[79]

Some Iranians ignored restrictions against eating in public during Ramadan and defied government sanctions of ten to sixty days in prison and seventy-four lashes.[80] In 2015, 2,699 people in Shiraz were given verbal warnings, 261 received written notices, and 500 were detained for eating in public.[81] Residents of other cities were arrested for consuming food and ignoring the Ramadan, including 92 in Tabriz,[82] 72 in Hamedan,[83] 32 in Sirjan,[84] 10 in Neka,[85] and 228 in Mahmoudabad.[86] In Ghazvin, 400 people were detained for eating in public during Ramadan in 2014; 200 of them were whipped, and the rest were given warnings.[87]

The regime's promotion of Islamic values and culture, and the public's ongoing resistance, even had an affect on people's sex life. One report revealed that 80 percent of high school girls in the country had boyfriends.[88] A survey of 141,555 high school students throughout the country by the Ministry of Education uncovered surprising facts regarding young people's sexual activities. More than 74 percent of students acknowledged "impermissible relationships with the opposite sex." In Tehran, 80 percent of high school girls admitted that they had engaged in relations with males.[89] The report also indicated that compared with thirty years earlier, relations between boys and girls prior to entering the university had tripled; this was according to Mahmoud Golzari, deputy minister of sports and youth.[90] Increasing numbers of young Iranians also began living together without getting married. The rising number of such cases— referred to in Iran as "white marriage"—led government officials to criticize the practice and begin devising mechanisms to prevent it. Mohammad Golpaygani, a cleric and head of the supreme leader's office, condemned white marriages and stated, "The Islamic ruler has to deal severely with such living."[91]

Iranians defied other social and cultural norms imposed by the regime after the revolution. People persisted in drinking spirits despite sanctions of eighty lashes for first-time offenders and execution for third-time offenders. Alcohol consumption was widespread and on the rise in the Islamic Republic, according to the Ministry of Health in 2012.[92] Estimates of the amount vary, but all sources confirm alcohol consumption in Iran.[93] According to the *Economist,* Iranians' rate of alcohol use ranked third among the majority Muslim countries as early as 2003–2005, exceeded on a per capita basis only by Lebanon and Turkey, where alcohol consumption was legal.[94] Other reports claimed that the actual amount of liquor consumed was even higher. In 2014, Hassan Taamini Liechaee, deputy head of the health committee of the Majles, stated that Iranians consumed more than 200 million liters of alcohol per year.[95] In a later report, Deputy Health Minister Ali Akbar Sayyari stated that Iran's annual alcohol consumption totaled 420 million liters.[96] These figures would place fifty million Iranians over the age of 15 among the highest per capita drinkers in the Middle East.

Alcoholic drinks were readily available throughout the country and could be purchased clandestinely. Many Iranians produced alcoholic beverages in their own homes, and citizens spent about $12 billion annually on liquor.[97] People also smuggled about $1 billion worth of alcohol into the country in 2014, according to Ali Reza Jamshidi, the deputy justice minister, who called it disgraceful for the country.[98] Some Iranians converted ethyl alcohol into alcoholic beverages, according to liquor producers in Iran.[99] Alcohol was served at weddings, according to cleric Jaafar Shajooni, who condemned the practice as shameless.[100] Alcohol consumption occasionally resulted in large-scale poisoning. A record number of poisoning cases were reported in the city of Rafsanjan, where 355 young people sought treatment at the same time.[101]

The rise of alcohol consumption among elementary and high school students in recent years has been a serious social problem, according to Dr. Ali Mohammadi, in charge of the alcohol abuse program at Kermanshah medical school.[102] A survey in 2012 by researchers at Tabiyat Moalem University in Tehran found that among high school students, 24.4 percent of males and 4.2 percent of females had consumed alcohol.[103] Despite the threat of severe punishment for drinking, some high school students readily admitted to consuming liquor and getting drunk in public.[104] Recognizing the severity of the problem, the government established the first publicly funded clinic in 2014 to treat alcohol addiction.[105] By early 2016, Iran had launched 150 clinics to deal with the problem of alcoholism.[106]

At times, the regime imposed harsh sanctions for drinking alcohol. The judiciary sentenced two people to death after drinking for the third time.[107] Authorities in Ghazvin arrested 35 male and female university students for drinking and other violations at a graduation party and punished each one with 99 lashes.[108]

Iranians' resistance also took the form of religious conversion, a phenomenon rare prior to the revolution. Ayatollah Khomeini declared repeatedly that Islam and Islamic values were undermined by the monarchy and that the Islamic Republic was established to rejuvenate Islam. But as the clergy successfully captured the commanding heights of Iran's economy and politics and enforced Islamic social and cultural practices, increasing numbers of Iranians chose to resist the theocracy by converting to Christianity and other religions. Religious conversions were frequent enough to attract the condemnation of the Islamic Republic's leaders. Supreme Leader Ayatollah Khamenei issued a warning in Qom in October 2010, stating that the enemies of Islam plotted to weaken religion by promoting carelessness and conversion to false religions such as Baha'ism and Christianity. Similarly, Mohammad Saeedi, Friday prayer leader of the religious city of Qom, warned of the rising conversion to Christianity: "The enemy is attempting to expand home-based churches."[109] President Rouhani presented a different analysis and blamed certain practices for people's move away from their religion. In a speech in Qom, the president declared that reactionary fanaticism and extremism not only destroyed peoples' lives but that, above all, they also destroyed their religion.[110]

It appears that Christianity has become the religion most commonly chosen by converts who defied the Islamic Republic. Although most conversions to Christianity were found in the cities of Tehran, Karaj, and Rasht, conversions also occurred in the major religious centers of Qom and Mashhad.[111] Christian converts often established churches in their homes, where they held religious events. An investigation revealed at least two hundred home churches serving converts in Mashhad.[112] Although Christianity was the preferred religion of those who defied the Islamic theocracy, some converted to other religions. Specifically, some reports pointed to "rapid" conversion, particularly of rural inhabitants in the eastern provinces, to the Baha'i faith, whose adherents were persecuted.[113]

Shiite conversion to the Baha'i faith caused alarm in the Islamic Republic. Ameneh Balangi, a member of the Basij paramilitary organization, expressed concerns and regrets about the growth of "false cultures," particularly Baha'iat (the Baha'i faith), in villages around the city of Kerman. She added that the Basij student organization had initiated a jihad and dispatched fifty-six female students to the region to educate women and counteract the spread of Baha'iat among Shiites, according to the Fars News Agency associated with the Revolutionary Guard.[114] The rising conversion of Shiites to other religions alarmed the rulers of the Islamic Republic who introduced measures to discourage conversion (see Chapter 5).

Religious conversion in the Islamic Republic has been remarkable for two reasons. First, people converted to other religions despite the fact that the Islamic regime spent billions of dollars annually to strengthen Shiite Islam through state-owned media, mosques and religious spaces, educational institutions from elementary schools to universities, and barracks and military centers. These efforts were reinforced by the spread of religious graffiti, which covered doors and walls in Iranian cities. Second, religious conversions took place despite the regime's regulation of churches and repressive measures, including imprisonment, execution, and murder.

Defiance by small groups of dissidents and by human rights activists against official policies produced some sympathy for the unrecognized religious minority of Baha'is. Dissidents engaged in a few unprecedented actions supporting their civil rights. A group of human rights activists, writers, and journalists—including Mohammad Maleki, Mohammad Nurizad, Nasrin Sotoudeh, Heshmatollah Tabarzadi, and Ayatollah Abdolhamid Masumi Tehrani—issued a statement demanding that the judiciary defend the rights of non-Muslims as enshrined in the constitution. The activists also called for an investigation of the persecution of Baha'is.[115] In Tehran in 2014, leading human rights activists and former political prisoners attended an anniversary event commemorating the arrest of the leaders of the Baha'i community, imprisoned in 2008. Maleki, Ayatollah Masumi Tehrani, Nurizad, Narges Mohamadi, Sotoudeh, Jila Baniyaghoub, and Issa Sahar-Khiz—along with others—participated in the event, sympathizing with the Baha'i community and condemning state repression.[116] Such activities would have been unthinkable soon after the revolution, and were forbidden under the Islamic Republic and by orders of the supreme leader.

Even prominent religious figures, including Ayatollah Masumi Tehrani, challenged and criticized discrimination and persecution of the Baha'is by the Islamic regime.[117] In an unprecedented undertaking, Ayatollah Abdolhamid Masumi Tehrani personally created a work of art, incorporating some Baha'is scriptures, and dedicated it to the world Baha'i community in consolation and sympathy with the Baha'is of Iran.[118] He hoped that his gift would help eliminate hatred and prejudice and foster peaceful coexistence among all the people in the nation.[119] Another example is that of Hassan Yousefi Eshkevari, a defrocked cleric and former Majles deputy, who defended Baha'is rights. In response to Ayatollah Mohammad Mousavi Bojnourdi's claim that Baha'is had no rights as citizens,[120] Eshkevari published a rebuttal.[121] Similarly, Ayatollah Dr. Mohsen Kadivar noted in an article that Mousavi Bojnourdi's claim concerning Baha'i citizenship rights did not have any legal or religious basis.[122]

Despite repeated fatwas that Baha'is were untouchable and Muslims should avoid interacting with them, some Iranians met with Baha'is and expressed support for their citizenship rights. For example, several female former political prisoners including Faezeh Hashemi, Nasrin Sotoudeh, a lawyer, and journalists Sajedeh Arabsorkhi, Mahsa Amrabadi, and Jila Baniyaghoob visited the home of Fariba Kamalabadi, one of the seven imprisoned Baha'i leaders, then out on furlough. Sotoudeh defended her visit and stated that given the suffering and injustices they endured, she should have made the visit. She added that she would do anything to help the Baha'is.[123] Faezeh Hashemi, former Majles deputy and daughter of former President Hashemi Rafsanjani, who had spent jail time with Kamalabadi, told a reporter that Baha'is deserved full citizenship rights, like all Iranians. "Unfortunately, they do not have the least rights."[124] In response to criticism of her visit, including by her father, Hashemi responded that she had done nothing wrong and did not regret her actions.[125] Five prominent Islamic theologians and intellectuals, including Abdolali Bazargan, Hasan Fereshtian, Mohsen Kadivar, Sadigheh Vasmeghi, and Hassan Yousefi Eshkevari, defended Hashemi and declared her visit against injustice as both moral and religious.[126]

Passive defiance also focused on social and cultural restrictions imposed by the theocracy. Women, particularly of the younger generation, remained among the most rebellious segments of Iranian society. They continued to push back at every opportunity. Women appeared in public spaces in Tehran and other cities without proper hejab, the Islamic headscarf. According to surveys in large cities, between 52 and 68 percent of women were not covered properly during the years 2007 to 2013.[127] A survey by the official Council of Public Culture revealed that 71 percent of women in Tehran did not properly observe this Islamic practice.[128]

Women's resistance has forced the regime to spend considerable resources annually and employ a special Guidance Patrol to ensure that they observe the Islamic dress code.[129] A large number of women are arrested every year and given fines or reprimanded for improper hejab. During three months in the spring of 2014, 220,000 women were taken to police stations to sign statements promising to observe the proper use of the headscarf, 18,785 women were given notices about their hair covering (or lack of it), and 8,629 women were detained, according to the interior minister.[130] Police announced that they would impound for one week the cars of female drivers who did not observe the Islamic rules for proper dress. During eight months in 2015, traffic police in Tehran stopped 40,000 women drivers who lacked proper cover and impounded the vehicles of most of them.[131]

In the face of widespread defiance by women, some high-ranking officials of the Islamic Republic questioned the effectiveness of enforcing the existing regulations for head covering. Shahindokht Molaverdi, vice president for women's affairs under President Rouhani, noted that twenty-six organizations in the three branches of the government were tasked in 2005 with promoting Islamic covering but had not succeeded. She concluded,

"National determination and collective will do not exist in the country to deal with the problem of chastity." Molaverdi added that neither families nor the educational system had succeeded in promoting proper covering.[132] Parviz Alizadeh, deputy head of Western Azerbaijan's judiciary, complained that violations were on the rise and that the struggle to contain them had become difficult.[133] Mohammad Bagher Olfat, deputy head of Iran's judiciary, regretted that the country seemed to be moving from bad head covering to no covering.[134]

Iranian women also resisted the ban against wearing makeup, considered Western decadence by the rulers. Makeup professionals estimated that Iranian women bought one tube of mascara per month, in contrast with one every four months purchased by French women.[135] In a population that ranked seventeenth in the world, Iran's consumption of makeup was seventh, according to the Ministry of Health. Iranians smuggled in at least $2.2 billion of makeup in 2013.[136] Although a Tehran police chief stated that the arrest of "100 street supermodels" would resolve the problem, Iranian women continued to defy the ban and risk arrest. "Many young women ignore the loose dresses recommended by the religious establishment and instead wear tight trousers, covered with short overcoats or flimsy cotton shirts. Their headscarves slip backwards to reveal as much hair as possible, and they wear heavy make-up."[137]

Iranians, particularly the youth, also resisted the regime's attempts to eradicate ancient cultural practices. The most important was the fire festival (mentioned earlier), a celebration that predated Islam and probably originated in Zoroastrianism. Religious prohibition and threats of arrest actually provoked Iranians to observe this annual tradition more widely and enthusiastically than ever before, often resulting in injuries. The celebration was held outdoors on the eve of the last Wednesday of the year, just before the Iranian New Year, Norooz. It involved jumping over a fire and chanting, "My yellow is yours, your red is mine," a phrase proposing to shed sickness and sadness in exchange for the color and warmth of fire.[138] Although fire or misuse of firecrackers during the festival annually injured some three thousand people, with 10 percent requiring hospitalization according to official claims, the resistance has continued. In spite of the criminalization of festival observances and the imprisonment of violators, millions of Iranians use the occasion every year to publicly defy the Islamic Republic's cultural restrictions. "Despite all the crackdowns over the past 30 years by the Islamic Republic, the ritual is still observed by an increasing number of people who go on to the streets to sing the traditional song: 'Give me your fiery red colour and take back my wintry sallowness.'"[139]

Nearly four decades after the revolution, Iranians continued their resistance to the regime's disapproval of the fire festival. As recently as March 2015, the Friday prayer leader of Tehran, Ayatollah Ahmad Khatami, urged Iranians not to observe the fire festival, especially because this year it occurred so close to an Islamic mourning period.[140] General Taghi Mehri, head of the police's prevention department, warned that fire festival gatherings were prohibited and violators would be arrested.[141] Other high-ranking police authorities declared that those arrested would be detained for the duration of the Norooz celebration, which lasts thirteen days. Nevertheless, Iranians defied the religious leaders and the police, and celebrated the fire festival. Revelers gathered in public spaces, built and jumped over bonfires, played music, and danced in the streets.[142] Despite all the warnings, the celebrations went ahead and resulted in at least three accidental deaths and hundreds of injuries.[143]

Passive defiance was also manifested in the widespread use of satellite dishes, prohibited by the Islamic Republic in 1994 to discourage Western culture and block access to dissident political views disseminated from abroad. Alizadeh, deputy head of the Western Azerbaijan judiciary, revealed that between 70 and 80 percent of people used satellite dishes and that removing them would not help because people routinely replaced them.[144] President Rouhani noted during his presidential campaign that satellite dishes were even visible in villages, and efforts against the dishes on rooftops were ineffective.[145] Ali Jannati, minister of culture and Islamic guidance under President Rouhani, noting that 71 percent of the residents of Tehran watched satellite television stations, warned, "Our society is gradually moving toward moral collapse, and many of the important values of Islamic society are losing their color."[146] Jannati also acknowledged that every time authorities confiscated a satellite dish, another was installed two days later. He noted that closing down all social networks was futile and impossible.[147]

Government officials struggled to enforce the banning of satellite dishes. Agents repeatedly raided Saadat Abad Taavoni, a government-owned cooperative housing complex, to seize the dishes of residents, all of whom were government employees.[148] An official declared that during nine months in 2015, the government confiscated more than 270,000 satellite dishes in the city and province of Tehran.[149] At the same time, many Iranians did not watch the state-owned television programs. According to Ramazan Shojaie Kiasari, a parliament member in charge of supervising state television, some networks had more employees than audience members.[150]

Iranians also defied the state prohibition against foreign music. The arrests and suspended sentences in 2014 against youths who produced

"Happy in Tehran," a dance video set to the global hit song "Happy" by American singer Pharrell Williams, demonstrated the results of the continued defiance of cultural restrictions.[151]

People's passive resistance at times included disrespect and insults toward the clergy. Respect for the clergy declined as early as the 1980s, before Khomeini's death. Surveyed in 1971, 86.7 percent of people venerated the clergy, but by 1986 only 32.3 percent had the same response.[152] Shortly after the revolution, some high-ranking clerics complained that even in the religious city of Qom, people occasionally insulted them.[153] By the mid-1990s, disrespect and resentment against the clergy reached a new peak. Taxi drivers often refused to provide service to the clergy.[154] "Stories were rampant in the capital about how some cabbies ran fingers across their throat to show contempt as they sped by mullahs waiting curbside," according to Robin Wright.[155] Disrespect toward the clergy increased after the 2009 presidential elections. Seyyed Ali Akbar Mohtashami-Pour (a cleric, former interior minister, and two-time Majles deputy) admitted, "Here as I walk in the street, some people come and disrespect me merely because I am a cleric, without knowing me; when they see the clergy, they disrespect them."[156]

Disrespect and defiance took other forms after the 2009 presidential elections. Some women were unwilling to marry clerical students, acknowledged Mehdi Daneshmand, an influential cleric, seminary teacher, and university professor.[157] People even beat up clerics who tried to tell citizens to correct their behavior, according to the New York Times.[158] Clerics Seyyed Mahmoud Mostafavi Montazeri, Farzad Forozesh, and Haj Agha Khair Andish were beaten for telling people to behave properly; some suffered irreversible harm. [159] Ali Khalili, a cleric, was severely injured in Tehran in 2011 when he tried to reprimand another man on his behavior. Khalili underwent complex surgery.[160] A young woman responded violently when Seyyed Ali Beheshti, the Friday prayer leader of Shahmirzad, ordered her to cover up. She told him to close his eyes; when he repeated his demand, she pushed and kicked him to the point that he required hospitalization.[161] When Mohsen Mirzaie, a cleric in Khorramabad, admonished a woman for creating an "immoral scene," he was attacked by four men and severely beaten. Mirzaie was hospitalized and underwent surgery.[162] In Eslamshahr, a man severely beat up Mohsen Farahaani, a young cleric, who scolded him about sexually explicit behavior in public with a female companion.[163]

Passive resistance was accompanied by the decline in the status of the clergy, as witnessed by some leading theologians. Ayatollah Seyyed Jalaleddin Taheri, Khomeini's appointed Friday prayer leader of Isfahan, wrote in his resignation letter of July 2002, "We are filled with sorrow witnessing the decline of the status of the clergy today and the collapse of the position of jurist."[164] Mohsen Rahami, a cleric and seminary professor, attributed the decline of the clergy's status to the fact that they had lost their mission and become engaged in commerce. "Now the kind of respect the clergy receives today is different from thirty or forty years ago by comparison; when the clergy is distanced from its main mission, people have the right to be pessimistic about them," Rahami noted.[165]

Passive defiance was also expressed in the popular criticism of the political system in a number of surveys. One poll found that only 6.2 percent of the respondents in Tehran were satisfied with the current state of affairs, 48.9 percent favored "reform," and 44.9 percent favored "fundamental change."[166] Another national survey, before the 2009 presidential election, reported that almost nine out of ten Iranians favored direct elections and the replacement of the supreme leader. Only 8 percent favored the conservatives.[167] Another survey found that Iranians had a proliberal values structure that was deeply at odds with the fundamentalist regime. This survey found that 94 percent of the respondents favored freedom to choose what was important to them.[168]

Dissatisfaction with the ruling clergy could also be seen in the composition of the Majles. Despite advantages given to clerical candidates for elected office, the number of clergy elected to the Majles declined dramatically over time. While clerics constituted 60.7 percent of deputies in the first Majles in 1980, their proportion in the 2016 elections declined to 5.5 percent.[169]

Finally, resistance sometimes led dissidents and activists to criticize the country's dire situation and demand genuine, democratic changes. For example, Davoud Hermidas Bavand, Kourosh Zaim, and Heshmatollah Tabarzadi, leaders of Solidarity for Democracy and Human Rights in Iran, issued a statement in November 2015 analyzing the various problems of the country and offering some solutions.

> We are a country that is socially injured and that in the past three decades has not been developing; we have become poor, addicted; we have been humiliated; we have lost our industry, agriculture . . . and in all we have lost everything. We have lost hundreds of thousands in the imposed war and tens of thousands in murders and executions. In bureaucratic corruption, number of executions, addiction, illiteracy, and unemployment we have reached among the first in the world, but we have turned two to three thousand ruling elite into super-rich. . . . . We all want a democratic government that is not dependent on the faith of the people, one that guarantees the civil freedoms and human rights of all the citizens and prepares conditions for the reconstruction of the ruins and for progress, well-being, and the pride of the nation. . . . We

want democracy for Iran—that is, the rule of the people for the people and with the vote of the people.[170]

The statement went on to underscore majority vote, minority rights, and equality of all before the law; laws devised by representatives elected by free, popular vote; laws that did not discriminate between majority and minority, men and women, different perspectives, and religions. Although they did not call for dismantling the theocracy, the statements made demands that would, in effect, require the separation of religion from politics and the removal of special privileges and powers existing in the theocracy.

Elite Reactions to Challenges and Future Developments

The rulers of the Islamic Republic introduced and emphasized new ideological claims in the wake of the erosion of popular support. Although a popular revolution established the Islamic Republic, the ruling elite claimed that the people were irrelevant in conferring legitimacy on the Islamic regime, contradicting the rights enshrined in the Islamic Republic constitution, which gave sovereignty to the people. Instead, the rulers maintained that the Islamic Republic's legitimacy had divine roots and derived from the prophets and the Twelfth Imam. The ruling elite also exalted and sanctified the status of the *velayat-e faghieh*, to a degree unprecedented in Shiite Islam, and demanded that everyone obey him. Some noted that following the jurist was the same as following the Prophet. Ayatollah Mohammad Yazdi, head of the powerful Assembly of Experts, noted that the "absolutist *faghieh* never makes mistakes."[171] Ayatollah Ahmad Khatami, a member of the Assembly of Experts and Friday prayer leader of Tehran, declared in public that Islam without the jurist would be an "incomplete blessing."[172]

The rulers of the Islamic regime became increasingly concerned about passive resistance in the social and cultural spheres. The Majles passed legislation to militarize social and cultural practices and established a new headquarters to "propagate virtue and prevent vice." It assigned the Revolutionary Guard and the paramilitary Basij to enforce the headquarters' orders.[173] Although the Guardian Council found the law unconstitutional,[174] the Majles passed additional legislation to make enforcement legal.[175] These policies prompted the development of a cellphone application that would alert people about the location of the morality police,[176] an innovation that quickly became popular.[177]

The rulers of the Islamic Republic expanded repression and went beyond the measures enacted shortly after the overthrow of the monarchy. In this round, they targeted moderate Islamic forces that had been members of the polity. Their actions surpassed that of Khomeini, who had repressed radical opposition elements outside the polity, such as secular and Islamic socialists and secular forces that advocated separating religion and politics. Thus, they dissolved the two reformist organizations, excluded them from the polity, and demanded that reformist political activists and protesters be imprisoned following the 2009 presidential election. They arrested thousands of dissidents at that time and placed the leaders of the Green Movement, referred to as "the sedition," under house arrest.

To counter the Green Movement after the 2009 presidential elections, the rulers of the Islamic Republic expressed concerns about the Movement and called for vigilance, repression, and the exclusion of opponents. The ruling clergy advocated continued vigilance, repeatedly noting that the sedition was not over and could be reignited at any time. Supreme Leader Ayatollah Khamenei warned Rouhani and his cabinet more than five years after the disputed election that "the problem of sedition and seditionists is one of the most important problems and a red line" and that cabinet ministers should maintain their distance from it and remain resolute.[178] Even though repressive measures had demobilized the Green Movement, the Islamic Republic's leaders called for severe repression. Some members of the ruling elite also called for the execution of the leaders of the Movement without any trial and conviction. In response to demands to try the Green Movement leaders or release them from house arrest, Ayatollah Ahmad Jannati, head of the Guardian Council, noted that the punishment for Mousavi and Karroubi should be execution and that they should have been executed when they were arrested. In an interview on national television, he maintained, "In the case of a trial, no just and informed judge would issue anything but an execution."[179] Mohammad Taghi Rahbar, Friday prayer leader of Isfahan, also noted that calls for the execution of Mousavi and Karroubi were correct and based on Islamic laws because the two had rebelled and challenged the Islamic system.[180] The ruling elite went ahead and, without any trial and conviction, called for the execution of the leaders of the Green Movement. Sadegh Amoli Larijani, a cleric and head of the judiciary, declared more than five years after the disputed presidential election that the sedition was a strong current that would have undermined the basis of the Islamic Revolution but that the wise people of Iran, in a timely manner, "blinded the eyes of the sedition."[181]

Repressive measures continued even after Ahmadinejad's presidency ended. The Islamic regime introduced a law requiring anyone arrested on security charges to choose a defense attorney from among lawyers

approved by the judiciary.[182] Security forces intimidated parents and sib-
lings of political prisoners and recommended that young wives divorce
their imprisoned husbands.[183] They even destroyed the prayer building of
Sunni Muslims in Tehran and prevented them from gathering.[184] Concerts
were routinely canceled throughout the country, and universities were
ordered not to hold concerts on campus, according to Mohammad
Mohammadian, a cleric and the supreme leader's representative in universities.[185] The Guardian Council, in charge of vetting all candidates for
office, disqualified most moderate and reformist candidates following the
2009 presidential elections. For example, the council eliminated 99 percent of 3,000 reformists who had registered to participate in the 2016
Majles elections.[186] Some of the disqualified candidates included former
Friday prayer leaders, who were eliminated because of an insufficient commitment to Islam, according to Masoud Pezeshkian, a Majles deputy.[187]
The council also disqualified Hassan Khomeini, grandson of Ayatollah
Khomeini, from running for the Assembly of Experts.[188] Some of the candidates eventually were reinstated, but others, including 296 academics,
declared that canceling an uncompetitive and unfair election would be
better than carrying it out.[189]

Summary and Conclusions

The people and the rulers of the Islamic Republic have fought for different
ends over the past several decades. Most Iranians have struggled for a
better standard of living, more egalitarian distribution of wealth and
income, and greater political rights and civil liberties. During the revolution, Ayatollah Khomeini and other leaders of the revolution repeatedly
promised to grant political freedom and serve the interests of the downtrodden. Once in power, however, the Islamic Republic's rulers pursued a
very different agenda. In lieu of fulfilling the revolution's fundamental
demands, the clerical rulers introduced social and cultural changes that
relegated women to second-class citizenship, imposed restrictions on civil
liberties, prohibited venerated cultural practices and expressions, and violated established rights and interests. None of these changes were part of
the demands of the major collectivities that took part in the overthrow of
the monarchy. Prior to the revolution, social and cultural issues largely
resided in the private sphere, outside the political domain. The clergy's
imposition of these changes sharply contradicted popular expectations.
The restrictions politicized many social and cultural institutions and

practices and generated widespread passive resistance, necessitating end-less repression. The changes rendered the state vulnerable to challenge and attack by broad segments of society.

The new rulers failed to resolve the underlying economic and political contradictions and conflicts that caused the revolution. Instead, they intro-duced traditional Islamic practices and restricted various social and cul-tural freedoms that Iranians enjoyed before the revolution. This disjunc-tion between popular demands and the formation of the theocracy and the imposition of an exclusive state contributed to the reform movement of the 1990s, student protests, and the Green Movement in 2009. Disjunctions also contributed to continuous passive resistance against the imposition of social and cultural restrictions, which the ruling clergy claimed to be fun-damental to the success of the revolution.

In the long run, intensification of repressive policies, the continued exclusion of moderates, and novel ideological claims may have serious implications for the Islamic Republic's future. The exclusion of former allies and rivals who were important members of the postrevolutionary elite has narrowed the scope of the polity and produced an exclusive state with a high concentration of power. These policies and transformations have violated the revolution's promises and undermined trust in the Islamic regime. Persistent repression of popular movements and democratic forces, especially after the election, has eroded the regime's social base of support. Repression contributed to ongoing resistance in social and cultural spheres that constitute the theocracy's cornerstone. More importantly, repression and exclusion—along with adverse economic conditions, declining standard of living, rampant corruption, and cronyism—have rendered the Islamic Republic vulnerable to challenge and set the stage for further conflicts.

In the context of unresolved conflicts and irreconcilable ideologies, the Islamic Republic's rulers face two broad options: political change or repres-sion. They could fulfill popular demands and promises dating back to the revolutionary struggles by implementing fundamental change. Such a course would require them to give up their special powers and privileges, expand and democratize the polity, and grant civil liberties and political freedom. Pursuing this option would reduce the intensity of the conflicts, prolong the stability of the Islamic Republic, and isolate the radical forces in society. Alternatively, the rulers could hold onto the exclusive polity; maintain their special powers and privileges; and continue to restrict access to the polity, repress dissent, and silence the populace and challengers alike. Following such repressive policies and refusing to carry out serious reforms would further polarize and radicalize the public and the opposition and set the stage for broader, more intense conflicts. State failure to resolve the contradictions and to fulfill the promises of the revolution will prepare the way for the rise of more radical democratization movements. Radical ideological claims that discount the role of the people in determining the legitimacy of the Islamic Republic will inevitably produce a radical counterpart among the people, who will reject the system. Pervasive, passive defiance against social and cultural practices imposed by the Islamic Republic already indicate the extent of the rejection of a system that denies people the right to self-determination enshrined in the country's constitution. Endless repression will inevitably radicalize future democratization movements that may pursue change through a revolutionary route.

In sum, more than three decades after the formation of the Islamic Republic, Iranian society is more polarized than ever before. On the one hand, the regime insists on the continuation of the theocratic structures. On the other hand, people are engaged in widespread passive resistance and refuse to live in accordance with the rules of the theocracy. The persisting conflicts have compelled the regime to resort to endless repression. More importantly, the contradictions have generated irreconcilable conflicts and set the stage for protests and clashes that have yet to reach a climax.

CHAPTER TWO

Alternative Routes to Democracy: Synthesizing Structures and Processes

DEMOCRATIZATION IS the process of empowering the civilian population vis-à-vis the state, thereby enabling people to influence and determine government's structure, personnel, and policies. Establishing liberal democracy involves limiting government powers and dismantling arbitrary authoritarian rule, which will empower the civilian population in the political sphere. More importantly, democratization requires political equality and the elimination of categorical inequalities that assign special powers and privileges to some portions of the population, enabling them to control the political system. Such a process may be especially complicated if the powers and privileges of the rulers are enshrined in the constitution, and the state has certain uncommon characteristics. Historically, democratization has taken one or another of two routes, reform or revolution. To understand the process, this chapter presents a new theoretical framework for analyzing these alternative routes to democratization. The framework synthesizes structures of the state, economy, and society, as well as processes that may lead to democratization.

A New Theoretical Framework through Comparative Analysis

A comparative analysis is essential for understanding Iran's democratization. Despite Iran's political features, exceptional in modern history, some aspects of its development can be compared and contrasted with highly authoritarian regimes in developing countries. Iranian intellectuals often compare Iran's development with that of South Korea. Iranian reformists have tried unsuccessfully for more than two decades to democratize Iran through reform, as occurred in South Korea, where the ruling military consented to constitutional change and gradual reforms. South Korea and Iran had roughly the same per capita GDP in 1979. South Korea's military rulers instituted a highly authoritarian political system that had some features in common with the Islamic Republic established after the 1979 revolution. For example, Park Chung-hee, a military officer, imposed a constitution, Yushin, in 1972 that granted him near-absolute powers as president for life. With special powers and privileges, he appointed one-third of the National Assembly, primarily from the military, thereby empowering a special category of the population in the political sphere. As a result, by 1975, the military held 66 percent of the cabinet posts and 22 percent of the National Assembly.[1]

At the same time, South Korea's development diverged from that of Iran in the 1980s, which provides a worthy case for comparative analysis. South Korea succeeded in developing industrially without the extreme corruption and economic inequalities prevalent in other developing countries. A movement arose in South Korea that united the moderate middle class and a powerful, radical, socialist student movement in their demands for democratic institutions. More importantly, the South Korean military, which had not rejected democracy in principle, agreed to constitutional reforms and thus paved the way for democratization. These features diverge sharply from that of Iran and thus make it unlikely that Iran would follow that path.

Iran may be more similar to Indonesia, where Suharto, the strongman of the country, had to be removed from office before democracy could be established. Thus, Indonesia also provides a good case for comparison, because Suharto pursued certain policies that resembled some of those of the Islamic Republic. Under Suharto, Indonesia did not succeed in industrializing, and its economy remained highly dependent on its oil industry. Because it controlled the supply of oil, the state intervened heavily in the country's economic development. Similarly, Indonesia's military—like Iran's Revolutionary Guard—controlled substantial economic assets that provided some measure of autonomy from the civilian population. At the end of Suharto's rule, Indonesian society remained highly unequal in the distribution of wealth and income. In the political arena, Suharto's regime, like the Iranian leadership, categorically rejected liberal democracy. Suharto was able to use the military as a coercive force to repress the people and deny them democratic rights. Thus, the two cases of South Korea and Indonesia can provide revealing comparisons for understanding Iran's failure to democratize through reform.

Predicting Iran's path to democracy requires a new theoretical framework for three reasons. First, despite decades of scholarship, a universally applicable theory of democratization across different historical periods and regions of the world does not yet exist.[2] A comprehensive theory has not emerged, in part because undemocratic regimes are diverse in nature and present dissimilar obstacles to democratization. Second, existing theories neither explain the determinants of the two alternative routes to democratization nor answer the question of why some countries democratize through reform while others must do so through revolution. Finally, most of the literature has focused on Europe and cannot be readily applied to all cases. Other theories have been developed to analyze democratization in the context of developing countries with colonial experience and those dependent economically, politically, or militarily on the United States or Western Europe.

The prevailing theories have difficulty explaining cases like the Islamic Republic of Iran. The Iranian political system has distinct features that make it different from other developing countries. Iran's political system has some democratic institutions, including universal franchise and the right to vote for president and the parliament (Majles). However, most Iranians are excluded from power. And because of onerous political and educational requirements and a vetting system that eliminates the candidacy of citizens who fall outside of acceptable ideological and political limits, most Iranians cannot run for office.

At the same time, Iran's political system has uniquely undemocratic features. The Islamic Republic of Iran is the only internationally recognized theocracy in the contemporary world. It claims to be a "government of God," as Ayatollah Khomeini labeled it, and enforces God's laws, as Ayatollah Ahmad Khatami, the conservative Friday prayer leader of Tehran, put it.[3] The ruling clergy assert that people have no place in determining the legitimacy of the system because it has divine support. According to its religious leaders, the Islamic Republic is a divine trust that was gifted to the revolution and must be protected by the servants of God, even if they are in the minority. Elected representatives, and even the president, have limited power. Real power rests with an unelected cleric, the supreme leader, who is infallible according to some clergy. Without the supreme leader, society would go astray, remarked Ali Saeedi, a cleric and the supreme leader's representative in the Revolutionary Guard.[4] Radical opposition to the regime is considered to be *moharebeh*, enmity against

God, and is punished by death. Apostasy, too, is forbidden in the Islamic Republic. Muslim men who convert to other faiths are condemned to death by law, and women converts are sentenced to prison for life.

The Islamic Republic differs from other authoritarian states in that the regime interferes in virtually all aspects of Iran's social and cultural practices, from gender relations to dress, drinking, singing, and dancing. Extensive state intervention in so many areas led President Rouhani to argue for a reduction in government intrusion into people's lives: "Let the people find their own way to heaven; it is not possible to take people to paradise by force and whip."[5] In response, Ayatollah Khatami, Friday Prayer leader of Tehran, and Ayatollah Ahmad Alamolhoda, Friday prayer leader of Mashhad, disagreed and criticized the president. Khatami opposed giving people freedom to do anything they want in the areas of morality, economy, and culture, proclaiming the government's duty to take the people to heaven even by force.[6]

Finally, the Islamic Republic differs from many developing countries because it is independent of the United States and the West. Unlike the previous monarchy, the current Islamic Republic does not depend on the West for political and military support. As a result, the regime is less vulnerable to external pressures to become more democratic. Moreover, the Islamic regime also has regional ambitions and even challenges the West and existing regional powers in the Middle East. These exceptional features of the case of the Islamic Republic require that we develop a new theoretical framework to understand Iran's political development and democratization.

Alternative Routes to Democratization

Democratization can proceed through one of two paths: reform or revolution. Democratization through political reform where power-holders maintain their power is often marked by gradual, piecemeal change in aspects of the political system. These reforms potentially involve various combinations of actors, such as the ruling elites and opposition challengers who may be engaged in negotiation or disruptive collective action. For example, Taiwan democratized in the 1980s through reform, and the mechanism involved both political negotiation and social protest. The contrasting route, political revolution, involves abrupt, forcible removal or the resignation of the political leader or leadership from office through noninstitutional collective action and protests. The people of the Philippines democratized in 1986 by removing Ferdinand Marcos from power through popular demonstrations and collective action. More recently, the people of Tunisia and Egypt forced their political leaders out of office and instituted political changes.

A reformist route to democratization may involve disruptive collective action, but political leaders maintain power and introduce changes in certain aspects of the existing political structure to ensure political equality and a broadening of the polity. In the reformist route, existing elites and power-holders often play an important role and may not trust or favor a substantial involvement of the population and the working classes in the democratization processes, even though these latter may be involved heavily in the initial disruptive processes that result in reform. This route to democracy may be undertaken by the elite to prevent complete transformation of the political system and the power structure. Conflicts in the reformist route tend to be relatively limited and primarily focused on the nature of the political system. In other arenas, the state and society are characterized by some degree of cohesion and, as a result, democratic challengers do not demand significant alterations in the social structure. Democratic forces in the reformist route may be more likely to reconcile their conflicts and reach compromise. We can hypothesize that the greater the extent of social, economic, and ideological cohesion between state and society, the greater the likelihood that democratization will proceed through the reformist route.

A revolutionary route to democratization involves noninstitutional, disruptive collective action and the abrupt removal of power-holders, paving the way for fundamental changes. In contrast with the reformist route that may largely be controlled by elites, the revolutionary route to democratization involves greater popular participation through disruptive processes. The revolutionary route to democracy often involves multiple conflicts that are irreconcilable and elite intransigence that rejects compromise.[7] These conflicts tend to reduce cohesion between the state and society and prevent contending forces from cooperating and compromising. Thus we can hypothesize that the greater the breadth of the conflict, the greater the likelihood that democratization will proceed through the disruptive revolutionary route.

The revolutions of the past century can generally be divided into two categories: social revolutions and political revolutions. Revolutionary overthrow of the state throughout much of the twentieth century was less predictable than reforms and more vulnerable to failure in democratizing, depending on the new postrevolutionary elite's ideology. Social revolutions led by radical leaders did not generally produce liberal democracies, as they often resulted in large-scale transformation of the social structures, centralization, and expansion of state power. In contrast, political revolutions frequently created liberal democracies in which revolutionaries dismantled undemocratic regimes, limited state power, and introduced the rule of law. The "colorful" revolutions of the past few decades fall in the category of political revolutions.

Although a revolutionary path to democracy may not be a desirable option from a reformist perspective, the determining factor in alternative routes has to do with the nature of the conflicts. The challenging issue is to identify which route is more likely given existing structural conditions and barriers. In other words, the task of scholars is to uncover the forces and variables that explain and predict the determinants of each route: under what conditions may contending parties reach compromise, and under what conditions is compromise not possible due to the irreconcilability of the conflicts? In what follows, I propose a model to specify the variables that determine the likely route to democratization.

To explain alternative routes to democratization, a comprehensive interdisciplinary and synthetic approach is needed to incorporate variables that analyze the social, economic, and political features of undemocratic states and societies. This work will focus on the following key variables:

- State structure, ideology, and their relation to the society
- State intervention in the economy and social and cultural arenas
- The ruling elites' economic position, occupational backgrounds, and social status
- The nature of economic development, inequalities, and corruption
- The ideology and politics of challengers
- The ideology of social movements
- The capacities of various social groups and classes for mobilization and collective action
- The extent of convergence of contradictions and conflicts
- The likelihood of consolidation of the opposition and the formation of broad coalitions

Finally, analyses of democratization must also explore the role of external factors and conditions such as wars and external pressures and influences.

Although predicting the future remains an inexact science, these conditions and variables will help us analyze Iran's likely route to democratization. If these variables remain contradictory and point in different directions, the analysis is inconclusive. But if most of the conditions and variables point in the same direction, they will strengthen the predictive value of the analysis. The work will address three important questions regarding Iranians' struggle to democratize. Why did the 1979 revolution fail to democratize Iran despite the prominent role of secular democratic forces in initiating the protests and their involvement throughout the revolutionary struggles? Why has the reform movement thus far failed to democratize Iran? What might be Iran's likely route to successful democratization?

Exclusive State and Political Repression

States characterized by exclusive rule tend to limit the extent of the polity, denying power to the vast majority of the population and rendering the rulers vulnerable in times of conflict and crisis. Exclusive states often centralize and concentrate power, which blocks access to the state and centers of political power. Even though exclusive states may grant universal suffrage and provide political contestation, they tend to eliminate or render irrelevant formal democratic institutions. These states also are inclined to assume a high level of autonomy from the underlying population and risk becoming unaccountable to the people that they govern.[8] Exclusive states are especially vulnerable to challenge, because they restrict access to the polity—often for prolonged periods and without providing options for real change.[9] To maintain these characteristics and their power, such states would have to rely on the coercive apparatus and repression. Exclusive states may be rooted in the power of a single ruler (personalistic) or a social category.

These alternative structures have different political consequences for democratization. Exclusive states that are based on personalistic rule may be able to democratize through reform because of the departure of the power-holder or weaknesses in the succession. But where exclusive rule is based on categorical inequalities, where a specific social group with certain characteristics rules, democratization might be more likely through a revolutionary transformation. The reason is that categorical inequalities in the political system tend to bestow special privileges on vested interests and thus polarize the political system, reduce cohesion between the state and society, and thus undermine the likelihood of cooperation and compromise. Challengers cannot expect democratic changes from the removal of the leader alone. They would need to change the entire system based on categorical inequalities, often enshrined in the constitution, and remove the entire category of power-holders from their positions of power and privilege. The scale of such an undertaking and resistance against it may require a disruptive, revolutionary movement toward democracy. In addition, the resistance of rulers and their employment of repeated repression tends to undermine the position of the moderate forces in the long run and favor the ascendancy of radicals.

Thus, exclusive states that are based on categorical inequalities and repress the opposition affect the alternative paths to democratization. If this analysis is accurate, persistence of exclusive rule characterized by special privileges for the rulers based on categorical inequalities often has the effect of channeling democratization through a revolutionary route. The extent of state repression may also affect mobilization options in future rounds of conflict and channel democratization through a reformist or disruptive, revolutionary route. We can tentatively hypothesize that while moderate repression of democratic opposition may permit democratization through reforms, high levels of repression may require a revolutionary route in order to achieve democratization. In South Korea, for example, the military repressed the moderate opposition in the name of national security and economic development but did not completely destroy opposition forces. The moderate opposition took the lead during the crucial period of conflicts and democratized South Korea through reform in the mid-1980s, despite the fact that the military maintained political control. In contrast, a number of governments in other developing countries— including Iran under the monarchy, Nicaragua under Somoza, Indonesia under Suharto, and Egypt under Mubarak—severely repressed the moderate opposition and eventually were forced out of power through disruptive revolutions led by their more radical opponents.

State Ideology and Intervention in Social-Cultural Arenas

State ideology generally articulates rulers' interest and orientation toward democracy. It reveals whether the state is willing to accept empowering civilians, guaranteeing political equality, and dismantling special privileges that result in categorical inequalities. As a result, the nature of state ideology may affect the route to democratization in at least two ways. First, the link between state ideology and the path toward democratization rests on the critical distinction between states that accept democratic institutions as long as they abide by certain conditions and states that reject democracy in principle. Undemocratic states may subscribe to democratic ideology but may postpone it under certain conditions, such as urgency of economic development, necessity for order, threats of internal "instability," or external threats. These regimes do not, as a rule, promote an alternative ideology, but neither do they repress the moderate opposition to the point of elimination. The acceptance of democracy in principle by such undemocratic states may allow for compromise and ultimately pave the way for democratization through a reformist route. Consequently, rulers and democratic challengers may agree on some commonality of interests and goals. Faced with internal and external pressures, such regimes may, in time, negotiate agreements with the moderate democratic challengers and relinquish power in favor of a democratic opposition.

The South Korean experience provides a good example. Early on, South Korean military leaders pointed to the necessity of economic development and prioritized economic development over political development and democratization. In his book, Park wrote,

> I want to emphasize, and re-emphasize, that the key factor of the May 16th Military Revolution was to effect an industrial revolution in South Korea. Since the primary objective of the revolution was to achieve a national renaissance, the revolution envisaged political, social and cultural reforms as well. My chief concern, however, was economic revolution. One must eat and breathe before concerning himself with politics, social affairs and culture. Without a hope for an economic future, reforms in other fields could not be expected to yield fruit. I must again emphasize that without economic reconstruction, there would be no such thing as triumph over Communism or attaining independence.[10]

More importantly, Park and his military associates never rejected liberal democracy; they emphasized that it had to wait until after successful economic development. Although they severely repressed the leftist students and the communist opposition, the military rulers of South Korea defended liberal democracy on ideological grounds. Park declared: "The military revolution is not the destruction of democracy in Korea. Rather it is a way for saving it."[11] He elaborated on his actions in his book: "We cannot deviate from the principle of opposing communism and building liberal democracy. So long as we adhere to democratic principles we cannot suppress the freedom of public opinion."[12] "The ultimate purpose of the revolution was to construct a sound democratic society."[13] Despite repressing the moderate opposition, the military never completely eliminated them. In the face of popular protests, the military agreed to the moderate opposition's demand for constitutional change and democratic reforms in 1987.

In contrast, states that reject democracy in principle and advocate a nondemocratic or antidemocratic ideology preclude any alternative for democratization except through a revolutionary route. Ideologically driven, antidemocratic regimes often develop authoritarian ideologies to justify and legitimize their rule. Antidemocratic states may go to the extreme of adopting ideologies that grant rulers absolute authority and thereby become autonomous from the underlying population, and reject accountability. In such cases, rulers may go so far as to invoke higher powers to bolster their legitimacy and deny popular sovereignty. By integrating religion and politics, these regimes empower the clergy or those who represent the higher powers, and they inevitably establish categorical inequalities. They may impose restrictive codes of political conduct, deny people the right to determine their own destiny, and attempt to punish deviations. Claiming to represent higher powers, these regimes may refuse any checks and balances that could restrict their political activities and undertake extremely repressive measures to maintain power. These undemocratic states continuously implement ideological indoctrination to control public interaction and behavior.

Regimes with these characteristics may also restrict political participation on ideological grounds and erect rigid boundaries between who can and who cannot be included in the polity. They may impose onerous criteria that severely limit the range of candidates for political office. To maintain purity, such states may continuously purge the polity and ultimately polarize the political sphere. Rulers in ideologically driven, antidemocratic states may refuse compromise and render moderate opposition irrelevant or ineffective. They have to rely on the coercive apparatus to maintain power.

These features have profound consequences for political conflicts and the route to democratization. The introduction of absolutist principles, categorical inequalities, and rejection of compromise undermine the likelihood of instituting democracy. Democracies operate on the basis of popular sovereignty and allow for reforms rather than absolute principles that are immutable. In addition, democratization involves empowering the civilian population vis-à-vis the state and has to reject categorical inequalities. Thus, any democratic opposition must abrogate undemocratic powers and special privileges. Democratization also entails maintaining common ground and political compromise as well as permitting moderate democratic opposition to remain active. But ideologically driven, antidemocratic states tend to reject all these conditions and consequently polarize and radicalize the opposition in the long run. As a result, antidemocratic regimes may inadvertently strengthen the position of radical forces, whose only remaining option to bring about democratization is to employ disruptive mechanisms. Prolonged exclusion and repression also have a tendency to radicalize ordinary people whose political shift may strengthen the position of radical democratic challengers. With broad popular support from the public, democratic challengers may press for a fundamental transformation of the polity through a disruptive, revolutionary route to democracy.

Indonesia under Suharto provides some illustration. Suharto in Indonesia created a political system that was highly authoritarian and rejected democracy in principle. For Suharto, Indonesia's political system provided no room for opposition for opposition's sake alone, only to voice differences. In his view, Western liberal democracy was wanting and had to be abandoned.[14] The state under Suharto became highly autonomous and unaccountable. Suharto's policies rendered the moderate, democratic opposition completely ineffective and irrelevant for thirty-two years. Unlike South Korean moderates, who organized many nationwide protests against the military government, the Indonesian opposition was unable to organize even a single major protest by the end of Suharto's rule. These policies in turn radicalized large segments of the students and the youth. In the absence of a viable, moderate democratic opposition, Indonesian students spearheaded the struggles for democratization.[15] They demanded Suharto's removal and refused to consider negotiation or compromise. Student protests in 1998 provoked large-scale riots by the unemployed and the urban poor that shook the foundation of the Indonesian economy. These developments in turn radicalized larger segments of Indonesian society, including segments of the business community, and led the armed forces to abandon support for Suharto, forcing him out of office.

State ideology also influences the extent of the leaders' intervention in social and cultural spheres and the route to democratization from another perspective. In the absence of direct state intervention in social and cultural arenas, the scope of conflicts remains relatively restricted. In times of crisis, such states may agree to reform and gradually democratize. The South Korean military regime did not intervene significantly in social and cultural spheres except to prohibit weddings in hotels and extravagance at funerals. The goal of these interventions was to promote savings and capital accumulation rather than impose strict social and cultural codes of conduct. Conflict during the rule of the military was restricted to the political arena. As a result, middle-class challengers and protesters in the 1980s limited their demands to political reform, and under disruptive pressures, the military agreed to constitutional changes.

In contrast, extensive state intervention in social and cultural issues transfers the locus of decision making from the private to the public sphere, thus empowering the government and subjecting civil society to antidemocratic processes, undermining personal liberties and civil rights. State-imposed cultural codes of conduct and social relations range from personal appearance, dress codes, and music and musical performances to gender and ethnic relations. These restrictions politicize multiple issues and subject them to public scrutiny, contention, and possibly resistance. They may polarize society and render the state more vulnerable to challenge and attack. These processes increase the likelihood that democratization will only be achieved through a disruptive, revolutionary path.

In particular, state imposition of religion and religious practices politicizes these spheres and eradicates freedom of thought and religion. The public, in turn, may regard the state's imposition of absolutist cultural and social standards as a violation of basic rights, leading to rejection of religious practices and even conversion to other faiths. Because absolutist standards cannot be negotiated, state imposition of such standards may produce resistance, necessitating state repression. The state may construe deviation from official edict as apostasy, "warring against God," and punish it accordingly, thereby criminalizing sin. Reliance on repression to enforce state religion may polarize society and reduce the likelihood of compromise and reform. As a result, a high degree of government intervention in social and cultural spheres may channel democratization movements along a disruptive, revolutionary route.

State Intervention in the Economy

State intervention in the economy may also affect the route to democratization by affecting the nature of social and political conflicts. Such intervention ranges from government regulation to ownership of state enterprises, vast economic resources, and involvement in various economic activities. In general, a low level of state intervention in capital accumulation, as occurs in market economies, reduces the probability that the state will become a direct target of attack and may facilitate a reformist route to democratization. In Western liberal democracies, democratization entails allocating the country's economic assets within the private sphere and the market system. These states generally refrain from intervening heavily in the process of capital allocation and accumulation. Where market forces determine these activities, they tend to reduce the scale and scope of political conflicts because markets are abstract, decentralized, depoliticized entities that cannot be overthrown. Disadvantaged collectivities may blame themselves or their fate. Where the state engages in narrow regulative activities, it may become an integrative rather than a divisive force if people perceive the government as an autonomous entity that serves general, societal interests. Adversely affected groups do not blame the state for market-generated disadvantages but instead seek government intervention to redress their grievances. Under such conditions, democratization struggles are more likely to adopt a reformist rather than a revolutionary character.[16]

In contrast, where state intervention in capital accumulation is high and the state controls vast economic resources, the likelihood is greater that democratization will proceed on a revolutionary route. In general, a high level of intervention and control by the state of vast economic resources empowers the power-holders and may undermine democratic forces. A state that is hyperactive and intervenes extensively in capital accumulation may become the single largest industrialist, banker, and employer in the country. States that own natural resources, such as oil and rentier states, may easily become hyperactive, expanding their economic activities and exerting enormous influence in the financial and industrial sectors. The high degree of state intervention contradicts a basic requirement of liberal democracy—that is, the empowering of the civilian population vis-à-vis the state in the economic arena. Thus, states that intervene extensively in capital allocation and accumulation may generate intense social conflicts that could produce revolutionary challenges.

More specifically, a high degree of state intervention in the economy and capital accumulation may have significant political consequences. A hyperactive state can readily become the target of attack because it replaces the abstract, decentralized, and depoliticized market mechanism with a visible, concrete social entity.[17] Where government intervention is high and the state controls vast economic resources, economic and political powers tend to converge in the political arena, and the scope of conflicts in the state expands. In addition to being targets of conflicts over political power, hyperactive states also become the center of economic conflicts. As inequalities increase in the early stages of economic development, state policies will be held directly responsible for rising inequalities. In times of economic downturn, the state—not market forces—will be blamed for failure and mismanagement, once again making the government vulnerable to challenge and attack. Those who are adversely affected tend to become politicized and may call for revolutionary change and the forcible removal of power-holders.

In addition, a high level of intervention by the government may adversely affect and radicalize the politics of two major classes: capitalists and workers. State intervention may weaken the private sector in situations in which government activities compete with and restrict the role of the private sector. The state's intervention may also co-opt a small segment of the capitalist class by offering special privileges unavailable to the rest of the class. When this government intrusion is in the area of capital allocation, it may politicize the financial system, because smaller entrepreneurs are likely to be excluded from the most favorable loans and government subsidies. As a result, the excluded capitalists may withdraw their support for the state and side with opposition forces in times of conflict.

A high degree of intervention by the government in capital accumulation may adversely affect the working classes. Where state intervention is high and the government is the principal employer, workers may quickly become politicized and direct their grievances against the state. Hyperactive states that intervene extensively in the economy to promote rapid industrialization may prevent workers from organizing and forming independent unions for collective bargaining. When the government bans labor actions and intervenes on behalf of employers during economic conflicts, class conflict is likely to become politicized, and the working class may join with revolutionary forces to overthrow the state.

In cases in which extremely repressive and corrupt regimes rely on the coercive apparatus to maintain a grip on power, they may permit or encourage the military to intervene in capital accumulation by undertaking lucrative economic activities. Repressive regimes may need to provide special privileges for military and paramilitary personnel who carry out the repressive tasks, particularly if the regime experiences erosion of social support. Military intervention in capital accumulation may in turn have important economic and political consequences. Economic privileges may give the military unfair advantage in competition with private sector businesses operating in a volatile market. Under such conditions, the military may control vast economic resources, develop monopolistic enterprises, or use its coercive instruments to undermine its competitors. Where special interests such as the military are permitted to engage in economic activities and accumulation of capital, they may undermine notions of state neutrality and reinforce a sense of injustice among civilian populations who are excluded from state protection and resources.

More importantly, the military may use its economic privileges to gain advantage in the political sphere and undermine democratic institutions. Economic privileges may generate a sense of autonomy and superiority among the military and undermine civilian rule. The military may also pursue antidemocratic policies and polarize the political sphere. Military intervention in the economy and capital accumulation may have significant consequences in the political arena. The military in both Indonesia[18] and Egypt[19] engaged in a great deal of economic activities, operated their own enterprises, and enjoyed economic privileges. Democratization movements in both countries went through a revolutionary path. President Suharto of Indonesia was forced out of office in part because his state and military intervened extensively in the economy and capital accumulation. President Mubarak of Egypt was overthrown through a revolutionary route that involved a popular uprising. The Egyptian military interfered in the political arena after the revolution and removed the elected president, Mohammad Morsi, from power, effectively blocking the democratic process. Thus, where state power is upheld by coercive forces that are also leading economic and political actors, the likelihood is greater that democratization movements will pursue a revolutionary, rather than a reformist, route.

In contrast to Indonesia and many other developing countries, the South Korean state gradually reduced intervention in the economy prior to the rise of the democratization movement, paving the path for democratization through political reform. State intervention in the economy and capital accumulation in South Korea was relatively high in the 1960s and early 1970s. The government privatized most banks and state enterprises in the early 1980s. The South Korean public share of fixed capital expenditure was roughly 19 percent, during 1978–1980, well below developing countries.[20] Private conglomerates known as "chaebols," not state-owned enterprises, dominated the economy when democratization struggles intensified in the mid-1980s. South Korean leaders engaged in some corrupt practices, but the military did not operate large economic enterprises or control vast economic empires of its own. Because the level of government intervention in the economy and capital accumulation was low, the scope of the conflicts was limited, and democratization proceeded through constitutional reform.

In contrast, state intervention in Indonesia under Suharto was very high and contributed to the overthrow of the government through disruptive protests. The Indonesian state intervened in every aspect of the economy. Article 33 of the constitution stated that all areas of the economy crucial to the welfare of the people should be controlled by the state. Under Suharto, the government owned the lucrative oil industry. It also established state-owned plantations, making the government the largest landowner in Indonesia. The state's share of fixed capital expenditures reached nearly 46 percent during the years 1978–1980, more than twice that of South Korea.[21] State enterprises contributed 25 percent of GDP by 1983 and paid roughly 50 percent of the total corporate taxes paid to the government.[22] The assets of state enterprises surpassed those of the swelling private conglomerates as late as 1995.[23] Suharto and the state were held responsible for the economic downturn of the latter part of the 1990s, and the opposition succeeded in removing him from power.

Economic Development, Inequality, Corruption, and Democratization

The nature of economic development may also influence the intensity and breadth of social conflicts and the route to democratization. Successful development—as measured by high per capita income and human capital—channels social conflicts in a reformist direction. Industrial development increases the resilience of the economy and renders it less vulnerable to sudden crises and disruptive political experiences. Successful economic development reduces dependence on monocrops and diversifies the economy, which becomes less vulnerable to the vagaries of the world market. Where economic development succeeds in transforming the social structure and improving the standard of living, major segments of the population acquire a stake in preserving the broad character of the social structure, thus expanding the social base of support for the state. Successful economic development also expands the middle class, an important, critical element for democratization.[24] Economic development also produces a stable, skilled industrial workforce, as well as a vibrant civil society, essential for democratization.[25] These two sectors may pursue moderate, reformist politics and avoid radicalism. Such conditions, in turn, may encourage moderation in politics and prevent radicalization of political actors. Under these conditions, democratization struggles are apt to assume a reformist character.

Successful economic development also affects the distribution of income and wealth in a more egalitarian direction. Although economic development in the short run may increase inequalities, it tends in the long run to reduce income inequalities and concentration of wealth, increasing the income of the middle and working classes. Thus, successful development may undermine forces advocating radical transformation of the social structure.[26] Economic development may also reduce inequalities in the agrarian sector by increasing productivity. Public policies such as land reform may generate an interest in the existing social order among agricultural workers. Finally, successful economic development has a tendency to reduce corruption and cronyism by producing well-off businesses and honest, competent civil servants who do not rely on corruption to perform their duties. For all these reasons, successful economic development is likely to reduce the intensity of social conflicts and generate moderate or reformist challenges rather than radical, disruptive and revolutionary movements.

On the other hand, failed economic development renders the system vulnerable to crises and sharp downturns, particularly where economies depend on monocrops. Economic crises and material deterioration tend to undermine popular support for the rulers as the public ends up questioning the competence of those in power. Thus, deteriorating material conditions and a declining standard of living have the effect of generating support for contentious politics and collective protests. Economic crises may impose heavy costs and sacrifices and violate established rights and interests. Repeated and prolonged violations of established rights and interests tend to polarize and radicalize disadvantaged collectivities and prevent a search for common grounds and compromise. As a result, these collectivities may also pursue political change through a revolutionary route to democracy.

Failure of economic development beyond an intermediate level will result in high levels of inequality in the distribution of income and wealth.[27] Extensive inequality tends to polarize social and political systems, intensify distribution conflicts, weaken or eliminate moderate forces, and prevent compromise and the search for common ground. If economic inequalities and a rising concentration of wealth are generated by state policies, conflicts may then politicize rapidly and target the state. In addition, if economic and political powers converge within the same collectivities, such convergence has a likelihood of revealing the roots of privilege and the accumulation of wealth. These conditions often politicize and radicalize the public. Victims of social and historical processes do not blame the market or fate for their misfortune. Instead, they may directly attack the state and the privileged during economic downturns and political crises, demanding radical redistribution. It can be hypothesized that the greater the association between political power and economic privileges, the greater the likelihood that disadvantaged collectivities will become politicized and radicalized. More importantly, these conditions encourage radical challengers to take center stage in the struggles for democratization. Thus, failed economic development tends to promote greater inequalities, greater polarization, and radicalization, increasing the likelihood of producing democratization movements that pursue a revolutionary route.

Failed economic development also stimulates corruption and cronyism, thereby further increasing the likelihood that democratization will take a disruptive course. Rampant corruption and cronyism are often by-products of state control over immense economic resources. Extensive state corruption and cronyism undermine trust and the legitimacy of the government and increase ill-gotten wealth. They also increase inequalities in favor of the privileged and power-holders at the expense of small business and the rest of society, polarizing the population. Corruption places an additional tax on businesses and the civilian population and skews the distribution of resources. Cronyism violates the basic principle of state impartiality by favoring certain constituencies and unfairly determining the distribution of privilege. Corruption and cronyism may lead to the politicization of ordinary people who may often view these manifestations as evidence of inequality and fundamental unfairness that need to change. Thus, high levels of corruption and cronyism may reduce the social base of support for the state and prevent finding common ground and compromise, encouraging democratization by means of a disruptive, revolutionary route.

The extent and locus of corruption may also play an important role in generating social conflicts. Where corruption is limited and concentrated at the elite level, it may be relatively inconspicuous and may not generate large-scale conflicts. However, where corruption is systemic and wide-ranging throughout the state and society, it may generate the perception that the system routinely serves special interests and cannot be reformed, a view that may polarize the public against the state and give rise to demands for fundamental transformations. Thus, the stronger the association between the state and corruption and the accumulation of ill-gotten wealth, the greater the state's vulnerability, the greater the possibility of radical attacks against the existing order, and the more likely that democratization movements will proceed via a revolutionary route.

In sum, successful economic development tends to reduce the intensity and breadth of social and political conflicts by reducing corruption, cronyism, and inequalities in the distribution of wealth and income, thereby increasing the likelihood that democratization will proceed by way of reform. In contrast, failed economic development tends to increase inequalities and promote cronyism and corruption, adversely affecting broad segments of the population. These developments increase the intensity and breadth of social and political conflicts and generate conditions for the consolidation and formation of broad coalitions, which may lead to democratization through a revolutionary path.

Among Asian countries, South Korea's successful economic development and democratization through reform highlight some of the issues discussed above and support these hypotheses. Following South Korea's military coup, the country's per capita income soared from $110 in 1962 to more than $2,370 in 1986, while South Korea's per capita GNP jumped from ninety-ninth to forty-fourth in the World Bank's sample of 135 countries.[28] South Korea's per capita income and economic development lagged behind that of Iran in the early 1970s but caught up with Iran's by 1980. Significantly, South Korea's per capita income far surpassed that of Iran when South Korea democratized in 1987 and hosted the Olympics in 1988. Admittedly, the state's development policies principally benefitted large enterprises, and the relationship between the government and big business was marked by considerable corruption. However, during South Korea's rapid economic development, income inequality was not very high by international standards, nor was corruption as widespread as in other developing countries such as Indonesia. In South Korea, corruption did not produce a group of highly visible wealthy government officials who attracted national and international attention. Economic conflicts and issues did not play a significant role during South Korea's democratization struggles because the focus of protesters, aside from radical students, remained primarily on political demands and reforms.

Other countries were not as successful in producing genuine economic development and therefore were overthrown by revolutionary struggles. The Philippines, Indonesia, and Egypt had periods of rapid economic growth promoted by oil boom, foreign aid, or borrowing. But none of these countries successfully industrialized or avoided dependence on oil and gas or, in the case of the Philippines, other raw materials. Although the standard of living improved somewhat for the population, state economic policies served the interests of large capital and generated extensive inequality in the distribution of income and wealth. States in all three countries engaged in corruption and cronyism to a considerable degree, undermining legitimacy and the popular trust that the power-holders could actually serve societal or national interests. Presidents Marcos, Suharto, and Mubarak used state power to enrich themselves and their allies but failed to develop their economies. Eventually, all three leaders were overthrown by popular struggles.

Alternative Mobilization Channels and Exit Options

The mobilization options available to challengers and the exit options for elites and power-holders also affect the route to democratization. Challengers pursuing democracy through political reform in highly authoritarian systems may be well positioned to seize the opportunity created by a decline in political repression. Relatively privileged segments of the population and even moderate factions of the regime may also support democratization through reform, which holds the promise of being accomplished within existing institutions without a massive cost in human lives in a disruptive revolutionary process. On the other hand, challengers interested in democratization may have limited options and be forced to abandon routes that prove unsuccessful and seek alternatives. If the power elites refuse to accept reform and counter with repression, democratic challengers may become radicalized and turn to a revolutionary route in pursuit of democracy, using noninstitutional, disruptive collective action to remove power-holders from office. Political repression and prolonged exclusion from the polity may exacerbate polarization and radicalization and push challengers to pursue democratization by means of revolution.

The elites' economic interests, occupations, and social position also affect the route to democratization. If the ruling elites' economic interests are relatively secure, they will be less dependent on the political system for survival. In times of conflict, elites may negotiate and agree to political reform and change. Hence, where elites' economic position is secure, democratization is more likely to advance along a reformist route. Conversely, ruling elites may resist political reform if they lack a secure economic position, depend on the political system to maintain their privileged status, or wield political power to enrich themselves and their allies. The greater the dependence of ruling elites on political power to maintain their economic status, therefore, the greater the likelihood that democratization will require a disruptive, revolutionary route to succeed.

Finally, the capacity of challengers and the vulnerability of the state may also affect democratization routes. Where democratic forces have limited capacity and the state is not vulnerable, they tend to demand minimal changes and prefer to pursue democracy through reform. In contrast, where democratic forces have a higher capacity to challenge the rulers and the state is vulnerable, challengers may demand radical changes and seek democratization through a revolutionary route.

Elites' occupational backgrounds may also affect the likely route of democratization. If ruling elites possess independent, viable occupations they can return to if they lose power, they may be willing to give up power and accept reform.[29] On the other hand, if the elites lack viable occupations to return to, they may resist reforms, forcing democratizers to pursue a revolutionary route. The social status of the elite, too, may affect the route of democratization. Ruling elites that enjoy positive social esteem may be willing to accept democratization if it includes a high probability that they can regain power through political contest and election. Under such conditions, the elites may give up power and negotiate democratization through a reformist route. In contrast, ruling elites without positive social esteem may reject democratic reform if it appears unlikely that they can regain power in a democratic political system. In this case, democratization movements may be more likely to proceed by way of a disruptive or revolutionary route.

South Korean democratization in the 1980s proceeded through reform because of several important factors. The military regime reduced repression for the moderate opposition, which enabled the latter to mobilize and press for reform. By June 1987, moderates were able to attract radical students to their camp and form an implicit coalition that proved to be successful in democratizing the country through reform. South Korea's military rulers agreed to democratic reform and, despite some corruption, did not use their power to build vast fortunes. They had the option of returning to military life in case they lost an election and had to relinquish power. The military elites eventually withdrew to their barracks, although they actually won the first presidential election following democratic reforms. In contrast, the shah of Iran, President Marcos of the Philippines, and Suharto of Indonesia held onto their power because, through control of the state, they succeeded in accumulating large amounts of wealth. All three insisted on maintaining power and refused reforms. In the end, all three were overthrown in revolutions.

Scope, Convergence of Conflicts, and Route to Democratization

Finally, the scope and the interaction among conflicts also influence the route to democratization. Where the state and society generate few conflicts and do not affect broad segments of the population at multiple levels, democratization movements may advance through a reformist route, seeking gradual, piecemeal resolution of contentious issues. For example, where state intervention in the economy and the cultural sphere is low and economic development has been successful, conflict may be limited to political rights and issues. Hence, democratic forces may be able to focus on bringing about incremental change in the political system alone, and therefore democratization will likely proceed through reform.

In contrast, convergence of multiple conflicts may channel democratization through a disruptive, revolutionary route. Convergence of multiple conflicts tends to expand their breadth and depth. Convergence of multiple conflicts between the state and society makes it unlikely that strife will remain localized around narrow issues or affect only small segments of society. Where conflicts involve both the state and society, they reduce cohesion between the two, broaden and expand the scale of confrontations, and intensify the impact of the conflicts. Multiple conflicts inevitably polarize the people and the state into mutually exclusive camps, reducing the likelihood of finding common ground and compromise through reform. Convergence of conflicts arising from a high level of state intervention in the economy and the cultural arena, together with an antidemocratic ideology and political repression, will likely focus broad dissatisfaction on the state. Even economically privileged classes may be adversely affected by converging multiple conflicts such as political exclusion, social restrictions, and state intervention in social and cultural practices. Where multiple conflicts converge and focus on the political system, the state must resort to widespread, endless repression, further antagonizing the people and reducing the likelihood of reconciliation. In addition, state repression may render the two sides irreconcilable and reduce the likelihood of compromise and reform. Thus, convergence of multiple conflicts may impose heavy costs on the populace and, in the long run, radicalize the people, with the result that they demand fundamental transformation.

The convergence of multiple conflicts also makes it difficult for democratic challengers to resolve the conflicts gradually or in a piecemeal fashion, because the discord is likely to assume an irreconcilable character. Where this occurs, a reformist route to democratization is less likely as conflicts become too numerous to be resolved through step-by-step changes. Reformist challengers can no longer argue that the system has advantageous elements or institutions that should be preserved. As a result, convergence of multiple conflicts tends to generate democratization movements that are likely to assume a revolutionary character focused on fundamental transformations in the political system. As broad segments of the population become increasingly polarized and politicized, they are more likely to consolidate, form broad coalitions, and demand radical transformation of the state. This process increases the likelihood that a revolutionary route will be necessary to achieve democratization.

South Korea's military rulers never rejected democracy in principle. Even as they repressed the opposition, they supported a democratic future when the country developed economically. State intervention in capital accumulation in the South Korean economy declined drastically by the early 1980s, and intervention by the government in social and cultural spheres was always very limited. Successful economic development, together with a relatively low level of inequality in income distribution compared with that of other developing countries, prevented convergence of multiple conflicts in South Korea during intense political conflicts. State repression of the moderate opposition declined a few years prior to the democratization agreement and facilitated mobilization and collective action. During the most intense political conflicts, the moderate opposition focused on a narrow demand for constitutional revisions to eliminate military privileges. The absence of multiple conflicts and the presence of moderation in political demands in South Korea facilitated democratization through a reformist route.

In contrast, the prerevolutionary rulers of Iran (the shah), the Philippines (Marcos), and Indonesia (Suharto) rejected democracy in principle and imposed exclusive states that denied access to the polity to the vast majority of the population. All three rulers repressed their country's moderate opposition and rendered them weak. State intervention in Iran under the shah and in Indonesia under Suharto remained very high. In the Philippines, it rose during Marcos's rule but afterward declined somewhat because of the economic crisis.[30] The three economies failed to develop and industrialize successfully, and in all three countries, economic development widened income inequality as wealth was highly concentrated. All three countries also had serious problems with state corruption and cronyism, and none could claim to serve national or societal, rather than particular, interests. As a result, once conflicts were under way, multiple grievances converged and prevented the countries from democratizing through political reform. The convergence of multiple conflicts produced revolutionary crises that led to the overthrow of the three regimes in 1979, 1986, and 1998.

Consolidation, External Pressures, and Democratization Outcome

While states and social structures set the stage for conflict and strongly affect the likely path of democratization, they do not actually determine either the process or the outcome. The process of democratization and its outcome depend heavily on the capacity, solidarity, scope, and ideology of the opposition, and the likelihood of consolidation and broad coalition formation. To initiate the democratization process, major collectivities and classes must have unifying organizations and solidarity structures to be able to mobilize, engage in collective action, and challenge the power structure. Collectivities that are subject to intense repression often fail to mobilize and join democratic coalitions. Such collectivities may have to wait for declining repression or favorable opportunities to mobilize. While strategically positioned actors, such as students, often mobilize and initiate democratization struggles against highly authoritarian regimes, they cannot by themselves effect a democratic transformation. They must expand their chances for success by forming coalitions with other collectivities that play crucial roles in the social structure and in the production and distribution of goods and services.

Broad coalitions and consolidation tend to isolate the government and reduce or eliminate the social basis of support for the regime, leaving it vulnerable. In addition, broad-based coalitions and movements have the potential to disrupt the normal functioning of the social structure through large-scale collective action such as general strikes and popular uprisings. Disruption of the social structure may broaden the scope of the conflicts and result in factionalism and the defection of some members of the polity, producing political instability. More importantly, broad coalitions can disrupt the functioning of the social structure and signal instability in the political sphere. Political instability may provoke defections from the armed forces and limit the ability of the state to repress the challengers. In the case of government intransigence, broad coalitions and the disruption of the social structure may provide greater social support for armed struggle as the last resort to defeat military forces.[31]

Forming broad coalitions is particularly essential under conditions in which regimes are highly repressive and elites are monolithic and enjoy the support of the armed forces and paramilitary entities. Such regimes are capable of erecting enormous obstacles to democratization. With consolidation and enhanced capacity, democratic challengers may choose to escalate their demands and proceed through revolution to overthrow governments that refuse to democratize.

Consolidation and formation of broad coalitions are infrequent because different social classes and collectivities have diverse interests and capacities for mobilization and collective action. Class or ethnic conflicts, which often fail to target the state, may impede coalition formation and consolidation. Intensified class conflict involving only economic demands may actually block democratization by preventing the capitalist class and workers from joining a broad democratic coalition. In fact, intense class conflict may force the capitalists to rely on the state for protection, thus making democratization struggles unachievable.[32] In addition, capitalists may not join the democratic coalition if they are heavily dependent on the state for resources, contracts, and protection from foreign capital.

Broad coalitions tend to emerge during periods of national economic crises that threaten or impose heavy costs on the interests of wide segments of the population. These crises may reduce state resources and disrupt the pact between an authoritarian regime and big capital in the private sector. Fearing economic decline, capitalists may lose confidence and refuse to invest in the private sector, producing further instability[33] and increasing the likelihood of consolidation and coalition formation. As declining economic conditions exacerbate disparities in the distribution of income and wealth, adversely affected populations can often mobilize and join in broad coalitions to demand a more egalitarian distribution of resources.

National political crises, too, influence the interests, opportunities, and capacities of major collectivities. Serious divisions and schisms among the dominant classes and elite may prepare the ground for fundamental transformations. Radical challengers may emerge from political crises to demand fundamental political change and mobilize excluded collectivities otherwise incapable of independent action. Political schisms among the ruling elite over alternative policies, reduced repression, or the rise of a reformist faction may produce favorable opportunities for popular mobilization and coalition formation. Violations of established rights or intensified repression against members of powerful or resourceful collectivities often produce popular collective action and consolidation, which may contribute to the transformation of the political system.

Finally, external pressures and conflicts may affect the likelihood of democratization by influencing the interests, capacities, and opportunities of the state and major social and political actors. External conflicts, particularly wars, tend to reduce the likelihood of democratization because they can promote nationalism and expand the power of the coercive organs within the state apparatus. Furthermore, during external conflicts, power-holders tend to repress their opponents and undermine the opposition's capacity to mobilize. Regimes that lack popular support at times may invoke external conflicts to shore up their domestic support. Short of defeat and collapse of the armed forces, external conflicts tend to adversely impact democratization.

Summary and Conclusions

Democratization involves empowering the civilian population against the state and requires elimination of all political inequalities. It can proceed through the alternative routes of reform or revolution. Despite great advances in understanding democratization, so far scholars have not been able to develop a comprehensive framework to predict the likely route to democratization in highly authoritarian political systems. The theoretical model developed in this chapter uses both structural and process variables focused on the nature of the state, the economy, and society to analyze the likely routes to democratization.

The model suggests that it is highly unlikely that the Islamic Republic of Iran would democratize through gradual reform. It is more likely that Iran's democratization would have to go though a disruptive process. There are a few reasons for this. First, the state is exclusive and grants special privileges to the clergy, a small portion of the population. Also, the Islamic Republic's rulers systematically used coercion to exclude increasing portions of Iran's political elite and population from the polity. Further, state ideology claims a divine basis for the theocracy and unequivocally rejects democracy or empowering the people. State intervention in social and cultural spheres imposes and enforces specific ideological precepts that cannot be altered by the people. Thus, the state denies people the right to pursue different historical, cultural practices. Following this ideology, the rulers are intransigent and reject change and reform.

State intervention in the economy and in capital accumulation has empowered the government or the elite, undermined the market mechanism, and rendered the entire system vulnerable to challenge and attack. State policies have failed to develop Iran's economy, exacerbated inequalities, and expanded unprecedented levels of corruption and cronyism. These conditions have polarized the system and undermined the possibility of finding common ground between the state and society. Moreover, the state cannot claim to represent the interests of society in the social, economic, and political spheres. Instead, state structures and policies have generated multiple conflicts in Iranian society, all of which converge around the theocracy and clerical rule. As a result, the theocratic regime is extremely vulnerable to challenge and attack.

In combination with the nature of the state and its ideology, these conflicts have undermined popular trust and support for the regime. Having lost a great deal of popular support, the rulers of the Islamic Republic are highly unlikely to agree to a democratic transition through reform. Faced with fair and free elections, they would likely lose all their powers and privileges; hence, the Islamic Republic's rulers have consistently refused to reform the state and the political system. Instead, they have preferred to provoke external conflicts to expand public support and enhance national cohesion. More importantly, the rulers of the Islamic Republic have chosen widespread, endless repression, adversely affecting broad segments of the population, reducing the likelihood of compromise and gradual reform, and undermining the long-term survival of the regime. If the model presented in this chapter is accurate, it is highly likely that successful democratization in Iran can only proceed through a disruptive, revolutionary route.

❧ II ❧

REVOLUTION AND THE POLITICAL
ECONOMY OF THEOCRACY

CHAPTER THREE

Ideologies, Revolution, and the Formation of a Theocracy

SCHOLARS HAVE OFTEN explained the Iranian Revolution in terms of the rise of a cohesive movement, inspired by Shiite martyrdom and the authority of the clergy, which overthrew the monarchy and established an Islamic republic.[1] These explanations tend to be tautological and analyze the revolution's cause in terms of its outcome. Such explanations implicitly begin with the establishment of the Islamic Republic and work backward to explain the root causes of the revolution. As a result, these explanations often pay inadequate attention to the revolutionary processes. They fail to account for the fact that major classes and collectivities entered the revolutionary struggles at different times and presented diverse claims and demands. These analyses ignore the fact that Ayatollah Khomeini articulated different ideological claims during the revolutionary struggles and following the overthrow of the monarchy. Finally, these analyses cannot explain the intense conflicts that erupted after the establishment of the Islamic Republic, provoking endless repression that still continues in Iran.

The revolution was the outcome of a struggle carried out by a broad coalition of major classes and collectivities differently positioned in the social structure with different interests and capabilities. The revolutionary struggles were for democracy and greater equality, and the principal demands were freedom and social and economic justice. The claims and demands of these collectivities were not different from the movements of the early 1950s when Iranians mobilized for political freedom, greater equity, and social justice.

An empirical analysis of the revolution reveals that it was too complex to be explained by an overarching ideology alone. Some Iranians certainly embraced Islamic principles and fought for an Islamic state. As in many social revolutions, others fought for freedom, civil liberties, social justice, and a more egalitarian distribution of wealth and income. The majority of those involved in the struggles expected to improve their lives socially, economically, and politically. Their deaths during the revolutionary struggles were the result of political repression by a regime intent on maintaining power. The majority of the Iranian people mobilized themselves through the mosque because of the relative safety and security it provided, not because they wanted to establish a theocratic state. In fact, none of the major classes that carried out the revolutionary struggles asked for the social and cultural changes that were imposed after the establishment of the theocracy. Iranians overwhelmingly supported Ayatollah Khomeini because he addressed their economic and political concerns and promised to resolve them in their favor.

Once the Islamic Republic was in place, however, its rulers imposed a highly authoritarian state upon the populace, thereby contradicting promises made during the revolutionary struggles. The ruling clergy and their allies eliminated their rivals and opponents through successive waves of repression. They established an exclusive theocratic state with a narrow polity and quickly banned and repressed secular political parties and autonomous organizations. They also intervened extensively in social and cultural affairs and attempted to Islamize significant aspects of the country's social institutions, even though none of the major classes had demanded greater state intervention in social and cultural arenas during the revolutionary struggles.

Clerical Students: Protest and Popular Indifference

The Qom clerical student uprising of 1975 provided an opportunity for those interested in promoting the cause of Islamic fundamentalism to give their lives in defense of an ideology subscribing martyrdom. Just two years before the eruption of the revolutionary struggles, the uprising offers a good test of the ideological hypothesis. The three days of protest have not garnered the attention of most scholars of the Iranian Revolution. Had broad segments of the population actually been driven to give their lives, the 1975 event would have provided a favorable opportunity for them to demonstrate their ideological orientation or conversion.

During a protest on June 5, more than one thousand clerical students in the religious city of Qom seized control of the Madraseh-e Faizieh-e, a school for training clergy, located near the shrine of Fatima visited by Shiite Muslim pilgrims from all over Iran. Fellow clerical students from an adjacent school, the Madraseh-e Khan, quickly joined the demonstration. The students raised a red flag symbolizing Shiite martyrdom high enough to be visible throughout the city and also unfurled a banner declaring, "We commemorate the anniversary of the great rebellion of Imam Khomeini." They even dared to broadcast tapes of Khomeini's fiery speeches against the shah. Their demonstration was deliberately timed to coincide with the twelfth anniversary of Ayatollah Khomeini's arrest in 1963 and the government's subsequent massacre of protesters.[2]

More importantly, the students were lucky to receive the support of Ayatollah Khomeini, then in exile in Iraq. Khomeini issued a message of condolence, lamenting the deaths of forty-five students during two days of protest and condemning the government's refusal to admit injured protesting students to Qom hospitals. At the same time, he congratulated the Iranian people on the "dawn of freedom" and the elimination of imperialism and its "dirty agents."[3]

News of the Qom events spread to other cities and sparked additional demonstrations. Two clerics and approximately thirty clerical students were arrested in the religious city of Mashhad, where the clerical student insurrection lasted for three days and nights. Tehran army commandos finally put down the protest, killing and injuring dozens of students and arresting more than five hundred.[4] Leftist students in Tehran and Tabriz also protested the repression of the clerical students. The state sentenced more than one hundred demonstrators to prison terms ranging from seven to fifteen years. SAVAK, Iran's secret police, shut down the school, which remained closed until the end of the shah's rule.

Despite press reports of the demonstration and heavy student casualties, popular response was limited and confined to the students. The vast majority of Iranians completely ignored the insurgency. Neither the clergy nor the public observed mourning ceremonies for the fallen students, nor did any bazaars close down in protest. The clerical students' failure to capture broad support—even with Khomeini's endorsement—challenges the hypothesis that the Iranian Revolution sprang from an ideologically driven Islamic movement.

The eruption of political opposition to the regime a few years later also challenges this assumption. The timing of the later collective actions further contradicts the ideological explanation. Political mobilization and opposition against the government became widespread in late 1977 and early 1978 only after the government eased repression slightly in response to President Carter's human rights campaign. People responded to declining— not increased—repression after a new government led by Sharif-Emami promised greater freedom and reforms. Under the previous government, some seventy Iranian cities witnessed political protests. Sharif-Emami's declaration of national reconciliation sparked demonstrations in one hundred additional cities. The link between the timing of popular protests and political repression was unmistakable. Had Iranians truly sought martyrdom, they would have protested when political repression was high and the risk of dying was higher (as in June 1975) rather than during declining repression when the risk of dying was lower.

Intellectuals and Students: Alternative Ideologies

The protests that led to the overthrow of the monarchy in 1979 were initiated not by religious clerics, but by secular, liberal, nationalist intellectuals organized under the National Front, which addressed an open letter of protest to the shah soon after President Carter took office in the summer of 1977. They publicly criticized the shah and called on him to observe the precepts of the constitution, free political prisoners, respect freedom of speech, and hold free and fair elections. Shortly thereafter, secular lawyers and writers formed independent associations of their own and demanded greater freedom and civil liberties. But the major collectivity whose protests captured the country's attention was comprised of students enrolled in the country's colleges and universities.

University students and intellectuals stood at the forefront of the 1979 revolution. Furthermore, students and the youth more generally were also the principal victims of state repression both before and after the revolution. More importantly, an analysis of the ideology of students and intellectuals and the nature of their collective actions calls into question the argument that the revolution was driven strictly by an Islamic ideology.

Like students in many other developing countries such as Nicaragua, South Korea, and the Philippines, the vast majority of Iranian student activists in the 1970s adhered to a secular, socialist ideology, although a sizeable segment of the students subscribed to Islamic socialism and, to a lesser extent, other varieties of Islam.[5] They displayed that ideology every year on Shanzdah-e Azar, the unofficial student day, observed in rallies and protests throughout the country. The event commemorated the slaying of three students by the government during the visit of Vice President Richard Nixon in 1953. Prior to the revolution, students had never observed the

June 5 commemoration of of Ayatollah Khomeini's 1963 arrest. Nor had they observed the date of Khomeini's exile from Iran. In contrast, student support for the Marxist Fedayeen, a guerrilla organization, was so intense in 1976 that the shah ordered closure of two major universities; but he quickly reversed himself for fear of sparking an even greater uproar.[6] Concerned about students' strong support for the radical political organization, the shah once remarked, "The dangerous young communists had made universities their primary bastions."[7]

Students' usual preoccupation with educational matters declined when repression eased somewhat and limited legal reforms were introduced in 1977. Early on, leftist students, acting independently of the clergy, undertook some of the most visible demonstrations. They quickly converted the universities and college campuses into centers for political opposition and information, and they also invited leftist intellectuals to speak on their campuses. Students never asked clerics to participate or speak at campus events, even later when the clergy began to mobilize and oppose the monarchy. When most other groups and classes were silent, students held at least twenty rallies and demonstrations and boycotted classes on twenty-one occasions during the first three-and-a-half months of the 1977–1978 academic year.[8] Student protests were so intense that many colleges and universities all but closed down by the end of the fall term. Student mobilization and collective action were critical in promoting mobilization by other groups, including the clergy, because most religious groups were slow to speak out against the government.

Both the government and opposition leaders were aware of the significant role of students in the political arena. To counter the students, the government organized a demonstration attended by five thousand people on the Tehran University campus condemning the student protests. Recognizing their crucial role, Khomeini praised student participation in political protests throughout the revolutionary struggles. Later, it became clear that Khomeini regarded students and the universities as unfriendly allies, if not enemies, because of their leftist politics. When Khomeini's clerical supporters scheduled him to speak at Tehran University upon his 1979 return to Iran, he refused and went instead to the cemetery to pay tribute to the martyrs of the revolution.

Not all student activists subscribed to secular leftist ideologies. Some students adopted an Islamic ideology following political repression in 1963. The Islamic Mojahedeen, influenced in part by Ali Shariati, an advocate of Islamic socialism, accepted the Marxist materialist interpretation of history and pursued a classless Islamic society. But Islamic socialists in the universities rejected this thinking when massive government repression targeted the Mojahedeen in 1972 and more than one hundred members and leaders were arrested.[9] The government unexpectedly shut down the Hoseinieh Ershad, an Islamic center, and arrested Shariati, who had criticized traditional Islamic clergy and Marxism alike. The Mojahedeen experienced another setback when some members discarded Islamic ideology and adopted Marxism-Leninism in 1975. In all, government repression and internal divisions largely disorganized and demobilized the Mojahedeen in the years before the revolution.

The fortune of Islamic students improved in the fall of 1978, when Sharif-Emami's government promised liberalization. As the Islamic student movement expanded, it generated divisions and competition on university campuses. Additional Islamic students arrived following the shah's ouster in 1979. A number of younger students, especially those from provincial towns and cities, gravitated to the pro-Khomeini camp and challenged the hegemony of the left in the universities.

But soon student politics shifted on campuses as the new rulers revealed their goals and plans after the overthrow of the monarchy. Student support for Ayatollah Khomeini and his fundamentalist faction faded rapidly, and many of the young students joined various leftist organizations and opposed the Islamic Republic.[10] They clashed with both the liberal and the clerical factions of the regime. Student movements supported demands by the opposition for democratic freedoms, workers' councils, land reform, women's rights, and autonomy for ethnic minorities. Government officials complained that the leftist Fedayeen and Islamic socialists, such as the Mojahedeen, used university resources to attack Islam and the Islamic Republic. Top clerical officials charged that the actions of these groups undermined the forces of Islam in the universities.[11] Khomeini, who had earlier lauded university students for their struggle against the monarchy, dictatorship, and imperialism, sounded like the shah when he declared that "universities were bastions of communists, and they were war rooms for communists."[12]

To counter the students, militant clerics—with the support of the government's liberal faction—unleashed a "cultural revolution" to Islamize the universities in April 1980. Government forces, assisted by club-wielders, attacked students on campuses across the country, killing dozens and expelling thousands of students considered leftist or antigovernment. In an unprecedented move, the government shut down all universities and colleges for at least two years, and many remained closed even longer. Students and youth became the principal targets of repression and violence, as they had been during the revolutionary struggles. When campuses finally reopened, Khomeini announced that only students without affiliations to either Eastern or Western ideologies would be admitted, unleashing a wave of purges of students and faculty throughout the country.[13] Nearly four thousand students involved in political opposition activities died by execution or in armed struggle between 1981 and 1985.[14]

Apart from students, the majority of Iranian intellectuals also subscribed to some form of socialism or liberal-nationalism (followers of Mosaddegh's National Front) throughout the 1970s. Intellectuals' ideological leanings were evident during a series of popular poetry nights organized by the Writers' Association in Tehran in the fall of 1977. Sixty-six percent of the sixty-four poets and writers who participated were secular-socialists, and 28 percent were liberal-nationalists.[15] Roughly 6 percent followed some sort of Islamic ideology that did not subscribe to the establishment of a theocracy. Government repression terminated the readings before the entire schedule of events could be presented.

A minority of intellectuals adopted some form of Islamic ideology in the years before the revolution, and some of them attempted to mobilize and challenge the regime. In addition to Ali Shariati, Jalal Al-e Ahmad also abandoned Marxism and encouraged intellectuals to join forces with clergy and resist "westoxication." Islamic intellectuals held a series of lectures of their own in Tehran's Ghoba Mosque in the fall of 1977. Speakers included Mehdi Bazargan, who later became the first prime minister of the Islamic Republic; Dr. Habibollah Payman; and others who attacked rival secular, materialist, and Marxist ideologies.[16] Student attendance at these religious lectures was much smaller and less enthusiastic than at the secular poetry nights.[17] The lectures also failed to capture the national attention to the same degree as the poetry readings, and the government did not intervene with the lecture program.

After the overthrow of the monarchy, the Writers' Association found itself to be in serious conflict with the Islamic Republic's ruling clergy. The association attempted to organize a new round of poetry nights in October 1979 to "defend freedom of thought and speech, and oppose absolutely any censorship of writing."[18] These events never materialized, because the government of Prime Minister Bazargan could not guarantee the safety and security of the meetings. The Islamic regime banned the association and executed one of its prominent founders, Saeed Soltanpour, in June 1981.

Bazaaris: Politics and Ideology

Unlike the industrial bourgeoisie, which was closely allied with the regime and did not join the political conflicts, the merchants, shopkeepers, and

artisans—known collectively as *bazaaris*—representing a substantial portion of Iran's capitalist class, were particularly active in Iran's political
conflicts. Concentrated in close to forty thousand shops and workshops
and controlling about two-thirds of the nation's domestic trade, bazaaris
played a significant role during the 1979 revolution. Despite their importance, however, bazaari ideology and politics have often been misunder-
stood and misinterpreted by recent scholarship. Bazaaris have been viewed
as a traditional social class strongly allied with the clergy and willing to
follow clerical leadership in political matters.[19] It is true that many bazaaris,
particularly of the older generation, were religious and that their religious
contributions were important in maintaining Islamic mosques, functions,
and ceremonies in the twentieth century.

However, the bazaaris' religious orientation did not always determine
their political ideology, nor did they pursue religion as a political ideology.[20] Some bazaari activists even claimed that bazaaris always dictated
the clergy's politics, rather than vice versa.[21] Bazaaris' mobilization and
collective actions can best be explained as a component of liberal-nationalism
not under the authority of the clergy. For example, during the political
conflicts of the early 1950s, bazaaris backed the liberal National Front led
by Prime Minister Mosaddegh and mobilized against the shah, despite the
fact that the vast majority of the clergy supported the monarchy. Bazaaris
took advantage of Mosaddegh's liberal policies in 1951 and organized the
bazaar organization Society of Merchants, Guilds, and Artisans (SMGA).
Bazaaris repeatedly demonstrated their support for the prime minister by
closing down the bazaar on at least fifty separate occasions between 1951
and 1953.[22] Bazaaris' loyalty to Mosaddegh never wavered after his arrest.
They closed their shops in protest[23] and refused to open their doors despite
assurances that they would not be jailed. Government duress eventually
obliged them to reopen.[24] All the while, the highest clerical leaders—
including the most preeminent Marja'a Taghlid, Ayatollah Boroujerdi—
issued public expressions of support for the shah.[25]

While Mosaddegh languished in prison, bazaaris formed a secret committee with a fund of 40 million rials in a vain effort to secure his release.[26]
The Tehran bazaar closed down on October 8, 1953, to protest the state
prosecutor's demand that Mosaddegh be executed. Police arrested one
hundred people during the strike and accompanying demonstration,
according to the government.[27] Four days into Mosaddegh's trial, bazaaris
went on strike again.[28] The government arrested more than 300 people,
mostly bazaaris and students, and exiled at least 218 of them to Khark
Island in the south.[29] Government forces destroyed the roof of the Tehran
bazaar in several places, and the new prime minister threatened to demolish
the entire roof if the strikes recurred.[30]

With the repression and decline of the liberal-nationalist movement in the 1950s, and particularly after the conflicts of the early 1960s, some bazaaris began supporting Ayatollah Khomeini. However, bazaaris' politics and ideology did not suggest any large-scale ideological conversion in favor of an Islamic theocracy in the 1970s. On the contrary, their contributions and participation in mosque activities, including prayers, declined dramatically during this period.[31] Bazaaris, like the vast majority of the Iranian public, ignored the protest by clerical students in Qom in June 1975 even though Ayatollah Khomeini swiftly endorsed the clerical students' actions from his exile in Iraq. No bazaaris anywhere in the country initiated a single shutdown, protest, or mourning ceremony to challenge the government's repression of the clerical students.

Bazaaris initiated mobilization and political activities in the latter part of the 1970s in response to economic and political changes, not because of requests from the clergy. Although economic and political divisions had reduced cohesion among bazaaris, the government's economic policies—and particularly the price controls and "antiprofiteering" campaign—enhanced solidarity within the bazaar. Bazaar activists such as Lebaschi and Manian who had long supported Mosaddegh and the National Front over religious activists, took the lead in mobilizing against the government. They illegally reestablished the Society of Merchants, Guilds, and Artisans of the Tehran Bazaar (SMGATB) in October 1977, before the clergy became involved in the conflicts. They were highly resourceful, encouraged religious bazaaris to issue public statements, and even printed their leaflets on their own printing machines.[32] The SMGATB leaders had honed their political skills during decades of political activism, enjoyed the respect of the bazaaris, and had name recognition because of their long involvement in politics and repeated imprisonment. Significantly, the SMGATB had the support of Azerbaijanis, the single largest group in the Tehran bazaar, and organized bazaar shutdowns and strikes throughout the revolutionary struggles.[33]

It is important to note that bazaaris did not initially mobilize through the mosque, nor did they act collectively in response to exhortations from Khomeini or other religious leaders. Instead, as declining repression presented favorable opportunities, bazaaris mobilized alongside modern secular groups that had earlier opposed the government. For example, bazaaris joined students to establish funds to pay striking university professors when the government suspended their salaries in March 1977.[34] Tehran bazaaris completely shut down their businesses when students called for a day of mourning to protest the death of a student killed in an antigovernment demonstration following Saeed Soltanpour's poetry night in the fall of 1977.[35] But soon bazaaris, like others, found it difficult to mobilize because of state repression. They gathered with National Front leaders in an orchard in Karvansara Sangi to celebrate Aid-e Ghorban, a religious holiday in mid-November. SAVAK, the secret police, concluded that the assembly was in fact a political gathering and dispatched 750 agents to disperse it, which resulted in a large number of injuries.[36] Subsequently, bazaaris, like other groups, turned to mosques as the only safe spaces insulated from state repression.

Bazaaris often initiated protests on their own against the government. They independently closed their shops in the religious city of Qom on the second day of student protests against an anti-Khomeini article in *Ettelaat,* a national newspaper, in January 1978, even though no deaths or arrests had yet occurred. After they went on strike, the country's religious leaders met but could not agree on a course of action. One preeminent cleric argued that the bazaar should reopen, but protesting bazaaris countered that they were willing to pay the fine to remain closed.[37] They remained closed for four days while the preeminent Qom ayatollahs refused to endorse their strike. Arrests and deaths occurred on the second day of the strike. Even bazaar leaders who assisted victims' families were arrested and exiled to different parts of the country.[38]

Bazaaris occasionally mobilized and protested against the advice of the clergy. When government forces massacred student demonstrators in Qom, Ayatollah Khonsari—Tehran's highest religious leader and one of the most prominent ayatollahs in the country—advised bazaaris not to go out on strike. But the SMGATB ignored him and called for a strike. Bazaaris from Azerbaijan, Shiraz, and Isfahan who had businesses in the Tehran bazaar soon joined the strikers. When the strike concluded, Khonsari was forced to seek protection from police bodyguards whenever he attended prayer.[39]

To be sure, a small minority of bazaaris actively supported Ayatollah Khomeini during the revolutionary struggles. This group consisted of approximately thirty bazaaris who worked closely with the clergy during the monarchy's final days. They included Sayyed Taghi Khamoushi, Pour-Ostad, Amani, Shafi'i, and Asgar-Oladi. But these bazaaris did not have a wide network in the bazaar and lacked broad support.

During the revolutionary struggles, many bazaaris willingly supported clerics and their activities as long as these individuals opposed the government. They distributed Khomeini's statements and tapes through their trading networks, and SMGATB leaders provided space for special prayers at the conclusion of the fasting month of Ramadan on September 4, 1978. When Khomeini was expelled from Iraq and went to France, leaders of the SMGATB brought one hundred baskets of flowers to the French embassy to urge that

France allow Khomeini to carry out his political activities. SMGATB leaders called for a demonstration to support Ayatollah Taleghani—a liberal cleric and an ally of Mosaddegh—who was released from prison in November 1978. The Tehran bazaar closed down, and many bazaaris joined more than 250,000 people in a march to Taleghani's residence.

Bazaaris' support for Khomeini and militant clerics was political in nature and also extended to other opponents of the regime and antigovernment activities. Bazaaris raised funds to support striking workers and sent flowers and publicly endorsed employees of the three national newspapers who declared their first strike ever to protest state censorship. The head of the SMGATB called representatives of the press, expressed support, and promised bazaar assistance.[40] Bazaaris continued to support students and faculty struggling for autonomy and democracy within the universities. Bazaaris shut their businesses and joined a rally at Tehran University to support students and faculty who called for a week of solidarity in early November 1978 against the government.[41]

The bazaaris' mobilization and protests were primarily political in nature and directed against the state. Bazaaris in major Iranian cities issued at least fifteen statements between January and December 1978; these statements unanimously protested government repression. Fifty-three percent of the statements also protested the despotic nature of the regime, and an equal percentage condemned imperialist interference and the government's dependence on foreign powers. The statements also condemned some of the government's economic policies, singling out corruption, governmental and international "pillaging" of national resources, and growing poverty and inequality. Three statements specifically supported the Islamic movement, and two backed the clerical community and its struggles. Only one statement by Isfahan bazaaris explicitly called for the establishment of an Islamic government. Two statements issued late in 1978 acknowledged Khomeini as the leader of the opposition movement.[42] Aside from the few statements referring to the Islamic movement and government, the issues were similar to those bazaaris raised in the 1950s, when bazaaris under Mosaddegh's nationalist banner protested the shah's dictatorial tendencies and British control of Iranian oil.

The bazaaris' support for Khomeini derived from his uncompromising opposition to "despotism" and the shah's regime. Nowhere in their statements did bazaaris support the Islamization of laws or clerical supervision of the government, or a theocratic Islamic state. One well-known bazaari activist, a devout Muslim who raised a great deal of money for Khomeini, declared, "Had bazaaris known about Khomeini's ideas on theocracy, they never would have supported him."[43]

The bazaaris' postrevolutionary politics and conflicts with the ruling clerics also reveal that many of them opposed the establishment of a theocratic state as promoted by Khomeini. In the final struggle against the monarchy, broad segments of the bazaaris shifted to favor an Islamic government, but their support for Islamic leaders was based on political considerations, not on an ideological conversion in favor of a theocracy. Sayyed Taghi Khamoushi, a leading pro-Khomeini bazaari and important government official, stated that the bazaars were not under the control of the "Hezb-Ollah" after the shah's ouster.[44]

Once in power, Khomeini and his allies had to devise a number of policies to gain control over the bazaaris and influence their organization. They formed a treasury to assist merchant guilds and extend interest-free loans to "needy" merchants and shopkeepers.[45] They established the Imam's Committee for Guild Affairs to guide and regulate the guilds' economic activities, select and supervise guild leaders, and prevent violations and "infiltration by counter-revolutionaries and their conspiracies."[46] The ruling clergy also tried to attract leading dissident bazaaris to their camp. Ayatollah Khamenei, Khomeini's successor, met with Abdolghasem Lebaschi, an SMGATB leader, and invited him to cooperate with the clergy as late as January 1981.[47]

Although bazaaris disagreed among themselves on political issues after the revolution, most opposed the fundamentalist clergy and militant clerical organizations. The political actions of bazaaris in Isfahan and Qom clearly revealed the problems. During the revolutionary conflicts, Isfahan bazaaris had called for the establishment of an Islamic government and even closed their bazaar to protest when the shah's government arrested Ayatollah Taheri. After the revolution, these same bazaaris again closed the bazaar, this time to protest Taheri's criticism of their liberal Majles deputy, Ahmad Salamatian. On another occasion, Qom bazaaris refused to close down their bazaar when requested to do so by fundamentalist supporters of the regime's clerical faction who opposed President Bani-Sadr.[48]

Most importantly, many bazaaris incurred harsh repression as a result of political and ideological conflict with the Islamic government. More than one hundred bazaaris were killed or executed following President Bani-Sadr's ouster in 1981.[49] The government executed two prominent bazaaris—Karim Dastmalchi, a leading liberal member of the SMGATB, and Ahmad Javaherian, a supporter of the Mojahedeen—in July 1981.[50] Leading bazaari activists such as Lebaschi and Mohammad Shanehchi were forced to flee the country. Mahmoud Manian, a founding member of the SMGATB, withdrew from politics and public life. After three separate attempts on his life, he eventually was killed in 1994 in a "traffic accident" in front of his own house.

Workers and White-Collar Employees: Economic Grievances and Political Mobilization

Workers' interests, conflicts, and resources differed significantly from those of students, intellectuals, and bazaaris. As the timing of their collective action demonstrated, workers were not in the forefront of the political struggles against the monarchy. Although the size of the urban labor force expanded during the monarchy, a substantial portion of the industrial working class was dependent on the state for employment and as a result could not mobilize and engage in collective action. More importantly, workers experienced severe repression and lacked solidarity structures to mobilize and initiate collective action. When students, intellectuals, and bazaaris protested against government repression during the fall of 1977 and also in 1978, workers struck for purely economic demands in thirty-nine unrelated cases. Workers did not join other collectivities or support their political protests and mourning ceremonies with solidarity strikes of their own. Yet, workers' concentration in large state enterprises facilitated their communication and enabled them to play an important role in the overthrow of the government in the final phase of the revolutionary struggles, when the political system grew increasingly unstable.

Sharif-Emami's appointment as prime minister in the fall of 1978 presented a fresh opportunity for workers' mobilization. He promised liberalization and political freedom for all political groups except communists but offered nothing to the working classes. A small group of politicized workers who had previously been arrested, imprisoned, or involved in past strikes seized the opportunity to mobilize and demand change. They formed secret cells and committees with trusted coworkers and organized collective action through informal workplace networks.[51] White-collar employees, representing a substantial portion of Iran's middle class, soon joined and initiated strikes of their own and made claims against the government.

The paramount concerns of workers and white-collar employees, unlike bazaaris, were economic. Virtually all striking workers and white-collar employees pressed for relief of their immediate grievances of mounting inflation and a declining standard of living. All strikers demanded higher wages, with job-related issues a close second. Most strikers also insisted on allowances or loans to cover housing expenses and medical insurance.

Many strikers expressed dissatisfaction over pay inequities, especially in industries where foreign workers were employed, and complained of arbitrary promotion rules and secret "rewards" granted by heads of state bureaucracies. Although the vast majority of these demands were purely economic, the strikes and the demands of the strikers also had a political aspect. Workers and white-collar employees often targeted the state as the principal employer of industrial workers and white-collar employees in state bureaucracies.

Confronted with mounting walkouts, the state attempted to respond positively to the demands of the strikers. The government initially chose to address the burgeoning number of strikes on the national level with some concessions, not repression. The government announced on October 10, 1978, that within six months all state employees' salaries would increase by 25 percent in two stages. Five days later, the government promised housing loans to twenty thousand government employees. The cost of the raises to about six hundred thousand employees was $4.5 billion, forcing the government to cut back on development projects.[52]

In the absence of nationwide labor organizations, workers' responses varied in different enterprises and different parts of the country. Some strikers accepted the offers and returned to their jobs, while others continued their strikes, doubting the government's promises. But most strikers regarded the state's concessions as insufficient, because many had demanded 50 percent to 100 percent salary increases along with additional benefits.[53]

The continuation of strikes had adverse political consequences for the state. As they continued, segments of the workforce concentrated in large enterprises and possessing greater skills and solidarity structures gradually raised some political demands. Striking workers in an oil refinery and in other industries—including a steel mill in Isfahan, a mine in the central Alborz Mountains, a railway in Zahedan, and Iran General Motors in Tehran—all demanded the expulsion of various department chiefs in their enterprises. In addition, workers in Tabriz Machine Tool Factory walked off the job on September 2, insisting that government-sponsored unions be dissolved and martial law be lifted.[54] They organized a joint strike with employees at Tabriz Tractor on November 4 and issued a political statement condemning government repression and martial law; calling for freedom for political prisoners and the dissolution of government-sponsored unions; and proclaiming support for political demands by students, teachers, workers, and government employees. Striking oil workers in Abadan and Ahvaz echoed these statements by demanding an end to SAVAK and martial law, release of political prisoners, formation of independent labor unions, freedom for all political parties, and other political concessions.

In the absence of a satisfactory settlement of the conflicts, workers increasingly adopted political demands, but their demands were neither Islamic nor revolutionary. Workers did not call for the overthrow of the government or the destruction of the capitalist class, nor did they endorse an Islamic movement or Islamic government. Nevertheless, workers' demands became increasingly radical in the Iranian context.

In response to increasing politicization, the regime changed tactics and attempted to repress the strikers. The rising politicization of striking workers and white-collar employees, coupled with spiraling popular protests, led the shah to dismiss the civilian prime minster and appoint a military government on November 6, 1978. The army attempted to force the strikers back to work by occupying strategic institutions—such as oil installations, radio and television stations, and newspapers—that had just completed a strike and gained positive results for their demands. The military government and its occupation of strategic enterprises had some success, as some strikers returned to work, and the number of strikes declined.

But the military could not maintain order for long. The imposition of a military government, in the context of promising reform and reconciliation, backfired. Within days, popular protests and bazaar shutdowns expanded in response to the installation of the military government and challenged the state. The protests had a positive impact on workers and white-collar employees who had developed a greater awareness of their conditions and the capacity to mobilize and launch collective action. Soon, workers and white-collar employees initiated extended politicized strikes in many parts of the country. Also, striking workers and white-collar employees in different enterprises and cities issued statements denouncing state repression.

Oil workers and employees played an important role in the final phase of the revolution because they controlled the nation's most vital economic asset. Their strikes differed from those of other workers because of the greater likelihood that their actions would have significant consequences for the state and for society at large. First, they controlled the lifeblood of the country, as both the state and society were dependent on oil revenues. Second, oil workers numbered more than thirty thousand and were heavily concentrated in specific oil-producing regions, adding to their ability to communicate, strategize, and engage in coordinated collective action. Third, oil workers had greater skills and a greater potential to become politicized during times of conflict because they were all state employees. Finally, some oil workers also shared a core of political experience stemming from oil strikes during the nationalization in the early 1950s. These features contributed to the politicization of oil workers during the final phase of the revolution. Oil workers and employees became increasingly militant in the fall of 1978. Their final strike began on October 31, 1978, when most of the thirty-seven thousand oil workers refused to go back to work despite government pressures.[55]

Leftist workers with secular and religious ideologies played a crucial role in the oil workers' organization and mobilization. Thirty-five percent of the leaders of the Ahvaz strike committee, for example, were self-avowed Marxists.[56] Some oil workers and employees also subscribed to some forms of Islamic socialism. It is noteworthy that Ahvaz oil workers respected Ayatollah Khomeini mainly because of his political opposition to the shah, not for his religious dictates.[57] One oil worker observed that Ayatollah Khomeini "brought the eyes of the world on our problem here and made them see that the shah is a puppet of the foreigners who are stealing our money." Another oil worker told an American correspondent, "We want Khomeini. He will take power from the rich and give it to us."[58] Oil workers regarded their movement and Ayatollah Khomeini's leadership as "anti-despotic, anti-imperialist."[59] They shifted still further to the left once the shah was overthrown and formed a workers' council in the oil sector. The composition of the oil workers' council reflected the trend: nine of fourteen members were Marxist, and four others advocated some form of Islamic socialism.[60] The oil workers' politicization inevitably affected the politics of the rest of the working class, undermined the monarchy, and encouraged radicalization among segments of the working class in the years following the overthrow of the monarchy.

Mosques, Popular Collective Actions, and the Ideology of the Clergy

In the years prior to the revolution, state policies repressed or rendered ineffective all major political organizations capable of mobilizing the people for political purposes and collective action. Furthermore, the state carefully monitored public spaces such as universities and labor unions to prevent political challenges against the regime. But the government did not severely repress the mosques. In fact, mosques were the only relatively autonomous institutions in Iran prior to the 1979 revolution, as most clergy remained apolitical and did not threaten the state. As conflicts erupted and government repression intensified, dissidents and protesters turned to the mosques to mobilize for collective action against the regime. Mosques proved to be the safest places to gather, communicate grievances, and mobilize for action.

Although they relied heavily on mosques during the revolutionary struggles, the majority of protesters did not actually intend to establish a theocratic state. In fact, an analysis of the slogans and ideological orientation of popular protests organized in mosques demonstrates that they were not predominantly fundamentalist. Mehdi Bazargan and his associates in the Freedom Movement used tape recordings of major protests organized through mosques during religious holidays to analyze the popular slogans shouted during these events. They found that antidespotic slogans were the most common, comprising about 38 percent of the total. The investigators combined a number of broad and diverse slogans into a second group representing 31 percent that included Iran's economic exploitation by other countries, Pahlavi corruption, "Independence, Freedom, Islamic Republic," and "Islamic Republic, Yes! Dictatorial Government, No!" Sixteen percent of the slogans recognized Ayatollah Khomeini's leadership, and 15 percent praised other leaders, including Ayatollahs Taleghani and Montazeri and the Mojahedeen martyrs.[61]

It is important to note that most of these events were organized in the last phase of the revolutionary struggles when substantial segments of the protesters were calling for the establishment of an Islamic republic. The crowds who repeatedly chanted, "Independence, Freedom, Islamic Republic," and "Islamic republic, Yes! Dictatorial Government, No!" saw no contradiction among the concepts of freedom, civil liberties, political rights, and an Islamic republic. Demands for freedom and independence had been the backbone of the nationalist movement led by Prime Minister Mosaddegh in the early 1950s. Protesters in the late 1970s appended "Islamic Republic" to the slogan because to them it signified social justice based on egalitarian Shiite ideals and resonated with the majority of citizens, given the growing inequality and increasing concentration of income and wealth in the country as demonstrated by the rising Gini coefficient.[62]

If the anti-shah protesters were not religious fundamentalists, neither were the vast majority of Shiite clergy revolutionaries. A small group of clerics opposed the monarchy, and a small minority—one hundred of whom were defrocked after the revolution—supported it.[63] After the revolution, Ahmad Khomeini, son of Ayatollah Khomeini, admitted that only a small minority of clerics initially opposed the regime and that they were slow to mobilize.[64] Most clergy were moderates and remained aloof from political matters. The highest echelons of the clergy in the religious centers of Qom and Mashhad, who played a significant role during the initial stages of the revolutionary conflicts, were indeed moderate in their politics. Their preeminent position and national recognition enabled them to activate mosque networks for approximately one hundred religious and mourning ceremonies observed annually.

These high-ranking Shiite clerics, in contrast with Khomeini, took a moderate course of action during the political conflicts from the late fall of 1977 to the fall of 1978. They emphasized proper implementation of the constitution. They also consistently advocated the elimination of anti-Islamic laws and practices by enforcing the constitution, not by creating a new Islamic government. The three leading clerics in Qom issued fifteen protest declarations that coincided with major political events or ceremonies. All of the statements condemned state political repression and violence, seven denounced despotism, and five deplored imperialist influences and the lack of national independence. Another five statements deplored the absence of civil liberties in the country, and four called for the abolition of anti-Islamic laws. Two of the statements called for improved economic conditions for workers and farmers, as well as clerical supervision of laws passed by the Majles, a feature of the 1906 Iranian constitution. Lastly, individual statements addressed several separate issues: nationalization of pillaged assets and wealth, poverty, and foreign exploitation. Significantly, only one of the statements demanded the formation of an Islamic government.[65]

Given their apolitical nature, most clerics did not join the political mobilization in the early phase of the struggles. Clerical inaction surprised Ayatollah Khomeini who encouraged clergy to write and protest, and he noted that others had already begun to mobilize.[66] But the clergy did not have a political organization through which to advance any agenda. The main political organization of the clergy, *jamehe rouhaniat mobarz*, was established several months before the revolution. The organizational weaknesses of the Islamic clergy were apparent during the Tasoua march in Tehran in 1978. As late as two months before the revolution, militant, pro-Khomeini clergy inside Iran lacked a wide network for mobilization, despite months of struggles. The militant clergy mustered 1,400 individuals to act as marshals for the Tasoua march of opposition groups in Tehran on December 10, 1978. The largest number came from the secular, liberal National Front, which supplied 2,500, followed by the Islamic liberal Freedom Movement with 800 marshals, and the supporters of the Islamic socialist Mujahedeen with about 500.[67]

Because the total number of marshals was inadequate for the huge crowd anticipated at the event, the march's organizers called for additional marshals on the day of the protest. More than seventy thousand volunteers, mostly unaffiliated ideologically, spontaneously turned out to act as marshals and received armbands from the organizers. At the conclusion of the march, the pro-Khomeini clergy used loudspeakers to direct the marshals to introduce themselves to their local mosques that evening to prepare for another march, to be held the following day on Ashura. [68] During the Ashura march, the pro-Khomeini contingent's enhanced capacity allowed it to control the streets of Tehran. Organizers and protesters called for the shah's overthrow and the formation of an Islamic republic. The shah was overthrown two months later, on February 11.

Ayatollah Khomeini: Freedom and the Path to Theocracy

Ayatollah Khomeini became the acknowledged leader of the revolutionary coalition despite years of exile in Iraq and later in France. The vast majority of the populace backed his relentless public statements opposing dictatorship and defending freedom and Iran's national interests. Although Khomeini was in financial straits, had few students, and did not enjoy the respect of other prominent clerics,[69] he did have greater freedom to issue political statements against the Iranian government. From the safety of exile, Khomeini demanded the shah's overthrow, borrowing the basic tenets of the liberal-nationalist movement—freedom from dictatorship and imperialism and an end to corruption and the pillaging of the country's national resources. He condemned the government's violation of Islamic principles and expressed concern over the clergy's declining status and the erosion of Islam. While in Najaf, Iraq, Khomeini responded in an interview with a French reporter to the shah's charges that he was a reactionary and against civilization: "It is the shah himself who is against civilization and a reactionary. Over the past fifteen years in my statements, I have insisted that I am in favor of social and economic development. But the shah implements imperialist politics and attempts to keep Iran behind and backward. The shah's regime is a dictatorial regime. In this regime, personal freedoms have been trampled, and real election, the press, and parties have been removed. The shah imposes representatives by violating the constitution, establishment of political and religious associations is forbidden, and judicial independence and cultural freedoms do not exist at all."[70]

Throughout the revolutionary struggles, Khomeini consistently promised that an Islamic government would guarantee national independence and political freedom for all citizens, adding that even Marxists would be free to express themselves.[71] As the revolutionary struggles began, Khomeini stated, "We will not abandon our struggle until we have a real democratic government that replaces the dictatorship and bloodshed."[72] In response to a question from a Reuters reporter about the relationship between the Islamic movement and opposition parties and groups, Khomeini responded: "All groups are free to express their ideas, but we will not permit treason."[73] In response to a French reporter who asked whether this was a religious movement that wanted to return to Islamic traditions, Khomeini replied that "when we speak of Islam, we do not mean to turn our back to progress, rather it is the opposite. In our opinion, basically Islam is a progressive religion, but we are enemies of regimes that under the guise of modernism impose dictatorial manners and oppression." He continued, declaring that "before anything, we think that force and repression are not the means to progress."[74]

Khomeini consistently emphasized the democratic aspect of an Islamic state and promised political freedom. "Islamic democracy will be more perfect than Western democracy," Khomeini declared in an interview with a Dutch reporter on November 5, 1978.[75] Interviewed by a group of international reporters on November 9, he declared that the Islamic government would be a democratic government in the real sense of the term. In his first press conference with Iranian reporters in Paris, Khomeini declared, "In Islamic government, there is no dictatorship."[76] Before he left Paris, Khomeini spoke to international journalists about freedom in Islam. "The 78 year old religious leader has given assurances from exile in France that 'Islam will . . . ensure freedom,'" reported Otto C. Doelling of the Associated Press.[77] Khomeini also said that "religious minorities will have complete freedom, and everyone will be able to express their opinions."[78]

Khomeini's supporters repeated his statements that the Islamic Republic would guarantee political freedom and civil liberties. Shortly before the revolution, the Society of Tehran Clergy invited the people for a march in Tehran in support of the establishment of an Islamic republic. While the clergy urged the marchers not to chant "communist slogans," they stated that the march was in support of "Iran's national independence and the guarantee of individual and social freedoms."[79] Ayatollah Beheshti, a cleric close to Khomeini, was known to be a strong advocate for political freedom. He reiterated during the final phase of the revolutionary struggles that "Islam was a religion of freedom and would not take away anyone's freedom."[80]

Upon returning to Iran, Khomeini repeatedly condemned the shah's dictatorship and affirmed that Islam was for freedom. In a public event, Khomeini remarked about the liberating aspect of the revolution. He noted that thirty-five million Iranians lived in a prison; Iran was a prison, and everyone lived in torment. "With the revolution, the door of the prison was opened and thirty-five million people were freed from that prison."[81]

Khomeini issued a statement on the occasion of the reopening of schools and urged children: "Never allow a small group to rule over you like in the bitter days of despotism of the past. Do not forget the principle of Islamic democracy." He went on to say that people should attempt to maintain unity so that they could establish an Islamic society, a society in which all were free to express their beliefs.[82] In a message to the Iranian people on April 1, 1979, after the approval of a referendum on the establishment of the Islamic Republic, Khomeini declared, "There is no repression in Islam. There is freedom in Islam for all classes—for women, for men, for whites, for blacks, for everyone."[83]

Khomeini repeatedly assured Iranians of the freedom of the press and of expression, maintaining, "We are not afraid of freedom of expression"— as long as there was no conspiracy against the government.[84] More importantly, he unequivocally declared publicly that the Islamic Republic would not repress the people: "Repression has been buried and will not return."[85] He repeated his promise that Marxists would be free to express their views in the Islamic Republic.

With so much sacrifice, Khomeini never expressed an interest in power. He repeatedly denied personal aspirations of a political nature during his years in exile. Khomeini instructed his clerical supporters to respect and work with students and intellectuals. "Tomorrow we will not become government ministers; our work is different. These [students] are the ones who become ministers and representatives."[86] Later, in France, he asserted that he would be merely a guide to the people as he had been in the past and had no interest in a role in the government.[87] In response to a question from a Reuters reporter about whether the clergy would run the affairs of the government in case the shah retired, Khomeini stated that the clergy would not run the government. They would be observers and guides to the leaders, and the government in every respect would be dependent on the vote of the people and their decision.[88] During his first year in Iran, Khomeini even declared that clerics should not become presidents.[89]

For a long time, Khomeini did not reveal his novel ideology. In his public statements addressed to Iranians in the years preceding the revolution, Khomeini never mentioned his radical theocratic and doctrinal views. Clerics and clerical students who supported him knew nothing about such concepts or his plans in the years prior to the revolution and during the revolutionary struggles.[90] Even some of Khomeini's closest political allies and advisors in Paris were completely bewildered after the revolution when they first heard of the concept of *velayat-e faghieh*.[91]

Once secure in power, however, Khomeini defended the integration of religion and politics and the clergy's authority to enforce Islamic laws and defend the Islamic system. The role of the Islamic state was to enforce sacred laws.[92] He castigated the Pahlavi dynasty for weakening the clergy's power and undermining Islam. Where the clergy were weak, dictatorship emerged, but in an Islamic republic, God alone would be sovereign. Without the clergy, Khomeini declared, Islam would have been destroyed. "We would know nothing about Islam."[93] He repeatedly emphasized the clergy's leadership role in guiding the Islamic system: "Until the end, we need the clergy; Islam needs the clergy until the end. In the absence of the clergy, Islam would disappear. These are Islam's experts who protected Islam and have to be present to protect Islam."[94] Khomeini also stated that maintaining the Islamic system was one of the most important obligations:[95] "Preservation of Islam itself is more important than the lives of Muslims." He added that spying to protect Islam and Muslims was necessary; even lying and drinking alcohol were necessary if performed in the service of Islam.[96]

In yet another shift, Khomeini rejected democracy on the grounds that it was based on the rule of humans who could fall into error.[97] Furthermore, democracy was unacceptable because it had a Western dimension. Khomeini even rejected the suggestion of calling the country an Islamic democratic republic. In a large public gathering in Qom, he noted, "We accept Western civilization but do not accept their corruption." He denounced those "aristocrats" who lived in the West and had no role in the movement but wanted to derail the revolution. Khomeini declared that those who weakened the government were traitors. He noted that it was the youth who created the revolution, not the lawyers. "Newspapers should correct themselves and not commit treason against Islam. . . . The thing we want is an Islamic republic, not just a republic, or a democratic republic, or even an Islamic democratic republic, just an Islamic republic, he stated."[98]

As the undisputed leader of the revolution, Khomeini greatly influenced the Islamic Republic's constitution, which empowered the clergy, prohibited the publication of views violating Islamic principles or public interests, and halted Iran's century-long popular struggle for freedom of expression and the press. When constitutional debates began, Khomeini fully supported the principle of *velayat-e faghieh*.[99] Asked about the likelihood of dictatorship under the newly debated principle, Khomeini asserted that the *velayat-e faghieh* and clerical rule would prevent dictatorship, not establish it.[100] With his backing, the principle was adopted in the second draft of the constitution. According to Article 5 of the Islamic Republic's constitution, the supreme leader was the Muslim nation's highest leadership position during the occultation of the Twelfth Imam. The position was reserved for clerics, which generated categorical inequality and solidified the monopoly of clerical power. When the Assembly of Experts appointed Khomeini as the republic's first supreme leader, Khomeini agreed to serve.

The supreme leader controls all three branches of government by virtue of his position at the apex of an elaborate network of councils and assemblies that reinforce theocratic, authoritarian decision making and leave no room for democratic checks and balances. The supreme leader exercises the preeminent role in determining the regime's top leadership by directly appointing six of the twelve members of the Guardian Council and the head of the judiciary. The Guardian Council vets and approves all candidates for the Assembly of Experts, who must also pass a religious examination. Only approved candidates for the assembly are presented to the public for nationwide popular vote. The Guardian Council also certifies that all legislation is compatible with Islam, thereby bestowing upon the supreme leader additional influence over these activities by virtue of his role in determining the Guardian Council's membership. The supreme leader appoints all members of the Expediency Council, which is constitutionally charged with resolving disputes between the Guardian Council and the Majles. Although the Assembly of Experts appoints the supreme leader for an indefinite term and can theoretically dismiss him in case of moral transgression or incompetence, such an outcome is highly unlikely because of the leader's influence over the assembly. The supreme leader is, for all practical purposes, accountable to no one.

The supreme leader is the commander in chief of all armed forces—the military, the national police, the judiciary, the chief of staff, the supreme commanders of the armed forces, the Revolutionary Guards, and the Basij (the paramilitary part of the Revolutionary Guard)[101]—which together total well over a million members. He has the ability to declare war and to veto all government decisions and can even dismiss a popularly elected president if the Majles or the Supreme Court impeaches him. The supreme leader effectively controls the country's powerful institutions, including the national radio and the television network. He oversees a staff of approximately six hundred, names the heads of many bodies that report to him, and appoints some two thousand representatives to all state ministries and educational, government, and military institutions.

The supreme leader has a great deal of power in the religious sphere, an autonomous realm prior to the revolution. He appoints all of the Friday prayer leaders, who are dependent on him for financial resources. He also supervises all mosques, clerical schools, and seminaries. He administers millions of dollars annually to seminaries to promote a particular interpretation of Islam that is compatible with the theocracy.[102] The supreme leader controls the Special Clerical Court, which is independent from the judiciary and ensures clerics' loyalty by punishing dissidents.

Khomeini's Ideological Shifts, Repression, and Theocracy

Soon after the establishment of the Islamic Republic, it became clear that the people of Iran and the new clerical leaders were fighting for different goals. The country's new Islamic rulers faced the uncomfortable fact that major segments of the population had mobilized to demand economic benefits, political freedom, and civil rights during the final stages of the revolutionary conflicts—and especially following the collapse of the armed forces. Workers, farmers, students, and national minorities called for major changes in the country's social structure.

Instead, Khomeini and his allies moved to establish a theocracy. They relied on ideological, political, and repressive mechanisms to gain popular support, demobilize the growing opposition, and repress it to establish a theocratic state. Khomeini adopted a new ideological stance to confront rising class conflict and the growing strength of both the radical secular and religious left. Shifting his prerevolutionary focus on independence from foreign powers and freedom from dictatorship, he borrowed from the basic tenets of the radical left and concentrated resolutely on economic and social justice. The day the referendum of the Islamic Republic was approved, he used for the first time the term *mostazafin,* calling the new system the government of the downtrodden, "which is the same as government of God."[103] The term *mostazafin* quickly became the most repeated word in Khomeini's vocabulary. Throughout history, he claimed, prophets had risen up along with the *mostazafin* and struggled against the oppressors.[104] Islam, Khomeini repeatedly affirmed, served the interests of the *mostazafin,* the oppressed, and the deprived. The feast of the oppressed, he noted, is when the oppressors are eliminated.[105] "God is determined to cleanse the earth of the oppressors and put the oppressed in power. Islam has come for this purpose."[106] The Islamic Republic, Khomeini declared, was established to serve the interests of the poor and the oppressed. He insisted that Islam intended that people should have both a material and a spiritual life.[107] "We want to improve your lives in this world and the next world," Khomeini declared upon his return to Qom.[108]

In these pronouncements, Khomeini moved further to the left than any established Iranian politician in the twentieth century, including Mosaddegh. Khomeini's ideological shift proved to be a critical component in the Islamic Republic's survival and the clergy's rise to political supremacy. He warned that "if we cannot reduce economic polarization and reduce the inequalities between the rich and the poor, and if consequently people get disappointed in Islam, nothing can prevent the resulting explosion; and we will all be destroyed."[109] He prevailed over liberals who had no plans to restructure the social order or redress social inequality. The shift also reduced the left's ability to mobilize students, workers, and farmers around social justice and equality. As Ervand Abrahamian has noted, Khomeini sounded more radical than even Karl Marx when the supreme leader declared on May Day 1979, "Every day should be considered Workers' Day for labor is the source of all things, even of heaven and hell as well as of the atom particle."[110]

More concretely, Khomeini announced specific measures to help the poor and urged the state to adopt policies favoring the lower socioeconomic classes. He repeatedly warned profiteers against raising prices but also established a committee to help bazaaris in economic distress.[111] Khomeini ordered the provisional government to provide free water and electricity for the poor who had been deprived under the monarchy. He quickly promised that "we will build houses for all the poor"[112] and ordered the expropriation of Pahlavi assets to provide housing and employment for the poor.[113] Declaring that everyone had a right to housing, Khomeini opened "Bank Account 100" for contributions to build housing for the poor.[114]

Khomeini's ideological shift toward social justice for the poor was coupled with repressive measures to eliminate his political rivals. He and his allies created the Revolutionary Komiteh (committee), the Revolutionary Court, and the Revolutionary Guard to demobilize and kill the regime's opponents. Khomeini declared that once the Islamic government was in full control of the cities, the Komiteh should relinquish its activities to the government and avoid interfering in government affairs.[115] The Komiteh was eventually merged with the police, but the Revolutionary Guard was never dissolved and instead expanded from a small band to hundreds of thousands during the eight-year war against Iraq. Along with its paramilitary wing, Basij, it remains an important repressive organ in the Islamic Republic. The clergy also organized Ansar-e Hezbollah, or Partisans of God's Party, which received funding directly from the office of the supreme leader, according to some reports. Hezbollah published various papers and newsletters, and many of its several thousand members were armed. Hezbollah's gangs of club-wielders were closely tied to the right-wing faction of the regime and were paid to attack dissident political rallies and demonstrations and to impose strict codes of behavior for women, according to Amir Farshad Ebrahimi, a former vigilante.[116]

During the political conflicts, the Islamic regime repeatedly used paramilitary forces to further their agenda. Hezbollah violently disrupted political gatherings of dissident organizations, torched "non-Islamic" bookstores that sold secular and critical books, and sacked offices and headquarters of dissident political organizations that did not advocate Islamic values.[117] For example, hundreds of religious zealots armed with clubs, knives, and brass knuckles attacked a march in Tehran organized by the National Democratic Front in defense of free press and the *Ayandegan,* the country's largest morning newspaper.[118] When tens of thousands of demonstrators marched in Tehran to Prime Minister Mehdi Bazargan's office shouting, "Death to censorship!" and "Death to fascism!" about two thousand religious supporters of Khomeini attacked them.[119]

The Islamic regime's repressive capacity quickly targeted publications that favored freedom of the press and presented alternative perspectives. Khomeini departed from his promises of political freedom and initiated the attack on the press. He insisted that the press should always promote the cause of Islam and avoid discord, disunity, and dissention.[120] Khomeini and his supporters declared that pens that were involved in treason and helped the hand of foreigners had to be broken.[121] As early as May 1979, a few months after the revolution, he called for the boycott of the *Ayandegan* newspaper, calling it "deviationist." Khomeini's denunciation provoked hardliners to organize attacks against the provincial offices of the *Ayandegan,* leading to its closure.[122] The regime eventually banned the *Ayandegan* in early August.[123] A few days later, pro-Khomeini workers barred twenty-two members of the *Kayhan's* editorial staff on charges of being "leftist or communist." In response, most of the 120 editorial staff struck in protest. The moves by the Islamic Republic were seen by some in the Iranian press as attempts to establish "absolute fascism," according to a *Washington Post* report.[124] Soon, the regime began purging the editorial staff at the *Kayhan.* "Within three months, nearly all of *Kayhan's* news staff, among the best in the country, were fired," according to Housang Asadi, deputy editor of *Kayhan.*[125]

The Islamic regime intensified repression of the press six months after the revolution. It announced a new press code that forbade publishing criticism of Ayatollah Khomeini and insults against recognized religions.[126] The law prepared the legal pretext for eliminating opposition press. In one day, on August 20, the Islamic Revolutionary Court banned twenty-two publications.[127] The banned papers were published by liberal and leftist political organizations and were shut down for failing to follow "an Islamic line or criticizing religious leaders."[128] The Islamic regime then expropriated both the *Ettelaat* and the *Kayhan,* the two oldest and largest dailies, on September 11, 1979, and put them under the ownership of the Mostazafan va Janbazan Foundation, a new organization created and controlled by the clergy.[129]

Repression of the press expanded in 1981 as political conflicts intensified. The state shut down 175 newspapers in 1981 alone,[130] arresting dozens of journalists. Of the nearly 450 newspapers and magazines that flourished in the year following the revolution, scarcely 100 such publications remained by the end of the Islamic Republic's first decade.[131] In April 1981, the regime banned the largest opposition newspaper, the *Mizan*, published by former prime minister Mehdi Bazargan. The ban followed the arrest of the *Mizan*'s managing editor, a former commerce minister named Riza Sadr, who was accused of "slander, libel, disturbing national security and printing false reports through his editorials."[132]

The Islamic rulers also began repressing dissident organizations almost immediately after the revolution, and by the end of June 1981, all political organizations and parties had been banned except the ruling Islamic Republican Party (the IRP). Ayatollah Khomeini maintained that Islam did not grant freedom to people to engage in any activity they wished: "Islam does not permit us to allow anyone the freedom to commit any mistake or any conspiracy they want to."[133] He repeatedly called for unity of words *(vahdat kaleme)*. Impatient with continuing conflicts, Khomeini declared in August 1979 that he had made mistakes by treating opponents leniently. He stated that he could no longer give freedom to political parties to continue their "corrupt activities." "We all made mistakes. We thought we were dealing with human beings, we behaved like human beings, but we are not dealing with human beings—we are dealing with fierce animals. It is not possible to treat fierce animals leniently; we will not do it any longer."[134]

The state began repressing many of the leftist and liberal organizations that directly challenged the Islamic theocracy. By August 1979, about six months after the revolution, many of the leftist, radical, and liberal organizations had been seriously disrupted.[135] The National Democratic Front, a center-left political organization, was among the first to be banned. The organization had opposed restrictions on the press, violations of people's democratic rights, and political repression. In an open letter to Ayatollah Khomeini, the National Democratic Front criticized many aspects of the Islamic Republic, including Khomeini's authoritarian proclamations and policies.[136] When the organization defended freedom of the press and organized a demonstration against the banning of the *Ayandegan* in early August, the Front was banned the next day.[137] Khomeini ordered the arrest of its leader, Hedayatollah Matin Daftari,[138] a grandson of former prime minster Mohammad Mosaddegh, and forced the organization to go underground.

The Islamic regime also repressed other organizations that struggled for greater autonomy. The Kurdish Democratic Party led the Kurdish struggles and demanded autonomy for Kurdistan, democracy for all of Iran, freedom for all political parties, and guaranteed freedom for the press.[139] Ayatollah Khomeini called the Kurdish Democratic Party "the party of the devil" and charged it with "collusion with the United States and international Zionism."[140] The Islamic regime then banned the Kurdish Democratic Party.[141] Khomeini sent Ayatollah Sadegh Khalkhali to the Kurdish region to try the rebels. Khalkhali found the rebels guilty of "corruption on earth and fighting against God and his prophet."[142] Khalkhali executed more than 130 Kurds,[143] and the Revolutionary Guard killed dozens of Kurds in armed clashes[144] in a couple of weeks in the summer of 1979. Eventually, the Islamic regime succeeded in suppressing the Kurdish struggle for autonomy. The Islamic Republic also repressed the autonomy movement of the Turkmen people in Gonbad Kavous. Ayatollah Sadegh Khalkhali, Khomeini's emissary, ordered the arrest and execution of ninety-four people, including four leaders of the Political and Cultural Headquarters of the Turkmen People, and suppressed their movement.[145]

The Islamic leaders also repressed organizations that supported alternative political visions and followed the lead of other religious leaders. The regime outlawed the Muslim People's Republican Party in Azerbaijan because they supported Ayatollah Shariatmadari and rebelled in Tabriz. The party demanded autonomy and greater democratic rights and had the backing of the population of Tabriz, as demonstrated in a general strike in which all schools and shops closed down.[146] But Khomeini blamed the troubles in Tabriz on "traitors," "stooges," and "plotters who receive their orders from America and other places."[147] Government troops attacked the rebellious forces in Tabriz, executed some members of the party, and eventually suppressed it.[148]

With the repression of the more radical and regional opponents, the Islamic rulers began to attack the more moderate, liberal organizations. Khomeini charged the moderate National Front, which had been an ally during the revolutionary struggles, with apostasy when the group called for a march against a parliamentary bill on the Islamic law of retribution (an eye for an eye). Khomeini declared that the Front had stood against the Islamic Republic and the Quran and that members were apostates, and were thereby expelled from the polity.[149]

As conflicts between liberals and the fundamentalists intensified, the Islamic regime decisively demobilized all political parties that did not subscribe to the fundamentalist interpretation of Islam. The regime banned all political parties in June 1981 except the Islamic Republican Party.[150] A "parties law," passed in September 1981, specified conditions under which parties could operate. The law effectively prevented the formation of new political parties until it went into effect in late 1988.[151]

To establish an exclusive state and an authoritarian political system, Ayatollah Khomeini and his allies took advantage of ideological and political divisions within the secular camp among liberals, social democrats, socialists, and communists. The new rulers benefitted from extensive, deep divisions within leftist organizations, including the powerful Islamic socialists and various secular leftist organizations. The political and ideological divisions were exacerbated by intense conflicts between workers and employers, which was often the state itself. In combination these divisions enabled the clergy and their allies to repress the leftists one by one as they failed to form coalitions to defend themselves.

Khomeini and his militant allies also took advantage of external conflicts to promote national cohesion, deflect attacks, divert attention from problems, and exclude their former allies, rivals, and opponents. Khomeini declared the Iraq war to be a godsend and a blessing that had many benefits, including national cohesion.[152] The clergy also used the hostage crisis and the Iraq war to promote nationalism and buttress their own powers. During the war, they were able to strengthen the Revolutionary Guard and improve their coercive apparatus. The ruling clergy forbade labor strikes, dissolved independent workers' councils, and imprisoned dissident workers, thereby weakening the labor movement and the radical left's influence. During the hostage taking, the regime attacked universities, which had overwhelmingly supported the revolutionary left in favor of fundamental changes. They closed down all universities for at least two years and, upon reopening, purged half of the faculty and thousands of students who did not support the Islamic Republic.

More importantly, during the hostage crisis, Khomeini and his allies succeeded in excluding their liberal, revolutionary partners and established a theocracy, narrowing the polity. Khomeini initially appointed Mehdi Bazargan—leader of the Freedom Movement, a Mosaddegh ally, and a devout Muslim—to form a provisional government. The provisional government prepared a constitution for the Islamic Republic without providing any position for the rule of jurisprudence, the centerpiece of Khomeini's innovation. The ideological divisions led the militant clergy to interfere and undermine Bazargan's role as prime minister. With the hostage crisis, Bazargan and his entire cabinet resigned to protest the students' takeover of the American embassy in November 1979. With the removal of the provisional government, Khomeini did not have much difficulty getting the theocratic constitution approved in early December 1979 in the midst of rising conflicts.[153] During the hostage crisis, the Islamic regime also intensified repression of former members of the polity that continued to oppose the theocracy. The ruling clergy and their allies in the Islamic regime arrested Abbas Amir-Entezam, spokesman and deputy premier of the provisional government. They charged him with spying for the United States on December 18, 1979, several weeks after the hostages were taken, and sentenced him to life in prison.[154] He was released in 1996 but was rearrested in 1998 because he criticized the regime and demanded a public trial to clear his name. While released for medical treatment, he gave a speech at Tehran University and called for a referendum to determine whether Iran should remain under religious rule, which led to his arrest.[155] He was eventually freed after serving about twenty-six years in prison.[156] Amir-Entezam has repeatedly demanded a public trial to clear his name, but his request has been rejected.

With the provisional government eliminated, the militant clergy and the Islamic Republican Party edged closer to a formal power structure. Khomeini asked the Revolutionary Council, composed of seven clerics and fourteen nonclerics (three other members were assassinated), to take charge of the government's operation until national elections for the president and the Majles. The clergy organized in the Islamic Republican Party used various tactics to exclude rivals. Charging that the Islamic socialist Mojahedeen had not supported the Islamic Republic's constitution, Khomeini barred Masoud Rajavi, the Mojahedeen's leader, from running for president.[157] As a result, Abolhassan Bani-Sadr, a liberal, won the presidential election of January 1980, but the IRP won control of the Majles.

The next Majles elections in 1980 favored the IRP led by the clergy, but the elections were criticized. Some observers and critics complained of voting problems and numerous alleged irregularities surfaced after the first round of elections. In violation of election rules, the clergy closed down polling stations where opposition organizations had been successful.[158] The Hezbollah attacked the offices of opposition political groups and organizations, disrupting and intimidating their campaigns. The regime further weakened secular forces in advance of the second round of elections by expelling campus leftists and closing down all colleges and universities throughout the country for more than two years. The IRP won 130 of 241 seats in the second round of Majles elections, liberals won approximately 40, and the rest went to independents.[159] Khomeini's brother telegraphed President Bani-Sadr, charging that "people were made to vote for the IRP candidates through the use of deception, intimidation . . . mass imprisonment and murder. . . . I am grieved to declare that at no period (in history) acts such as these been witnessed. People did not expect the Islamic government to act in this manner."[160]

With the Islamic socialists largely excluded from the Majles, Khomeini and his militant supporters sought to undermine the liberals, who were led by President Bani-Sadr. The regime clashed regularly with Bani-Sadr and his allies, who advocated formal democratic institutions, civil liberties, economic development, and appointments based on expertise and competence in relevant fields. When Bani-Sadr addressed a rally at Tehran University commemorating the death of former prime minister Mosaddegh, a group of his opponents stormed the crowd and attempted to disrupt the rally. Mojahedeen militias subdued dozens of the assailants and confiscated their identification cards, which Bani-Sadr displayed to the audience and live television cameras, revealing most of the attackers to be members of the Revolutionary Guard and associated with the IRP.[161] Clergy in the IRP accused Bani-Sadr of abusing his authority, defying Ayatollah Khomeini's orders, and refusing to sign a bill passed by the parliament. They organized a large demonstration and demanded Bani-Sadr's resignation, trial, and execution.[162] The Majles held two days of impeachment hearings and voted 171 to 1 against Bani-Sadr. A few days later, Khomeini dismissed Bani-Sadr from the presidency.[163]

Khomeini then reversed his previous position that it was beneath the dignity of clergy to hold the office of president or any other governmental post. Declaring that no one else was competent or willing to advance God's cause, he announced that clergy would occupy political offices and run the country. He explained his decision thus: "In those days, we thought that there would be people among the educated intellectuals and religious strata who would be willing to advance God's wishes and run the country along God's lines. But we realized that we were mistaken and that some of these people had foisted themselves upon us and some of them had different views from us; thus, the clergy should run the country at least temporarily until nonclerics could take over."[164]

Bani-Sadr's ouster unleashed a reign of terror unprecedented in modern Iranian history. Khomeini and his followers turned loose the Revolutionary Guard and the Hezbollah to demobilize liberal and leftist opposition. With the help of the security forces, they arrested thousands of dissidents.[165] The Islamic Republic then launched a campaign of executions. The state accused twenty-three political prisoners of the crime of *mohareb* (warring against God) and sentenced them to death. Saeed Soltanpour—a former political prisoner under the monarchy, a poet, and the first secretary of the Writers' Association—was arrested at his wedding and charged with what the Tehran revolutionary prosecutor described as having "bad records and being a plotter."[166] The regime executed him and the other twenty-two prisoners on the day Bani-Sadr was removed from office.[167] Although the regime primarily targeted the radical left, it also attacked the business sector by putting to death a few bazaar merchants to discourage opposition. Ali Asghar Zehtabchi, a supporter of the Mojahedeen, was also executed the day Bani-Sadr was removed as president.[168] A few weeks later, the regime executed Ahmad Javaherian and Karim Dastmalchi, who supported Bani-Sadr and were accused of having encouraged the bazaar merchants to stage shutdowns and other protests.[169]

State repression was even directed at the youth. Assadollah Lajavardi, prosecutor general of Tehran, warned parents to watch their children closely because even 12-year-olds would be executed for demonstrating against the regime.[170] Iran's revolutionary prosecutor, Musavi Tabrizi, announced over Tehran Radio that terrorists would be tried and sentenced "on the spot" when arrested. "They will be tried in the streets," Tabrizi said, so as not to waste government money feeding them in prison.[171]

A veritable bloodbath soon followed. The clerical regime put to death 2,665 political prisoners over the next six months, seven times more than the number of promonarchists slain in the previous sixteen months.[172] In one day alone, on September 19, 1981, the government executed 149 political dissidents.[173] Between June 1981 and September 1985, the Islamic regime killed or executed about twelve thousand dissidents in its relentless objective to solidify the Islamic Republic and clerical rule.[174] The revolutionary prosecutor general observed, "We cannot practice forgiveness or leniency when faced with so many people."[175]

The regime did not halt the execution of dissidents once the Iran-Iraq war ended and the Islamic regime was stabilized. Authorities executed thousands of political prisoners and prisoners of conscience in the summer of 1988.[176] Most executed prisoners were about to complete their sentences, according to Amnesty International.[177] Although the regime never provided a full account of the executions, Amnesty International estimates that between 4,500 and 5,000 men, women, and children were executed in the summer of 1988 in Iran's prisons. According to the Iran Tribunal—an "international people's tribunal" organized by legal experts, lawyers, and academics from all over the world—more than five thousand people were murdered in the summer of 1988 in thirty-two Iranian prisons. After hearing testimony from nearly one hundred witnesses, the tribunal issued a verdict at the Peace Palace in The Hague declaring that the Islamic Republic of Iran had committed crimes against humanity in the widespread, systematic torture and execution of political prisoners and prisoners of conscience.[178]

In their struggle for power, the ruling clergy extended repression to their former allies and important members of the polity. The government executed Sadegh Ghotbzadeh—Khomeini's aide in Paris, a former member of the Revolutionary Council and Iran's foreign minister during the hostage taking—for plotting to assassinate Khomeini and overthrow the government.[179] Dr. Kazem Sami, Iran's first postrevolutionary health minister, became a victim of power struggles, according to a report. Sami's name had been mentioned in political circles as the next prime minster, and he had traveled to Qom to meet with Ayatollah Montazeri. The next day, in November 1988, a man who appeared to be a Hezbollah agent murdered Dr. Sami in his office.[180] A few weeks later, the regime put to death nine people, six of whom were clerics, including two former Majles deputies— Omid Najaf-abadi[181] and Seyyed Ali Naqi Khavari Langarudi—who were charged with corruption.[182]

With the elimination of much of the opposition, division within the ruling Islamic Republican Party intensified. To end the schism, Rafsanjani, speaker of the parliament, and Khamenei, the president, asked Khomeini to dissolve the IRP because opposition to the Islamic Republic no longer existed in Iran. The country had "'no need' for the IRP, and it should be dissolved to prevent internal differences." In response, Ayatollah Khomeini dissolved the IRP, which had played an important role in the formative years of the theocracy, but asked the ruling group to remain vigilant against those who wished to "insult Islam."[183]

Political and ideological conflicts even engulfed rival and dissident clerics. Ayatollah Taleghani, a liberal cleric, became an early victim of the Islamic Republic. Taleghani favored helping the poor and working classes through radical economic innovations such as worker and agricultural laborer councils organized to run factories and farms. He supported the rights of women and autonomy-seeking ethnic minorities and advocated city and regional councils comprised of ordinary people in charge of their own affairs. Imprisoned during most of the fifteen years preceding the revolution, he helped forge a critical, temporary alliance between the clergy and liberal-nationalists in the final stages of the anti-shah struggle. Taleghani's political standing and popularity after the revolution led to his selection as Tehran's prayer leader. He received the highest number of votes for the Assembly of Experts, charged with drafting the new constitution, but he boycotted most of the assembly's sessions out of concern that the Islamic constitution would be much inferior to the constitution written in the early twentieth century.[184] It was public knowledge that Taleghani voted against adopting the Islamic constitution. In his last sermon, Taleghani warned the public of the dangers of autocracy promoted under the guise of religion. He died a few days later under mysterious circumstances.[185]

Even the highest religious leaders were not immune. The regime targeted Grand Ayatollah Shariat-Madari, who had saved Khomeini's life during the 1963 conflicts but was among the first clerics to fall victim to the revolution.[186] As the country's highest religious leader, he rejected the claim that Shiite religious doctrine provided for the *velayat-e faghieh* and observed that the very concept contradicted other constitutional provisions that granted sovereignty to the people. He and his supporters in Azerbaijan came under attack. The regime stripped Shariat-Madari of his title of Marja'a Taghlid, "source of emulation," in 1982 and placed him under house arrest until he died three years later. The government sentenced Ayatollah Rastgari to two years in prison in 1986 for supporting Shariat-Madari. The regime attacked other prominent clerics as well. Grand Ayatollah Tabataba'I-Qomi was sent into exile and lived under house arrest for more than a decade.[187] Grand Ayatollah Mohammad Sadegh Rouhani was also placed under arrest for several years.[188] Grand Ayatollah Seyyed Mohammad Shirazi was placed under house arrest for his opposition to the rule of jurisprudence and eventually poisoned by the agents of the intelligence ministry, according to a report provided by dissident clergy.[189] Over the years, hundreds if not thousands of Shirazi's supporters and relatives suffered harassment, and scores if not hundreds were arrested, some on more than one occasion, according to Amnesty International. "Many have reportedly been tortured. Some were released without charge, whereas others were sentenced to prison terms after unfair trials."[190]

The Islamic Republic also targeted leading members of its own polity, such as Ayatollah Montazeri, Khomeini's designated successor. When Montazeri criticized some aspects of state repression, the regime began attacking him, arrested hundreds of his followers, and executed at least twelve.[191] These included Mehdi Hashemi, a cleric who was the former head of the Global Islamic Movement and Montazeri's relative. The government accused him of corruption on earth, "the most serious possible charge in Iran's Islamic theocracy, with specific counts of murder, kidnapping, plotting to overthrow the Government."[192] Given his views for a more open political system and his criticism of the 1988 executions, the regime began attacking Montazeri and accused him of transforming his house into a "nest of plotters."[193] Ayatollah Khomeini removed Montazeri from his designated position in 1989 and in 1997 placed him under house arrest for several years. No one was immune from repression during the intense struggle for power.

Summary and Conclusions

The empirical evidence presented in this chapter demonstrates that simplistic, overarching theories are inadequate to explain the complexities of the Iranian Revolution. Such explanations tend to be tautological. This chapter refutes explanations that the revolution was caused by a cohesive, fundamentalist Islamic movement. If such a movement had been growing and an ideological conversion was underway, Iranians would have risen up in 1975 when clerical students rebelled in Qom. Instead, the vast majority of the Iranian public ignored the dramatic protests that were swiftly endorsed by Ayatollah Khomeini. When the revolutionary conflicts erupted two years later, various segments of the population joined the struggles at different times and made distinct claims and demands. The overthrow of the monarchy was accomplished by a broad, nationwide coalition of diverse interests.

Overarching explanations of the revolution fail to account for Khomeini's shifts and the successive rounds of political repression directed against dissidents, challengers, and even members of the polity. As the undisputed leader of the revolution, Ayatollah Khomeini articulated alternative analyses of the conditions in Iran at different times and offered varying remedies. For years prior to the revolution, Khomeini stressed national independence, freedom from dictatorship, and an end to corruption and pillage of national resources. When the referendum was approved, he shifted his emphasis to serving the interests of the *mostazafin* or downtrodden. He subsequently shifted his focus once again and pressed for the establishment of a theocracy. The mere fact that Ayatollah Khomeini and the Islamic regime put to death more Iranian citizens after the revolution than the shah killed during the revolutionary struggles underscores the absence of an ideological consensus as the cause of the revolution.

Students, along with dissident intellectuals, stood at the forefront of the struggles for democracy in Iran in 1979, confirming the theoretical claim in this work that in highly repressive regimes in developing countries, students often play leading roles in democratization struggles. While the industrial segment of Iran's bourgeoisie did not join the political conflicts against the shah's regime, the bazaaris were very active. Adversely affected by state policies, bazaaris engaged in a large number of collective actions early on and pressed for democratic changes. In contrast, the working and middle classes (white-collar employees) were not in the forefront of the political struggles. They joined during the latter stage of the conflicts and played an important role in overthrowing the monarchy.

The clergy did not initiate the revolutionary struggles, but a faction, led by Ayatollah Khomeini, played a significant role in the final phase of the revolution. As was noted earlier, the clergy's role became important because much of the mobilization had to take place through the mosque, the only institution with relative autonomy from the state. But the dissident clergy in Tehran did not have a wide network of activists to enable them to assemble enough marshals for the Tasoua and Ashura processions just two months before the revolution. They had to rely on their allies, including the secular National Front, which provided the largest number of marshals. The clergy also benefitted by the fact that state repression severely undermined the position of existing political organizations, enabling Khomeini to become the undisputed leader of the revolution. From relative safety and greater freedom in Iraq and Paris, Khomeini was able to issue political statements against the shah and promote mobilization of the opposition.

The overthrow of the monarchy and the establishment of the Islamic Republic unleashed multiple contradictions and large-scale conflicts. Social classes, collectivities including ethnic minorities and women, and political organizations each pursued different ideological ends as the postrevolutionary conflicts unfolded. Liberal organizations and privileged social strata advocated civil liberties and political rights, whereas secular Marxist and Islamic socialists and some labor organizations pressed for radical economic change. In the ensuing political and ideological conflicts, opposition organizations advocated alternative tactics and strategies and targeted diverse entities rather than focusing on the state. As a result, the opposition failed to consolidate and press for democratic institutions.

Taking advantage of opposition divisions and external conflicts, the hostage crisis and the Iran-Iraq war, the clerical leaders of the Islamic Republic expelled their former revolutionary allies—as well as their rivals—from the political system and constructed an exclusive polity. Soon after the revolution, the three principal allies of the clergy who had organized the Tasoua march during the revolutionary struggles—including the liberal Freedom Movement and the National Front—lost their positions in the polity. The clerical rulers pursued policies that forced the Freedom Movement to relinquish power during the hostage crisis. The regime also banned the liberal National Front in June 1981. The rulers of the Islamic Republic began repressing the powerful Mojahedeen Khalgh, the Islamic socialists, and severely repressed them.

With the breakdown of the revolutionary coalition, the clerical rulers had to use state repression to establish and maintain the theocracy, resulting in a great deal of bloodshed. While estimates differ as to casualties incurred during the revolutionary struggles that overthrew the monarchy, none exceeded three thousand deaths.[194] In contrast, the Islamic regime killed at least fifteen thousand Iranians (excluding the monarchists and nonpolitical Baha'is) between 1981 and 1988, to establish and maintain the theocracy. The scale of repression and violence demonstrated ideological and political divisions in the revolution. The new rulers used violence to empower the clergy and prevent instituting liberal democracy or some form of socialism. Leftist students and intellectuals were the principal victims of repressive violence.

During the revolutionary struggles, the people demanded independence, political freedom, social justice, improvements in economic conditions, and a more egalitarian distribution of income and wealth. The revolutionary leaders promised to meet these demands and also guaranteed an end to political repression. However, none of the major collectivities called for the establishment of an Islamic theocracy during the revolutionary struggles. Even Khomeini did not call for clerical rule in his public statements to the Iranian people.

Although Khomeini promised political freedom and democratic institutions during the struggles, the new rulers delivered power to the clergy and created an exclusive, theocratic state that established categorical inequalities within the polity. Khomeini repeatedly insisted on the necessity of the clergy's political role in the Islamic Republic and justified its privileged position. He asserted that the concentration of power in the hands of clerics in the newly created position of the *velayat-e faghieh* would prevent dictatorship. He argued that maintaining the Islamic Republic was one of the most important religious obligations, thereby dismissing his prerevolutionary promises of freedom and democracy. Furthermore, he noted that to preserve Islam, it was necessary even to lie, spy, and drink alcohol. Khomeini's shift away from democracy and his subsequent statements prepared conditions for cycles of conflict and endless repression.

The outcome of the revolution was unforeseeable to the majority of the actors in the revolutionary struggles, except perhaps to Ayatollah Khomeini and some of his closest allies. The new rulers imposed an Islamic theocracy in which the ruling clergy controlled the most important political institutions in the country. Under the new theocratic system, secular liberal intellectuals and leftist students who initiated the revolutionary struggles were among the principal victims of the revolution, while others who contributed little or nothing until the last phase of the revolution became the principal beneficiaries. The theocracy effectively restricted social, cultural, intellectual, and religious freedoms, which people had been relatively free to pursue their own choices under the monarchy. Yet by repressing their former allies, forming an exclusive and authoritarian state, and restricting social and cultural freedoms, the rulers of the Islamic Republic reduced social cohesion and rendered the new system vulnerable to challenge and attack in future conflicts.

CHAPTER FOUR

Politicization of the Economy
and Declining Performance

THE MAJOR GROUPS and classes that joined in political struggle in the
fall of 1977 sought a transformation of the country's distribution of
wealth and income. Bazaaris, students, liberal nationalists, and leftist intellectuals all demanded changes in state economic policies. In their collective
actions, working and middle classes each demanded improvements in their
standard of living, a greater share of the country's economic resources, and
improvements in working and living conditions. Farmers and rural workers
expressed their own economic grievances by demanding redistribution of
land and nullification of debt after the monarchy's ouster. Some Iranian
intellectuals and revolutionary leaders also called for reduced economic
dependence on oil and on the world market and agricultural improvements to achieve self-sufficiency in food production. They argued that
dependence on oil rendered Iran's economy vulnerable to the vagaries of
the world market, and deteriorating food production led to rising imports
of food that consumed some of Iran's foreign exchange. Despite some differences, major segments of the Iranian population and the leadership all
agreed on the vital importance of changing these aspects of the country's
economic structure. The Iranian people expected the revolution to transform Iran's economy and its policies.

In response, Ayatollah Khomeini and other revolutionary leaders emphasized the need to alter the economic structure to improve the standard of
living of the *mostazafin* and reduce inequalities. Khomeini promised to

change the distribution of wealth and income and repeatedly condemned high levels of corruption and pillage of the country's resources by the powerful elite as well as foreign countries. Khomeini promised that the Islamic Republic would serve the interests of the *mostazafin* and the oppressed. He specifically warned authorities to reduce inequalities or risk the Islamic Republic's destruction. Article 43 of the constitution also called for increasing agricultural and industrial production and for achieving self-sufficiency. It stressed uprooting poverty and providing interest-free loans through the banks for everyone who lacked the means to start their own business. The article also noted that the country's economic system should prevent concentration and circulation of wealth in the hands of specific individuals or groups.

Through revolutionary expropriations, the role of the state in the economy expanded, as the clergy and the Revolutionary Guard seized substantial economic resources. The high level of state intervention in the economy and the existence of powerful monopolies prevented the market from functioning efficiently. Iran's economic realities under the Islamic Republic continued to adversely affect the vast majority of the population, in spite of articulated intentions and some successes. The country's economic development was insufficient to achieve independence from oil and the world market. More than three decades after the revolution, Iran's real per capita GDP was below prerevolutionary levels. Continued difficulties in the agricultural sector forced Iran to import food from abroad. Both the state and the economy remained highly dependent on oil. Despite unprecedented oil revenues during Ahmadinejad's first term, Iran's economy suffered from multiple problems. More importantly, Western sanctions combined with heavy state expenditures led to stagflation during Ahmadinejad's second term in office.

The Islamic Republic failed to fulfill its promise of an egalitarian society. State capital allocation remained highly concentrated within a small circle and deprived small- and medium-sized businesses and ordinary people. Widespread corruption and cronyism persisted more than three decades after the revolution, adversely affecting the country's economic development. The state also failed to reduce inequalities in the distribution of wealth and income as promised. These conditions, in turn, generated intense feelings of injustice among major segments of the population, which viewed the state as a tool serving particular interests, not general societal interests. Even Ayatollah Khamenei acknowledged that the continued presence of high economic disparities in the Islamic Republic indicated the regime's failure to fulfill the promises of the revolution. Educated Iranians left the country in large numbers, causing brain drain and hampering the country's development. A declining standard of living and a failure to meet the revolution's promises undermined the credibility of the new regime, and people wondered whether the regime had the capacity to change Iran's economic conditions. The Islamic Republic's economic development eroded state legitimacy and rendered the system vulnerable to challenge and attack.

State Policies and Economic Concentration

Despite promises to improve economic conditions for the people, state policies weakened Iran's economic performance and resulted in technological inadequacy and failure to compete in the world market. Ali Akbar Torkan, senior advisor to President Rouhani, declared, "Our technology is not on par with the [rest of the] world, and we are behind the world's technological development."[1] Sadegh Zibakalam, Iran's leading political scientist, agreed, adding that without state protection, domestic producers would not be able to compete with their foreign counterparts in quality and cost in fields ranging from petrochemicals and steel to garments, tires, and plastics. He noted that much of the domestic production would go out of business in the absence of government protection.[2]

Weaknesses of technological development were rooted, in part, in the revolutionary process and the establishment of the theocracy, which undermined the country's human capital formation and retention. To fulfill the revolution's promises, the regime had to promote the education and capability of the population and retain educated people for scientific and technological innovation. The theocratic state discouraged freedom of thought and imposed restrictions on intellectual activities and scientific research. The regime pursued ideological purity and subordinated all aspects of society and culture to the clergy and their particular interpretation of Islam. Attempts to discourage Western science and promote Islamic sciences were driven by ideology and impeded scientific and technological advancement. Policies designed to Islamize the universities resulted in the loss of university autonomy, essential for scientific advances achieved in the final months of the monarchy. Clerical domination of universities led to large-scale purges of many competent faculty and students in the universities and other institutions of higher education shortly after the revolution, downgrading the quality of Iran's higher education. The cultural revolution closed universities and colleges for approximately two years and purged thousands more faculty and students on ideological grounds. The political conflicts of the 1980s also resulted in the execution of thousands of intellectuals and students who did not support the Islamic Republic, further depriving the country of human capital. State policies led to purges in the state bureaucracy that replaced skilled, experienced employees with unskilled individuals whose only qualifications were ideological.

To be sure, the Islamic Republic expanded Iran's higher education, essential for human capital formation and economic development. Like South Korea, the Islamic Republic established many new universities and colleges throughout the country and educated millions of Iranian students who otherwise would have attended universities abroad. However, unlike successful economic miracles in South Korea, Taiwan, and Singapore, the Islamic Republic's efforts did not result in the retention of human capital. At times, political and ideological factors played an important role in admission policies and undermined the quality of educational standards. The admission of thousands of students to obtain doctoral degrees based on ideological or political criteria with no regard for competence during Ahmadinejad's presidency, discussed in Chapter 5, degraded the quality of Iran's higher education and capital formation.

Out-migration, which began soon after the revolution, intensified in the 1990s and continued into Ahmadinejad's presidency, depriving the country of much-needed expertise, innovators, and managers who could contribute to the country's development. Shortly after the revolution, many skilled and educated managers, employers, and employees left the country. Moreover, a large number of Iranian students who were studying abroad never returned. According to an international comparison, the Islamic Republic of Iran had one of the highest incidences of brain drain.[3] Another report revealed that 15 percent of all graduates of higher education left Iran, costing the country an estimated $150 billion annually.[4] Officials in the Islamic Republic were very aware of the problem and expressed concerns. Between 150,000 and 170,000 educated elites departed every year, according to an estimate by Javad Haravy, a Majles representative and head of the Committee on Higher Education, who called the phenomenon a potential danger.[5] In some fields, between 30 percent and 40 percent of the educated elite left the country,[6] according to Dr. Seyyed Hassan Hosseini, an official in the National Elite Foundation. He declared that 30 percent to 40 percent of Iran's highly educated elite left to find employment elsewhere.[7] Fifty percent of elite students in the medical sciences at Tehran University left the country, estimated Shahin Akhondzadeh, a university professor and acting minister of health, labeling the situation a "disaster."[8]

Most importantly, 90 of the 125 students (72 percent) who won medals in international olympiads emigrated.[9] Maryam Mirzakhani, Stanford

University math professor, was one example. While a student in Iran, she won gold medals in the International Mathematical Olympiad in 1994 and 1995. She later immigrated to the United States, where she became the first female winner of the Fields Medal in 2014.[10]

Officials agreed that the cost of brain drain was enormous. Iran's minister of science, Reza Faraje Dana, stated that if international estimates were accurate, Iran was losing $150 billion annually due to the flight of human capital.[11] Haravy, a Majles deputy and head of the Committee on Higher Education, agreed that brain drain cost billions of dollars annually, in an amount equivalent to the government's annual budget.[12]

Recognizing the significant impact of human capital flight on Iran's economy and society, Ayatollah Khamenei urged the elite to stay in the country and work to solve the problems. He also urged the National Elite Foundation to help these Iranians stay in the country.[13] President Rouhani also acknowledged the adverse impact of the problem on Iran's economic development. He complained about persistent brain drain in a public gathering honoring twenty-eight distinguished faculty members, researchers, and artists. Intellectual elites, Rouhani asserted, are the sources of national power and wealth, being two sides of the same coin. Countries that can attract these elites would be in a position to advance and succeed. He criticized the fact that Iran could not attract and retain its own elite, let alone absorb elites from other regions. Rouhani argued that capital was invested to produce elites and lamented that various excuses such as ethnicity, religion, morality, and politics were used to exclude and prevent them from contributing to the country.[14]

A shortage of skilled managers persisted more than three decades after the revolution, prompting Ayatollah Khamenei to instruct the government to encourage Iranians living abroad to return and invest in Iran so that the country could benefit from their capabilities.[15] Recognizing the significance of human capital in economic development and the shortage of skilled managers, President Rouhani also invited Iranians living abroad to return.[16] The government announced new steps to change conditions and ease laws and regulations to encourage the return of expatriates and their expertise to help develop the provinces.[17] Sorna Sattari, vice president for science and technology, urged those who left the country to return and invest in the country's development.[18]

Another obstacle to economic development after the revolution was the increased politicization of the economy. State intervention in the economy expanded after the revolution, with the government, the ruling clergy, and the Revolutionary Guard controlling the commanding heights of Iran's economy. Article 44 of the constitution specified a large role for the state in the economy. The state sector included all the nationalized industries—major mines, banking, insurance, energy sources, dams and large water irrigation networks, radio and television, post, telegraph and telephone, aviation, navigation, roads, railroads, and more. With the revolution, the state gained exclusive control over vast resources comprising roughly 80 percent of Iran's economy. State intervention in the economy and capital accumulation expanded beyond levels that had existed under the monarchy. The new government nationalized all private banks and expropriated the assets of the top echelon of the capitalist class that had been closely connected to the monarchy and foreign capital. The ruling elite seized assets from the royal family and their wealthy associates, foreign investments, the Islamic regime's political opponents, and some religious minorities. "The mullahs seized virtually everything else of value—banks, hotels, car and chemical companies, makers of drugs and consumer goods," according to a report by Forbes.[19] As a result, the state became the most important economic actor, banker, and industrialist in the country.

After the revolution, the Islamic state continued to expand public enterprises and government bureaucracy, becoming the largest employer in the country. The number of state-owned enterprises rose from less than 200 before the revolution[20] to 779 by 2015.[21] Employment in the state sector also continued to increase after the revolution. By 1996, the state employed more than 29 percent of the workforce, compared to 19 percent in 1976.[22] As economic conditions deteriorated, the Islamic state continued to absorb the workforce, expanding government employment to some eight million people in various ministries.[23] In all, the state provided income for 50 percent of the country's households, including more than two million retirees and 312,000 individuals who received war casualty benefits, according to Ali Sadrolsadat, a high-ranking official in the human development branch of the government.[24]

Although the Islamic regime's rulers spoke of privatizing state enterprises, the privatization process remained limited and the privatized enterprises remained rather small. The supreme leader issued a decree in July 2006 privatizing 80 percent of state-owned enterprises but exempted the oil and gas sectors, which were controlled by the state and the Revolutionary Guard. Only 17 percent of such enterprises had actually gone over to the private sector by 2013, according to the minister of economics and finance.[25] Critics countered that the number was less than 5 percent, with the majority going to powerful entities, adding to the power of monopolies, according to Abbas Shakeri, professor of economics.[26]

Expanded state intervention and the failure of privatization inevitably led to the domination of the economy by monopolistic entities under the control of the government, the clergy, and the Revolutionary Guard. The ruling clergy and the Revolutionary Guard controlled an increasingly large share of the country's economic assets as they became the principal beneficiaries of expropriations after the revolution and the privatization of some state-owned enterprises. These monopolies, unlike the chaebols that led South Korea's technological innovation and economic development, did not engage in technological innovation and did not play a significant role in the country's development. Instead, they used their powerful positions to extract assets and accumulate capital. These monopolies, along with state enterprises, had great advantages over the private sector because of state ownership of the banks, preferential duties designated for these entities, and exemption from taxes, according to Mohammad Behzadian, former head of the chamber of commerce.[27]

Control of monopolies under favorable political conditions inaugurated the most prosperous epoch for the ruling Shiite clergy in Iranian history. When the clergy regained control over the Owghaf, or religious endowments, their resources expanded significantly. Cleric Ali Mohammadi, head of Owghaf, stated that revitalization of vaghf (donations) was one of the "greatest blessings of the revolution." Mohammadi added that vaghf belongs to the Ulama, religious authorities, the needy and the sick, and no one else should exploit it. He also noted that assets privatized during the land reform were re-expropriated after the revolution and returned to Owghaf.[28] An Owghaf administrator, Hassan Rabiei, stated that by 2011, the entity controlled one-third of the country's land.[29] Owghaf's spokesperson, cleric Mohammad Mehdi Hatami, admitted that the organization was a large landowner, but noted that its expansion was due to land donations, which had recently multiplied tenfold.[30] Rabiei also acknowledged that the number of shrines increased sevenfold after the revolution, from 1,500 to about 11,000 in 2011.[31]

Owghaf's expanding assets generated complaints and criticism. Mohammad Ali Poourmokhtar, head of a Majles committee, stated that Owghaf declared some property "donated" to the entity without providing any documents.[32] He noted Owghaf's behavior in parts of the country undermined public trust, [33] generating voices of protests by the people and Majles deputies.[34] Thus, the Majles formed a committee to investigate people's complaints.[35] Some Majles deputies charged that Owghaf had seized land and was illegally involved in commercial activities and development projects.[36] Rasht deputy, Gholam Ali Jaafarzadeh Imanabadi, charged that Owghaf had become a corporation and even seized public land and converted some of it into shrines. The number of shrines multiplied several times since the revolution. [37] The deputy remarked that the number of shrines jumped from four thousand to eleven thousand in just two years. [38] He added, Owghaf "seized so much land that it could soon declare itself an independent country."[39] As a religious entity, Owghaf enjoyed special privileges. Like other religious entities, Owghaf was exempt from paying taxes.[40] Vice President Bagher Nobakht recently argued that religious entities should pay taxes.[41]

Expansion of Owghaf land and shrines generated conflicts in some areas of the country. Villagers in Arak disputed Owghaf's claims of ownership.[42] In the city of Koohdasht, Owghaf registered all residential and agricultural property and converted longtime residents who had lived there for generations into renters, prompting a massive dispute.[43]

Supreme Leader Ayatollah Khamenei administered the greatest assets in the country. Seizures following the revolution enabled him to control the domestic wealth of the shah and his cronies combined. The state converted these assets into about 120 foundations distributed across every major economic sector in the country. The foundations included, among others, shipping lines based in London and Athens. Another foundation, the *Mostazafin* and Janbazan Foundation (for the deprived and the martyrs), was established to succeed the Pahlavi Foundation. That foundation ranked as the second-largest economic entity in Iran behind the state-owned National Iranian Oil Company and was one of the largest in the Middle East. It comprised more than four hundred companies, with assets amounting to roughly $12 billion.[44]

In addition, Ayatollah Khamenei controlled a "financial empire" through the Setad Ejraiye Farmane Hazrate Emam, "Headquarters for Executing the Order of the Imam," according to three reports by Reuters. Created to help the poor, the organization amassed assets in part by expropriating wealth from the Iranian people, including religious minorities. The Headquarters collected all confiscated assets from criminals and smugglers, along with government-assessed fines from their activities. It also took in all expropriated assets of political opponents and religious minorities, particularly those of the Baha'is. According to Reuters, "The Supreme Leader, judges and parliament over the years have issued a series of edicts, constitutional interpretations and judicial decisions bolstering Setad."[45] The Headquarters was organized like South Korean conglomerates and created to be a national champion, generating billions in revenue annually.[46] The Headquarters "now holds stakes in nearly every sector of Iranian industry, including finance, oil, telecommunications, the production of birth-control pills and even ostrich farming"—and was estimated to be worth $95 billion.[47]

Beyond these assets, the supreme leader received a government budget, though the amount was never publicly revealed. The supreme leader also took in Khoms, a religious tax, from many economic activities as well as the income of all religious endowments throughout the country. A liberal critic of the regime estimated that Khamenei's annual receipts ranged from several billion to as much as $18 billion.[48] Indeed, the supreme leader's office controlled the largest share of the country's property, financial capital, and industrial assets.[49]

A few crucial features stand out about the foundations controlled by the supreme leader and other clergy. First, the supreme leader administered and supervised the foundations, and the resources were then used as slush funds for the clergy and their supporters, according to Forbes.[50] Second, the supreme leader was not obliged to account for the administration of the country's largest properties under his control. Third, Khamenei publicly refused to allow members of the Assembly of Experts to examine the details of his economic activities and decisions.[51] Lastly, despite controlling huge foundations, the supreme leader's assets were exempt from paying taxes, according to Hasan Mansour, an economist.[52]

The existence of such vast assets in the hands of the clergy had important consequences for Iran's economy and development. Operating independently from the executive branch, the foundations absorbed about 58 percent of the state budget[53] and amounted to close to 50 percent of Iran's gross national product.[54] Some foundations did not even pay for utilities. But no one dared to disconnect services to these entities, according to Mohsen Safaie Farahani, a former Majles deputy and a prominent reformist leader.[55] The economic activities of monopolistic foundations and enterprises adversely affected the private sector. The foundations competed unfairly against private enterprises by accessing government resources, including subsidized foreign currency and low-interest loans from state-owned banks. Through the foundations, the clergy solicited successful businesses for funds, allegedly for charity work. If businesses refused to contribute, the clergy imprisoned the owners and seized their assets for allegedly insulting the Prophet or the supreme leader, according to a report by Forbes.[56]

Access to power and state resources proved to be the key to the accumulation of capital and wealth. High levels of intervention in the economy produced great wealth for some members of the new ruling elite, despite the country's economic problems. Some of the revolution's clerical leaders, their families, and their associates accumulated vast fortunes from their commercial activities and access to state power. Hashemi Rafsanjani, twice elected president, privatized some state-owned enterprises during his first term, benefitting individuals closely connected to the regime. Originally from a modest background, Rafsanjani became one of the country's wealthiest men and ranked among the "millionaire mullahs,"[57] with assets worth $1 billion. The Rafsanjani family controlled economic assets ranging from mining, farming, and oil to communications, airline, and industrial activities. Many other religious leaders and their children also accumulated substantial wealth, according to dissident sources. Among these was Ayatollah Makarem Shirazi, considered one of the wealthiest clerics in Iran.[58] He and his family influenced state policies and were able to control the sugar industry.[59] His family was known as the "sultan of sugar," according to an opposition source.[60] Dissident Mohammad Nurizad stated that other clerical families whose children accumulated vast fortunes and benefitted greatly from the revolution included Ayatollah Abbas Vaez Tabasi, Ayatollah Dorri Najaf-Abadi, and Ayatollah Mahdavi Kani.[61]

The ruling elite's heavy involvement in economic activities and accumulation of wealth antagonized some of the most distinguished senior clerics and supporters of the revolution. Ayatollah Taheri, Friday prayer leader of Isfahan, in an open letter of resignation in July 2002, stated that the "hellish gap" between poverty and wealth and the "deep and increasing class division threatened the life of the nation." Taheri noted, "When I remember the promises and pledges of the beginning of the revolution, I tremble like a willow thinking of my faith. . . . When I hear that some of the privileged progeny and special people, some of whom even don cloaks and turbans, are competing amongst themselves to amass the most wealth . . . and those who plunder the property of the people, and those who assume that the wealth of the nation is theirs and think that the country is their inheritance, . . . I spill the sweat of shame."[62] Some clerics also claimed that the clergy's involvement in economic activities lowered the status of the clergy in the eyes of the people. Dr. Mohsen Rahami, a clergy and seminary professor, noted that the principal work of the clergy was not to trade in meat, steel, and sugar. He stated that when the clergy distances itself from its main duty, "people have the right to become pessimistic about them."[63]

The Revolutionary Guard also engaged in capital accumulation and successfully competed against the private sector. The Guard, along with the government and the clergy, controlled the pinnacle of Iran's economy. As the theocracy's social base of support declined, the Islamic regime turned increasingly to the coercive power of the Revolutionary Guard and provided it with ever-greater resources. As a result, the Revolutionary Guard became the first armed bourgeoisie in the country, controlling a substantial portion of Iran's economy. Unlike South Korea, where military leaders did not become capitalists, Iran's Revolutionary Guard joined the ranks of capitalist investors by establishing and taking over conglomerates. "The

IRGC is so deeply entrenched in Iran's economy and commercial enterprises, it is increasingly likely that if you are doing business with Iran, you are somehow doing business with the IRGC," Henry Paulson, U.S. Treasury secretary, noted.[64]

The Revolutionary Guard became the principal beneficiary of privatization as it purchased many formerly public enterprises, which, although privatized, remained within the state apparatus. It built a multibillion-dollar business empire that controlled hundreds of firms operating in virtually every sector of the economy, often free from constraints such as taxes or duties. "Across Iran, public works projects involving pipelines, roads, bridges and, increasingly, oil and gas are dominated by the Guard's engineering arm, the equivalent of the U.S. Army Corps of Engineers, or by companies with which the Guard has a close relationship."[65] The Guard invested heavily in lucrative enterprises, including oil, gas, and the black market trade in consumer goods. One of the Guard's largest entities, Khatam al-anbia, established in 1989, had hundreds of firms in Iran and abroad, "cooperated" with five thousand private corporations, and directly employed 135,000 people.[66] Companies associated with the Revolutionary Guard amassed considerable wealth by undertaking large government-sponsored development projects every year.

The Guard's economic activities expanded during Ahmadinejad's presidency. In 2005 alone, more than 750 government contracts were granted to the Revolutionary Guard.[67] A construction subsidiary linked to the Guard received a contract amounting to about $7 billion to develop gas and oil fields and refurbish the Tehran metro in 2006.[68] The Guard continued to receive contracts after Ahmadinejad's term ended. The mayor of Tehran, Mohammad Bagher Ghalibaf, a former Guard commander, awarded a contract worth nearly $8 billion to the Guard for development projects in Tehran without consulting the city council or obtaining bids, provoking criticism from city council members.[69]

The Revolutionary Guard engaged in activities that only the most powerful could undertake. The Guard seized thousands of hectares of land across the country.[70] For example, the Guard expropriated 818 hectares of land in Shimranat, one of the most desirable areas, according to Governor Ezzatollah Khanmohammadi.[71] The Guard reneged on a development project in Gheshm Island in the Persian Gulf worth 860 million euros (more than 1 billion dollars) awarded by Ahmadinejad's administration, for which they had received a portion of the payment. The contract was to have been completed by 2013, but the Guard turned over the work to the government with only 3 percent of the construction completed, stating that it could not finish the project. The government of President Rouhani was unable to enforce the terms of the contract. Akbar Torkan, chief advisor to President Rouhani, publicly complained that the contractor, Khatam al-anbia, a Guard corporation, "is powerful, and our power does not match theirs."[72]

Revolutionary Guard corporations and former members of the Guard continued to engage in questionable practices after international sanctions intensified. Khatam al-anbia, along with other enterprises, became involved in the sale of oil although it was not connected to the national oil company. Some former members of Khatam al-anbia and retired Guard members sold nonexistent oil, "engaging in fraud" *(kolah bardari)*. Another unnamed corporation linked to the military apparatus sold some of the country's oil by order of the commander of Iran's armed forces but failed to turn over the proceeds to the government, according to a report by Iran's semiofficial Labor News Agency.[73]

A few Revolutionary Guard leaders, including Mohsen Rafighdoust and Sadegh Mahsouli, have accumulated massive fortunes. Rafighdoust, who was from a working-class background, began his activities as Ayatollah Khomeini's driver. He eventually became a commander in the Revolutionary Guard and used his business dealings to become one of the richest men in Iran.[74] Dubbed a "billionaire general," Mahsouli was a close friend of Ahmadinejad and served as interior minister during his first term.[75] Mahsouli was said to have accumulated massive sums, although he has denied the figures given in the media.[76] One report ranked him among the richest ten Iranians.[77] The Majles rejected his nomination as oil minister in 2005, partly because "Mahsouli could not provide a satisfactory answer to the question of how he, a dirt poor IRGC officer in 1988 at the end of the Iran-Iraq war, could amass such a large wealth during such a short time."[78] Mahsouli told the Majles oil committee in 2005 that he had accumulated his wealth through property development during the previous ten years.[79] His six mansions and estates were estimated at 10 million British pounds.[80] Mahsouli's total wealth in 2005 was at least as much as 86 million British pounds,[81] although some sources placed it even higher.[82] Mr. Mahsouli has acknowledged that he was a rich man but was quoted saying, "What Imam [Ayatollah Khomeini] has prohibited is the attitude and demeanour of living in palaces, not the actual living in palaces."[83] Mahsouli has also noted that his wealth belonged to the Imam of the Age. "It is in trust, to be returned to his Highness upon his manifestation."[84]

The Guard's heavy involvement in the economy and in capital accumulation drew criticism and objections from some members of the elite. Ayatollah Hashemi Rafsanjani, former president and speaker of the Majles, stated publicly, "Now the Guard has taken control of the economy and foreign and domestic politics, and is not satisfied with less than the entire country."[85] President Rouhani and his administration also became concerned about the Guard's involvement in so many aspects of Iranian society. Ahmad Khorram, former minister of roads and transportation, in an interview, implicitly criticized the Guard's heavy involvement. He noted the fact that "ruling entities" carried out between 70 percent and 80 percent of the development projects. "The ruling entities were not supposed to dominate the field and compete against the private sector in projects that the latter is capable of carrying out."[86] Without naming the Guard, President Rouhani stated in a public event that concentrating guns, money, media, and other sources of power in one entity would encourage corruption.[87] Rouhani also expressed concerns about the impact of the Guard's economic activities on the private sector. When the Guard expressed interest in continued involvement in economic activities after Ahmadinejad's presidency, President Rouhani's administration asked the Guard not to compete against the private sector in small-scale projects. Vice President Mohammad Bagher Nobakht recommended that the Guard participate only in projects that the private sector was not capable of undertaking.[88] In response, the Guard agreed not to participate in projects smaller than 100 million *tomans* (about 3,000 tomans equal $1).[89] President Rouhani then invited the Guard to participate in some large, national projects and help the government in economic activities.[90] Vice President Bagher Nobakht challenged the tax-exempt status of corporations held by the Revolutionary Guard and declared that they should start paying taxes.[91]

Ties to the government and the state also proved to be a source of accumulation of wealth for others. Asaddollah Asgaroladi, a bazaar merchant, who came from a working-class background, was able to accumulate vast fortunes after the revolution. Through his ties to the state, while his brother Habibollah was Commerce Minister, he received a trade license that enabled him to buy hard currency at an artificially low price and use it for his business. His wealth was estimated at over $9 billion, making him the second wealthiest man in Iran,[92] though he claimed to be only the country's seventh richest person.[93]

State Corruption and Cronyism

High levels of government intervention in the economy and state control of huge assets produced graft, corruption, and cronyism in both the public and private sectors. State corruption resulted in an added tax on businesses and consumers. Corruption also contributed to accumulation of wealth and increased inequalities. Cronyism affected state capital allocation and led to the concentration of the country's financial assets in a small portion of the population. In addition, cronyism pointed to the unfair operation of the power structure and contributed to the existing inequalities. More importantly, widespread state corruption and cronyism eroded the legitimacy of the regime and undermined public trust in the state.

Corruption has been a problem in Iran for decades and noticed by observers. Ayatollah Khomeini had repeatedly condemned corruption and the pillage of the country's resources during the revolutionary struggles. People expected the country's revolution to put an end to such practices. Yet, more than three decades after the revolution, corruption remained rampant. The Islamic Republic repeatedly has been deemed "highly corrupt" by Transparency International, which ranked Iran 79 out of 133 countries in 2004, lowered it to 105 in 2006, and dropped it to 168 of 180 countries in 2009.[94] Corruption cost the economy $34 billion a year, expanded poverty, concentrated wealth, and undermined regime legitimacy, according to Ahmad Tavakoli, a Majles deputy.[95]

The supreme leader and prominent government officials publicly complained of the extent and depth of corruption. Ayatollah Khamenei likened financial corruption to cancer and AIDS that had to be dealt with.[96] As early as 1997, he declared war on corruption. "The judiciary must combat those who are bent on amassing huge fortunes by breaking the law," Khamenei stated.[97] When a big financial scandal was exposed in 2011, he vowed that there would be "no mercy" for anyone found guilty.[98] The supreme leader demanded concrete steps in dealing with corruption. "There is no point in talking about corruption. By saying 'thief, thief,' the thief will not give up on theft. Officials are not newspapers to be talking about corruption. We have to take real steps to prevent corruption," his website stated.[99]

Other officials of the Islamic Republic also spoke against corruption. President Rouhani noted that people launched a revolution to get rid of corruption and that "we have to struggle against corruption."[100] Ahmad Tavakoli commented that the state had reached the stage of "systematic corruption," as the agencies that were supposed to fight corruption had themselves become corrupt to some degree.[101] Eshagh Jahangiri, Rouhani's vice president, likened corruption to a leprosy that was destroying the system when people could see how one individual pocketed 8 or 9 billion tomans in oil revenues.[102] Judiciary spokesperson Gholamhossein Mohseni Ajei warned that the economic, political, and bureaucratic corruption could threaten the system and cause serious difficulties for the state.[103] Majles deputy Gholamali Jaafarzadeh, a member of the committee investigating corruption, said that the dimensions of the corruption were so extensive that they were afraid of discussing the issues publicly due to the fear of causing shock to society and the system.[104]

Reports of corruption often implicated the elites. Ayatollah Jannati, head of the Guardian Council, charged that some in the upper echelon of the country and in the private sector had transferred massive wealth to Indonesia, United Arab Emirates, and Europe. He complained that they should not have been allowed to spend billions of dollars from unknown sources so easily.[105] Two reports, in particular, charged that the supreme leader's family was involved in irregular activities. President Ahmadinejad uncovered a document revealing that Mojtaba Khamenei, son of the supreme leader, received 1.6 billion euros from the country's oil revenues, according to a dissident source.[106] In addition, Mohammad Nurizad, a dissident, in his twenty-sixth letter to the supreme leader, claimed that the supreme leader's son had received 800 million tomans from Shahram Jazayeri, an entrepreneur who was imprisoned and charged with corruption.[107] Nurizad declared his readiness to present supporting documents in court if Mojtaba Khamenei were to sue him.[108]

Other reports implicated the family of Hashemi Rafsanjani—specifically his son, Mehdi Hashemi. According to Houshang Bouzari, advisor to Iran's oil ministry, Mehdi Hashemi had demanded a bribe amounting to $50 million from him. When Bouzari refused to pay, he was arrested and tortured by government agents in 1993.[109] His family was forced to pay $3 million to the Ministry of Information to obtain his release from prison.[110] Hashemi was implicated again in a 2003 report for taking $5.2 million in bribes.[111] Ahmad Tavakoli, a Majles deputy, stated during a public session of the parliament that Hashemi had taken $5.2 million in bribes from Statoil between 2002 and 2004. He added that Statoil continued to give Hashemi $1 million per year for the next ten years.[112] Mehdi Hashemi was arrested and detained for two months and twenty-three days in 2012 on corruption and other charges, and in 2015, he was sentenced to ten years in prison for embezzlement and security charges by the judiciary.[113]

Documents obtained by Bamdadkhabar revealed that two Larijani brothers, Mohammad Javad (head of the judiciary's human rights council) and Sadegh (member of the Guardian Council) unlawfully seized 342 hectares of "national" (public) land in Varamin. The brothers dug illegal wells and maintained nine hundred sheep and two hundred camels on the property. A complaint was filed on May 17, 2008, to investigate these illegal activities, but it was never carried out.[114] While Ali Larijani, speaker of the Majles, defended his brothers and demanded that the accusers reveal their documents, farmers in the area complained that the deep wells ruined their agriculture.[115] Sadegh Larijani was later appointed head of the judiciary in

2009, but he did not order the judiciary to investigate the case until 2013, when he did so in response to media reports of corruption. Under pressure, he ordered the head of Tehran's judiciary to investigate the matter, which is still under investigation.

Other reports implicated powerful entities engaged in activities and use of corruption laws to expropriate assets of private companies. One report revealed the arrest and imprisonment of Mohammad Saeedi, executive of Iran Marine Service, in August 1997 on charges of tax evasion and bribery. Critics disagreed with the charges and noted irregularities. The head of the Committee Principle 90 of the Majles, Hussein Ansari Raad, noted that if the committee decided to publicize the entire file on this case, it would reveal the kind of legal and moral violations that had been committed against citizens' rights and the public interest in the name of maintaining the treasury. He also noted that if the company executive was guilty as charged, he should have served a sentence of two years, not five years with no apparent end. Another irregularity involved the takeover of the company's property by the Intelligence Ministry, which sold some corporation assets, shut down other parts, and operated the rest profitably.[116] Saeedi's wife filed a complaint about the illegal sale of her husband's assets, but her complaint was unsuccessful.[117]

Multiple reports revealed that corruption extended to one of the highest offices in the country. The city of Tehran spent about $100 million in the 2005 presidential campaign on behalf of its mayor, Mahmoud Ahmadinejad. No receipts were available for the expenditures, according to Mohammad Ali Najafi, a member of the city council.[118] Other reports indicated that several other violations occurred during Ahmadinejad's rule, ranging from $1 billion to $53 billion. Billions of dollars of oil revenues were not deposited in the treasury, according to Saeed Zamanian, a Majles deputy. Zamanian remarked, "Under Ahmadinejad, they treated oil like a beverage."[119] Rouhani's presidential transition team found that much of Iran's oil revenues had not been deposited in the state treasury during the last few years of Ahmadinejad's term in office, but instead ended up in the accounts of sixty-three individuals, thirty-two of whom did not even reside in Iran. All of the individuals were associated with Esfandiar Rahim Moshaie, Ahmadinejad's relative and his chief of staff.[120]

Other investigations also revealed unprecedented irregularities in the handling of budget and state revenues during Ahmadinejad's presidency.[121] In his first year in office, Ahmadinejad committed two thousand budget rule violations,[122] including failing to deposit $1 billion from oil revenues into the treasury, according to a report by the Supreme Audit Court (Divan Mohasebat).[123] The Court also reported that Ahmadinejad's government embezzled and wasted billions of dollars between 2008 and 2011. The high level of corruption in the government led a majority of Majles deputies to vote and demand an investigation into illegal payments to nine million citizens by the president just before the tenth presidential elections.[124] Some accused Ahmadinejad of buying votes. He defended the distribution of the money, claiming that it represented "justice shares," created by privatizing state-owned enterprises to help forty-five million needy Iranian families, according to a report.[125] But the government failed to distribute additional money to the needy after the election and instead placed the funds under the control of 250 individuals without obtaining parliamentary approval. Rouhani's administration could not recover the funds, according to Iran's official news agency.[126] Some of the privatized enterprises were given to Ahmadinejad's relatives, according to Mohammad Reza Behzadian, the former head of Iran's chamber of commerce.[127]

Reports directly implicated Ahmadinejad and members of his administration in corruption, despite his claim that his government was the "cleanest government in Iran's history." Morteza Baank, a high-ranking official in Rouhani's government, announced that Ahmadinejad had inappropriately granted 9 billion tomans to a foundation whose members were individuals close to Ahmadinejad's government.[128] Baank also mentioned that Ahmadinejad had illegally deposited 16 billion tomans from the government budget to an account belonging to him and his former vice president, Hamid Baghaie, for the purpose of establishing the Iranian University, to be run by Ahmadinejad himself. Other examples of illegal appropriations mentioned by Baank included loans from Martyrs Raja-ie and Bahonar Fund, designated to provide loans to needy members of the president's office.[129] An investigation revealed that high-ranking officials and even cabinet members repeatedly took out loans from the fund. Some never repaid these, according to Mohammad Reza Jalilian, coordinator of the investigating committee.[130]

Government corruption also involved other state assets. In an unprecedented move, the government of Ahmadinejad transferred $22 billion to Turkey and Dubai, according to Vice President Jahangiri.[131] Prime Minister Recep Tayyip Erdogan announced the arrival of over $18 billion in Turkey but did not specify the source of the transfer.[132] Jahangiri noted that the government transferred the money to stabilize the foreign exchange market and then sold it to other countries at a low price.[133] The vice president also charged that government officials withdrew 17,000 miliard (billion) tomans from the Central Bank.[134] Members of Ahmadinejad's administration took more than forty cars and refused to return them to the government.[135] In another case, the government sold a house that was worth 106 billion tomans for only 30 billion tomans, according to Ali Rabiei, the labor minister.[136]

The National Audit Office implicated the president's allies and the head of his office in an unprecedented case of graft after about $2.6 billion (3,000 milliard tomans) was embezzled from Saderat, Iran's second-largest bank, which was partially state owned.[137] Mohammad Reza Khavari, managing director of state-owned Bank Melli and one of Iran's leading bankers, fled to Canada to avoid arrest, according to reports.[138] More than one hundred government officials involving the three branches of the government and the board of directors of Saderat and Bank Melli were involved in the scheme, further investigation revealed.[139] In addition to some Majles deputies, the assistant director of Iran's judiciary was also implicated in the scandal, according to Mohseni Ajei, judiciary spokesperson.[140]

Of thirty-nine people investigated in the Saderat case, four were sentenced to death, two were given life in prison, and the rest received sentences of up to twenty-five years.[141] Mah-Afarid Amir Khosravi, a wealthy businessman, was sentenced to death for embezzlement, forgery, money laundering, and "disruption of the economic system."[142] He responded to the charges by claiming that certain government officials had asked him by letter to start a new bank to help circumvent sanctions. Khosravi wrote a letter to the supreme leader to ask the judiciary's permission to disclose the letter's contents to authorities and the public, according to his defense lawyer. Less than seventy-two hours after his lawyer revealed the existence of such a letter, Khosravi was executed on May 24. Khosravi's quick execution without prior notice to his lawyer or his family, along with the acquittal of a few other players, led critics and opponents of the regime to accuse authorities of a cover-up.[143]

Another investigation found an even bigger case of corruption that involved five banks and at least twenty officials in the Ahmadinejad's administration. The perpetrators formed a phantom corporation and obtained loans of nearly $4 billion (12,000 milliard tomans), four times larger than the Saderat embezzlement, between 2006 and 2012, according to Ali Tayebnia, Iran's minister of economics and finance.[144] At least twenty people were arrested in connection with the case.[145]

Some highly publicized cases of corruption were investigated by the country's parliament. In one case, the social security organization, which covered more than thirty-seven million people, was accused of corruption, squandering resources, making appointments based on connections and cronyism, and providing "gift cards" of substantial sums to powerful members of the government, the parliament, and the media.[146] The case generated protests by those who were adversely affected. One thousand workers filed a lawsuit charging fraud and embezzlement by Saeed Mortazavi, former public prosecutor and head of the social security organization, together with two vice presidents and thirty-seven Majles deputies. Workers rallied in front of the parliament to demand that Mortazavi be put on trial.[147] Pressure from parliament forced Ahmadinejad to remove Mortazavi from his position, but he subsequently reappointed him as caretaker. Mortazavi later denied some of the charges and boasted that he had given gift cards not to 37, but to more than 180 parliament deputies.[148] Mortazavi's case is still pending.

Rising reports of corruption prompted the Majles to launch another inquiry that uncovered twenty-four violations on the part of the president and the executive branch during Ahmadinejad's second term and referred them to the judiciary for investigation, according to the Majles news agency.[149] The Majles also investigated a corruption case involving Iran's Central Bank and found that, with the help of the bank, three currency exchange agents made a profit of some $6.2 billion in 2011.[150] The Majles released its findings to the judiciary and demanded accountability on the part of government officials involved at the time, according to Arslan Fathipour, head of the Majles committee on economics.[151] President Rouhani's government formed a preliminary committee to investigate the case of corruption in Ahmadinejad's administration. "We witnessed a great deal of rent seeking and abuses of the treasury in the previous government, which called itself the cleanest government in history," according to Mohammad Ashrafi Esfahani, a cleric and the head of the committee. Esfahani added that the committee had begun investigating more than seven hundred files of violations in the government.[152]

Corrupt activities were not limited to the public sector but involved private corporations as well as government officials. Babak Zanjani, a young businessman worth over $13 billion who owned some seventy companies that employed seventeen thousand people, was accused by the United States and the EU for using his companies to circumvent international sanctions and the oil embargo. Iran's parliament began investigating his business dealings after he was accused of withholding $1.9 billion of oil revenue that had been channeled through his companies. Zanjani was subsequently arrested and imprisoned in December 2013.[153]

Zanjani's case, the largest financial file investigated by the judiciary since the revolution, was three times larger than the $3 billion embezzled from Saderat, uncovered in 2011, according to the Tehran prosecutor, Abbas Jaafari Dolatabadi.[154] Bijan Zangeneh, oil minister under President Rouhani, revealed in 2014 that several ministers and the head of Iran's

Central Bank approved depositing $2.7 billion in a fake account in Tajikistan belonging to Zanjani. The money disappeared completely.[155] Further investigation by the parliament found that a few of Ahmadinejad's ministers, including the minister of oil and finance and the head of Iran's Central Bank, were implicated in Zanjani's case, according to Amir Abbas Soltani, a Majles deputy.[156] Zanjani was sentenced to death for corruption and owing more than $2 billion to the government,[157] prompting the opposition to charge that the officials who collaborated with him were relieved.[158] Majles deputy Hossein Dehdashti argued that executing Zanjani without also investigating his "hidden collaborators" would allow them to go free.[159]

Another case of corruption involved the state and importers who worked with authorities to abuse Iran's currency allocation. The state provided $22 billion in foreign exchange to importers at subsidized rates to buy essential goods. According to Kazem Palizdar, head of the office for coordinating the fight against corruption: "They would get a large amount of currency at a prime rate to acquire essential goods. Not only did they not do this, but also we realized that these import companies did not even exist. It's not even clear where this currency went."[160] In another instance, an individual received $400 million from the government to import spare parts for airplanes but never delivered the parts, according to Majles deputy Moayed Hosseini Sadr.[161]

Corrupt dealings also affected Iran's state-owned oil sector. According to oil minister Zangeneh, authorities paid $87 million in 2012–2013 to purchase an oil rig, which could not be located. The Iranian buyers even issued a receipt for receiving the rig at the time the contract was signed, but the rig was never delivered. Further investigation revealed that the company that was to supply the rig, Dean International Trading, had been established in the British Virgin Islands only twenty-two days prior to the sale and had never actually owned any rigs.[162] Iran's oil minister revealed an investigation was launched into the disappearance of a second oil rig in October 2015.[163]

As a result of widespread reports, at least two of Ahmadinejad's vice presidents were implicated in corruption and imprisoned. Vice President Mohammad Reza Rahimi was charged with corruption for his involvement in Iran Insurance, the country's largest insurance company. In that case, more than seventy others were prosecuted and sentenced to long prison terms, had their assets confiscated, and were barred from government employment.[164] Ahmadinejad drew a red line around his cabinet and publicly threatened to "break his silence." He went even further and appointed Rahimi as head of the Headquarters against Economic Corruption in 2013, despite the fact that the corruption case against

Rahimi dated back to 2009. In 2013, Ahmadinejad even rewarded Rahimi for his valuable service.[165]

But some members of the elite criticized the judiciary for failing to take action on the matter. Ali Motahari, the outspoken deputy, publicly criticized the handling of the case in the Majles on December 29, 2013, and charged that the judiciary had failed to come to a decision after more than four years. The judiciary finally took action. A Revolutionary Court prosecutor announced that the Court had initiated an investigation and that Rahimi had been questioned and was on bail. Subsequently, Rahimi was tried, given a jail term of fifteen years, and fined 3 billion and 850 million tomans.[166]

In another corruption case, Hamid Baghaie, Ahmadinejad's vice president, was charged with embezzling 300 million tomans in June 2015.[167] A judiciary official, cleric Mohammad Ashrafi Esfahani, revealed that Baghie had been arrested for removing sizeable wealth from the country, which he invested in some ten countries. Esfahani quoted a security official, saying, "He has embezzled and looted so much that it would take us several years just to locate the pillaged wealth. Reports also revealed that Baghaie's case was larger than that of Babak Zanjani."[168] Baghaie was arrested in June 2015 but released on bail in January 2016.[169]

The frequency and severity of graft led a number of officials to criticize persistent state corruption in the Islamic Republic. Majid Ansari, a cleric, Rouhani's vice president, a former Majles deputy, and a member of the Assembly of Experts and the Expediency Council, noted in an interview that anyone looking from outside wonders, "What kind of sacred system is this where in the past thirty-four years all its managers except the supreme leader have been involved in deviation and corruption?"[170] Mohammad Ashrafi Esfahani, a clergy and Majles deputy, stated that Ahmadinejad's government was the most contaminated *(alodeh tarin)* since the revolution.[171]

Without naming anyone, President Rouhani publicly criticized people in powerful political positions. He stated, "Some people, in the name of resistance to the powerful and the superpowers, robbed the pockets of the people and pillaged the nation's property."[172] Rouhani noted, "They informed us that in such and such a foreign account we have billions; we couldn't find millions, or thousands, or even one dollar."[173] Similarly, Motahari, Majles deputy, pointed his finger at government officials. He observed that it was impossible to embezzle $3 billion without coordinating with the government, because banks did not readily lend money to anyone.[174] Interior Minister Abdolreza Rahmani Fazli went even further and asserted that some of the money from dirty economic activities like drug dealing entered the political arena and affected political campaigns and elections.[175]

Some prominent members of the clergy also criticized state corruption. Grand Ayatollah Dastgheib, a member of the powerful Assembly of Experts, protested against the problem. He refused to participate in the assembly's sixteenth gathering, in September 2014, to protest the lack of investigation of corruption during Ahmadinejad's presidency. In a statement, he declared that he had urged President Rouhani, the judiciary officials, and other heads to investigate corruption between 2005 and 2013. He noted that his calls went unanswered, suggesting that those officials lacked full independence to investigate the violations.[176] In another statement, Dastgheib called upon the Assembly of Experts to break their eight-year silence and demand trials for those who pillaged the national treasury during the eight years of Ahmadinejad's rule.[177]

To prevent government corruption, the state implemented transparency measures. The Expediency Council voted to enact a law that would require all high officials of the government and their immediate relatives—including the president, members of the cabinet, parliament deputies, and bank executives—to disclose their assets before and after taking office.[178] Under this law, more than 153,000 people would be required to report their assets publicly.

Official statements also revealed caution in reporting corruption. Ayatollah Hashemi Rafsanjani stated at a public gathering that the eleventh (Rouhani) government was the "meekest" since the revolution and that it could not publicly reveal all the problems it had inherited because of its religious convictions: "Only occasionally pieces of the iceberg of corruption are mentioned, and to prevent the enemies' abuse, they restrain themselves from stating all the problems." Ahmad Khorram, minister of roads and transportation under President Rouhani, said that corruption was widespread in the previous government. He quoted the head of the country's general inspectorate, who said, "There were more than one hundred files like the one with $3 billion."[179] "Some people tell us not to talk about the injustices. What we have talked about is less than 5 percent of the injustices committed against the country; we have not even spoken about past abuses," declared Vice President Jahangiri, at a gathering of bank executives.[180] He later noted that "slogans against corruption were shouted more frequently during the last round [of elections] than at any other time in history; nevertheless, the biggest and the most widespread corruption of the century occurred then."[181]

Nevertheless, new reports of corruption continued to surface. In just two weeks, thirteen major cases of corruption that occurred during

Ahmadinejad's two terms came to light. The new cases implicated the former president, his ministers, and high-ranking managers and executives across the country.[182] One report revealed that corruption had expanded to academic institutions, where doctoral degrees—particularly in the humanities and the social sciences—were sold. Many people, including judges and lawyers, bought their doctoral degrees, according to law professor Reza Eslami.[183] In 2014, Vice-Minister of the Sciences, Vahid Ahmadi, pledged to stem the practice,[184] but the problem continued.[185]

Fighting corruption became complicated during Ahmadinejad's presidency. Ahmadinejad temporarily assumed control of the Intelligence Ministry and gained access to crucial files. He uncovered weaknesses and vulnerabilities of many officials who then could not speak out against him, according to Majles deputy Fazel Mousavi.[186]

Cronyism, too, ballooned to unprecedented levels. Appointments and resources in the Islamic regime were allocated on the basis of strong personal connections and cronyism as well as ideological criteria. Networks of government officials, the clergy, and the Revolutionary Guard were the principle sources of cronyism. Ahmadinejad, who had campaigned on a platform to promote justice and fairness, actually appointed his relatives and friends to many more positions of power than had any previous government in the Islamic regime, further expanding political cronyism.[187] Relatives, including children, with connections to clergy had an advantage in social, economic, and political arenas, whereas those without such connections were largely excluded. Bahram Biranvand, a Majles deputy from Boroujerd, charged in a speech in the parliament that when "the children of the powerful" got involved in oil contracts, corruption became widespread.[188] Another aspect of cronyism involved high level government officials who were paid exorbitant salaries, which led to widespread criticisms and resignations.[189]

Cronyism also played an important role in capital allocation and the operation of Iran's financial sector. Credit allocation in the banking system, primarily owned by the state, was carried out through widespread cronyism and led to a high level of concentration of the country's resources. President Ahmadinejad disclosed that three hundred people horded 60 percent of the country's financial capital.[190] A further investigation by the Majles revealed an even higher concentration in lending. Mustapha Afzali-Fard, a deputy and committee speaker investigating the issue, charged that thirty people had borrowed 80 percent of the country's financial resources.[191] Labor minister Rabiei observed that 90 percent of the country's financial capital was under the control of 5 percent of the population.[192]

Ezzatollah Yusefian Molla, a member of the official Headquarters against Economic Corruption, revealed that a quarter of the country's total liquidity was in the hands of about six hundred people, children of influential individuals. He hoped that exposing them might prevent them from monopolizing the country's treasury.[193] In response to public debate, Iran's banking authorities eventually submitted the names of 575 of the largest borrowers to Vice President Eshagh Jahangiri, who referred the list to the judiciary for investigation. He noted that the Central Bank had singled out the twenty largest borrowers on the list.[194]

Cronyism also affected other aspects of Iranian society. During Ahmadinejad's presidency, powerful people in the state used their position to hire relatives and friends. High-ranking officials, ministers, and governors illegally hired their relatives and friends, according to a report by Gholamali Jaafarzadeh Eemanabadi, Majles deputy from Rasht.[195] Of the 650,000 people hired by the government during Ahmadinejad's final years, about 450,000 were hired on the basis of connections and without due process or qualifying examinations, according to the report.[196] Mokhtar Mohammadi, advisor to the High Council Supervising Bureaucratic Violations, declared that 56 percent—some 499,000—of all hiring during Ahmadinejad's presidency was illegal.[197] Hiring in the Education Ministry in the last few years of Ahmadinejad's presidency was a disaster, according to reports. Of seventy-six thousand people hired, 2 percent were illiterate, 14 percent had completed only elementary school, 19 percent had finished middle school, 1 percent had high school diplomas, and 33 percent had received degrees beyond high school.[198] A governor's daughter was hired to teach Arabic despite not knowing the Arabic alphabet. She was assigned to teach geography.[199]

Cronyism also affected academic institutions. During Ahmadinejad's presidency, more than three thousand individuals who took no qualifying exams were admitted to pursue doctoral degrees based on their political connections or for ideological and political reasons.[200] One report alleged that the president of Azad University enabled some government ministers and Majles representatives to obtain doctoral degrees without high school diplomas or a master's degree, and at times without studying.[201] Mojtaba Sadighi, deputy minister of science, revealed that the Ministry of Science found that many students were admitted or were given scholarships because of their family connections, not because of merit, as quite a few lacked the qualifications for admission to universities.[202] Another report found that ten recipients were husbands and wives and another fifteen were brothers and sisters.[203] Vice President Jahangiri revealed that scholarships were granted based on favoritism and constituted an abuse of power.[204]

The publicity attracted national attention and led to a Majles investigation. The investigation drew criticism from the Majles and led to the dismissal of the minister of science that had revealed the irregularities. Ayatollah Khamenei entered the debate and criticized the science minister for drawing attention to irregularities in granting scholarships.[205] In the end, a new minister announced that only thirty-six scholarships had been illegal.[206] Subsequently, Mahmoud Sadeghi, a Majles deputy that had investigated the entire affair while he worked at the science ministry, corroborated the original accusations of impropriety that involved more than 3,700 individuals. He went further and stated that a prosecutor had filed charges against the science minister that had issued the scholarships but was afraid to proceed legally.[207] Another prosecutor in the Supreme Audit Court that had investigated the matter filed a complaint against seventeen individuals, including the science minister, who had issued about 3,700 scholarships amounting to over $2 million.[208]

Economic Performance and Inequality in Wealth and Income

The particular structural features of Iran's economy—combined with the nature of state policies, economic mismanagement, and international sanctions—undermined the country's economic performance and adversely affected the vast majority of the population. More than three decades after the revolution, the Islamic Republic failed to fulfill the demands of the middle and working classes who had fought for the revolution. The rulers of the theocracy also failed to carry out Ayatollah Khomeini's promises to improve conditions for the *mostazafin*.

Under the Islamic Republic, Iran's economic performance declined from its prerevolutionary level. Most citizens' standard of living either stagnated or deteriorated due to economic mismanagement, high unemployment, and inflation. Iran's prerevolutionary per capita GDP in 1976 was ranked fifty-fourth in the world, higher than that of South Korea, which ranked ninety-third. By 2009, even before international sanctions intensified, Iran's ranking had dropped to ninety-fifth, while South Korea moved up to fifty-sixth.[209] Iran's per capita GDP was less than a third of South Korea's. Based on Iran's prerevolutionary growth rates and the economic performance of neighboring countries, the opportunity cost, due to the revolution, ranged from 25 to 50 percent in per capita real GDP, according to a study of Iran's performance between 1979 and 2010.[210] Iran's real per capita GDP (in 2005 US$) peaked at $13,329 in 1976 and declined to $9,644 in 1978.[211] Just over thirty years later, in 2009, it was $9,421, slightly below the 1978 level and well below the 1976 peak. Iran's GDP declined by 20 percent between 2012 and 2014, according to Ali Tayebnia, Iran's minister of economics under President Rouhani.[212] For Iran's 2015 per capita GDP to return to its 1976 level, it would need to rise by 76 percent.[213]

Multiple factors contributed to Iran's economic problems. One was that the Islamic Republic's external conflicts and foreign policy affected the country's economy. Iran's nuclear policy had a negative impact on the country's currency and the economic well-being of its people. International sanctions beginning in 2006, during Ahmadinejad's presidency, were particularly devastating because of Iran's dependence on oil and a variety of imports. The rial, which was devalued soon after the revolution from about 80 per dollar, depreciated to approximately 10,000 per dollar in November 2008, several months before the disputed presidential elections. It plummeted to roughly 34,000 per dollar by early October 2012, losing 57 percent of its value in three months.[214] The currency depreciation adversely affected all sectors of the economy and the vast majority of the population.

Currency depreciation provided an opportunity for the country to increase exports, but intensified sanctions, and Iran's technological dependence prevented Iranian producers from expanding. The auto industry, a sector that began to develop before the revolution, revealed Iran's technological weaknesses. Despite decades of production, the auto industry was not self-sufficient and could not manufacture all the parts necessary for domestic automobile production. Before sanctions intensified, Iran exported cars to Iraq, Azerbaijan, and Ukraine, but sanctions undermined producers' ability to obtain necessary parts from China and South Korea, resulting in a decline in exports. Furthermore, the quality of Iran's automobiles was substandard, complained Iraq's government-owned auto-importing company.[215]

Large-scale capital flight after the revolution had led to the near-collapse of banks and financial institutions. Subsequent political conflicts and endless repression increased capital flight and adversely affected the value of Iran's currency. To stem capital flight and address the foreign exchange gap in the context of the Iran-Iraq war, the government devalued the currency.[216] Periodic political conflicts also generated a climate of uncertainty that prevented or limited foreign investment in the country and was a factor in capital flight in later years. The rate of capital flight increased 150 times between 2004 and 2011, according to Farshad Momenie, an economist at the Allameh Tabatabaie University.[217] Some $600 billion in capital left the country during the eight years of Ahmadinejad's government, according to Mohammad Reza Khabbaz, a government official at the time.[218]

The Islamic Republic's leaders promised to reduce dependence on the oil sector, but failed to deliver. Iran's economy remained highly dependent on oil and international markets more than three decades after the revolution. Although the country's relatively cheap labor and heavily subsidized fuel made it possible to export some manufactured goods to the world market, the economy failed to achieve economic independence. In 2005, before international sanctions intensified, 88 percent of Iran's exported merchandise consisted of raw materials and only 9 percent were manufactured goods, including Persian handicrafts and handwoven Persian rugs. Iran's performance contrasted sharply with that of South Korea, where 91 percent of exports were manufactured goods and 9 percent were raw materials.[219] Iran's manufactured goods were largely exported to Asian countries, whereas South Korea was able to export high-tech products to developed, industrial countries. Despite international sanctions, oil still constituted 85 percent of Iran's exports in 2013, according to Iran's head of the chamber of commerce.[220]

The adverse impact of dependence on oil and the world market was exposed during the global recession and the imposition of international sanctions. Iran's GDP growth rate declined from 7.84 percent in 2007 to .83 percent in 2008, due to a reduced international demand for oil during the Great Recession. Iran's dependence on oil was further underscored when intensified Western sanctions reduced Iran's GDP growth rate from 3.2 percent in 2011 to −5.4 percent in 2012, according to the Statistical Center of Iran.[221] Still worse, the heavy dependence on oil and the world market led to stagflation during Ahmadinejad's second term, as Western sanctions intensified and factories closed because they could not import parts and raw materials (*reuters.com*, December 8, 2013). The dependence on oil rendered Iran's economy vulnerable and adversely affected people's material well-being.

To be sure, oil revenue increased during Ahmadinejad's presidency, providing an opportunity for the state to promote the country's economic development and reduce unemployment and poverty. Iran's oil revenues rose by sevenfold between 1979 and March 21, 2011, to $976 billion, compared with $139.537 billion in the prerevolutionary years from 1908 to 1979. In the first seven years of Ahmadinejad's presidency, oil revenues peaked at an all-time high of $531.882 billion, compared with $445.472 billion accrued between 1979 and 2005 when Ahmadinejad took office, according to an official government report.[222]

However, the opportunity was lost as corruption and government mis-management undermined Iran's economic performance. The government owed huge debts to bankers, contractors, and the Retirement Fund by the end of Ahmadinejad's presidency. Government debt to banks alone increased eightfold during Ahmadinejad's presidency.[223] Dariush Ghabari, a Majles deputy, stated that Ahmadinejad had divided Iran into two cate-gories: unemployed and indebted.[224] State economic policies were directly responsible for the country's economic problems, according to a statement by forty-three Iranian economists. Between 2005 and 2010, Iran had $630 billion in oil revenues but still had a debt of $200 billion to banks and the private sector.[225] The economists noted that state policies and mis-management also disrupted the functioning of about 1,750 industrial enterprises in 2012.[226]

A specific example of the expansion of state intervention in the economy and mismanagement was the Mehr housing project. With increased oil revenues, the government offered free government land to developers to build over two million houses for first-time home owners in order to reduce housing pressures in Tehran and other large cities. Ahmadinejad borrowed over $16 billion from the Central Bank to carry out the project. After eight years of Ahmadinejad's rule, the project remained unfinished. The areas chosen were isolated and had little provision for services to meet the needs of the people who bought the houses, making living conditions very diffi-cult for residents in seventeen new cities across the country, according to reports.[227] By August 2014, hundreds of thousands of the houses lacked water, electricity, gas, and toilets.[228]

The Mehr housing project was driven by Ahmadinejad's vision of an egalitarian and just society and sought to make homeownership available to the economically "oppressed." Instead, "the project caused prices to soar, enabled corruption and profiteering, and made affordable housing more expensive" not only for the poor, but also for the relatively well-off, according to observers and experts (*theguardian.com*, January 30, 2014). President Rouhani noted that the Mehr housing project was one of the largest hurdles to Iran's economic recovery. Abbas Akhondi, minister of roads and city construction in President Rouhani's administration, esti-mated that it would take more than fifteen years to finish the "ill-conceived" housing project.[229]

Another example of government mismanagement was rooted in the allo-cation of capital from increased oil revenues. State policies provided sub-stantial resources for businesses to import cheap foreign goods, which undermined domestic production. Although increased funds served large traders, importers, and consumers, the rapid import of industrial goods led to factory closures, adversely affecting the industrial sector. As a result, industrial growth during Ahmadinejad's presidency was −12 percent, according to Ali Tayebnia, minister of economics in the Rouhani administration.[230] Mohammad Gholi Yusefi, a professor of economics, criticized state trading policies for adversely affecting domestic industrial production.[231] Experts and members of Iran's chamber of commerce warned that continued unregulated imports could shut down the country's factories.[232] Imports of cheap textile goods led to the closure of massive, long-established textile factories, prompting the head of the textile association to urge changes in government policies.[233] State policies also adversely affected small and medium-size enterprises, which comprised about 92 percent of Iran's industrial sector and employed about 45 percent of the industrial labor force.[234] Unregulated imports were largely responsible for the closure of about 70 percent of small industries and enterprises in industrial cities between 2005 and 2012, according to Mohammad Ali Abrishami, deputy minister of industry.[235] Mohammad Reza Naamat Zadeh, minister of industry in Rouhani's administration, noted that fourteen thousand small and medium-size enterprises in industrial zones had stopped operating.[236]

Given the deteriorating condition of the industrial sector, the government announced a decision to allocate 10 percent of cash subsidies to the manufacturing sector. But the state did not make good on its promise after fuel subsidies were terminated in 2010. Lack of capital and investment, along with sanctions and economic stagnation, had a severe impact on Iran's industrial sector by the end of Ahmadinejad's presidency. The situation resulted in the closure or underutilization (less than 50 percent use) of 52 percent of the factories in the country's industrial cities, according to Iran's Central Bank. The bank report also revealed that between 7,700 and 9,300 industrial units had closed. Other observers claimed that the actual figure was even higher, with more than 75 percent or even 80 percent of the country's productive units closing their operations. Some industrial enterprises put their assets up for sale to repay bank debts and the salaries of their employees.[237] Lack of state support and the economic difficulties also led to the closure of about 40 percent of the country's handicraft industries, according to Behman Namdar Motalgh, deputy head of the Organization of Cultural Heritage.[238]

Economic difficulties also undermined the state's capacity to improve the agricultural sector. Iran's attempts to achieve self-sufficiency in agriculture and food production failed. Despite some food exports, Iran became a major buyer of food on the international market, importing about 56 percent of its food.[239] Thirty-five years after the revolution, President

Hassan Rouhani lamented the fact that a substantial portion of the country's population was needy or lived below the poverty line. He noted that as soon as he took office, the government realized that the country needed to import seven million tons of wheat. The president complained that the government must continue to search for imports of basic food items to feed the people. In a public gathering, he stated, "No nation can take pride in the fact that its government has to think about finding its people's bread in the wheat markets of others."[240]

Although the Islamic Republic greatly expanded the infrastructure of rural communities through development projects, the revolution brought little change for Iran's small farmers and rural poor—or for the agricultural sector as a whole. The state failed to carry out land reform, the principal demand of the agrarian population and the rural poor. Despite approval by the first Majles, the highest religious leaders declared land reform to be un-Islamic, and the Guardian Council failed to approve the bill. At the same time, various government policies had an adverse impact on agricultural production and the rural population, according to Hussein Mohajeran, head of the Association of Fruit and Vegetables Traders.[241] Artificially low exchange rates for certain items made imported agricultural products cheaper than domestic ones, undermining domestic producers. In addition, the government at times guaranteed the purchase of agricultural goods at very low prices, which discouraged production. Mohammad Gholi Yusefi, professor of economics, noted that state import policies undermined domestic food production in ways that had not been seen for nearly four decades in Iran's history.[242]

The government under Ahmadinejad distributed free food such as potatoes to the urban population to gain political support, an act that affected prices and undermined production. Alireza Mahjoob, a Majles deputy, told the Islamic Consultative Assembly News Agency that difficult economic conditions in the countryside caused a rising exodus from rural areas. He noted that the rate of out-migration of the agrarian population increased by seventeen times in the three decades following 1982, causing enormous social problems.[243] Other government policies also adversely affected the agricultural sector. Acting head of the Farmer Syndicate, Enayat Biabani, noted that a lack of support, rising costs of production, higher fuel and transportation costs, and low prices for agricultural products caused farmers in some parts of the country to abandon their lands. He pointed out that as farmers became unemployed, agricultural land was being converted to other uses, driving farmers to migrate to the cities.[244] Mehrdad Lahouti, Majles deputy from Langroud, noted that excessive government imports of food undermined the country's agriculture. Hungry farmers were forced to sell their lands in order to live (*ilna.ir*, February 23, 2015). According to a deputy of planning and employment of Semnan province, only 548 of 2,227 rural units were inhabited; the rest were empty.[245]

Conditions for Iran's urban working class did not improve after the revolution and failed to fulfill the promises made by the Islamic Republic's leader. The failure of the country's economic development, persistently high levels of unemployment and inflation, and government repression over decades adversely affected the working classes most particularly. Labor activists and leaders called attention to the absence of independent labor organizations that could improve workers' bargaining power and economic conditions. Mansoor Osanloo, a prominent labor leader, noted that some five hundred trade unionists were executed in the first decade of the Islamic Republic.[246] Even state-organized "Islamic councils" that emerged after the revolution and had been permitted to operate and counter the leftist and independent unions were dissolved in many factories, and in the best of circumstances, they were replaced by weaker organizations, according to a labor activist.[247] Workers complained that articles of the constitution regarding labor wages were not enforced.[248] Labor activists also pointed out that labor organizations had no support and were opposed by employers, who often fired organizers and activists in workplaces.[249] A judiciary lawyer, Houshang Pour Babaie, noted that the state, the principal employer in the country, interpreted in its own favor the labor laws enshrined in the constitution.[250]

Rising unemployment also adversely affected working-class conditions. The economic stagnation, international sanctions, and cheap Chinese imports led to rising unemployment. During Ahmadinejad's presidency, the unemployment rate never fell below 10 percent.[251] The closure of factories producing steel, textiles, shoes, sugar, and other products resulted in the loss of many industrial jobs. Before the end of 2013, more than 40 percent of Iran's steel factories were closed.[252] The closure of fourteen thousand industrial units in industrial cities resulted in the loss of 112,000 jobs between 2005 and 2013, according to deputy minister of industry Abrishami.[253] Between 2005 and 2013, the timeframe of Ahmadinejad's terms, the number of Iran's unemployed declined by only 273,000.[254] During the same period, Iran's economy added only 542,308 people to the actively employed population of the country,[255] as the total number of the employed rose from 20,618,579 to 21,160,887, according to the Statistical Center of Iran.[256] Between 2007 and 2012, the country did not create net employment: the number of people who found employment was equal to the number of people who lost their jobs, according to President Rouhani.[257]

The plight of the working class was exacerbated by the fact that a substantial number of workers had to hold temporary jobs that prevented them from organizing and forming solidarity, a situation that rendered them vulnerable to job loss. The number of workers with temporary contracts increased when international sanctions intensified and the economy went into stagnation. For example, one million workers lost employment in 2012.[258] The situation deteriorated in the following years. Observers noted that between 70 percent and over 90 percent of the country's workers held temporary jobs by 2013. Majles deputy Mahjoob from Tehran and executive director of the Labor House, stated that 70 percent of Iran's workers held temporary contracts in 2012.[259] The figure given by Seyyed Hassan Hefdah Tan, undersecretary of labor, was about 90 percent.[260] According to Mohammad Reza Baghaian, labor representative at the High Council of Work—an agency composed of nine representatives of government, employers, and workers—the figure was still higher, at 93 percent.[261] These workers lacked benefits, insurance, and were not protected by labor laws.

Working-class income was often inadequate for a family of four. Workers in large cities like Tehran spent about 70 percent of their income on rent, according to a labor representative. As a result, their income was short by about 1 million tomans per month (3,000 tomans equaled $1).[262] The low minimum wage set by the state also adversely affected workers' income and fostered widespread poverty. The country's minimum wage in 2012 sufficed to pay living expenses for only ten days of the month in large cities, according to an official analysis carried out by the Statistical Center of Iran.[263] Not surprisingly, 90 percent of workers lived below the poverty line, according to Mahjoob, Majles deputy. The remaining 10 percent of workers lived very close to the poverty line.[264]

Workers became increasingly vocal, pursuing their interests through collective action. They regularly complained about the low level of the minimum wage and the fact that increases still left it below inflation rates, failing to improve workers' economic conditions. Growing numbers of workers protested over economic conditions to the labor minister: ten thousand workers presented a petition criticizing the government's new value-added tax, which deposited 5 percent of their income—already below the poverty line—into the government treasury.[265] Another petition—also signed by ten thousand workers—demanded higher wages; protested the widespread use of short-term contracts and worker dismissals instead of steady employment; criticized rising prices, inflation, and the planned discontinuation of government subsidies; and blamed the government for the country's economic plight.[266] Thirty thousand workers signed a third petition to the labor minister complaining of antilabor laws and declining wages, demanding an end to the workers' precarious situation, and requesting a higher minimum wage and other benefits.[267] In another attempt, forty thousand workers signed a petition and demanded that the labor minister raise the minimum wage for workers: "Your Excellency, honestly, governments and employers have guaranteed their fabulous profits by imposing poverty on us, the workers."[268] The workers even threatened to shut down the "wheels of production" if authorities did not reconsider their position.

Poverty continued to plague Iran. The country's economic growth rate in the past thirty to forty years (as of 2014) was limited and inadequate to fight poverty, improve the country's international position, or provide jobs for the younger generation, according to economic minister Tayebnia. He also said that the combination of stagnation and 45 percent inflation had caused a great deal of difficulty for the economy.[269]

Iran's poverty rate declined somewhat after the revolution but edged up again during Ahmadinejad's rule. Under the monarchy, in 1977, 25 percent of urban households and 43 percent of rural households lived below the poverty line.[270] The poverty rate began to drop after the war and especially when the reformists assumed power in the latter part of the 1990s. By 2005, the poverty rate had declined in both urban and rural areas of Iran.[271] However, economic mismanagement and international sanctions quickly pushed it back up. Ahmadinejad campaigned to establish social justice, but the percentage of the population living in absolute and relative poverty, by the government's definition, increased to 55 percent in 2010, according to the head of the Statistical Center of Iran.[272] By 2012, about 40 percent of the population lived in absolute poverty and 10 percent suffered from hunger, according to Professor Hussein Raghfar, a leading Iranian economist.[273] Raghfar also noted that a high inflation rate, rising unemployment, and a lack of antipoverty policies produced an underclass in the country. By 2013, the last year of Ahmadinejad's rule, seven million Iranians lived in extreme poverty, without food security, according to labor minister Rabiei.[274]

Rising poverty spread to the middle class. Iran's middle class became poorer and grew closer to the lower class in the past two decades, according to the labor minister.[275] During Ahmadinejad's presidency, a large segment of the middle class became poor, Professor Raghfar noted.[276] As many as half of the country's medical general practitioners lived below the poverty line, according to Dr. Iraj Najafi, professor at Tehran Medical Sciences, Iran's premier medical school.[277] The majority of Iran's teachers also suffered from poverty, provoking recurring protests. Average pay for a university-educated high school teacher was well below the poverty line—and below the pay for public employees in other sectors, such as oil.[278] Inadequate compensation placed three-quarters of all teachers under the poverty line. Only one-quarter lived above the poverty line—because of second or third jobs or the income of their spouses—according to a statement issued by a nationwide teachers' association.[279] Rising poverty among the middle class also forced some of the country's highly educated people to take menial jobs, as in the capital city of Khorramabad in Lorestan, where 23 of the 150 people hired to sweep the streets had bachelor's and master's degrees, according to the mayor of the city.[280]

Growing poverty in Iran's middle class gave rise to an unprecedented development: homelessness. A considerable number of Tehran's homeless included members of the middle class who had long worked in professional careers. High-status individuals such as translators with several published books and people who had graduated in the 1990s with degrees from state-run universities were homeless in Tehran, according to the city's mayor Mohammad Bagher Ghalibaf.[281] Some of the two hundred thousand homeless in Tehran's twelfth district, the oldest part of the city, had doctoral degrees from reputable foreign universities, according to a city official.[282] Unemployment was a major cause of economic hardship for highly educated people; 43 percent of the unemployed at the end of Ahmadinejad's presidency were people with higher education, according to labor minister Rabiei.[283]

Low wages, high levels of poverty, and unemployment made economic conditions difficult for large segments of the population. Over 40 percent of the country's employed population held more than one job to make ends meet during Ahmadinejad's first term, 2005–2009, according to government statistics.[284] The number of Iranians forced to sell their kidneys legally rose, even though the price dropped from $10,000 to $2,000 in 2011, according to Professor Raghfar.[285]

Economic conditions deteriorated for many Iranians when the government cut subsidies on fuel, electricity, and basic food items such as bread, rice, cooking oil, and sugar. Although it claimed to promote social justice, Ahmadinejad's government in 2010 eliminated subsidies to producers that had survived from the Iran-Iraq war and had helped the poorer segments of the population. Instead, the government distributed a direct monthly subsidy of $40 to all Iranians in 2012. The elimination of subsidies to producers increased prices of everything, including food.[286] The prices of electricity and natural gas tripled.[287] More importantly, the policy change adversely affected the less well-off segments of the population, as the elimination of subsidies inflated prices of food and basic necessities, which constituted a larger portion of this group's expenditures, according to a report by the Majles Research Center.[288] Similarly, the Ministry of Economics reported that the elimination of subsidies by the government during Ahmadinejad's presidency adversely affected Iran's poor and increased the ratio of the population living under the poverty line. In addition, the ministry noted that the policy change led to the bankruptcies of factories and the other industries in the productive sector.[289] Thus, subsidy cuts worsened economic conditions for many, increased unemployment, and—along with the stagflation—adversely affected the poorer segments of the population.

To be sure, the Gini coefficient declined after the revolution, indicating some reduction in income inequality.[290] Expropriations played an important role in reducing income inequalities after the revolution. Specifically, the seizure of the assets of the royal family and the top echelon of the capitalist class and their appropriation by entities under the control of the supreme leader contributed to the decline in the Gini coefficient. This reduction can also be partially attributed to government policies subsidizing food and fuel during the Iran-Iraq war. The Gini coefficient for urban Iran at the end of reformist rule in 2005 was .401.[291] The country's Gini in 2009, the end of Ahmadinejad's first term, was .41, a figure that resembled Iran's income distribution in the early 1970s.[292]

Although the government claimed greater social justice during Ahmadinejad's presidency, this interpretation was contradicted by a closer examination of the facts. In the first place, the expropriated assets were not distributed to the people, but went directly to the supreme leader and were thus removed from the equation, giving only the appearance of greater social equality. Second, some scholars maintained that the decline of the Gini did not actually represent improvement in the conditions of the poor. Rather, it resulted from the decline in the income of the middle class, according to Professor Raghfar, the leading Iranian academic expert on income and poverty.[293] Professor Farshad Momeni challenged the government's claim of the decline of the Gini coefficient, noting that Iran's rising unemployment and inflation adversely affected income distribution. Momeni added that the rising cost of education and health care deprived some segments of the population, forcing them into poverty. These developments could not have resulted in the lowering of the Gini coefficient.[294]

It should be noted that the Gini coefficient does not reveal the broader picture of inequality in the distribution of resources. Thus, any analysis of income distribution based on the Gini coefficient must take into account a few important points. Iran's coefficient is based on household expenditures, not household income, which is a more direct measurement of the extent of inequality. The Islamic regime provides data on household expenditures only, and this measure often results in underestimating the incomes of the rich; thus, it does not accurately reflect inequality. Moreover, the Gini coefficient does not reflect the high concentration of Iran's wealth in the hands of a small portion of the population. "We have five to six million high-income individuals whose wealth is not very dissimilar to the wealth of rich people in countries like America," labor minister Rabiei reported.[295] Rising inequalities and conspicuous consumption on the part of the wealthy invited public attention. Even the supreme leader criticized ostentatious public displays of wealth, noting that "the flaunting of expensive motor vehicles in the streets by some youths drunk with the pride of wealth created psychological insecurity in society."[296]

The reduction in inequalities revealed by government statistics may not have been as substantial as Iranians expected or were promised by the revolutionary leaders. Thus, it is also important to understand how people viewed their situation and made choices when they were given clear options. Iranians have been keenly aware for years of the unequal distribution of wealth and income. Many believed that high levels of inequality and corruption were the main causes of the revolution. To many ordinary Iranians, the prevalence of corruption and cronyism in the state, the financial institutions, and the private sector demonstrated that the system did not operate in the interest of everyone. Disproportionate access to the state and to the country's financial institutions by the privileged and the well-connected played an important role in the concentration of wealth and was evident to the population. Ordinary Iranians considered widespread corruption, cronyism, and graft throughout the state and society as evidence of the polarization in Iran's economy as large segments of the population were pushed into poverty while those with connections accumulated great wealth.

More than 77 percent of Iranians expressed an intense sense of injustice over economic disparities, according to a 1992 national survey.[297] Many citizens were of the opinion that the gap between rich and poor was wider during Ahmadinejad's presidency than ever before.[298] The elimination of subsidies and the intensification of sanctions worsened economic conditions for broad segments of the Iranian population. Fifty percent of respondents in a later survey said that there were times in the previous year when they had trouble paying for adequate shelter and food. This percentage was the highest among nineteen populations surveyed in the Middle East and North Africa region in 2012 and 2013.[299] The vast majority of the Iranian people responded negatively to President Rouhani's request in 2014 that they forgo the subsidy if they did not need it. Only 2.4 million of the country's population turned down the cash payment, which had been reduced to $14, whereas 73 million (or roughly 95 percent) decided to take it.[300]

Aware of inequalities and rising hardships, the Islamic Republic's rulers have repeatedly called for remedies, but the government has not adequately addressed these problems. Ayatollah Ahmad Jannati, conservative head of the Guardian Council, severely criticized the government for the country's economic conditions, which forced the poor to sell their children while the rich spent "astronomical" sums on corrupt lifestyles.[301] Ayatollah Abdollah Javadi Amoli—a source of emulation, seminary teacher, and former Friday prayer leader of Qom—complained about the failure of Iran's economy, saying, "In this country we have everything, but what we do not have is competence and integrity. What we have is corruption and incompetence."[302] Other prominent leaders of the Islamic Republic emphasized similar points. Seyyed Hassan Khomeini, Ayatollah Khomeini's grandson, declared that it was the task of the government to struggle against poverty and class inequalities *(faseleh tabaghati)*.[303]

Both of Iran's supreme leaders have acknowledged the severity of economic problems and high levels of inequality. Ayatollah Khomeini warned the government early on: "If we cannot reduce economic polarization and reduce the inequalities between the rich and the poor, and if consequently people get disappointed in Islam, nothing can prevent the resulting explosion; and we will all be destroyed."[304] Ayatollah Khamenei, Iran's current supreme leader, called on officials to stem poverty and narrow the gap between haves and have-nots. "Dispensing economic justice has been one of the regime's most cherished yet unrealized goals since its establishment nearly a quarter-century ago."[305] He urged action in a keynote address during Persian New Year, saying "disparities were intolerable and not accepted in Islam."[306] State economic policies and the country's economic performance have thus far failed to fulfill Khomeini's promises to serve the downtrodden and lift up the *mostazafin*.

Summary and Conclusions

During the revolutionary struggles, major segments of the Iranian population mobilized and demanded improvement in the standard of living and changes in the country's distribution of wealth and income. The middle and working classes joined the revolutionary struggles in the fall of 1978 and called for a greater share of the country's resources. Revolutionary leaders also agreed that Iran's economy needed major changes to make the country more independent from the rest of the world, including reducing reliance on oil and promoting the agricultural sector to achieve food self-sufficiency. With the overthrow of the monarchy, Ayatollah Khomeini and his allies responded positively to the people's demands and promised changes in the economic arena. In particular, Khomeini repeatedly declared that the Islamic Republic would serve the interests of the oppressed and the downtrodden.

However, the new regime pursued policies that undermined the likelihood of success. To develop, Iran had to expand the physical and human capital of the country. But deteriorating economic conditions, along with recurring political conflicts, economic mismanagement, political repression, and the absence of democratic institutions, led to periodic capital flight and large-scale brain drain from the Islamic Republic. The Islamic government, unlike prerevolutionary leaders, expanded higher education to unprecedented levels and educated many Iranian students inside the country. However, many highly educated Iranians left for the West, depriving the country of human capital vital for the country's development.

State intervention in the economy expanded after the revolution as the revolutionary government nationalized banks to promote Islamic lending and other financial transactions. Expanded intervention in the economy increased state ownership of economic assets, and attempts at privatization did not fundamentally change the economic structure. The state's increased role enhanced the power of the rulers at the expense of civilians and the private sector. More importantly, it politicized capital accumulation and allocation, undermined the market mechanism, and rendered the state vulnerable to challenge and attack in times of crisis. The high level of state intervention was accompanied by the rise of monopolistic foundations controlled by the clergy. State intervention expanded with the entry of the Revolutionary Guard as a major player in Iran's economy, commanding enormous assets and resources. Unlike South Korea, where the military regime promoted the interests of the business elite and the chaebols, the Islamic regime fostered the economic activities of the Revolutionary Guard.

State economic policies did not promote the private sector, which failed to become a major economic player in Iran. Despite declarations of policy changes, privatization of state enterprises remained limited. The Islamic Republic occasionally imprisoned businessmen for political reasons or corruption and, at times, even executed them. State policies during Ahmadinejad's presidency promoted the interests of importers and often ignored the industrial sector. It also bypassed the private sector for development and infrastructure projects in favor of the Revolutionary Guard. The country's private sector was able to export some manufactured goods abroad, but Iran failed to industrialize as South Korea did. Iran could export some industrial goods, largely due to cheap labor and subsidized fuel, but made no major advances in industrial capacity. By the end of Ahmadinejad's rule, Iran was not an industrial economy. In contrast to Korea, Iran's economy remained dependent on oil exports, and the country had to import manufacturing parts from the Korean Hyundai conglomerate. Failure to make advances in the industrial sector or reduce dependence on oil rendered the economy and society vulnerable to the vagaries of the world market and Western sanctions.

The high level of state intervention in the economy and capital accumulation had important consequences. In essence, the high level of state accumulation of capital further empowered the rulers vis-à-vis the civilian population and the private sector. The state received huge sums of capital from the sale of oil and was able to influence the direction of the rest of the economy and society. In addition, expanded government influence in the economy politicized capital accumulation and allocation and undermined the market mechanism. More importantly, the high level of intervention rendered the state vulnerable to challenge and attack during conflict and crisis. Instead of blaming the market, people routinely blamed the Islamic regime for their economic problems.

The revolution produced winners that controlled economic monopolies. It generated a new economic elite composed of the ruling clergy and the Revolutionary Guard. These twin pillars of the Islamic regime controlled the commanding heights of Iran's economy. The clergy and the Revolutionary Guard acquired vast fortunes through political power and state control. Supreme Leader Ayatollah Khamenei alone controlled more assets than the combined wealth of the shah and the top echelon of the prerevolutionary capitalist class. The Revolutionary Guard also gained control over substantial assets and became the country's first armed corporation, while the regime became increasingly dependent on the Guard for maintaining the system. It competed unfairly against the private sector and at times even reneged on its contracts, rendering the government powerless because the Guard had greater power, as President Rouhani's chief advisor noted. Possessing independent economic resources, the Guard developed strong interests in maintaining the Islamic Republic and intervened extensively in the political process, which was outside its original sphere of activity.

Despite Ayatollah Khomeini's repeated condemnation of corruption and pillaging of national resources prior to the revolution, corruption actually expanded after the revolution. The supreme leader declared war on corruption as early as 1997 but failed to eradicate it. Iran's state, economy, and society experienced unprecedented levels of corruption and cronyism as power-holders used their positions to gain resources and influence. Reports implicated virtually all the Islamic Republic's ruling elite and families. Corruption and cronyism gave rise to inequalities and resulted in an extra tax on businesses, consumers, and the public. Access to resources, major contracts, and good jobs all required connections and access to those who held power. Corruption also threatened economic stability, reduced business confidence, and undermined the country's economic development. More importantly, high levels of corruption and cronyism undermined state legitimacy, as many considered the state to be an instrument that served particular, rather than general, societal interests.

Economic mismanagement, corruption, capital flight, currency devaluation and depreciation, and the expansion of monopolies undermined Iran's economic performance. The standard of living declined as sanctions intensified during Ahmadinejad's second term as president. While Iran's per capita GDP was slightly higher than South Korea's in 1979, by 2009 Iran's per capita GDP was less than one-third of South Korea's. Real per capita GDP (in constant 2005 dollars) was lower in 2009 than in 1978, the year before the revolution, and considerably lower than its peak in 1976, resulting in a major drop in Iran's international ranking. Deteriorating economic conditions undermined popular confidence in the regime's capacity to fulfill revolutionary promises to improve the standard of living.

The lack of economic development led to the regime's failure to fulfill popular demands for improved living standards and a more egalitarian distribution of wealth and income. A substantial portion of the population lived in poverty. To be sure, income inequality declined after the revolution, in part because the assets of the former elites were expropriated by the government and the ruling clergy, thus generating the appearance of greater equality. But by 2009, income distribution had declined only modestly from the prerevolutionary period and resembled its levels in the early 1970s. Furthermore, by the end of the third decade of the revolution, Iran's Gini coefficient was still higher than during South Korea's decade of rapid development between 1975 and 1980, when the Gini averaged 0.36.

More importantly, the distribution of wealth remained very unequal and mirrored the concentration of political power. State capital allocation—conducted through government-run banks and financial institutions—operated in ways that increased the concentration of wealth. Financial institutions allocated capital to a small portion of the population, increasing inequalities. Thus, a combination of political power and selective allocation of capital intensified the concentration of wealth.

Although the revolution transformed the economic status of the clergy and the Revolutionary Guard, the Islamic Republic undermined the livelihood of large segments of the population. A larger proportion of Iranians lived in poverty than before the revolution. Poverty and homelessness affected the middle class, including doctors, teachers, and professionals. The unfulfilled promises, along with deteriorating economic conditions, generated an intense sense of injustice among major portions of the Iranian population. High levels of inequality in the distribution of wealth undermined popular trust in the state and generated intense feelings of injustice. Many Iranians viewed the state as an instrument of power serving particular, rather than general, societal interests. Unprecedented corruption and cronyism have undermined public confidence that the Islamic regime will ever be able to fulfill the revolutionary promises.

These conditions rendered the state vulnerable to challenge and attack, and set the stage for large-scale conflicts. To fulfill the revolution's promises and reduce state vulnerability, the Islamic Republic had to introduce fundamental changes. But, despite decades of promises, the rulers of the Islamic Republic refused to tolerate either challenge or reform.

CHAPTER FIVE

Failure to Reform and a Return to Repression

T HE FORMATION OF the Islamic theocracy politicized Iranian society and all aspects of social life, generating multiple contradictions and conflicts. The conflicts inevitably affected the country's ruling elite, which had held differing political and ideological views during the revolutionary struggles. Their divisions remained contained in the Islamic Republic's earlier years by external conflicts, including the hostage crisis and the Iraq war. But the conflicts intensified following the war and Ayatollah Khomeini's death, at which point the conservative faction attempted to narrow the scope of the polity and exclude some of its former allies. The conservatives introduced measures to further restrict political power to a small minority, thereby reinforcing categorical inequalities. These measures and the ensuing conflicts led to the rise of a reform movement that mobilized large portions of the population.

The reformers gained power in the latter part of the 1990s—in both presidential and parliamentary elections (2000)—challenged the conservatives at the ideological and political levels, and pressed for change. President Mohammad Khatami and the sixth Majles attempted to introduce reforms, expand freedom and civil liberties, and enforce the rule of law. In response, conservatives reasserted the powers of the supreme leader, claiming his supremacy and even infallibility. Opponents of reform created dozens of obstacles, producing a crisis for Khatami and the country every nine days, according to reformists.[1] More importantly, the ruling conservative faction intensified its repression of reformists, prosecuted a number of Majles deputies from the reformist camp, and actually imprisoned some of them. In the end, reformists proved powerless to democratize the political system. Following a conservative victory in the parliamentary and presidential elections, the regime inaugurated a new wave of repression against dissidents and large segments of the population to enforce Islamic rule and silence the opponents. The conservatives expanded state intervention and further politicized social and cultural issues, adversely affecting many segments of the population. These policies and developments in turn set the stage for large-scale conflicts.

Ideology and Politics under Ayatollah Khamenei

In the ideological arena, the supreme leader and his allies continued to reject liberal democracy, political reform, and expansion of civil liberties. As reformists and political activists pressed for greater democratic rights and civil liberties, Ayatollah Khamenei resisted change and repeatedly criticized democracy and liberalism. He maintained, "The present governments claiming to be democratic are in fact the same old dictatorships but in a new guise. Today, the same old tyranny is being exercised by political groups and parties. Even if there is competition, it is between the political groups and parties themselves, and the public plays no effective role in the arena of politics."[2] When Khamenei endorsed Khatami for a second term, he declared, "Liberalism is promoted by our enemies . . . we must stand against it."[3] He further asserted, "The bitter and venomous taste of Western liberal democracy, which the United States has hypocritically been trying to portray through its propaganda as a healing remedy, has hurt the body and soul of the Islamic Ummah and burned the hearts of Muslims."[4] Khamenei exhorted the clergy not to embrace Western ideals because, with the rise of liberalism, humanism, and democracy, "the worst wars and killings took place and human beings behaved in the most horrible ways toward one another during this period."[5]

Instead, conservatives emphasized continuity in Islamic institutions and the need to obey the supreme leader. The Assembly of Experts reaffirmed the supreme leader's powers, including his absolute command over the three branches of the state, granted to him by the 1989 constitutional revision.[6] "The word of the leader is final and it ends all disputes. This is the fundamental tenet of Islam."[7] Several days later, Ayatollah Khamenei claimed that the supreme leader, his own position, was infallible and his authority was indisputable. He stated that the true meaning of the concept

of *velayat-e faghieh* was that "the person in charge of the Islamic government does not make mistakes and if he does he will not be the supreme
leader from that moment." He added, "This is an obvious point that must
be understood well and spelled out properly."[8] Conservatives also rejected
calls for the supervision of bodies under the control of the supreme leader.
Ayatollah Sadegh Larijani, head of the judiciary, declared that the constitution of the Islamic Republic did not allow for the supervision of the
leader. He noted that such an action would be illegal.[9]

Ayatollah Khamenei and other leaders repeatedly stressed the institu-
tionalization of Islamic culture and values more than three decades after
the revolution. In a meeting with President Rouhani and his cabinet, the
supreme leader noted that it was the duty of all three branches of the government to enforce Islamic values and culture to prevent the enemy from
destroying Iran's identity.[10] Ayatollah Khamenei reminded the president
and his cabinet that cultural transgressions could not easily be redressed.
He emphasized that any changes in the cultural sphere would disturb the
identity of the system.[11] Other Islamic leaders, too, had little regard for
liberalism and emphasized state intervention to ensure the observance of
Islamic values and culture. Ayatollah Mohammad Taghi Mesbah Yazdi, a
member of the Assembly of Experts, disparaged liberal culture. He repeatedly emphasized the spread of Islamic values and culture in society. Yazdi
noted that although the revolution had been an Islamic cultural uprising,
work on cultural problems were inadequate.[12] He maintained that those
who were ignorant or were hirelings insisted that in order to advance
materially, Iran should eliminate Islamic morality and culture.[13] In a public
gathering, he called on the state to take responsibility for providing a
healthy culture in a system that was based on Islam. He complained that
in his family some youths, who formerly prayed, entered the university,
graduated, and became unbelievers. "If you open your eyes, you will see
that the youth, brought up in the lap of the Islamic Revolution, shun religion and saying prayers when they enter universities."[14]

Yazdi also maintained that culture was more important than economics
and that an economy without culture would not go very far.[15] He noted
that secularity and worldliness had no place in Islamic culture. He reminded
the people that this world should be seen as valuable as long as it can
ensure happiness in the next life.[16]

Other religious leaders also opposed liberal cultural freedoms. Ayatollah
Ahmad Khatami, a Friday prayer leader of Tehran, opposed granting
people the freedom to do anything they wanted in cultural matters. He
advocated state intervention to institutionalize Islamic culture and values,
saying, "It is the government's duty to take the people to heaven even by

force or whip."[17] Ayatollah Ahmad Alamolhoda, Friday prayer leader of Mashhad, argued that religion and religious beliefs had a higher priority for the people than economic well-being or security. He noted that the enemy had initiated a wide-ranging assault on Islamic culture and that if Iranians could not institutionalize Islamic culture, they would be defeated.[18] Ayatollah Alamolhoda called upon the state to intervene and spread Islamic culture.[19]

To promote Islamic culture, the Islamic Republic's rulers continued to censor artistic and intellectual activities. Ali Saeedi, a cleric and the supreme leader's representative in the Revolutionary Guard, stated that the Ministry of Culture and Islamic Guidance was created to promote the cultural health of society and prevent damage to the religious and national culture. He singled out films, newspapers, books, magazines, and the Internet as avenues for foreign influence.[20]

The regime also pursued other policies to reduce the autonomy and independence of religious organizations. The state began to provide economic resources for religious bodies that had been economically independent of the state in Iran. The state budget revealed major funding for seminaries beginning in 2000, although such funds had also been provided in earlier years. The revelations caused concerns among some clerics who argued that Shiite seminaries should be independent in contrast to Sunni seminaries.[21] Beginning in 2005, the state formally allocated a budget for seminaries and institutionalized the practice.[22]

More importantly, the Islamic Republic's conservative faction took steps to expand the supreme leader's power by reinforcing categorical inequalities following Khomeini's death in 1989. Under Ayatollah Khamenei, the power of the supreme leader increased as the Guardian Council's power grew. The council's function expanded from supervising elections to vetting all candidates—approving those committed to the Islamic Republic, the constitution, and the supreme leader, and disqualifying others. In addition, although the Guardian Council ruled in 1998 that nonclerics could be candidates for the position of supreme leader, in practice, candidates required such a high standard of religious expertise that practically all nonclerics were ineligible. Rulers of the Islamic Republic also introduced new legislation that discouraged people's access to power but facilitated the rise of the clergy to positions of power. The constitution initially required candidates for elected office only to be literate high school graduates. Conservatives imposed more stringent educational and ideological qualifications that excluded most citizens from the Majles and the power structure. They raised the educational requirement for officials to a master's degree or a bachelor's degree with five years of executive experience.[23]

Clerics thereby gained a substantial advantage in provincial cities and towns where a limited number of people possessed the advanced degree required for holding office. At the same time, the regime relaxed the educational requirement for clergy, who they deemed qualified to run for the Majles without a university degree and without being subjected to a stringent entrance exam as was required for admission to all state-run universities.

To reinforce exclusive rule, some ruling clerics discouraged organized political constituencies and recommended obedience to the supreme leader. For example, Ayatollah Mohammad Reza Mahdavi Kani, head of the Assembly of Experts, remarked in a public gathering, "If you want the revolution to survive, you should stay alongside the clergy and not build parties against the clergy."[24] Ayatollah Mohammad Ali Movahedi Kermani, Friday prayer leader of Tehran, in a sermon, recommended that people should obey the imam and the *velayat-e faghieh* and elect representatives to the Assembly of Experts that were 100 percent "full of obedience to the leader of the Muslim world," meaning the supreme leader.[25]

The country's conservative rulers also imposed political and ideological criteria that disqualified many citizens from ever running for office. All potential candidates must be loyal to the supreme leader and the constitution. The Guardian Council routinely disqualified thousands of candidates in every election for Majles, president, or other public office.[26] The council eliminated 46 percent of the candidates in the first Majles elections in 1980, 20 percent in the second in 1984, 19 percent in the third in 1988, 28 percent in the fourth in 1992, 39 percent in the fifth in 1996, 26 percent in the sixth in 2000, 44 percent in the seventh in 2004, 37 in the eighth in 2008, and 35 percent in the ninth in 2012.[27] Ideological purity combined with the arbitrary veto of the council blocked some candidates who seemed to the public or the reformists to be very qualified. In 2008, the council even disqualified Ali Eshraghi, a grandson of Ayatollah Khomeini, although he was later reinstated. He eventually withdrew but told reporters that the council had questioned his neighbors whether he fasted and prayed.[28]

The conservative Majles passed additional restrictive measures to silence the opposition. It approved a penal code in 1996 that rendered dissent a crime. The new law imposed the death penalty for acts against state security and any attack on Iranian leaders, as well as spying—notably for Israel and the United States. The death penalty was also given to defendants found guilty of unspecified "offenses" against Ayatollah Khomeini and his successor, Ayatollah Ali Khamenei. A charge of "propaganda against the Islamic Regime" could bring a sentence of up to one year in jail.[29]

The rulers of the Islamic Republic also reduced the power of the Majles, the principal elected body of the government. In 2005, the supreme leader granted new authority to the Expediency Council to supervise the three branches of the government, including the Majles.[30] By this change, the supreme leader extended his own power over the democratic entity by virtue of his authority to appoint the members of the Expediency Council.

Narrowing the polity, rejecting democratic rights, and bolstering the clergy's power reflected growing conflict within the Islamic Republic. These changes inevitably led to increasing reliance on repression and the expansion of the Revolutionary Guard's role in the political sphere. Although the Guard was created as a nonpolitical force, its leadership fully embraced military intervention in the country's political affairs, often claiming that the Guard was created to protect the revolution. Mohammad Ali Jaafari, commander of the Guard, rejected calls by reformists who cited Khomeini's prohibitions on the involvement of the Guard in political affairs. He noted that the Guard paid no attention to critics' statements and conducted its own work.[31] He declared, "The Guard is responsible for the defense of the Islamic Revolution and its outcomes." He added that "the imam prohibited the Guard from supporting any specific faction."[32]

The continued ideological and cultural orthodoxy, restriction of the polity, and increased Guard intervention in the political arena set the stage for contentious politics in the Islamic Republic. The end of the Iran-Iraq war and the death of Ayatollah Khomeini contributed to intense conflicts in the second decade after the revolution.

Schism in the Polity and Demands for Change

Although the Islamic Republic's ruling elite managed to contain its political and ideological conflicts in the first decade following the revolution, divisions eventually emerged that set the stage for intensified factional conflict. When factional conflicts intensified in 1987, Ayatollah Khomeini dissolved the Islamic Republican Party, the IRP, a clerically dominated party important in the theocracy's formation. He warned, "Sowing discord is one of the greatest sins."[33] Khomeini's death, coupled with social and economic crises, deepened the gulf between two competing factions, each holding different perspectives on social, economic, political, and cultural issues, although some did not precisely fit in either group.[34] The leftist Association of Combatant Clergy advocated state control over the economy, supported limitations on the private sector, and opposed normalized relations with the West. The more conservative Society of

Combatant Clergy favored less state intervention in the economy, a greater role for the private sector, and fewer state subsidies. This faction was allied with the Coalition of Islamic Societies, which represented a wealthy segment of the bazaar merchants.

Factional disputes mounted as conservatives attempted to exclude members of the leftist faction in the early 1990s. Leftists predominated in the second and third Majles, but their fortunes began to shift by the fourth Majles election in 1992. During the 1992 elections, the Guardian Council began vetting the qualifications of Islamic candidates who had been members of the polity since the revolution. The council's screening committee initially disqualified many leading leftist candidates, including forty sitting Majles deputies, but reinstated many of them when leftists protested.[35] The growing strength of the more conservative faction in the executive branch, coupled with the influence of the supreme leader, prevented leftists from winning any of Tehran's twenty-eight parliamentary seats. Only twenty leftists or 7 percent of all deputies, were elected nationwide to the Majles in 1992. Many leading leftists, including Mehdi Karroubi, Mohammad Mousavi Khoeiniha (spiritual advisor to students who took American hostages), and Ali Akbar Mohtashemi Pour failed to win seats in the Majles.[36] As a result, well-known leaders from the leftist faction were excluded from the polity for several years.[37]

As conservatives imposed Islamic ideals upon democratic institutions and attempted to narrow the polity by excluding the opposing faction, dissidents reacted by demanding change. Individuals and groups formerly linked to the government challenged the conservative ascendancy and pressed for political change even before the 1992 election. Ebrahim Asgharzadeh, one of the three student masterminds of the 1979 takeover of the American embassy, criticized Majles conservatives as early as 1989 and called for greater political freedom and democracy.[38] The government imprisoned him and barred him from running for public office in 1992. He continued to pursue protections for individual rights, a democratic vote, and cultural freedom, which he claimed were the ideals of the revolution. Abbas Abdi, a leading student in the embassy takeover, became a critic of the government and was imprisoned in solitary confinement for nine months. His name appeared on a "death list" of reformers disclosed in 1998 by a defector from the Intelligence Ministry.[39]

A number of individuals and groups also spoke out and called for change. Gholamhossein Karbaschi, mayor of Tehran in 1988–1998, published a newspaper, *Hamshahri*, that openly criticized the conservatives. He argued that Iran encompassed two very different versions of Islam. "One of them is a very advanced political Islam, which has to do with everyday life." The other, he said, "is stagnating in the old traditions."[40] Others who were outside the polity began voicing their criticism of the system. In a daring move, 134 leading writers signed an acclaimed declaration against censorship in November 1994 and planned to revive the banned Writers' Association.[41] Abdol Karim Soroush, once part of Khomeini's cultural revolution, began criticizing the Islamic regime. He maintained that Muslim clerics were not superior but equal to the people: "They should not gain politically or socially from religion, nor should they be supported economically by the state or the people."[42] Journalists also criticized national shortcomings. Mashallah Shamsolvaezin and Mohsen Sazegara launched the outspoken reformist newspaper *Jameah*. The former was a proreform journalist and the first postrevolutionary editor of the rigid Islamic daily *Kayhan*, while the latter had been a founding member of the Revolutionary Guard and had held high-ranking positions under Prime Minister Mir Hossein Mousavi. Both men turned reformist and advocated social and political change. The judiciary banned *Jameah* in 1998 for publishing articles deemed detrimental "to the country's national interests and security." Shamsolvaezin and the director of the paper's publishing company, Hamid Reza Jalipour, were arrested.[43]

University students openly discussed political reform and democratization. In December 1996, the Association of Islamic Students called on President Hashemi Rafsanjani to guarantee free speech and free presidential elections the next year. "Mr. President, before the end of your term make arrangements so that the freedom and security of the press will be guaranteed," the newspaper quoted a statement as saying. "Provide guarantees so that newspapers aren't closed down and telephone lines are not tapped."[44]

Some of Khomeini's descendants also were critical of the Islamic government by the mid-1990s. Ahmad Khomeini publicly expressed skepticism that the United States and its sanctions were to blame for Iran's problems. He criticized Iran's economic mismanagement, growing bribery and corruption, and increased foreign borrowing and national debt. "It's time we stopped blaming America for our own shortcomings and corruption," he declared, a week before his death.[45] Hossein Khomeini, Khomeini's oldest grandchild, began criticizing the regime as early as 1981, arguing that the new Islamic government was "worse than that of the shah and the Mongols."[46] "People were desperate in the days of the shah to attain freedom, which was the basis of the revolution. . . . But, they did not get it," he argued.[47] He told a BBC interviewer that the Islamic regime was guilty of oppressing the Iranian population, "killing people or jailing them for no reason." He added that "if his grandfather were alive today, he would have opposed all of Iran's current leaders because of what he described as their excesses and wrongdoings." He also proposed a referendum to determine how Iran should be governed.[48] He told an audience in the United States, "Today, Iranian people again want democracy, they want freedom. Furthermore they have experienced everything, they have experienced theocracy in Iran and they have come to understand that religion and government cannot be one and the same."[49]

Threatened by internal challenges and a rising wave of democratization movements throughout the world, the Islamic government unleashed measures to suppress Iran's secular and nationalist dissidents. Employing potassium cyanide, knifing, strangling, or shooting, repressive forces killed or caused the disappearance of as many as eighty dissidents during President Hashemi Rafsanjani's two terms, according to reports.[50] Separate, suspicious car accidents killed Shams Amir Alaie, a leader of National Front, and Mahmoud Manian, a National Front leader and bazaar activist, in 1994. Ali Akbar Saidi Sirjani, an eminent writer, died in prison. Sirjani had been charged with homosexuality, gambling, smoking opium, drinking alcohol, and having ties with the CIA. He was later charged with activities against the Islamic Republic. A heart attack was announced as the cause of death, although a doctor who had treated him earlier said that he had been in good health.[51] It was later revealed that a potassium suppository caused the heart attack, according to a PBS report.[52]

According to dissident sources, the regime even attacked important members of the polity who criticized or threatened the Islamic order. They claim that Ahmad Khomeini—Ayatollah Khomeini's son, chief of staff, and closest confidant—had died under mysterious conditions in March 1995 after criticizing Khamenei, his father's successor as supreme leader. The official explanation of his death was a heart attack, but subsequent dissident analyses blamed it on poisoning. According to the opposition, Saeed Emami, deputy to the intelligence minister, later testified that Intelligence Minister Ali Fallahian, a cleric, had ordered Ahmad Khomeini's death.[53]

Secular individuals and groups were also targeted by repressive entities. Security forces detained twelve writers that had gathered to draft a new charter for the Iranian Writers' Association in 1996. After interrogating them for several hours, security forces released them on condition that they cease organizing activities.[54] Professor Ahmad Tafazzoli, a prominent secular academic at Tehran University, was murdered in Punak, a suburb northwest of Tehran, in January 1997.[55]

In response to rising repression, the leftist clerical camp, which had been excluded from power, regrouped and presented fresh challenges in the fourth Majles election in 1992. Leading leftist activists and clerics formed a diverse coalition with moderate technocrats and leftist Islamic intellectuals who had pressed for radical action in the revolution's early years. Eschewing state intervention in the economy, the leftists now advocated social, economic, and political reforms and called anew for political freedom, the rule of law, and the strengthening of civil society.

Reformist Ascendancy and the Failure to Reform

In the wake of rivalry between clerical factions, President Rafsanjani and Ayatollah Khamenei responded positively to demands that the 1997 presidential election be free and fair.[56] President Rafsanjani noted years later that he had prevented cheating during the 1997 presidential elections, "leading extremists to criticize me."[57] A high voter turnout—especially among students, young people, and women—was sparked by the presence on the ballot of Mohammad Khatami, a candidate from the leftist, reformist faction that had been marginalized in the early 1990s.

Mohammad Khatami entered the race reluctantly after no other viable opposition candidate surfaced because the Guardian Council had disqualified many of the reform-oriented candidates.[58] A midranking cleric, he belonged ideologically to the clergy's leftist faction, which advocated egalitarian distribution of economic resources through state intervention in the economy and restriction of the private sector. Khatami had served briefly as the head of a publishing house, won a seat in the first postrevolution Majles, and was appointed minister of Islamic guidance and culture in 1982. In the latter capacity, he earned a national reputation for easing restrictions on films, music, art, and literature. He was forced to resign in 1992 when the conservative majority gained control of the Majles and was "banished" to the National Library in Tehran where he faded from public view.[59]

Khatami was no radical revolutionary who would overthrow the Islamic Republic. He accepted the theocratic regime's basic foundations and condemned those who demanded constitutional change, but he supported the rule of law, greater social and political freedom, tolerance for opposing views, and the creation of a civil society.[60] Khatami favored freedom of the press and a more democratic system in which people could openly express their views and determine the political processes. He leaned toward greater openness and some reforms, but at other times he expressed dissatisfaction with the people and their expectations. At one point in 2000, he stated that Iranians expected too much reform.[61]

His challenger, Nategh Nouri, was the choice of the conservatives. Nouri, as speaker of the parliament, was the designated winner. He enjoyed the support of the religious establishment, the majority of the parliament, and the bazaar merchants.[62] During the campaign, conservatives mobilized all their resources, including state-owned media and the mosques, to encourage the public to vote for their candidate. Nategh Nouri had the support of the supreme leader and the Revolutionary Guard.[63]

A larger-than-expected voter turnout of 80 percent of the electorate thwarted the conservative plan. Students, intellectuals, women, and the youth, along with the middle class, participated heavily and changed the outcome of the election. Khatami won the presidency with 69 percent of the vote.

Like Mosaddegh, Khatami opposed repressive aspects of Iran's politics. He told reporters, "Our country emerged twenty years ago from the heavy weight of dictatorship, but unfortunately we are not yet completely delivered from it, and dictatorship continues to haunt us all."[64] But, unlike Mosaddegh, Khatami never mobilized the public on behalf of his reforms and greater freedom. Although charismatic, he did not call for demonstrations and street protests to press for change. His promises of reforms and change, however, encouraged students, women, and other segments of society to mobilize and act collectively, which threatened conservatives and sparked further repression.

President Khatami and his reformist cabinet challenged the conservatives in ideological and political arenas and pressed for reforms and openness. The president repeatedly criticized the conservatives for being narrow-minded: "There is a rigid-minded group that sees its existence as dependent on the people's ignorance," Khatami told thousands of students gathered to mark the one hundredth anniversary of the birth of Ayatollah Ruhollah Khomeini. "They think the more ignorant a society, the more it protects the religion. They try to inculcate the belief that learning is against religion.'"[65] On the twenty-second anniversary of the revolution, Khatami told a gathering, "Those who claim a monopoly on Islam and the revolution, those with narrow and dark views, are setting themselves against the people." He continued, "They are putting religious values against the wishes of people, religion against freedom and disregarding the rights of people. They seek to suppress views that are not in agreement with their own narrow and dark views."[66] Members of Khatami's cabinet also criticized the conservatives. In an appearance before the conservative Majles, Mohajerani stated, "We have to create an atmosphere where all citizens can express their ideas. Islam is not a narrow, dark alley. Everyone can walk freely in the path of Islam."[67]

Conservatives reacted against relative openness and reformist efforts to introduce change. The factions disagreed over many issues, including freedom of the press. To fulfill a campaign promise for greater freedom of the press, Khatami's government granted licenses to a large number of new publications, newspapers, and magazines advocating reform and civil liberties. The Revolutionary Guard issued explicit threats, despite criticism that it was not supposed to interfere in politics or take sides. The commander of the Revolutionary Guard bitterly complained, "Liberals have entered the foray with cultural artillery. They have now taken over our universities, and our youth are now shouting slogans against despotism."[68] He also said, "We are seeking to root out counterrevolutionaries wherever they are. We have to behead some and cut off the tongues of others. Our language is our sword. We will expose these cowards."[69]

A wave of mysterious deaths labeled "chain murders" surfaced in 1988. A defector from the Intelligence Ministry disclosed a list of the names of people to be killed.[70] Two liberal-nationalist opposition leaders, Parvaneh and her husband, Daryoush Forouhar, former minister of labor, were murdered in November of 1998. An Islamic court warned Mohammad Mokhtari and Mohammad Jafar Pouyandeh, secular writers who sought to revive the banned independent Writers' Association, that they could be tried for antistate activities. The bodies of both men were discovered two months later, separately, in different parts of Tehran.[71] An Iranian security chief confessed to ordering the killings of dissidents, according to a Reuters report.[72] Two secret service agents were found guilty of murdering the four and were sentenced to death, but Iran's Supreme Court commuted their sentences to ten years in prison.[73] Other prominent writers—including Majid Sharif, Mohammad Mokhtari, Mohammad Pouyandeh, Pirooz Davani, Ebrahim Zalzadeh, Ghaffar Hosseini, and Ahmad Alaie—were murdered between 1996 and 1998.[74]

Under intense pressure from the press and reformists, President Khatami replaced the intelligence minister and ordered the prosecution of those responsible. "Rogue agents" of the Ministry of Intelligence carried out the murders, according to a government investigation. Saeed Emami, deputy to the intelligence minster, was accused of being the ringleader. Emami was arrested and imprisoned in a maximum-security jail, where he was found dead by his own hand, according to government reports.[75]

Twenty-four Revolutionary Guard commanders sent a letter to Khatami during student protests in July 1999, warning that they were losing patience with "democracy" that was turning the Islamic Republic into "anarchy." "Mr. President, if you don't make a revolutionary decision today and [you] fail to abide by your Islamic and nationalistic duty, tomorrow

will be too late, and the damage done will be irreparable and beyond imag-
ination." They threatened to take matters into their own hands, saying,
"How long do we have to stand by idly watching, with extreme sadness,
what is happening in the country?"[76]

Conservatives in the Islamic Regime reacted to Khatami's presidency
with attacks against his administration, opposition groups, and individuals across all sectors of society. Leading members of the Majles and even
other important clerical leaders were not immune from repression. They
attacked Abdollah Nouri, a midranking cleric who had served as vice president and Khomeini's personal liaison, was twice elected to the Majles, had
served twice as interior minister, held important posts in the Revolutionary
Guards, and received the highest vote in the Tehran city council.[77] He was
attacked in part because he became immensely popular as his newspaper,
Khordad, advocated free debate, democracy, and tolerance.[78] The judiciary
convicted Nouri on a wide range of charges, including insulting Islam,
distributing propaganda against the Islamic regime, questioning Ayatollah
Khomeini's rulings, offending the present supreme leader, advocating normalized relations with the United States, and supporting Ayatollah
Montazeri and former prime minister Mosaddegh.

Nouri's trial was open to the news media, and he used the occasion
against the conservative rulers of the Islamic Republic. He subverted the
legal proceedings, dominated the hearings, and put the Islamic system on
trial.[79] Nouri contended that the Islamic Revolution was hijacked by hardliners who broke the promises of democracy and instead instituted a
system of rigid clerical rule. "From the early days of the revolution, our
belief was that there is complete compatibility between Islam and democracy," he argued. "Power has a tendency to breed authoritarianism, and
Iran's powerful clerics have perverted the democratic revolution to serve
their own interests," Nouri remarked.[80]

More importantly, Nouri stunned the country and the court by calling
for an end to a system known in Iran as *velayat-e faghieh,* rule of the religious jurist. Nouri stated that the 1980 Islamic constitution did not con-
template placing religious leaders above the law. He declared that the
supreme leader, who appointed the Special Court for the Clergy, was "in
essence equal with the general population." Like anyone else, the leader
had "an obligation to obey the law and had no powers not specifically
granted to him by the constitution."[81]

Nouri was sentenced to five years in jail in November 1999, five years'
banishment from political activities, immediate closure of his newspaper,
and seventy-four lashes. The lashes were set aside in favor of an additional
year in jail. Concerned about protests, authorities called out the police to

line up along the one-mile stretch from the court to the prison to prevent possible demonstrations in Nouri's support.[82] Nouri never retracted his statements and never asked to be forgiven. But he was pardoned in 2002 by the supreme leader when his brother, also a Majles deputy, died in a car accident three years after his imprisonment.[83]

Conservatives attacked other moderate and reformist officials, including the moderate, popular Tehran mayor Karbaschi. He was arrested on charges of embezzlement and mismanagement, provoking demonstrations by his supporters.[84] At his trial for corruption, several dozen hardline conservatives chanted slogans including "death to Karbaschi" and "looters of the public property should be executed."[85] Karbaschi was forced out of his position, sentenced to five years' imprisonment, and banned from holding office for twenty years.[86] He was pardoned by the supreme leader after serving seven months in prison. Attaollah Mohajerani, the reformist culture and Islamic guidance minister, also came under attack for urging greater openness, reducing press censorship, and issuing permits for more liberal publications. Although he survived an impeachment attempt, Mohajerani eventually resigned.[87] His resignation was in part related to a lawsuit launched against him. Mohajerani's wife, Jamileh Kadivar, a leading reformist in the parliament, was also put on trial for harming Iranian national security by participating in a conference in Berlin, Germany.[88] She was acquitted.[89] Conservatives also attacked government officials in the media and the press. A special government employees' court ordered the arrest of Fereydoun Verdinejad, the director of Iran's official news agency, IRNA, on charges of embezzlement, "mockery of public organizations, and spreading lies, slander and groundless accusations against others."[90]

Conservatives in the state also targeted other individuals interested in civil rights and democratic changes. The judiciary convicted two leading lawyers, Shirin Ebadi, Nobel Peace Prize winner, and Mohsen Rahami, of producing a videotape alleging that prominent conservative figures supported the activities of violent right-wing vigilante groups. They were given fifteen months of a suspended prison sentence and banned from practicing law for five years.[91]

In the electoral arena, conservative forces also made an unsuccessful effort to prevent the election of reform-minded candidates to the sixth Majles in February 2000. They used all state-owned media, the mosques, and the pulpits of Friday prayer leaders to dissuade the public from voting for reform candidates. Nevertheless, proreform candidates won about three-fourths of the seats in the sixth Majles. The Guardian Council initially refused to endorse the election, alleging fraud, but eventually accepted the results under pressure from the supreme leader.[92]

The sixth Majles passed dozens of bills reforming women's rights and expanding civil and political rights. Reformists introduced legislation barring security forces from entering the universities, defining political crimes, making arbitrary arrest more difficult, empowering the president to stop legal proceedings he deemed contrary to the constitution, and blocking the Guardian Council from vetting candidates for election. In an attempt to rein in the powers of the supreme leader, the Majles refused to extend a special budgetary privilege to state bodies controlled by the supreme leader.[93] President Khatami also pressed for democratic rights. He stated that democracy was necessary for Iran: "Democracy is a must in today's world. Those who negate pluralism do not understand the spirit of the times," he said.[94] But many of the bills did not go very far, because conservatives in powerful bodies rejected the attempts at reform. The Guardian Council rejected the law banning the entry of security forces into universities and the Majles bill defining political crimes.[95] The supreme leader quashed the press reform bid: "If the enemies infiltrate our press, this will be a big danger to the country's security and the people's beliefs. I do not deem it right to keep silent," the supreme leader said in a letter.[96] Mohsen Mir-Damadi, a reformist member of the Majles, complained that in the first six months of the sixth Majles, the Guardian Council rejected seventeen of forty-four bills passed.[97] The Guardian Council rejected and vetoed 111 of the 295 bills approved by the Majles and supported by President Khatami between 2000 and 2004.[98]

The conservative faction continued the intimidation and repression of journalists. During Khatami's eight-year presidency, hardliners closed down more than two hundred newspapers.[99] Between 2000 and 2004, over fifty journalists were detained.[100] A few days after the sixth Majles took office, the judiciary closed down eighteen newspapers, leading 151 members of the parliament to write a letter of protest to the head of the judiciary. The letter was read during the public session of the Majles.[101] The U.S.-based Committee to Protect Journalists placed Khamenei at the top of its list of ten worst Enemies of the Press in 2001.[102] Reporters Without Borders stated in 2003 that Iran held twenty-one journalists, making it the "biggest prison for journalists" in the Middle East.[103] Siamak Pourzand, a journalist, was arrested in 2001 and was charged with "spying and undermining state security" and "links with monarchists and counter-revolutionaries." He was sentenced to 11 years imprisonment and 74 lashes.[104] Zahra Kazemi, an Iranian-born Canadian journalist, died in custody from a brain hemorrhage resulting from beatings, but a court acquitted the intelligence agent, Mohammad Reza Aghdam, of the "semi-intentional murder" on grounds of a "lack of proof."[105] More than 120 reformist Majles deputies demanded an end to the crackdown against writers.[106]

The judiciary arrested seventeen proreform individuals who participated in an April 2000 Berlin conference examining the prospects for reform in the Islamic Republic. Eight of the dissidents were convicted of conspiring to overthrow the regime. The Special Court for the Clergy defrocked Hassan Youssefi-Eshkevari, a cleric and former Majles deputy, and sentenced him to death following the Berlin conference for "actions threatening national security and anti-Islamic statements." An appeals court eventually overturned the sentence.[107] He was released after serving four years of a seven-year prison sentence but could no longer serve as a cleric.[108] Akbar Ganji, another Berlin conference participant, had defected from the Revolutionary Guard and written about state-sponsored death squads and the "chain murders." Ganji was sentenced to ten years.[109] He spent six years in jail and nearly died from a seventy-three-day hunger strike.[110]

As factional conflicts continued, repressive measures escalated against leading reformers. In March 2000, an unidentified assailant attempted to assassinate Saeed Hajjarian, a former intelligence official, member of the Tehran city council, and a prominent reformist.[111] Although he survived, Hajjarian was permanently paralyzed. Conservatives lashed out at President Khatami's moderate policies and demanded the execution of his culture minister, Mohajerani, in response to a political cartoon portraying hardliner Ayatollah Mesbah Yazdi as a crocodile, a symbol of treachery and deception. Mohajerani, who had eased restrictions on the press, was forced to resign.[112] Hashem Aghajari, a reformist intellectual, university professor, and war veteran who had lost a leg in battle, also came under attack. A court sentenced him to death for blasphemy in June 2002 after he called for a popular reformation of Shiite Islam and declared that Muslims were not "monkeys" and should not "blindly follow" religious leaders. Student protests and international pressures led the supreme leader to order a new trial.[113] Aghajari's death sentence was commuted, and he was eventually released after spending twenty-three months in prison, much of it in solitary confinement.[114]

Conservatives in the judiciary targeted members of the Freedom Movement. According to a *New York Times* report, many observers speculated that the movement was attacked because members had done well in the 2000 parliamentary elections, and had won seats the first time they actively participated in the political arena.[115] A Revolutionary Court ordered the arrest of about sixty members of the Freedom Movement. According to the court, some of the dissidents "aimed to set up a Western-style government, and, to achieve this sinister goal, they were considering active resistance and eventually armed resistance."[116] Most of those arrested were elderly men who had spent decades opposing the shah.[117] Their numbers included important members of the Islamic regime, such as Mohammad Tavassoli and Hashem Sabbaghian; Majles deputies and former cabinet ministers of the provisional government; and Ezzatollah Sahabi, a former cabinet minister and former member of the Revolutionary Council. The court dissolved the Freedom Movement and sentenced twenty-one members to up to ten years in jail.[118] Another twelve were sentenced to jail terms of from four months to two years and ordered to pay fines of more than $1,200.[119] Sahabi was sentenced to four years in jail.[120]

The judiciary also prosecuted some sixty reformist deputies and imprisoned a few for expressing their opinions.[121] The president's brother, Mohammad-Reza Khatami, who was elected to the Majles with the largest number of votes in 2000, was accused of libel for publishing insulting articles in his newspaper.[122] A Tehran administrative court sentenced Mehdi Mousavinejad, a reformist deputy, to one year in jail for staging an "illegal rally" and delivering an "inciting speech" during student unrest in Khorramabad.[123] Hossein Loghmanian, Majles deputy from Hamedan, was sentenced to ten months in jail in December 2001, on charges of insulting the judiciary.[124] When lawmakers demanded that the supreme leader intervene and prevent Loghmanian's arrest, he refused and let the Guardian Council decide. The council ruled that the judiciary "could override the parliamentary immunity of lawmakers if they insulted the authorities."[125] In response to Loghmanian's arrest, the majority of the 290 deputies, including Speaker Mehdi Karroubi, walked out of the Majles in protest, leaving fewer than fifty members behind.[126] Karroubi protested and noted that the decision on Loghmanian's imprisonment was a violation of Article 57 of the constitution. Three deputies resigned their posts in response to the arrest.[127] Ayatollah Khamenei pardoned Loghmanian after the Majles protests. Two other deputies were given sentences, including Mohammad Dadfar, a deputy from Bushehr, and Fatemah Haghighatjoo, from Tehran. The latter was sentenced to twenty-two months in 2001 for "misinterpreting" the words of Ayatollah Khomeini and insulting the supreme leader and the Guardian Council. She appealed and was cleared of the first charge, which reduced her sentence to a suspended ten months. She relocated to the United States, but her case was still pending more than a decade later.[128]

Repression sparked a reaction from one prominent Shiite cleric. Ayatollah Seyyed Jalaleddin Taheri, Friday Prayer leader of Isfahan appointed by Khomeini, resigned from his post and condemned developments in the political arena. In his letter, Taheri portrayed the system as "deeply corrupt, self-serving, hypocritical and repressive."[129] He maintained that "the principle of republicanism meant the continuous circulation and replacement of the country's managers; and civil society meant the continuous review and criticism of the plans of the government; and revolution meant guarantee and fulfillment of the demands of the people, conditions that do not exist in reality." Taheri asked why the Islamic regime's rulers ignored sympathetic criticism now that the shah and America were no longer in control of Iran or to blame for its shortcomings. Why didn't they utilize expertise? Taheri then directly targeted the rulers and their repressive paramilitary forces: "Those who ride the untamed camel of power and in the political arena gallop on two horses . . . encourage the club-wielders . . . the louts and fascists, who are a mixture of ignorance and insanity and whose umbilical cord is connected to the center of power; they are completely uncontrolled and beyond the law and go unpunished by the judiciary. They are jurisconsults [legal experts] and philosophers, sheriffs and governors, muftis, and judges. They do what they like and rule as they please."[130]

Reformists continued to demand political change after the United States invaded Iraq in 2003, raising the external threat level. A group of 127 reformist Majles deputies, in an open letter to the supreme leader on May 21, 2003, criticized hardliners for using violence to prevent reforms and block the people's will. The letter declared that most people were dissatisfied and disappointed and that most intellectuals were either silent or departing Iran as foreign forces surrounded the country on all sides. The letter charged that since President Khatami's election, his attempts to promote reform had been undermined by an orchestrated campaign of serial murders, arrests, and the repression of reformists, students, journalists, and dissidents. The deputies noted that their most important task was to eradicate poverty and improve the economic condition of the people. "This cannot be done without investing capital, human resources, and competent management; these goals cannot be accomplished without political and economic stability, both of which require a government that has emerged from the people's preference." Time was running out for a peaceful transition, the writers warned, and the letter asked the supreme leader to intervene and save the country from political deadlock.[131]

Conservative Ascendancy and Intensified Repression

Reformists in the sixth Majles, 2000–2004, continued to challenge and protest against the Guardian Council's disqualification of a large number of candidates, who it deemed lacking in sufficient commitment to the constitution and the supreme leader. The council disqualified 3,600 of 8,150 candidates, or more than 44 percent.[132] Most of those disqualified were reformists, and eighty-seven were sitting Majles deputies. They included Mohammad Reza Khatami, deputy speaker and brother of the sitting president, and his wife, Zahra Eshraghi, granddaughter of Khomeini.[133] Approximately one-third of the deputies held a sit-in at the Majles building in protest for twenty-one days.[134]

Failing to achieve their goal, 124 deputies, representing more than a third of the 290 Majles members, symbolically resigned their posts in protest. In a strong statement read aloud during that session of Majles and broadcast live across the nation on Iranian radio, the deputies that resigned accused powerful conservatives of seeking to impose a religious dictatorship like that of the Taliban in Afghanistan. "We cannot continue to be present in a parliament that is not capable of defending the rights of the people and that is unable to prevent elections in which the people cannot choose their representatives," the statement said.[135] In an unprecedented letter to the supreme leader, more than one hundred Majles deputies stated, "The popular revolution brought freedom and independence for the country in the name of Islam, but now you lead a system in which legitimate freedoms and the rights of the people are being trampled on in the name of Islam." The statement continued, "Institutions under your supervision, after four years of humiliating the elected parliament and thwarting [reform] bills, have now deprived the people of the most basic right—the right to choose and be chosen."[136]

After this effort failed to effect any change, the protesting deputies called for a boycott of the Majles elections. Others soon joined them. A group of 1,179 people who had been approved by the Guardian Council to run for seats for the seventh Majles announced that they would not be running.[137] Shirin Ebadi, 2003 Nobel laureate, also called for a boycott of the Majles elections.[138] The European Parliament weighed in and declared the elections illegal because unelected bodies had disqualified elected bodies. It noted that the process dealt a serious blow to democracy: "[E]fforts towards the establishment of democratic structures have suffered a severe setback as unelected structures have shown themselves to be stronger than those institutions directly legitimated by the people of Iran."[139]

The supreme leader responded that elections represented the freedom and national determination of the people and would go ahead without delay. He also noted that dereliction of duty by resignation or by any other form was against the law and forbidden by religion.[140] In Ayatollah Khamenei's response to the European Parliament, he maintained that if its words interfered with the country's internal affairs, "Iranian people [would] hit them hard in their mouths."[141]

The supreme leader prevailed, and elections for the seventh Majles proceeded as scheduled, leaving reformists excluded. Protests were futile as conservatives reasserted their power in the run-up to the 2004 Majles election. With a boycott by some opposition groups and divisions in the reformist camp, conservatives won most of the Majles seats. Voter turnout was low: only 23,440,000 out of the 44,351,000 people voted across the country.[142] The 51.21 percent turnout was the lowest for a Majles election in the history of the Islamic Republic.[143] Voter participation in Tehran was a mere 28.1 percent. Conservatives won at least 149 of the 290 seats and wrested control from reformists, who had held 210 seats in the previous Majles. Approximately eighty new deputies were elected, many with backgrounds in various military and revolutionary institutions.[144]

The 2005 presidential election was also contentious. As conflicts grew, 624 of the most prominent political activists called for a boycott. The signatories included academics, students, doctors, engineers, lawyers, journalists, women, and workers, as well as former government ministers and Majles deputies. Prominent signers included Ali Afshari, Mansoor Osanloo, Abbas Amir-Entezam, Simin Behbahani, Fariborz Rais-Dana, Naser Zarafshan, Akbar Atri, Hadi Kahal-Zadeh, Bahareh Hedayat, Abdolfattah Soltani, Soraj Eddin Mir-Damadi, Mohammad Maliki, Shahrokh Zamani, Ali Akbar Mousavi Khoeniha, Hossein Shah Hosseini, Fatemeh Haghighatjoo, and Parviz Vajavand. The statement criticized the intervention of unelected bodies, which blocked the people's will and their aspirations, and also the inability of reformists to make good on their promises. The activists urged the boycott of an "election that would not result in democracy and popular sovereignty."[145] The Islamic Iran Participation Front, the largest proreform party, also boycotted the election.

The presidential election benefitted the conservatives. Voter turnout was 63 percent in the first round, but declined in the second round to 60 percent, according to academic analysts,[146] the third lowest for presidential elections in the history of the Islamic Republic.[147] Although many political activists and liberals boycotted the election, populist politics and promises to improve conditions for the poor probably helped Mahmoud Ahmadinejad attract some segments of the electorate. The elections resulted in Ahmadinejad's victory.

All three losing candidates—Hashemi Rafsanjani, Mehdi Karroubi, and Mostafa Moin—declared the election a fraud.[148] Rafsanjani's election headquarters publicly identified a number of Guard commanders that had actively promoted the conservative candidates, including Ahmadinejad.[149] Karroubi, former speaker of the Majles, claimed that the results in the first round were rigged.[150] In an open letter, he accused one of Ayatollah Khamenei's sons of exerting his influence in the elections through the Revolutionary Guard and the paramilitary Basij.[151] Significantly, Jaafar Habib Zadeh, the highest legal official of the Interior Ministry, declared that "violations by the military forces in these elections, such as chain murders, are cancerous tumors that have grown in the system." He added, "Eliminating the root of the tumor would be in the interest of the national security."[152] Years after the 2005 election, Rafsanjani repeated his fraud allegations. In a speech, he stated that, during the second round of the voting, reformist provincial governors completely gave up election oversight and lost interest. "Whatever they [unspecified] wanted, they stuffed in the boxes, and whatever they wanted, they read."[153]

Ahmadinejad, a conservative with a background in the Revolutionary Guard, pursued policies that exacerbated the state's growing authoritarian nature and cut short hopes for political reform. During his rule, state intervention in social and cultural arenas expanded and further politicized some issues that had been relegated to the private sphere during the reformist rule. Ahmadinejad's presidency also amplified corruption and cronyism in political, economic, and academic institutions. More importantly, during Ahmadinejad's first term, the security forces launched a concerted attack against political dissidents and reformists that posed a threat to conservatives. The regime also attacked and attempted to repress nonpolitical collectivities that simply differed from and did not follow the fundamentalist agenda. Most importantly, Ahmadinejad's presidency set the stage for the conflicts that unfolded after the subsequent presidential election.

The new president lost no time in introducing key changes that reflected state interest in greater control, politicization, and militarization of society. Ahmadinejad packed his cabinet with fourteen former Revolutionary Guard commanders, of the total twenty-one cabinet appointees.[154] To solidify his power, he reshaped the top echelons of state bureaucracy, government ministries, provincial governorships, and universities, replacing thousands of reformists and technocrats in critical government posts with conservatives from the clergy and the Revolutionary Guard. Ahmadinejad also appointed many more relatives and friends to positions of power than had any previous government in the Islamic regime.[155]

Ahmadinejad's government politicized many issues and instituted repression on a wide scale, intimidating anyone interested in changing any aspect of the Islamic regime and system. The state was quick to repress reformists and political dissidents in a campaign to demobilize all opposition. The state suppressed human rights proponents, labor leaders and activists, and women for the next eight years. Government agents cracked down on cultural practices they deemed non-Islamic. Conservatives expanded control over the universities, repressing academics and expelling students. The state also increased its persecution of ethnic and religious minorities, Dervish and Sunni Muslims, and even Shiite theologians.

Ahmadinejad's government outlawed the annual gathering of liberal activists at the tomb of former Prime Minister Mohammad Mosaddegh, a tradition that began after the revolution.[156] The conservative government also targeted individual reformers, including Ali Akbar Mousavi Khoini, a deputy in the sixth Majles and head of the Alumni Association of Iran, who was arrested for demanding an end to discriminatory laws against women during a demonstration in June 2006. Authorities accused him of "disturbing public order" and "defamation" and reportedly tortured him in Tehran's Evin Prison before releasing him after several months.[157] A mob attacked the popular former president Mohammad Khatami in 2009 two days after he announced plans to challenge Ahmadinejad for the presidency.[158] Intimations of further repression eventually persuaded him to withdraw his candidacy.

State repression of the more radical opponents was even harsher. The government arrested a few dissidents that were members of the Kingdom Assembly of Iran in April 2009 and convicted them of being "enemies of God." The government executed two men, Arash Rahmanipor and Mohammad Reza Ali-Zamani.[159] The judiciary sentenced Payman Arefi to death for supporting the Kingdom Assembly but commuted his sentence to fifteen years, to be served in exile.[160] Other political prisoners—including Amir Hossein Heshmat Saran, Valiollah Faiz-Mahdavi, and Abdolreza Rajabi—died mysteriously in prison, according to Human Rights Watch.[161]

The regime politicized a large number of cultural practices and imposed many cultural restrictions on the populace. During the eight years of Ahmadinejad's presidency, Iranian filmmakers made more than ninety films, but none received permission to be shown to the public, leading many filmmakers to leave the country.[162] The state shut down the biggest cinema guild, House of Cinema. Jafar Panahi, a prominent filmmaker, was sentenced to six years in prison for propagating dissension against the Islamic Republic of Iran. The regime also intensified prohibitions against watching television programs from other countries and listening to Western music, and it confiscated satellite dishes in mass raids. To prevent Iranians from watching programs broadcast outside the country, the regime jammed international broadcasts, leading the UN to demand that Iran and other countries halt such practices, which violated people's rights to receive and impart information.[163]

The Islamic state also imposed restrictions on the music industry. Ahmadinejad banned Western music from state radio and television stations in 2005.[164] Musicians complained that the president did not support the music community.[165] Although state schools had always been prohibited from teaching music, the government also barred private schools from teaching music to children because it interfered with Islamic values. Schools were told that, if they taught music, they might be closed permanently.[166] The government specifically banned rap music as an example of Western decadence, raided and shut down rappers' studios, incarcerated some musicians in 2007, and drove many rappers underground.[167] Authorities banned Mohammad Reza Shajarian's immensely popular Ramadan song, "Rabbana," because of his critical political statements.[168] When Ahmadinejad's term ended, Shajarian, Iran's most prominent singer (known as "master singer") said that music should not be regulated by the state. He noted that he had not performed on stage for a few years and expressed an interest in resuming concerts under suitable conditions.[169]

The state also launched a new attempt to regulate dress codes, harking back to the curtailments that followed the 1979 revolution.[170] Beginning in 2005, the government designated twenty-six organizations in the three branches of the state to promote Islamic dress, according to the vice president for women's affairs.[171] The interior minister allocated $1.5 billion to promote a moral code, and enforce dress codes to solve the country's cultural and social ills, according to Mostafa Mohammad-Najar, the minister.[172] Every spring and summer, the regime unleashed its agents to enforce gender and dress codes and punish violators. Starting in 2006, a year after Ahmadinejad took office, special "moral guidance" teams patrolled shopping centers and popular squares, stopping and sometimes arresting women that were inadequately veiled.[173] More than 30,000 women were arrested and over 460,000 were reprimanded for improper hejab between 2003 and 2013.[174] Tehran police arrested women wearing short coats or improper veils and fined them up to $800 for immodest dress.[175] The government detained 150,000 people for "immoral behavior" and Islamic dress code violations during late March and April of 2007. Most signed "letters of commitment" pledging to honor public behavior and dress codes, and only a few were actually referred for trial.[176] Authorities ordered barbershops not to provide Western hairstyles for their customers. Police closed more than twenty barbershops in a two-week crackdown in Tehran for encouraging un-Islamic behavior by offering men Western hairstyles, tattooing, and eyebrow plucking.[177] The policy drastically reduced the activities of barbershops in the northern part of the capital, where barbershops had invested substantial sums in their businesses.[178]

The intensification of gender discrimination and inequality during Ahmadinejad's presidency provoked protests. Women's rights defenders met in June 2006 to begin a campaign to collect one million signatures to repeal laws discriminating against women. Tehran police attacked them, arresting seventy and summoning others, including Noushin Ahmadi Khorasani, Parvin Ardalan, Bahareh Hedayat, and Sussan Tahmasebi.[179] Many of those detained were given jail sentences and lashes. Consideration of a controversial bill legalizing polygamy in 2007 led women's rights activists to more subtle action. Just before the parliament was scheduled to vote on the bill, the activists called the wives of parliament members and asked, "Would you mind if I married your husband—just for a week?"[180] To date, the bill has not passed.

The regime attempted to impose further limitations on cultural activities. Thirty-nine hardline Majles deputies introduced legislation in 2011 regulating dogs, considered unclean in Islam. The legislation prohibited people from walking dogs in public spaces or even keeping them as pets, on the grounds that they posed a threat to public health.[181] Police and security forces launched an extensive campaign to confiscate canines. They took a large number of dogs to the Kahrizak detention center where some died, provoking criticism from the Iranian veterinary society.[182]

The government also politicized academic issues, expanded control over the universities, and intensified the repression of academics with a number of unprecedented actions against faculty and students alike. President Ahmadinejad appointed Ayatollah Abbasali Zanjani as chancellor of Tehran University. Zanjani had been a notorious prosecutor during the 1980s and lacked academic credentials, which provoked unsuccessful student protests. Once in office, the new chancellor dismissed dozens of professors, forced hundreds into retirement, and recruited thousands of pro-regime faculty. The Ministry of Science also drove a large number of the faculty into retirement in order to Islamize the universities yet one more time.[183]

Expulsion and forced retirement of university faculty produced criticism and protests against the government. Former president Mohammad Khatami complained to former educators and administrators in higher education in a public event about conditions in academic institutions during Ahmadinejad's presidency. "Many of the distinguished faculty have been set aside. Some have left Iran, and others face a great deal of restrictions. Many others have been injected into the universities without proper standards. Also, a large number of accomplished and worthy students have been barred from continuing their education, and in their place, many students with lower qualification have gained the privilege of receiving continuing education."[184] The expulsion of more than twenty faculty at Sharif University led to a lawsuit that prompted the Administrative Justice Court (Divan Edalate Edari) to reverse some forced retirements.[185]

The government also intensified repression of politically active students and interfered in universities to demobilize them and prevent protests. Authorities at Amir Kabi University ripped up pictures of Mosaddegh, Bazargan, and Shariati; confiscated the school's library and other assets; demolished the student activities office on July 28, 2006; and declared the student association illegal.[186] The government expelled dozens of students who protested Ahmadinejad's presence at Amir Kabir University and designated them for compulsory military service.[187] As a result of repression, by 2007 many Islamic student associations had been dissolved or become inactive.[188]

The government actively discouraged students from engaging in protests. The judiciary sentenced Soroush Sabet, a medalist in both computer and math Olympiads, to two years in prison for participating in a demonstration in 2007.[189] The regime also arrested and imprisoned Bahareh Hedayat, a student leader, several times for participating in political protests and working to gather one million signatures for the cause of women's rights. She was sentenced to ten years' imprisonment on charges that included "insulting the president."[190]

Authorities routinely expelled students from universities because of their political activities or beliefs. Universities barred hundreds of students.[191] Mohammad Yousef Rashidi was suspended from Amir Kabir University after he displayed a placard reading "Fascist president, the Polytechnic is not a place for you," during Ahamdinejad's visit. He was later arrested and sentenced to one year in prison.[192] The situation worsened in the aftermath of the 2009 presidential elections, and one report claimed that universities expelled more than one thousand students from universities in Iran during Ahmadinejad's presidency.[193] Officials expelled Sayed Ziaoddin Nabavi from Noshirvan University in Babol in 2007 because of his political activities. He was arrested in 2009 and sentenced to ten years' imprisonment.[194] Allameh Tabatabai University suspended Majid Dorri in 2008 for his activities. He, too, was subsequently arrested and sentenced to ten years in prison. While serving his sentence, the university expelled him, but he was released from prison after serving only five years.[195] Amir Amir Gholi, a leftist student, was arrested on August 29, 2009, for political activities and subsequently expelled from the university, according to the Committee of

Human Rights Reporters.[196] A Revolutionary Court sentenced him to twenty-one years in prison for insulting the sanctities and making propaganda against the system.[197] He had to serve seven and half years.[198]

Beginning in 2006 and continuing every year thereafter, the government blocked students who had passed qualifying exams from enrolling in universities and colleges because of their beliefs, political activities, and participation in demonstrations. Yazdan Mohammad Baygi, who had passed the qualifying exam for a doctoral degree, was not admitted to Tehran University because of his past political activities.[199] Some students were told that they could enroll only if they promised to refrain from participation in political protests.[200] Authorities demanded that all doctoral students sign a letter promising to do nothing against the religious establishment during their studies, according to Iranian scholar Saied Golkar.[201] The Ministry of Science, Technology, and Research declared Daftar Tahkim-e Vahdat, a student organization inspired by Ayatollah Khomeini, illegal in 2009.[202]

Even elite *(nokhbeh)* students—those who were gifted and had performed extremely well in national competitions—were not immune to these attacks. Mitra Aali, member of the National Elite Foundation (Bonyad Melli Nokbegan), was arrested in the aftermath of the 2009 presidential elections and spent five months in prison. She was reincarcerated in 2012 to serve the rest of her one-year term.[203] Mohammad Mehdi Sajedifar, an elite graduate student in genetics, was arrested in 2010 and sentenced to ten years for contact with foreign professional associations.[204] Security forces arrested and imprisoned Omid Kokabee, a distinguished graduate student at the University of Texas, in January 2011. He was charged with "contact with enemy states" and sentenced to ten years in jail.[205] Kokabee denied the charges and maintained that he was imprisoned because he refused to work on military projects with nuclear application.[206]

The government also suppressed labor leaders, activists, and their supporters, resulting in bitter complaints from workers about government repression. The secretary of the Isfahan labor house, Asghar Breshan, told reporters that labor organizations had never been so intensely repressed as during Ahmadinejad's presidency. Breshan declared that Ahmadinejad's government, during its two terms, intended to eradicate all labor organizations.[207] Mansour Osanloo, one of the country's most prominent labor leaders, noted that "in Iran, advocating for the rights of workers and the poor is out of question. Even contemplating organizing union meetings or engaging in strikes, for example, can bring about devastating consequences."[208] He was a founding member of the independent Syndicate of Workers of the Tehran and Suburbs Bus Company, representing more than seventeen thousand workers and was arrested in September 2005. He served more than five years in prison for his organizing activities and endured more than seven months of solitary confinement and torture.[209] Security forces arrested 150 labor leaders and activists during a May Day rally in Tehran in 2009. Mehdi Farahi Shandeez, Ahmadinejad's wife's cousin, a supporter of worker rights and the labor movement, was among those arrested. He was kept in solitary confinement for several months.[210] Released after nine months, he was rearrested in 2011 for threatening national security, propaganda against the system, and insulting the supreme leader. He claimed that he was also mistreated and tortured in prison for shouting slogans such as "Death to Khamenei, death to dictator, long live freedom."[211] Reza Shahabi, treasurer of the Syndicate of Workers of the Tehran and Suburbs Bus Company, was arrested in June 2010 on vague charges and sentenced to six years' imprisonment, according to Amnesty International.[212]

During Ahmadinejad's presidency, the state also arrested, exiled, and imprisoned teachers. The antiriot police and the military arrested about one thousand teachers who demonstrated for higher pay in front of parliament on March 14, 2007.[213] That same day, security forces arrested protesting teachers in other cities, including Kermanshah and Rasht.[214] At least forty teachers were arrested between 2009 and 2012, according to a partial list provided by a human rights organization.[215] Rasoul Bodaghi, a teacher and member of the Teachers' Guild board of directors, was arrested and charged with "propaganda against the establishment" and "assembling to disrupt national security." He was sentenced to six years in prison and barred from "social activities" for five years.[216] While in prison, three more years were added to his sentence.[217] Mahmoud Bagheri, a physics teacher and union activist, was arrested and sentenced to six years in prison for his union activities.[218] Alireza Akhavan, a teacher and labor rights activist in Tehran, was arrested by intelligence officials, who confiscated his personal belongings, including books and computers.[219] Alireza Hashemi, executive director of Iran's teachers' association, was sentenced to five years in prison in 2010 and was taken to prison in 2015 to serve his term.[220] The Teachers' Guild of Iran issued a statement and demanded that President Rouhani release the imprisoned teachers.[221] The same teachers' group also held a nationwide rally in March 2015 and demanded the release of Bodaghi, Bagheri, and others.[222]

The state also clamped down on human rights activists. Abdolfattah Soltani, a human rights lawyer and cofounder of the Defenders of Human Rights Center, was imprisoned for seven months in 2005.[223] Soltani was eventually acquitted of all charges against him, but the government forcibly closed down the center in December 2008, shortly before it was to commemorate the sixtieth anniversary of the Universal Declaration of Human Rights. Authorities subsequently prevented Soltani from traveling to Germany to accept the prestigious Nuremberg International Human Rights Award.[224] He was rearrested in 2011 and accused of spreading propaganda against the regime, "establishing the Defenders of Human Rights Center," "assembly and collusion against national security," and "accepting an unlawful prize."[225] Soltani was sentenced to eighteen years in prison and barred from practicing law for twenty years.[226]

The regime restricted freedom of the press and the Internet. Islamic leaders often warned against publishing un-Islamic material. One source belonging to a Majles faction following the Imam's line reported that seventy-seven daily publications were closed down between 2005 and 2009, including thirty-four in 2006, twenty-eight in 2007, five in 2008, and ten in 2009.[227] The managing editor of the newspaper *Ebtekar* declared Ahmadinejad's first four years to be the "blackest days" for Iran's press.[228] Reporters Without Borders labeled Iran "one of the world's most repressive countries" in 2012. The organization accused the regime of using the Ministry of Culture and Islamic Guidance to interrogate and repress journalists during Ahmadinejad's presidency.[229] Faezeh Hashemi, former Majles deputy, head of the Association to Defend Press Freedom, and daughter of former president Hashemi Rafsanjani, criticized the repression of journalists, involving what she called "harshest punishments," and declared that Iran's freedom of the press had deteriorated to the point where conditions were worse than they had been one hundred years earlier after the Constitutional Revolution.[230]

State restrictions on intellectual activities led to a decline in the publishing industry. Iran published 11,363 books in 1980, but the Islamic regime quickly moved to censor all publications and banned the Writers' Association the following year. The number of published books dropped dramatically in the following years. Publishers issued only 2,075 books in 2013—Ahmadinejad's last year in office—the lowest number since the revolution.[231] Iranian writers often lamented government censorship of the press and publishers. Mohammad Djavad Mozaffar, a writer and publisher, condemned state censorship and declared that president Ahmadinejad's eight years were the darkest of the postrevolution period for writers and publishers.[232]

The government routinely arrested, tortured, and issued harsh sentences against writers and bloggers who published books and articles critical of the regime. Husain Derakhshan, an Iranian-Canadian leading blogger, tried to promote censorship-free access to the Internet in Iran until the Revolutionary Guard arrested him in 2008. He was sentenced to nineteen and a half years in prison, charged with "cooperation with hostile states, propagating against the regime, propagation in favor of antirevolutionary groups, insulting sanctities, and implementation and management of obscene websites." He was pardoned by the supreme leader in 2014.[233] Security forces arrested Vahid Asghari, a student blogger who was studying in India, as he was leaving the country in 2008. A Revolutionary Court sentenced him to death for launching a website that contained propaganda against the Islamic order and religion.[234] A higher court later overturned the sentence. Security forces arrested Hussein Ronaghi Maleki, a 28-year-old blogger and computer programmer on December 13, 2009. He was sentenced to fifteen years' imprisonment on charges of spreading propaganda against the regime and insulting Ayatollah Khamenei. Already in failing health, Ronaghi went on a hunger strike and explained his reasons: the authorities' "blatant disregard for the life and health of political prisoners and prisoners of conscience," their "failure to address the medical needs of sick prisoners," mounting pressure on his family, and the "arbitrary and illegal transfer of political prisoners to substandard prison facilities [where they were] held among criminals."[235] Authorities also arrested Saeed Malekpour, an Iranian student residing in Canada, who returned to Iran to visit his ailing father. Authorities charged him with "Internet offences" after a software program he developed was used by an adult website. In solitary confinement, he was tortured, forced to make false confessions, and sentenced to death for "taking action against national security by designing and moderating [an] adult content website, agitation against the regime and insulting the sanctity of Islam."[236] The judiciary later commuted his sentence to life imprisonment.[237]

The Islamic Republic intensified repression and discrimination against ethnic minorities, often targeting activists who were involved in civil rights or autonomy movements. The government prohibited ethnic minorities from teaching their languages in schools and repressed organizations that advocated for autonomy or independence. Kurds, Arabs, and Azeri ethnic minorities were often targets of intense state repression.

The Islamic regime banned the Democratic Party of Iranian Kurdistan as early as 1979. Kurdish politicians occasionally accused the Islamic regime of repression and murder. Jalal Jalalizadeh, a deputy representing the Kurdistan provincial capital of Sanandaj, launched an unprecedented attack on the floor of the Majles in November 2000, "accusing the regime of murder and religious repression of the nation's minority Sunni Muslim Kurds." He denounced what he called a "campaign of repression, serial murders, and the banning of the faith" of the Sunni Kurds. Jalalizadeh also condemned the destruction of the Sunni Feiz mosque in Mashhad.[238]

The government arrested many activist Kurds and others who sympathized with dissident Kurdish political organizations. Security forces arrested Habibollah Latifi, a Kurdish student activist, in October 2007 and sentenced him to death for supporting a separatist organization, although his family claimed that the charges were fabricated.[239] Latifi's death sentence was overruled by the supreme leader in 2015.[240] The judiciary convicted Ali Heydariyan, Farhad Vakili, and Farzad Kamangar, three Kurdish activists, of being *mohareb*—enemy of God—and sentenced them to death in 2008.[241] In May 2010, the government executed Kamangar.[242] Mohammad Sadigh Kaboudvand was sentenced to eleven years in 2007 for establishing the Kurdish Human Rights Organization.[243] Security forces arrested Zeynab Jalalian in 2008 and kept her at the Intelligence Ministry for eight months, where she was tortured according to Amnesty International; in January 2009, she was sentenced to death for the crime of *moharebeh* (enmity against God) for her alleged membership in a Kurdish organization (PAJWK) and waging armed struggle against the Islamic Republic. Jalalian's sentence was commuted to life imprisonment in late November 2011, according to Amnesty International.[244] Ali Jilan, an elderly Kurd, was sentenced to twelve years in prison.[245] At the age of 103, as of 2013, he remained confined in jail in Makoo.[246] The government banned more than two dozen Kurdish teachers[247] from teaching and prevented some Kurdish medical students from continuing their studies.[248]

The Islamic regime also attacked Arab and Azeri activists. The state executed four Arab activists in the province of Khuzestan.[249] Authorities imposed "punishments" on the families of activists, according to a BBC report.[250] Five Azeri activists were given combined jail sentences of forty-five years in 2013.[251] At least sixty Azeri activists were arrested in February 2014, in advance of International Mother Language Day.[252]

The Islamic Republic tried to curtail religious conversion and deviation, thereby politicizing matters that formerly were confined to the private sphere. Despite billions of dollars spent every year to disseminate Islamic values and principles, the number of Shiites converting to other faiths increased, provoking Islamic regime leaders' attacks on religious minorities. Ayatollah Jannati, head of the Guardian Council, publicly warned, "Non-Muslim people are animals who graze on the earth and cause corruption."[253] Ayatollah Mesbah Yazdi repeatedly reminded Iranians that in Islam, non-Muslims were not equal to Muslims. "We should not for the sake of citizenship say that Baha'is, Jews, and Muslims do not differ," Yazdi declared.[254]

To prevent religious conversion, the state defined it as a political security crime. The Islamic Republic's new penal code explicitly called for the

execution of men and life imprisonment for women in cases of apostasy.[255]
The state also persecuted and repressed religious groups that proselytized.
Although these measures did not end religious conversion, they inevitably
politicized discrimination and persecution. Prior to the revolution, discrimination and persecution of religious minorities were social matters.
With the exception of officially sanctioned discrimination against the
Baha'is, the state did not intervene in religious matters and disputes. The
revolution and subsequent establishment of the theocracy politicized
religious discrimination and persecution and contributed to a new set of
conflicts.

With Ahmadinejad's election, the government intensified its persecution
of the Baha'i community, the largest non-Muslim religious minority in
Iran. Persecution of Baha'is grew after the revolution, with the execution
of a few hundred people, expropriation of sacred sites, and destruction of
their cemeteries.[256] Security forces arrested all seven elected leaders of the
Baha'i community in 2008 and charged them with "espionage for Israel,
insulting religious sanctities, and propaganda against the regime," and
they were sentenced to twenty years' imprisonment.[257]

The Islamic regime expelled Baha'i students from universities, prompting
Baha'is with academic degrees to establish separate educational facilities in
1987. But the regime banned this institute and jailed thirty of the Baha'i
professors. They were charged with "membership in the deviant Bahaist
sect, with the goal of taking action against the security of the country, in
order to further the aims of the deviant sect and those of organizations
outside the country."[258] The court sentenced seven Baha'i professors to
several years in prison.[259] Authorities expelled Navid Khanjani, a Baha'i
student from the university and arrested him in March 2010.[260] The judiciary sentenced him to twelve years in prison in 2011 for his activities to
end discrimination in education.[261] Khashayar Zareie, a Baha'i student and
three-time national champion in judo, was expelled from Shiraz University
and forbidden to participate in the Asian and world championships
because of his faith.[262] Leva Khanjani was convicted on charges of "gathering and colluding with intent to harm state security," "spreading propaganda against the system," and "disturbing public order" for her alleged
participation in antigovernment demonstrations at the time of the Ashura
religious observance in December 2009. A Revolutionary Court sentenced
her to two years' imprisonment.[263]

Supreme Leader Ayatollah Khamenei issued a fatwa declaring Baha'is to
be unclean and untouchable and ordered Muslims to avoid interacting
with them.[264] He issued a similar fatwa two years later, sparking further
persecution.[265] As of 2014, the government held at least 136 Baha'is in

prison. Authorities desecrated Baha'i cemeteries, including one in Shiraz, which the authorities began excavating in April of that year.[266] Authorities in various cities closed down Baha'i-owned businesses. In some cities, authorities went even further and introduced new repertoires of persecution. The Friday Prayer leader of Rafsanjan declared that conducting business with Baha'is was forbidden. He also stated that Baha'is were untouchable and must leave the city.[267] The Agricultural Ministry sold fifty hectares of land to Ziaollah Motearefi, a Baha'i, who paid in installments. Once he made the last payment, the Ministry confiscated his land, declaring he had failed to pay rent.[268] Individual Baha'is were physically attacked at least fifty times between 2005 and 2013, resulting in some deaths.[269] Intelligence officials and the Friday prayer leader of Bandar Abbas threatened Ataollah Rezvani a number of times. He was eventually murdered.[270]

As growing numbers of Iranian Shiites converted to Christianity, the state persecuted Christians, particularly when church members and officials proselytized. At least a dozen Christians were murdered or executed in Iran after the 1979 revolution.[271] Arastoo Sayyah was the first Christian clergyman to be murdered in Shiraz shortly after the revolution.[272] Bishop Hasan Dehghani survived a murder attempt, but his son, Bahram Dehghani, was kidnapped and murdered in Tehran in 1980.[273] The Islamic regime arrested Hussein Soodmand in 1990 for converting to Christianity in 1960 when he was 13. Soodmand was given the option of denouncing his Christian faith, but he refused and was hanged.[274] Agents of the regime allegedly threatened Ghorban Tourani, a Christian convert who established a church in his home in Gonbad Kavous. They eventually abducted and murdered him in November 2005.[275]

The Islamic Republic reacted strongly against increased conversion to Christianity during Ahmadinejad's presidency. Security forces arrested hundreds of Christian converts and, in at least two cases, burned hundreds of copies of the New Testament.[276] The judiciary sentenced Yousef Nadarkhani, a protestant minister, to death for apostasy for renouncing his Islamic faith.[277] The Supreme Court blocked his execution on technical grounds. Government agents arrested at least 285 Christian converts throughout the country in the second half of 2010.[278] Security forces arrested Behnam Irani, a Christian convert and minister, in December 2006 for crimes against national security for holding church services in his home that could lead Muslims to convert to Christianity. He was released on bail in January 2007 only to be rearrested in February 2008 and given a five-year suspended sentence. Irani was arrested once again in 2010 to serve a six-year jail sentence for "preaching against the system." The Revolutionary Court sentenced him to a second six-year term in 2014.[279]

Security forces arrested Reverend Vruir Avanessian, of the Assemblies of God, along with approximately fifty recent converts in Tehran.[280] The Revolutionary Court sentenced him to three and half years in prison for antigovernment activities and promotion of ideas contrary to the sanctity of the Islamic Republic of Iran.[281]

To discourage conversion, the government restricted evangelical church meetings to Sundays only and ordered church officials to inform the Ministry of Intelligence and the Ministry of Islamic Guidance before admitting new members.[282] In addition, the Intelligence Ministry prohibited Christian churches from performing services in Farsi. In some cases, authorities even closed down churches to put an end to attendance and conversion by Muslims.[283] The Intelligence Ministry closed the Rabbani Church, one of the oldest in Tehran, and arrested one of its spiritual leaders.[284] Powerful Islamic organizations exploited powerless, minority Christians. An Islamic organization expropriated a church's land in Tehran in 2013, with the intention of erecting an Islamic center, according to Yonathan Betkolia, a deputy representing Assyrian and Caledonian minorities. The vice president for minority affairs told church officials who complained, "My hands cannot help you in this matter."[285] Intensified repression against converts had a negative outcome as more people established Christian churches in private homes.[286]

Zoroastrians, who had lived peacefully among Muslims for centuries, also came under attack. As increasing numbers of Iranians, particularly the youth, expressed interest in Zoroastrianism—the religion of ancient Persians that introduced eschatology to world religions—the regime interrogated, intimidated, insulted, and restricted Zoroastrians, warning them not to permit outsiders to participate in their cultural and religious observances.[287]

Denominations and sects within Islamic were also targeted for persecution. The regime intensified repression of Dervishes because their religious practice lacked clergy and organizational hierarchy, which appealed to some Shiite Iranians. The regime destroyed Dervish houses of worship in cities throughout the country and, in February 2009, bulldozed the Isfahan house of worship.[288] Dozens of Dervishes were persecuted and flogged throughout Iran. The judiciary in Qom sentenced Amir Ali Labbaf to seventy-four lashes, five years in jail, and ten years' exile for insulting the highest religious leaders and sanctities of Islam.[289] Security forces arrested a large number of protesting Dervishes in Tehran.[290]

In reaction to the repressive measures, about five hundred imprisoned Dervishes went on hunger strike.[291] Authorities ordered imprisoned Dervishes to shave their mustaches, which Dervishes considered insulting and a violation of their traditional practices.[292] The government initiated a campaign to fire Dervishes who worked in the public sector[293] and refused to grant state contracts to members of this group.[294] The Intelligence Ministry demanded that a Semnan Dervish employed in the environmental protection agency spy for them. When he refused, he was fired from the position he had held for years.[295] In reaction, a group of Dervishes wrote to the leader of the Islamic Republic and demanded constitutional changes so that they could be considered a religious minority.[296]

The Islamic regime also persecuted and discriminated against Sunni Muslims. Sunnis had no mosques in Tehran, but in 2011 the state closed down one prayer building and threatened two others with closure.[297] In Sunni regions of the country, the regime refused to allow people to select their own mosque prayer leaders and instead appointed them.[298] The government arrested dozens of Sunnis and put at least twenty on execution row for "acting against national security" in their proselytizing activities.[299] Security forces arrested Loghman Amini in Sanandaj in 2009 and kept him in solitary confinement, according to his father. State-run news broadcast a documentary in which Amini described himself as a Salafi; human rights organizations believed that Amini's confession was made under torture.[300] The Sunnis in Iran suffered the highest number of executions in 2013, according to one report.[301] Shahram Ahmadi and five other Sunnis were executed on December 28, 2011, and Bahram Ahmadi remained on death row.[302]

State intervention in religious matters targeted Shiite theologians who opposed the system or criticized the government. Even the highest religious leaders were not immune from attacks by the state or paramilitary entities. Raids on the offices and households of Grand Ayatollahs Montazeri, Saneie, and Javadi Amoli were ignored for twenty years by Qom authorities, according to Sayed Hadi Hosseini, a Majles deputy. He complained that the clerical sources of emulation in Qom had never been attacked in that way during the shah's reign. "Unfortunately, extremists during these years do not even hesitate to knock off the turbans of the grand ayatollahs."[303] Amnesty International reported that in the 1980s, after Ayatollah Montazeri was relieved of his position as heir to Ayatollah Khomeini, at least twelve of his followers were executed.[304] The report also stated that hundreds, if not thousands, of Grand Ayatollah Sayed Mohammad Shirazi's supporters and relatives had been harassed.[305] Ayatollah Mohammad Reza Shirazi and some of his followers were arrested in December 2012.[306] Other dissident theologians were treated far worse. Sayyed Mohammad Reza Shirazi, a dissident cleric, was murdered in his home after the 2009 presidential elections.[307]

A number of clerics were imprisoned and defrocked. The court charged Ayatollah Sayyed Hossein Kazemeyni Boroujerdi with *moharebeh,* enmity against God, for advocating the separation of state and religion, a ban on stoning adulterers, and an end to the Islamic practice of amputation as punishment for some crimes. Boroujerdi and seventeen of his followers were sentenced to death.[308] Authorities defrocked him, but he remains in prison. According to Amnesty International, prison officials told him that unless he wrote a letter and recanted his beliefs, he would never be released.[309] Security forces arrested Arash Honarvar Shojaee, a clergy and faculty member at Qom Seminary in October 2010 on charges of espionage, propaganda against the regime, acting against national security, and disrespecting the clergy. The clerical court defrocked and sentenced him to four years in prison.[310]

Even Shiites who held different interpretations of Islam and the scriptures were harshly repressed. Mohsen Aslani was arrested on April 30, 2006, and charged with being "corrupt on earth." He was a psychologist and a devout Muslim and taught the Quran to people interested in learning Islamic scriptures. Aslani was accused of presenting an interpretation that differed from the Quran's account of Jonah and the whale in one of his classes.[311] The judiciary initially sentenced him to four years in jail.[312] But in subsequent trials he was accused of additional crimes and twice sentenced to death. Aslani, 37, was eventually executed in September 2014.[313]

An important consequence of the increasing politicization and repression of the opposition was the growing number of executions, particularly during Ahmadinejad's second term.[314] Iran carried out some of the highest numbers of executions in the world. The head of the judiciary rejected calls from some citizens for the abolition of capital punishment, countering that "opposition against executions is opposition against Islam."[315] Amnesty International listed Iran as the second most prolific executioner in 2008 after China.[316]

Long sentences and harsh prison conditions inevitably imposed a heavy toll on political prisoners and prisoners of conscience. At least twenty-three such prisoners died between July 2003 and June 2013.[317] More than half of the prison deaths occurred in the three years following the 2009 presidential election. Zahra Kazemi, an Iranian-Canadian journalist, died in prison from a beating.[318] Arash Arkan, 26, died in jail as a result of deliberate neglect of a medical condition, according to a report by a human rights organization.[319] Mansour Radpour and Seyyed Mohammad Mehdi Naghshbandian died in Rajaie Shahr prison in May and June 2012.[320] Ramin Agha-Zadeh Ghahremani was allegedly tortured while incarcerated and died shortly after being released.[321]

Persistent, systematic repression of political prisoners and restrictions on their families drew statements of concern and condemnation from people in Iran and abroad. In response to increased reports of harsh conditions and deteriorating health of prisoners, Iran's Islamic Medical Association requested in vain that the chief of the judiciary allow independent physicians to examine political prisoners.[322] Shirin Ebadi, Iran's Nobel laureate, declared that Iranian prisoners of conscience and political prisoners had fewer rights than ordinary prisoners.[323] Ebadi and six human rights organizations—Amnesty International, Human Rights Watch, the International Campaign for Human Rights in Iran, Reporters Without Borders, the International Federation for Human Rights, and the International League for the Defense of Human Rights—called on Iranian authorities to allow all prisoners access to the medical care and family visits to which they were entitled under international law.[324] "Bullying a prisoner's child or denying the prisoner family visits and medical care only makes Iran look even worse in the eyes of the world, stated Amnesty International."[325]

Summary and Conclusions

From its inception, the Islamic regime used repressive measures in successive rounds of conflict to eliminate its rivals and challengers and expel its revolutionary allies from the polity. The ruling clergy attempted to expel their former most important ally, the leftist faction, from the polity as early as the second decade of the Islamic Republic, in order to construct a political system even more exclusive than the one established by Ayatollah Khomeini. However, attempts to exclude leftists had the effect of intensifying conflicts. After the first decade of the revolution, the regime further restricted access to the political system by introducing new qualifications for candidates for political office, making the system more elitist and reinforcing existing categorical inequalities. These policies gave rise to a reform movement in the 1990s. Reformists quickly gained popular support and attempted to introduce changes to strengthen civil society, reduce repression, enforce the rule of law, and expand democratic freedoms. Their attempts failed, and they were unable to introduce serious changes.

The conservative faction reacted to reformist efforts by increasing repression. The Revolutionary Guard, created as a nonpolitical entity, intervened more frequently in ideological struggles and threatened reformers. In the ideological arena, the Assembly of Experts reasserted the authority of the supreme leader. Ayatollah Khamenei attacked Western liberalism and claimed that the supreme leader would not make mistakes, implying his own infallibility.

With the failure of the reformist government, conservatives captured the presidency with the election of Ahmadinejad. During his presidency, the scope of the polity—which had expanded under Khatami's government—narrowed again. Ahmadinejad's rule further politicized many social and economic issues. The ruling clergy and the conservative forces used state power to enforce Islamic norms and practices. At the same time, the government intensified political repression against numerous social groups, including religious minorities and even Shiite sects. The intensification of repression confirmed that the rulers of the Islamic Republic were not interested in reform and change. Ahmadinejad's policies further polarized Iran's society and politics. By intensifying repression and failing to modify the system, Ahmadinejad and other hardliners demonstrated the regime's lack of commitment to the promises of the 1979 revolution. After more than three decades in power, the Islamic regime refused to tolerate either challenge or reform.

Endless political repression enhanced the power of the ruling clergy and their allies in the short run, but it violated revolutionary promises. Repression also antagonized the vast majority of Iranians and undermined support for the Islamic regime among segments of the population. The failure to ensure political freedom and civil liberties, along with deteriorating economic conditions, increased popular opposition to the regime and rendered it vulnerable to challenge and attack.

❧ III ❦

CHALLENGES AGAINST
THE ISLAMIC REGIME

CHAPTER SIX

Students: Vanguard of Struggles for Democracy

STUDENTS HAVE ALWAYS been in the vanguard of Iran's political and ideological struggles. They have also played leading roles in democratization movements in other developing countries with highly authoritarian and repressive regimes. Where state repression prevented the rise of well-organized civil associations such as independent political organizations and parties—for example, the Philippines, South Korea, and Indonesia—students were at the forefront of the democratization movements.

Students share a number of characteristics that set them apart from other social collectivities and increase the likelihood they will take a leading role in democratization. Unlike capitalists who often depend on the state and attempt to influence government policies to their advantage, university students do not constitute a class with significant economic assets to protect. Because most emerge from the middle and working classes, students often forge coalitions with the middle and working classes against the state and sometimes the dominant classes. Unlike workers who depend on employers for economic survival and thus are subject to workplace restrictions, students enjoy greater autonomy and are not bound by such restraints. Consequently, they have a greater capacity for collective action within institutions of higher education. Students from diverse backgrounds bring a variety of experiences and problems that strengthen their solidarity and enhance their awareness about issues confronting the population and affecting broader societal interests. Although students from disadvantaged and less well-off backgrounds historically have not had a significant presence in most countries' institutions of higher education, they are often among the most active participants in the democratization movements and have at times played leadership roles.

Students enjoy academic freedom and greater social space in which to participate in ideological debates about the shape of the social structure and allocation of power and privilege. Actively involved in producing and reproducing ideas, theories, and knowledge, students often develop a robust interest in theoretical issues and skill in analyzing existing conditions and alternative social structures. Students benefit from the elite nature of institutions of higher education, the fact that students historically originated from relatively privileged social backgrounds, and the relative autonomy of universities—where it exists. These factors convey some measure of immunity from government repression compared to other groups.

Compared to other collectivities, students have a greater capacity for mobilization and collective action. The high concentration of students with extensive communication networks facilitates mobilization and collective action. The expansion of higher education and the Internet, the spread of social media, and new means of communication create dense networks of interaction and a lively interest in events and issues around the world. Contact with fellow students from diverse backgrounds in classes, libraries, cafeterias, and dormitories generates endless opportunities for interaction and contributes to intellectual debates and challenges on campus. Not surprisingly, higher education institutions have commonly been the wellspring of radical ideologies, challengers, and revolutionaries. Intense student mobilization, collective action, or repression on one campus can spark protests on other campuses. Students' mobilization has the potential to escalate conflict elsewhere in the society, given the considerable social prestige and respect that students and universities usually enjoy.

In contrast to other collectivities, students are more inclined to break with the past, gravitate to large-scale transformations, and advocate a reconstruction of the entire social order.[1] Students in less-developed countries consistently resist exclusive rule, centralized state power, and highly authoritarian and repressive regimes. Because the state is a critical actor in the development of their societies, students are also concerned about the nature of the state and often favor promoting democratic systems that are inclusive and accountable to the public. Students oppose social and economic inequalities and the concentration of wealth produced institutionally or by state development strategies. Unlike some other collectivities, students often lack a vested interest in the existing social structure but possess a strong interest in constructing a better future for themselves and their countries through a more egalitarian social structure.

Iranian students stood at the leading edge of political and ideological struggles in the latter half of the twentieth century.[2] As early actors in the nationalist movements of the 1950s and 1960s, students created and supported guerrilla organizations opposing the government in the 1970s. Prestigious Tehran University, the country's oldest institution of higher education, was popularly referred to as the "bastion of freedom" in 1978. Marchers during religious observances paid tribute to students' contributions to political freedom by pausing in front of the gates of Tehran University to hail the students.[3] Students' active participation in the vanguard of the revolutionary conflicts attracted the attention and admiration of Islamic leaders. Ayatollah Khomeini and his clerical supporters repeatedly praised students and commended the universities as bulwarks of struggle against the shah's dictatorship and imperialism. Khomeini called for an alliance between university people and the clergy.[4] The student movement produced important political organizations and leaders. Some led radical or moderate political and professional organizations, while others joined the Islamic Republic's leadership.

Students' efforts on behalf of freedom and social justice continued after the establishment of the Islamic state. The students quickly mobilized to spearhead the democratization struggles and battled for women's rights, workers' councils, and the rights of ethnic minorities. Inevitably, students became the principal victims of government repression. They were far and away the single, largest social category arrested, tortured, and slain during acute postrevolutionary political conflict. The government killed dozens of students in the spring of 1980 and, in an unprecedented move, closed all universities for some thirty-two months.

Two decades after the revolution, Iranian students once again streamed into prominence in the democratization struggles. They intensified their political activities during the presidency of Khatami, who promised reforms. As the number of universities and student enrollment increased during Khatami's eight-year rule, students organized more than two thousand groups and participated by the tens of thousands in social and political events. Although the reformists in power did not favor insurgency or radical change, students challenged the foundations of the Islamic Republic in 1999 and again in 2003, opening a new chapter in the democratization of Iran.

Student Politics in the Islamic Republic

As their opposition to the Islamic Republic mounted, student politics gravitated to the left. Students opposed the clergy's imposition of a theocracy and ceased attending mosques and religious functions soon after the revolution. Alarmed by the absence of students and intellectuals in mosques less than four months after the establishment of the Islamic Republic, Ayatollah Khomeini encouraged students to return to the mosques. Addressing Shiraz University students on June 5, 1979, Khomeini declared, "People, protect your mosques. Intellectuals, protect your mosques. Intellectuals should attend the mosques. They are not going to the mosques; they should attend the mosques so that this movement succeeds and the country is saved."[5] A year later, Khomeini again criticized those who abandoned the mosques: "The lewd ones have emptied the mosques," he lamented. "In Islam no obligation is above prayer. Why are people so careless about prayer? All you students should go to the mosques and fill up the trenches."[6]

Although Khomeini earlier lauded university students for their struggle against the monarchy, dictatorship, and imperialism, he soon complained that "universities were bastions of communists, and they were war rooms for communists."[7] He denounced leftist influence in the universities and demanded that they "be reconstructed from the beginning so that our youth have Islamic training."[8] Iran's ruling Revolutionary Council announced on April 18, 1980, that non-Islamic groups must close their university offices within the next three days, or President Bani-Sadr, the council, and the Iranian people would shut them by force. The Revolutionary Council dismantled the headquarters and offices of various groups, along with their libraries and facilities for art, sports, and other activities.[9] When students resisted, the government killed dozens and injured hundreds in clashes.

In an unprecedented move, the Islamic regime closed down all universities in the spring of 1980 and kept them shuttered for some thirty-two months while it pursued a cultural revolution, purging universities of leftist and liberal influences and activities. The government expelled thousands of students and faculty during the cultural revolution. The number of university students dropped from 174,217 to 117,148, according to Amnesty International.[10] Authorities dismissed some 3,500 university faculty— nearly one-half of the teaching staff—deemed liberal, leftist or antigovernment. One government official boasted that while he served as minister of education, twenty thousand primary and secondary school teachers were fired.[11] Nearly four thousand students involved in political activities against the regime were executed or killed by the government between 1981 and 1985.[12] The Cultural Revolution Council, with Khomeini's approval, conducted a thorough review of university curricula to ensure that Islamic laws and precepts were being taught.[13] When the universities reopened in fall 1982, all students were required to take courses on Islam, taught primarily by clergy.

The Islamic regime developed a near monopoly on educational institutions and established a complex system to screen student admissions to colleges, universities, and subsequent public sector employment. Students seeking admission had to meet educational criteria and also be recommended by a local mosque or a respected member of the religious community. Only students who passed the initial scientific examination could proceed to the political and ideological evaluation. Security and political concerns initially motivated the ideological phase of the examination, but the political screening policies eventually were used to distribute educational and economic opportunities to government supporters—particularly war veterans and their families.[14] Special college admission quotas were established for Basij militias, Revolutionary Guards, and high-ranking government officials whose academic performance and competence were far below the level traditionally required for admission. War veterans and their family members also received special quotas in the years that followed.[15]

The regime imposed various measures on entering students to ensure they would support the Islamic Republic. Authorities banned independent student organizations and encouraged students to join government-sponsored Islamic student associations, represented in all colleges and universities by the Office of Consolidation Unity (OCU) or the Office to Foster Unity. Students who staffed the associations received special privileges, grants, scholarships, good jobs after graduation, and an easier time entering graduate schools.

The associations often spied for the government, generating fear and apprehension among students who remained under political surveillance throughout their educational experience. Islamic student associations prepared students for government rallies, reported antigovernment activities, and identified faculty members who criticized official ideology. The associations implemented the state's gender policies by monitoring male–female interactions on campuses and pressuring female students to observe proper dress codes and behavior toward male students. The associations occasionally issued warnings and referred nonobservant students to the Enzebat Komiteh, or disciplinary committees, empowered to expel those who failed to follow the regulations.[16] The Komiteh became a major source of censorship and suppression of freedom of thought. Students who raised questions were later called in for violating unwritten speech codes. The regime dealt harshly with those who espoused alternative views. In 1994, agents of the regime murdered Zohreh Yazdi, a female student at Tehran University medical school, for advocating secular viewpoints.[17]

Many students suffered economic hardships. Most came from middle-class families that could ill afford the tuition and expenses to attend the university. Provincial students had to pay high rents or stay in dormitories, which were in short supply. Lacking advantageous connections to power-holders, these students could not obtain scarce university loans or scholarships. High unemployment rates among college graduates added another grievance and uncertainty to the situation of college students. Most students knew they could not obtain good jobs after graduation without access to the government or powerful clerics. In response to these conditions, some of the country's best students opted to leave the country. An investigation by *Shargh* newspaper found that from 1993 to 2007, more than 62 percent of Iranian students who won medals at international science olympiads left the country to continue their education.[18]

The ruling elite attempted to retain student support and Islamize the universities during the second decade of the Islamic Republic, but grew alarmed by student apathy and lack of interest in Islamic cultural practices. The supreme leader warned of student indifference on the 1994 anniversary of the occupation of the American embassy. The official student magazine of his representative at Amir Kabir University cautioned that lack of student enthusiasm and activism would negatively affect the revolution.[19] Mohammad Mohammadi Golpayegani, a top aide to the supreme leader, noted in 1999, "The first generation of the 1979 revolution has not been able to transfer values to the second generation. This is a threat, and we must not let it slip by easily." He urged educators, clerics, and mosques to do more to inform the youth about the country's revolutionary past.[20] Hojatoleslam Mohammad-Ali Zam, head of the Cultural and Artistic Organization of the city council of Tehran, reported that 86 percent of young students did not say their daily prayers, which are obligatory in Islam.[21] Mohammad-Taghi Mesbah Yazdi, a high-profile Islamic cleric, complained, "If you open your eyes, you will see that the youth, brought up in the lap of the Islamic Revolution, shun religion and saying prayers when they enter universities."[22]

The Rise of a New Student Movement

State policies designed in part to counter the impact of the steady departure of educated Iranians to other countries, population growth, and the rise of private educational institutions enhanced the capacity of students for mobilization and collective action. Whereas Iran had only ten universities with a total of about 160,000 students in the early 1980s, the country established dozens of new universities by 1995 and enrolled about 1,150,000 students—far surpassing the growth of Iran's population—just before President Khatami was elected in 1997.[23] There were more than 1.5 million students in public or private institutions of higher education by September 2000. The number of universities exceeded two thousand and the number of students topped 3.5 million by 2009. As the number of students grew, so did their capacity to act collectively. Students had an even greater interest in mobilizing and acting collectively because many university graduates could not find employment after graduation.[24]

The end of the war, the expansion of universities, and an increase in students transformed student politics. Islamic student associations eventually subdivided and diversified. Heshmatollah Tabarzadi, former Revolutionary Guard and war veteran who had worked with Hashemi Rafsanjani, broke ranks with the OCU in 1987 and established the Islamic Union of University Students and Higher Education Centers. After graduating from the university, he renamed his organization to enable it to remain active. The new Union of Islamic Students and Alumni of Universities and Other Higher Education Centers drew its membership from six diverse groups: university students, teachers, educated individuals, university alumni, workers, and civil servants. Although the organization's following was much smaller than the OCU, its strength derived from the vocal, ambitious, and astute character of its secretary, Tabarzadi.[25]

New divisions within the ruling elite generated important developments in the decade following Khomeini's death in 1989. The regime's right-wing faction led by Ayatollah Khamenei and President Rafsanjani decided to end the radicalism of the earlier phase, eliminate instability in the system, and promote development. When the OCU rejected new economic policies, the government responded harshly. Rafsanjani publicly criticized the OCU during Friday prayer in April 1991 for having monopolistic tendencies in the universities and preventing the emergence of new constituencies.[26] A few weeks later, on May 21, agents occupied the OCU office and arrested six OCU members, detaining them for several hours. The agents confiscated documents and about 5–6 million tomans in OCU assets and forced the students to evacuate the building at the legal affairs college—a location they had used for years.[27] The new policies were intended to weaken and marginalize the OCU, an organization that had played an important role in clerical dominance during the hostage crisis.

OCU ideology and politics began changing in response to a number of factors, including state attacks, exclusion of the leftist faction in the 1992

parliamentary elections, the rise of a new category of dissident intellectuals
with new and critical publications, a decline in enforcement aspects of the
cultural revolution in universities, and a reduction in the number of war
veterans attending universities.[28] OCU ideology diversified and generated
three distinct trends.[29] A small group supported the conservative faction as
the true representation of Islamic ideals and saw their actions to be in the
interests of the state. The majority continued to support the leftist faction
of the political elite and, as revolutionary vanguards, remained vigilant
against the penetrating forces of the enemy and upheld the revolution's
original ideals.[30] A third, prodemocracy faction emerged to criticize corruption, government economic mismanagement, and the absence of political freedom. It eventually became the mainstay of support for reform. In
1996, even before Khatami was elected president, this faction of the OCU
protested repression and demanded that law enforcement personnel and
security forces stay off university campuses.[31]

The prodemocracy faction was supported by former members of the
OCU who, as students, were directly involved in the embassy takeover.
They included some of the masterminds—Abbas Abdi, Mohsen Mirdamadi,
and Ebrahim Asgharzade. Others voicing similar viewpoints included
Mohammad Reza Khatami (brother of Mohammad Khatami) and
Maassoumeh Ebtekar, who, as "Mary," was the students' spokesperson
during the hostage crisis.

Outside the OCU, new student constituencies emerged. A small group of
students acting independently formed a secular organization for political
change. Manouchehr Mohammadi, Gholamreza Mohajerinejad, and
others created the Organization of Intellectual Students in 1994.[32] Most
members came from relatively modest backgrounds in less well-off provincial cities. They launched their activities in student dormitories, which provided interaction, solidarity, and communication networks to mobilize
and act collectively. They distributed nationalist songs to dormitory residents. They also handed out literature advocating freedom of expression
and civil liberties; separation of religion from politics; the cessation of discrimination based on religion; ethnicity and language; equality of men and
women; social justice; and egalitarian distribution of national resources to
reduce the rising gap between rich and poor.[33] These students also initiated
a petition drive to ban the violent Ansar-e Hezbollah from university campuses. When agents of the Intelligence Ministry discovered the organization, they severely beat the two founders, who managed to escape.
Mohammadi went into hiding for months. They were allowed to return to
their studies when university authorities guaranteed that both men would
refrain from political activities.

Mohammadi and Mohajerinejad continued their campus activities covertly, escaping surveillance on mountain-climbing excursions where they were free to sing nationalist songs and discuss political issues. They recruited new members and established connections to secular, liberal-nationalist forces outside the university, such as the National Front, the Iran Nation Party, and the Freedom Movement. They participated in weekly meetings of the National Front's youth divisions and introduced fellow students to the Front's politics.[34] When Khatami became president in 1997, they formed the Student Committee for the Defense of Political Prisoners as well as an umbrella organization, the United Student Front, to bring together other student organizations[35] and expand their political activities. Students initiated a number of rallies and demonstrations to bring about change in colleges and universities in the late 1990s. The protests often turned violent as hardline vigilantes intervened and attacked the students.

The proportion of activist students within the universities remained small, but they played a vital role in the presidential election. In December 1996, the Islamic student association in Tehran signified its growing opposition to the regime by calling on President Rafsanjani to guarantee free speech and elections before leaving office the following year. The Association's newspaper had been temporarily banned for criticizing officials earlier that year. The organization asked the president to ensure that journalists and writers would not be imprisoned or punished for their ideas. "Mr. President, before the end of your term, make arrangements so that the freedom and security of the press will be guaranteed," the newspaper quoted the organization as saying. "Provide guarantees so that newspapers aren't closed down and telephone lines are not tapped."[36]

Students seized the opportunity to mobilize created by Khatami's election and promises of political reform and liberalization.[37] They organized a rally in November 1997 at which Tabarzadi issued an unprecedented call for the popular election of the supreme leader and restrictions on presidential powers. Tabarzadi was severely beaten, and his office was vandalized.[38] At a rally of the Union of Islamic Students and Graduates six months later, Tabarzadi told a crowd of two thousand that women and nonclerics should be permitted to run for election to the powerful Assembly of Experts.[39] He demanded that the constitutional right to freedom of speech be respected. "The purpose of our revolution was to allow us to breathe in a free atmosphere," he said. Even as he spoke, hostile slogans from fundamentalists repeatedly drowned out his voice. Police officers stood by and watched as fundamentalists attacked the students, injuring several and dragging others away. On another occasion, students protested with chants of "Khatami, come to our aid" and "death to the Taliban, the fascists," who were then in power in Afghanistan.[40]

In March 1998, student supporters of President Khatami demonstrated at Tehran University, urging democratization with slogans including "One country, one government, determined by the vote of the people." The students criticized the law that allowed the Guardian Council to apply stringent qualifications to potential candidates for election and accused conservatives of seeking to "monopolize" power. They called for the supreme leader to stop threatening the press. Fundamentalists once again attacked the demonstrators.[41] Proreform students at another event proclaimed their intention "to create a peaceful space with emphasis on dialogue and the rule of law," as well as a country for everyone, not just one sector, and a society without intolerance.[42]

Liberal-nationalist students, too, mobilized for collective action and political change. The Independent Student Association of Amir Kabir Industrial University joined the Society of Intellectual Students to organize a rally commemorating the death of Mosaddegh, leader of the country's nationalist movement. The event, held at Mosaddegh's birthplace and place of exile, drew thousands, including political leaders Dariush Forouhar, Abbas Amir-Entezam, and Ebrahim Yazdi. The organizers declared, "With the memory of Mosaddegh, we will support the Mosaddeghs of our time to prevent the victimization of law, freedom, and justice." Manucher Mohammadi, a student organizer, announced that the sheer number of participants deterred any attack from thugs.[43]

As conflicts intensified, students protested against political repression and engaged in collective action to support political prisoners. About one thousand students and professors demonstrated in Isfahan in February 1999 against the beating of students at a rally earlier in the month. Protesters criticized law enforcement personnel for negligence after a student was stabbed.[44] Students also demonstrated repeatedly on behalf of imprisoned dissidents. They called for the release of the popular mayor of Tehran in April 1998.[45] Students rallied to support Mohsen Kadivar, an intellectual cleric sentenced to one and a half years in prison for his antiestablishment views. They shouted, "Kadiver must be released" and "Death to the monopoly" in reference to hardliners who controlled the state.[46] The Islamic student association of Tehran University's Technical College demanded that Friday Prayers be held at another location, off campus.[47] The conflicts and protests set the stage for further mobilization and confrontations.

Conservative forces intensified their own activities. The Majles passed a law in October 1998 to establish the student branch of Basij, paramilitary arm of the Revolutionary Guard, to defend the achievements of the Islamic Revolution and clamp down on the OCU's activities.[48] Conservative publications hinted that the OCU and nonuniversity groups such as those led by Tabarzadi and Mohammadi were out of control, and spread the idea of massive intervention to intimidate the supreme leader's enemies.[49] Conservative students demanded that the Majles impeach the moderate interior minister. They demanded the expulsion of liberal activist students and accused the OCU of "betraying" revolutionary principles by inviting liberal intellectuals and dissidents to speak at universities.[50] New government units were tasked with university "disciplinary activities." Their disruptive, suppressive, and militaristic presence on campus became a major grievance for students.[51]

Conservatives in the ruling elite used repressive measures against liberal students. They seized Manuchehr Mohammadi shortly before he could speak at a protest rally at Tehran University on May 25, 1999. Fellow student leader Mohajerinejad was detained five days later. Both were released at the beginning of June, but others who attended the rally feared for their own safety. After Tabarzadi criticized aspects of government policy in a radio interview the same month, he and four colleagues were arrested and charged with publishing "deceitful and offensive" articles contrary to "public order and the public interest."[52] He was tortured while in custody, according to a report by Amnesty International.[53] Vigilantes attacked liberal newspapers, broke up prodemocracy demonstrations, and even attacked senior officials allied with Khatami. In one incident, about one hundred people attacked Hadi Khamenei, younger brother of the supreme leader. He was a press advisor to President Khatami and, unlike his older brother, had moderate political views.[54]

Radicalized Students

On July 7, 1999, the Majles approved a tough new law censoring press freedom. It sparked open and deadly confrontations between students and conservatives in the regime. The new press law stipulated that foreign agents, foreign spies, and members of counterrevolutionary groups were forbidden from working in the Iranian press.[55] The following day, a reformist newspaper, *Salaam*—whose editor in chief, Mohammad Mousavi Khoiniha, was a cleric that advised the American embassy hostage takers— published a letter allegedly written to the intelligence minister, insinuating that the repressive law originated with the ministry. The paper was quickly shut down, sparking student protests. Some two hundred students, mostly affiliated with the OCU, gathered in front of a Tehran University dormitory housing some 6,500 students to protest the newspaper's closure. Local security forces ordered the students to end the demonstration. Most did so, although a small number of students stayed to converse in front of the dormitory. Tehran's acting police chief and a large group of security forces arrived on the scene shortly after midnight to speak with the remaining students. Security forces, riot police, and Ansar-e Hezbollah soon surrounded the dormitory. Neighborhood residents came out to support the students and defuse the confrontation. Several officials from Khatami's office also appeared on the scene and persuaded the students to return to their dormitory.

More contentious events unfolded. At approximately 4:00 a.m., an organized force of some four hundred uniformed men carrying distinctive blue batons broke into the student dormitory to teach the students a harsh lesson. "Security forces and vigilantes stormed a dormitory at Tehran University on Thursday night and beat students as they slept, pushing some from the second- and third-story windows. Although the official death toll stood at two, Iran's newspapers, quoting students, claimed that between five and eight students had died," according to a *New York Times* report.[56] A former student, Ezzat Ebrahimnejad, who was visiting friends at the dormitory, was killed.[57] Raamin Karimi, a student, was beaten and suffered broken bones after being tossed out of a third-floor window. As he fell, he heard his attackers offer him up as a sacrifice to God.[58] Karimi later testified in court and stated that vigilantes and police officers dragged him from his room in the early hours of July 9. The corridor was filled with police who beat him with sticks and threw his semiconscious and bloodied body out a window. "By chance my head hit the grass, but the rest of my body hit the concrete," said Karimi.[59] Mohsen Jamali, a medical student, was blinded in one eye when tear gas was fired directly at him. "A teargas canister hit my eye. It was like a bullet," said Mohsen Jamali.[60] Some attackers broke into a dormitory that housed foreign students, asked individuals whether they were Shiite or Sunni, and then beat them up.[61]

As news of the attacks on students in Tehran spread, student protests erupted in at least eighteen cities in a matter a matter of few days, including Tabriz, Shiraz, Isfahan, Mashhad, and Yazd.[62] Tabriz University students held large demonstrations and chanted slogans such as *"Nirouy-e Entezami, Hamdast-e Hezb-e Shaytan"* (Security forces, allies of the party of Satan) and *"Simay-e Enhesari, Mamnu Bayad Gardad"* (Monopolistic radio and television must be forbidden). A theology student was shot dead and dozens of students were injured during clashes between students and the security forces.[63] According to an Agence France-Presse (AFP) report, ten to fifteen students needed hospital treatment.[64] A later report noted that at least fifteen people had been shot, including three women. One source said that "80 people had been injured by stones, clubs and knives when security forces began opening fire into the crowd."[65]

Students also demonstrated in other large cities, including Mashhad, Isfahan, Shiraz, Zanjan, Shahroud, and Oroumiyeh.[66] In some cases, women and children joined them. Students at Yazd University organized several sit-ins, and Zanjan University students held a mourning ceremony and demonstration to commemorate slain and injured students at Tehran University. Students of Azad ("free") Islamic University in Khomeini-Shahr condemned the repression of students. Students staged demonstrations and rallies in the provinces of Bushehr, Hormuzgan, Sistan-Baluchestan, Ardabil, Mazandaran, Gilan, and Lorestan, as well as the cities of Hamedan, Rasht, Birjand, Gorgan, Semnan, Shahroud, Maragheh, Khorram-Abad, Bandar Abbas, and Kashan.[67] Student protesters demanded the dismissal of top-level officials and General Hedayat Ollah Lotfian, the chief of police.[68]

As conflicts unfolded, students presented a number of specific demands. Many demands resembled those of the 1979 revolution, including freedom of the press, release of political prisoners, accountability of state institutions, and public investigations into intelligence and security operations against dissidents. Some slogans—"Down with dictators," "Death to despots"—were identical to the slogans of the revolution. Other demands included the transfer of key institutions, such as the military, from the supreme leader to the executive branch.[69]

Leaders of the Islamic Republic initially denounced the attacks on students and expressed sympathy for the victims. Ayatollah Khamenei condemned the violence, saying, "The young people of this country, whether they are students or no-students, are my sons and daughters. They are my children. For me it is very difficult and hard to bear anything that causes our young people inconvenience, dissension and mishap."[70] He declared that no one should use violence against opposition groups and that those responsible, including any police officials, would be punished.[71] Former president, Hashemi Rafsanjani stated that "college students are the greatest national assets, and to humiliate them or to question their moral uprightness would be to cast doubt on the values and merits of their future accomplishments."[72] Mohsen Rezaie, secretary of the Expediency Council, publicly noted that virtually all the country's political leaders had sympathy with the university in a noncompromising environment.[73]

Other important constituencies joined in and condemned the attacks, including members of Tehran's city council.[74] Various scientific and political organizations also expressed sympathy with the students. The governing board of Tehran University threatened to resign collectively in protest against the attacks.[75]

Students were not satisfied with official condemnations and wanted quick, decisive action. Tehran University continued to be a scene of great contention for several days. The OCU and the Islamic student associations of the university, which the OCU once helped to close down, condemned the attacks and called for a campus protest.[76] Tehran University students held a sit-in and took over the street adjacent to a dormitory. Male students broke open the gates to the women students' dormitories, which had been locked by security forces to prevent them from joining the demonstrations. Once freed, women students joined the demonstration. As law enforcement agents watched, students chanted the nationalist song "Ay Iran, Ay Marze Por Gohar" and shouted slogans such as "Freedom of thought, forever, forever," "Ideas can never be suspended," "Freedom of the press, health of society," "Closure of thought is not possible," and "Death to autocracy, death to monopolists."[77] A group of students demanded that July 9 be named "Student Victimization Day."

Many members of the government's reformist faction sympathized with the student protests. Mostafa Tajzadeh, vice president for political and social affairs, cautioned students that their sit-in and takeover of the adjacent street might provoke law enforcement agents to open fire, but the protesters refused to return to their dorms. The interior minister visited the scene and ordered law enforcement forces to retreat, but he was ignored. The ministers of higher education and health appeared to express sympathy for the students, and the former promised that he would resign if he could not do anything about the situation. To calm the students and prevent further attacks, a number of government officials—including Tajzadeh; Mehdi Karroubi and his wife, Fatemeh Karroubi; Faezeh Hashmi; Mosavi Lari; and Moin, the minister of education—spent Friday night and the next day on campus.[78]

Thousands of students continued to demonstrate on Saturday, July 10, breaking through Tehran University's gate, which authorities had closed. In the afternoon, a group of about two thousand students and a large number of other people marched to the Interior Ministry building. Marchers chanted slogans such as "Oh, free people, your students have been killed," "Oh, courageous people, support, support," and "Security forces, shame on you."[79] The protesters issued six demands: remove Lotfian, the hardline chief of police, identify and punish those responsible for the attack on the dormitory, issue an apology from the National

Security Council, release all jailed students, transfer control of the security forces to the elected government, and provide an honorable funeral for the students killed in the attacks.[80]

The crowd swelled over the next two days as the nation's attention was riveted on the protesting students. Numerous visitors to the students' dormitories expressed condolences and lent support. Ordinary residents from the city brought food for the students. Supporters of small, secular political organizations such as Marze Por Gohar and Pan Iranist joined the assembled students, along with a group of young people wearing headbands proclaiming "Iran Nation's Party."[81] Some of the parents of students who lived in other cities came to Tehran University and joined the students.[82]

With increased public support, the students threatened to take their protests beyond the campus and into the streets. They organized security units to protect themselves from attack by paramilitary forces.[83] Throughout the day, students shouted new slogans, including "Freedom of thought cannot exist with dictatorship"[84] and "Either Islam and the law, or another revolution."[85]

At Tehran University, students installed a free microphone for any interested person who wished to address the crowd. City council members and proreform political figures including Abdollah Nouri, Hadi Khamenei, Akbar Ganji, Faezeh Hashemi, Habibollah Payman, and Mostafa Moien addressed the gathering, asking students to be patient and pursue a legal resolution of their grievances.[86] Proreform activists and leaders Ezatollah Sahabi, Abbas Abdi, and Saeed Hajjarian warned students to remain vigilant and stay out of the streets because certain elements would use the situation as an excuse to impose martial law.[87] Tehran University's chancellor told the students that "July 9 was the worst day of his life because the sanctity of the university was violated and students were attacked."[88] When it was announced that the minister of higher education had resigned, students chanted, "Revolutionary minister, thanks, thanks."[89] Mehdi Karroubi, speaker of the Majles, a leader of the Association of Militant Clerics, and an advocate of reform, attended the students' gathering that evening. He told the students that compared to repression under the shah, "this is unique and heartrending. This attack is not in line with the revolution. I never imagined such a horrible incident."[90] Students responded by protesting that his association said nothing about the fact that each attacker had received 300,000 tomans.[91]

The governing board of Tehran University, heads of various colleges, and university professors called for a rally at the university mosque the following day. Thousands of students attended the event. Many demonstrators urged President Khatami to appear and address the students. "Khatami, where are you? Your students have been killed," they shouted. Students drowned out a message of condolence from the supreme leader with even more radical chants: "Commander in chief, resign!" and "Down with the dictator." Other student slogans added, "Cannon, tanks, and machine guns no longer have any effect" and "Students choose to die before they yield." The chancellor of Tehran University addressed the crowd, declaring, "Conscientious students will continue their struggle to reach their goals but will not allow others to take advantage of their movement."[92] Some students left campus to demonstrate in the streets, vowing to keep up the pressure until the authorities met their demands, which included designating July 15 as a national day of mourning for slain students, holding a public trial for police officers who ordered and carried out the dormitory attack, and releasing the bodies of the fallen students. Students' demands grew and became more radical.[93]

Throughout this conflict, numerous organizations criticized the violence directed against the students. Professors, deans, and university presidents across the country denounced the attacks and demanded the arrest and prosecution of those responsible. Groups of writers, the Association of Journalists, and even an association of researchers and teachers at Qom seminary decried the attacks.[94]

As conflicts escalated, fifteen proreform political organizations announced a protest at Tehran University on July 13.[95] The announcement condemned the brutal attack on Tehran University students by a group of "willful" law enforcement forces and their club-wielding hooligans. The signatories accused the attackers of being part of a premeditated plan to target the May 23 presidential election and demanded the arrest of the attack's masterminds and perpetrators. *Neshat,* the leading reformist daily, announced that newspapers would not print on July 14.[96]

But hardliners reacted decisively to prevent the formation of a broad coalition of protesters and the escalation of conflicts. The threat of a coalition between students and large elements of the reform movement alarmed the conservatives. Tehran's governor banned demonstrations and protests on July 13. Antiriot and security forces stormed Tehran University on July 12 with tear gas, intending to demobilize the students and put an end to the protests. Students responded by burning various objects to neutralize the tear gas.

Political divisions between the OCU and more secular and radical students emerged as protests continued. The OCU tried unsuccessfully to limit the protest to the government's conservative faction. Others wanted to direct their slogans against the entire system. Reformist students argued against creating trouble for the president, which might block his reforms; they favored limiting their protests to within the university campus. More radical students argued that the president had little power and had been unable to block political repression and murder. They labeled the OCU an organization of compromise and preferred instead to take their protests to the streets.[97]

Unable to control the pace or the direction of events, the main prore-form Islamic student movement, the OCU, washed its hands of the whole affair. "Now that the striking students have chosen their representative council, this office has no longer any responsibility with regard to the student movement."[98] The OCU and the Islamic Association of Students at fourteen colleges at Tehran University announced that they would pursue their demands through legal means and would not support any extremist moves outside of the legal process. They declared that anyone involved in demonstrations or marches would be responsible for their own actions. The next day, the council of students at the sit-in reiterated its position on violence and destruction, declaring that "these actions are made by individuals who wish to point the finger of blame at the students' movement." The council requested all supporters to refrain from engaging in sit-ins and street demonstrations until July 17, to provide time for negotiations between students and officials. The OCU discouraged students who wanted to continue the protest.[99]

As security forces banned protests, a large segment of the prodemocracy student body took to the streets around Tehran University, shouting radical slogans. Ignoring the OCU's retreat, the government's ban on demonstrations, and a police crackdown that had begun a day earlier, thousands of students clashed with volunteer, club-wielding Islamic militiamen known as Basiji and antiriot police on major streets around the university on July 13. Student activists and other protesters used mobile telephones, as they had done throughout the protests, to coordinate their actions and warn one another of impending threats from police and vigilantes. Students' radical slogans on July 13 attacked the very foundations of the Islamic Republic: "The people are miserable! The clerics are acting like gods!"[100] "Ansar (knife-wielding Hezbollah militias) commits crimes, the supreme leader supports the crimes," "Khamenei, shame on you, we want you to abdicate," "Khamenei, shame on you, let go of the country," "We want no despotic polity, we want no mercenary mulla," and "mulla's rule, overrule, overrule."[101] Some Tehran residents also joined the protests, shouting slogans like "Students, students, we support you. Iranians die before they accept humiliation" and "Army brothers, why kill brothers?" a slogan of the 1979 revolution.[102]

While students battled security forces around Tehran University, Basij militias and Hezbollah club-wielders rioted throughout the city, causing significant damage and injury. Some attacked and looted shops and banks in Tehran's business district. Some hardline Islamic militiamen carried automatic weapons and were supported by the security forces, according to reports.[103] Armed with clubs, chains, batons, and knives, the militias wore white shirts and were organized and operated in distinct groups. They attacked and injured spectators with automatic weapons fire and used obscenities against girls and women. Several uniformed individuals entered the clothing bazaar and told merchants to close their shops or face imminent attack. Within minutes, vigilantes arrived to set fire to shops that were still open. The remaining businesses—including banks, gas stations, shopping centers, office buildings, and the Tehran bazaar—shuttered their doors.[104]

The council representing students at the sit-in issued a statement declaring that the people knew full well that those behind the riots on July 13 were the same instigators that had attacked Tehran University's dormitory on July 9 with the intention of halting the reform process and defeating the president.[105] Other students bitterly criticized President Khatami for tricking them with empty promises and allowing the regime to crush their growing movement.[106]

Within days, as the government crackdown expanded, the language and message of official pronouncements changed from sympathy for the students to rebuke. The protesters were no longer "university students," but instead became "rioters and bandits" backed by terrorist groups.[107] Supreme Leader Ayatollah Khamenei stated, "The people will not allow acts of destruction and the Islamic Republic will repress it." His statement, read on national radio, blamed "bandits supported by bankrupt political groups and encouraged by foreign enemies" of being behind the unrest.[108] Khamenei later claimed in a sermon that the United States sought a new coup in Iran. "The head of the CIA said that big events would take place in Iran in 1999. They planned it. There were hidden hands behind the scenes directing this and they were waiting for a spark."[109]

President Khatami read a statement on state-controlled television, criticizing the degeneration of a peaceful protest into riots led by people with "devilish aims." The protests, he added, threatened national security and were "intended to attack the foundations of the system and lead the country into anarchy." He pledged to stop the protesters, saying, "We shall stand in their way."[110] Khatami's message characterized continued demonstrations as "deviations which will be repressed with force and determination." Some of the demonstrators' slogans "very clearly targeted the fundamental principles of the government and political progress," the president said. He accused student leaders of "attacking the foundations of the regime and of wanting to foment tensions and disorder. . . . The slogans of these groups are demagogic, provocative and aimed at creating social divisions and attacking national security."[111]

Other officials of the Islamic Republic joined in the condemnation. Hassan Rouhani, deputy speaker of parliament and secretary of the Supreme Security Council, warned a huge rally at Tehran University that "bandits and saboteurs" who clashed with the security forces and were behind the recent violent disturbances in Tehran could be executed.[112] "Those involved in the last days' riots, destruction of public property and attacks against the system will be punished as *mohareb* [fighters against God] and *mosfed* [people spreading corruption]," Rouhani declared.[113] "Among those arrested are insurgents, individuals with a long history of crime, people linked to defeated (antirevolutionary) groups and those who have somehow been fed by secret hands," he said, in an apparent reference to possible foreign involvement in the disturbances.[114] The intelligence ministry vowed to "uproot those opportunists and bandits" responsible for the bloody clashes between security forces and students at Tehran University[115] and appealed to citizens to turn in anyone involved.

At the same time, the regime mobilized its own supporters for a huge event in Tehran. The Organization for Islamic Propaganda called upon the populace to join a mass demonstration and march to the university on July 14. Hundreds of thousands of people took part in the official demonstration. The rally was broadcast on national television, and patriotic music played in the background. The slogans of the protests changed. "Death to America" replaced "death to dictators," wrote Geneive Abdo.[116]

The protests subsided, but repression against activists and protesters continued. The secret police arrested Manouchehr Mohammadi, an outspoken student dissident often interviewed on Persian-language broadcasts of Western radio shows. The intelligence ministry accused him of fomenting the recent unrest at the behest of exiled dissidents and foreign powers. Mohammadi and Mohajerinejad, a colleague, were charged with traveling to the United States and Turkey to meet with "counterrevolutionaries and so-called Western human rights groups."[117] In a report monitored by the BBC, Iranian television said that the interior ministry alleged that he met in the United States with "spies and fugitive Zionist elements" who helped him organize student groups to "spearhead disorder and violence."[118]

Several students disappeared during the antigovernment protests, including Fereshteh Alizadeh, Tara Haami, and Saeed Zinali.[119] Zinali's mother, Akram Neghabi, claimed that at least five other families were searching for their children who were arrested and then disappeared during the student protests.[120] Zinali was detained on July 14, 1999, in Tehran and has not been seen since. His mother and sister were arrested in 2010 by security forces, who confiscated their passports, money, computers, and books to prevent them from publicizing Zinali's case. Authorities refused to provide any information about his whereabouts, telling his mother in 2012 "to place herself in the situation of mothers whose sons went to war and never returned."[121]

Repression was also directed against those who had supported the reform movement and the dissidents. Some attorneys who defended activists and students were targeted, including two prominent lawyers, Shirin Ebadi and Mohsen Rahmani, who were arrested shortly before the first anniversary of the attacks. According to a report, they were held regarding alleged fake video cassettes that implicated leading officials in a number of incidents of terrorism.[122] Roozbeh Farahanipour, a journalist and leader of the Marze Por Gohar, and twelve other members of the party, were arrested after they joined the protests at Tehran University. Farahanipour was tortured and held in solitary confinement for thirty-six days. He was charged with endangering national security and insulting the supreme leader. He fled the country before his trial.[123]

Some leaders and activists of the secular student organizations were rearrested or kept in jail, often in solitary confinement under harsh conditions. Some claimed that they were tortured. Akbar Mohammadi wrote to Mahmud Hashemi-Shahrudi, the judiciary chief, and complained that he was tortured and treated badly after his arrest. "I was hit with an electric cable, hung up by a rope and violently beaten," he charged. He went deaf in one ear, lost two toenails, and suffered kidney pain. "The prison doctor ordered me to hospital but until now I have not been taken there and I continue to suffer," Mohammadi said.[124] He faced execution for his part in the July protests, but his sentence was reduced to fifteen years. Freed in 2005, he was rearrested the following year. He went on hunger strike and died in prison in July 2006, while his lawyer was denied access to visit him.[125]

Several protesters, including Mohammadi, Mohajerinejad, Afshari, and Batebi, who had spent time in prison, were able to escape the country and tell their stories. Batebi was arrested during a demonstration when he held up the bloody T-shirt of a fellow student to warn other students against marching. The picture was published on the cover of the *Economist*, leading to Batebi's arrest.[126] He was kept in solitary confinement for seventeen months. Authorities tortured and threatened him with execution if he did not admit to falsehoods, including that the famous T-shirt was stained with paint or animal blood.[127] He refused. Batebi's trial lasted for just three minutes while the prosecutor presented the photo of him as evidence that he had jeopardized the reputation of the Islamic Republic of Iran.[128] He was initially sentenced to death, but the supreme leader commuted his sentence to fifteen years in prison. Batebi's sentence was further reduced to ten years. He was temporarily released for medical care in 2008 and managed to escape the country, according to an interview he gave the *New York Times*.[129]

Students who were released from jail faced expulsion from their schools and workplaces, which created economic hardship for them and their families. Hamid Alizadeh, a medical student who had completed his studies and his internship at Shariati Hospital, was arrested and imprisoned during the July 1999 student protests. He was given a ten-year suspended jail sentence and told that he would have to serve the sentence if he engaged in political activities. He could not get his degree because he was expelled from the university and was not allowed to submit his thesis.[130] Dr. Farzad Hamidi, a new medical school graduate, lost his license to practice medicine due to his political activities with the outlawed National Association of Iranian Students.[131]

The suffering, injuries, and death produced by six days of conflict were substantial. According to a human rights organization report, seven people were killed in the course of the protests.[132] One of the dead was Mahmoud Khabasian, a businessman, who died of a gunshot wound to his head.[133] The greatest repercussions were felt in Tehran, where hundreds of students were injured and arrested. According to *Neshat,* many dormitory windows were broken. Students' personal belongings—including computers and refrigerators—were destroyed. One student complained that his books were burned.[134] A university official stated that ten dormitories, totalling eight hundred rooms, were completely destroyed.[135] At a ceremony reopening the university, on September 20, the mayor of Tehran, Morteza Alviri, said, "The reopening of the Tehran University dorms marks the end of the dirty face of violence in academia." He also noted, "We worked 24 hours a day to remove the ugly remains of July 9."[136]

In the aftermath of the protests, authorities attempted to intimidate the opposition by imposing stiff sentences. A Revolutionary Court sentenced four protesters to death for involvement in the demonstrations.[137] The court later commuted the death sentences.[138] Ezzat Ebrahimnejad, a former student and visitor killed during attacks on the dormitory, was prosecuted. He was tried in absentia, on charges he participated in an unlawful demonstration that led to sedition, and chanted slogans, and threw stones at security forces on July 8, 1999—all of which qualified as acts against national security.[139] A number of students and activists were sentenced to jail terms and tortured during imprisonment, including Tabarzadi, Akbar Mohammadi, Manouchehr Mohammadi, and Mohajerinejad, among others.[140] Protesters in other cities were also tried and given jail terms. For example, in Tabriz, a Revolutionary Court sentenced twenty-one people, including twelve students, to up to nine years' imprisonment.[141] Some of the detained students went on a hunger strike to protest their treatment and the fact that many of them were housed with murderers and drug traffickers.[142]

In contrast, the agents responsible for the attack on the student dormitory that killed several and injured hundreds faced little sanction. The supreme leader relieved Brigadier General Hedayat Lotfian of duty as head of the law enforcement forces ten days before the first anniversary of the attack in order to curtail commemorations and appease students. A military court acquitted General Farhad Nazari who directed the police chief and seventeen other officers involved in the attacks.[143] Fifteen plainclothes agents, accused of attacking local universities, were "acquitted on charges of acting against state security and therefore freed."[144] One report revealed that ninety-eight policemen were arrested for their role in the raid on student dormitories,[145] but most of them were freed. Only two policemen were found guilty. One was found guilty of stealing an electric razor from a dormitory, fined $125, and sentenced to ninety-one days in prison. Farhad Arjomandi, the other policeman, was found guilty of insubordination and sentenced to two years in prison for refusing to obey orders to beat students during the attack.[146] Students had considered him a hero.

The fate of the vigilantes who were arrested provoked national attention. A Revolutionary Court acquitted fifteen of them. "The suspects were released . . . after being found innocent because there were no private plaintiffs," the court chief concluded.[147] In 2001, a report of the acquittals provoked a strong reaction from a group of Majles deputies: 159, representing a simple majority in the parliament, expressed "deep regret and dissatisfaction" with the verdict in a petition to Ayatollah Mahmud Hashemi-Shahrudi, the judiciary chief. The deputies declared to the reformist-dominated Majles, "The crime which claimed one life, had one eye gouged out and bones broken, and oppressed students thrown out of the building has not healed the old wounds after two years."[148] A student leader at Tehran University, in a speech in 2013 given in the presence of the supreme leader, complained that the principal agents responsible for the oppression of students had not yet been identified fourteen years after the attacks on the student dormitory.[149]

Ideological Shift and a New Round of Protests

The growing influence of secular democratic students, state repression, and the reformists' failure to enact change led to a shift in the politics of the OCU. The organization supported reformist candidates in the 2000 Majles election and President Khatami in 2001, but internal divisions and conflicts beset the OCU and the Islamic student associations. Radical students advocated a boycott of the election, arguing that the president was required by the constitution to abide by the rules of the theocratic system and thus was unable to carry out the people's demands. This ideological shift garnered enough backing that the majority of the OCU's members favored withdrawing support from the reformist faction. At a rally, Afshari, OCU's leader, called for a referendum on the Islamic Republic's foundation, the rule of *"velayat-e-faghieh,* or the supreme leader in December 2000 leading to his arrest."[150] The majority of rank-and-file university students accepted this radical position and opposed the entire Islamic establishment.

A survey carried out by the OCU at Bu Ali Sina University asked students in the provincial capital of Hamedan to vote for one of three constitutions drafted after the monarchy's ouster. Ninety-five percent favored the provisional revolutionary government's first draft of the constitution (1979), which had no provision for the *velayat-e faghieh.*[151]

Early in the first decade of the twenty-first century, student ideology and politics further diversified and radicalized. For the first time in years, universities witnessed the rise of a group of students espousing Marxist ideology, which had declined in appeal after the universities were closed in the early 1980s. Marxist students advocated socialism, social justice for workers, and struggles against imperialism. The Islamic regime initially tolerated the new radicals, perhaps because they differed from reformist students who sought to democratize the political system.[152] These ideological changes within the student ranks emerged during a period when both the presidency and the Majles were controlled by reformists that proved incapable of changing the political system or expanding democratic rights.

In the context of growing radicalism, a new contentious issue emerged to activate students. A proposal to privatize some universities ignited another round of student protests in 2003. Tehran students mobilized on June 10 to condemn the plan. Thousands protested for ten consecutive nights, often fighting security forces and vigilantes. Students and some residents demonstrated against the regime in at least twenty other major cities, including Tabriz, Mashhad, Isfahan, Shiraz, Hamedan, Yazd,

Orumieh, Sabzevar, and Kermanshah. Student associations vowed to continue the protests until July 9, the fourth anniversary of the 1999 student protests. Chanting the most extreme slogans since the revolution, students disregarded the threat of imprisonment for even mild criticism of the supreme leader: "Khamenei, the traitor, must be hanged,"[153] "Death to dictators," "Dictator, shame on you, give up the reign," "The clerical regime is nearing its end," "The people are miserable! The clerics are acting like gods," "Freedom, freedom," "Democracy, democracy," "Justice, freedom, this is the slogan of the nation," "Khatami resign."[154]

Fighting vigilantes armed with sticks and chains, students quickly attracted support from the Tehran public. Older government workers joined the students, as did women in billowing black cloaks from poorer neighborhoods.[155] Thousands looked on, sometimes clapping along with the protesters' chants. Residents near the university hospital left open their doors to offer shelter in the event that security forces attacked the protesting students.[156] The protests extended to Tehran Pars, a poor neighborhood, and Narmak, both of which were located several miles from the university.[157] Security forces fired machine guns into the air to disperse protesters and attacked middle-class supporters and bystanders, injuring many. Shiraz vigilantes killed Ali Moini, a student.[158]

A large number of Majles deputies sympathized with the students, and 166 deputies signed a statement condemning vigilante violence against the protesters.[159] They deplored an attack on a dormitory at Allameh Tabatabaei University and the arrest of students and political activists. Four Majles deputies criticized the judiciary and police officials for allegedly failing to deal with the vigilantes. When the judiciary threatened to arrest the four deputies for provoking the protests, they staged a two-day "self-imprisonment" in the Majles building to protest the treatment of the students. One of the deputies, Haghighatjoo, told reporters that "the sit-in was a protest against the detainment of the students, insufficient information about their whereabouts and their treatment during interrogations."[160]

In reaction, hardliners and the media blamed the United States for the protests, labeling the demonstrators hooligans and mercenaries. Khamenei publicly accused the United States of trying to turn disgruntled people into mercenaries in order to cause trouble. He threatened additional repression, warning, "Leaders do not have the right to have any pity whatsoever for the mercenaries of the enemy."[161]

Security forces arrested four thousand people across the country.[162] Tehran prosecutor Saeed Mortazavi stated that the judiciary would also deal with any Majles deputy found guilty of instigating the unrest.[163] Officials also declared that most people who stirred up trouble were "thugs and hooligans" and that very few students were among those arrested.[164] Some hardliners called for harsh punishment of "hooligans" arrested in the protests. One senior cleric, Ayatollah Mohammad Yazdi, said that "those taking part in the current wave of protests were not bona fide students but hooligans who were instigated, and possibly even paid, by the United States." He urged the judiciary to show the offenders no mercy. "The judiciary should treat them like the opponents of God, *mohareb.*"[165] In the end, Ayatollah Khamenei ordered the prosecutor general to exercise clemency toward dozens of jailed students, notably those who had "dissociated themselves from the trouble-makers" in the protests and declared their loyalty to the Islamic regime.[166]

Subsequently, student politics radicalized further. Groups of students in Tehran, Isfahan, and Mashhad declared a hunger strike to demand the release of their classmates who had been arrested. One hundred six student leaders wrote President Khatami, warning that the Islamic regime would face a full-blown confrontation unless political prisoners were released and a protest rally scheduled for July 9 was allowed to proceed. "We openly declare that these words are the final words of dialogue between the student movement and the ruling establishment. . . . We call on you . . . to react before it is too late and adopt a reasonable solution, or otherwise have the courage to resign so that you do not justify oppressive policies and allow students to settle their accounts with the establishment."[167] Khatami did not resign, and students boycotted the 2005 presidential election. Student politics moved increasingly to the left, as revealed by a student demonstration on the official Student Day *(shanzdah azar)* at Tehran University in December 2006. During the event, students called for freedom, equality, and an end to political repression. A placard read, "The student movement is allied with the labor and women's movements." Another stated, "Even if bullets and sedition rain down from the skies of the university, the movement will continue."[168]

Summary and Conclusions

Iranian students stood at the forefront of the pursuit for democracy during the revolution and after the establishment of the Islamic Republic. Early on, students chose passive resistance by refusing to participate in religious activities and obligations. Students in major universities mobilized after the revolution and resisted the imposition of a new authoritarian and antidemocratic system, but they lost the battle when the regime closed the universities for some thirty-two months and purged dissident students from campuses. Students became the principal victims of repression, and student political activities declined sharply in the following years. It appeared that the cultural revolution's repression and purges had success-fully forced Iran's universities to accept the theocracy. However, this understanding was proven to be inaccurate. As events in the 1990s demon-strated, complex factors and developments had altered student orientation and political activities to oppose the Islamic theocracy.

Important factors prepared conditions for renewed student collective action and opposition. The expansion of universities and the growing number of students in higher education enhanced students' capacity to mobilize and act collectively. Political repression and disciplinary action against students generated grievances on university campuses. The rising levels of unemployment among college graduates—in part due to an over-supply of highly educated people—caused concerns among students about their future. Widespread cronyism and corruption created problems for most students because they lacked ties to powerful individuals to obtain prestigious jobs. Factional political conflicts sparked attacks against the OCU in the early 1990s, generated opportunities for students to mobilize, and set the stage for opposition.

Students played an important role in the electoral victory of reformists in the latter part of the 1990s. Students intensified their struggles for democracy when reformists assumed power. They mobilized and advo-cated greater political freedom and civil liberties. Over four years, students launched two major series of protests that seriously challenged the Islamic regime. Reformist student organizations had greater resources and support from the government and mainly attacked the regime's conservative fac-tion. In contrast, a handful of secular democratic students began a struggle for democracy, adopted an uncompromising stance and determination, and confronted the entire regime. They battled the repressive forces in the context of rising social tensions.

The majority of the student population became radicalized, in part because of state repression. While some student demands and slogans resembled those of the 1979 revolution, others were new. Radicalized stu-dents quickly broke from the reformists and the Islamic system, demon-strating the growing polarization and mounting political conflicts within the Islamic Republic. The regime's reformist faction, in power at the time of the protests, initially sympathized with the students' grievances. But as students were radicalized, reformists refused to endorse their demands. This refusal, along with some divisions among the students, and their failure to mobilize broad segments of the population to their cause, facilitated the repression of students. Students were eventually demobilized by repression and forced to abandon their protests.

Nevertheless, as vanguards of the struggles for democracy, students succeeded in challenging the economic, political, and ideological foundations of the Islamic Republic. Reflecting the contradictions and conflicts of the Iranian state and society, students sounded the alarm and raised the voices of democratic forces. During the conflicts, many students abandoned hope of working within the existing framework of the Islamic Republic and demonstrated the means and the path by which the people could challenge the system. Several years later, the Green Movement took up that challenge.

CHAPTER SEVEN

The Rise and Demise
of the Green Movement

THE VOLATILE AMALGAM of political exclusion, heightened repression, unbridled corruption, and unfulfilled promises rooted in the revolutionary struggles set the stage for a new round of conflicts by the end of the Islamic Republic's third decade. After Mahmoud Ahmadinejad was elected president in 2005, he demonstrated that he had no interest in liberalizing the Islamic system. He suppressed civil liberties and political freedoms and politicized numerous social, cultural, and economic issues. These restrictive policies mobilized the reformist faction and large segments of the population to challenge Ahmadinejad and the conservatives during the 2009 presidential campaign. When Ahmadinejad was declared the winner by a huge margin, a substantial part of the opposition, organized as the Green Movement, claimed election fraud and protested the official count and outcome. Protests erupted in every major city and persisted for twenty months. The regime arrested thousands of demonstrators and refused to rescind the election results, radicalizing many protesters to demand fundamental change. The protesters' radicalization, in turn, emboldened the relatively moderate leaders of the reformist opposition, who moved beyond the election results and demanded the political freedom and popular sovereignty that had been promised during the revolutionary struggles and enshrined in the constitution.

In the context of democratization movements in the region, calls by the Green Movement leaders to protest the very nature of the Islamic rule alarmed conservatives and led them to silence the leaders. After President Mubarak of Egypt was overthrown in February 2011, Supreme Leader Ayatollah Khamenei made a fateful decision to place the opposition leaders under house arrest and prevent them from communicating with their supporters. The regime dissolved the largest reformist political parties, arrested many leading reformists and dissidents, and suppressed the symptoms of larger conflicts in the Islamic Republic.

The Tenth Presidential Election

In 2009, the Guardian Council followed a pattern familiar from the previous election, dismissing nearly all the 470-plus would-be candidates and approving only 4. Mahmoud Ahmadinejad, the incumbent, and Mir Hossein Mousavi, prime minster from 1981 to 1989, emerged to represent the two major political factions. The outcome of the elections would have significant consequences for the future of the Islamic Republic.

Ahmadinejad enjoyed a number of advantages. As the former mayor of Tehran and member of the Revolutionary Guard, he had maintained ties with the latter organization and its paramilitary constituency, the Basij, after he took office in 2005. He funneled hundreds of government contracts to companies associated with the Revolutionary Guard.[1] One construction subsidiary of the Guard received $7 billion in 2006 alone to develop gas and oil fields and refurbish the Tehran metro.[2] Not surprisingly, the Guard and the Basij backed Ahmadinejad's reelection. The highest bureaucratic echelon also provided considerable support, because during his first term, he replaced ten thousand government employees and all thirty governors with new appointees loyal to him.[3]

Other officials of the Islamic Republic likewise threw their support behind Ahmadinejad. The Supreme Leader Ayatollah Khamenei repeatedly stated his support for Ahmadinejad in various private meetings, commenting, "Ahmadinejad's defeat is my defeat."[4] Such statements by Khamenei led officials to mobilize their resources to ensure Ahmadinejad's victory, according to dissidents.[5] The conservative Society of Combatant Clergy, which had supported right-wing candidates in the past, did not support any of the candidates,[6] although some powerful senior clerics, including Mahdavi Kani, backed Ahmadinejad.[7]

Ahmadinejad possibly gained some support from poorer segments of the population because of his humble background and increased subsidies the government provided to low-income families. As president, he had access to substantial resources and promoted his campaign by distributing cash to supporters on his provincial travels.[8] The provision of cash and the distribution of foodstuffs including potatoes among his supporters before the election softened the negative impact of the country's poor GDP growth rate during 2008 and early 2009. Ahmadinejad also had direct access to state-run media and received an extra forty-five minutes to address the nation before the election.

The reformist camp appeared in disarray at the outset of the campaign but managed to improve its image and attract popular support. What Mousavi lacked in charisma he made up for with a good reputation for managing the economy when he served as prime minister during the Iran-Iraq war. He gradually garnered broad support from students, women, and sizeable segments of the middle class and bazaar merchants with his message of greater freedom, gender equality, improved economic conditions, and an end to corruption. He also received contributions from wealthy businessmen interested in defeating Ahmadinejad. In the absence of access to state media, Mousavi organized effective rallies by relying on the Internet and cell phones to reach young people and get out the vote. Cell phone text messaging reached 110 million per day, which was double the preelection period in 2005.[9]

Mousavi's campaign also benefitted from his popular and charismatic wife, Zahra Rahnavard,[10] a proponent of greater rights and political power for women. Her presence often energized the public. When she addressed a rally in Tehran, thousands of people chanted, "Mousavi, Rahnavard, equal rights for men and women."[11] She proclaimed a revolution within the revolution and promised to modernize the country. "You are looking for a new identity for Iran that will bring you pride in the world, an Iran that is free, developing, and full of vitality. We seek peaceful relations with the rest of the world, not senseless attacks and uncalculated friendships."[12]

Ahmadinejad appeared to have momentum early in the campaign. He stressed the significance of the revolution's values and serving the deprived and the downtrodden. He was articulate, animated, and energetic during the June 3 debate with rival Mousavi.[13] He touted his domestic achievements and defended his confrontational stance vis-à-vis the West and his denial of the Holocaust. He claimed success for his foreign policy, claiming that after twenty-seven years of planning regime change in Iran, the United States had now given up that goal. He also took credit for the fact that 118 member countries of the Non-Aligned Movement supported Iran's nuclear program. Criticized for failing to reduce certain social and economic ills, he countered that those problems also existed when Rafsanjani and reformists were in power, and especially when Mousavi was premier in the 1980s. Ahmadinejad vigorously attacked corruption by former elites, specifically Rafsanjani and Nategh Nouri, accusing them of becoming "billionaires" since the revolution. Such corrupt people were part of Mousavi's political circle and base of support, he asserted. He also charged that Zahra Rahnavard's doctorate degree was awarded at a university that lacked a qualifying exam. Addressing censorship and political repression, Ahmadinejad stated that during Mousavi's rule, the country had only one newspaper critical of the government, and no Majles deputy dared to say anything against the prime minister.[14]

For his part, Mousavi promised to introduce change. He declared that he was concerned about Iran's international standing and internal problems. He criticized Ahmadinejad's foreign policy, which, he charged, isolated Iran. He chided Ahmadinejad's confrontational policies with the West and his denial of the Holocaust, which tarnished Iran's international reputation. He also criticized Ahmadinejad's claims that the United States was being destroyed and that Israel was near collapse. Mousavi denounced Ahmadinejad's surveillance policies, repression of students, press censorship, and treatment of some of the clergy, noting that the government had created a division between those who were treated as insiders and those who were considered outsiders. He also promised to put an end to corruption and cronyism in the system and accused Ahmadinejad of mismanaging the nation's economy. Mousavi debunked Ahmadinejad's claims of accomplishments, charging him with breaking laws, disrespecting the people, and moving the country toward a dictatorship.[15]

Popular enthusiasm for Mousavi was unmistakable. The televised presidential debate between the incumbent president and his challenger energized many citizens and catapulted Mousavi to front-runner status. In an unprecedented event, Mousavi's Tehran supporters protested existing conditions in dramatic form on June 8, donning green sashes and creating a human chain that stretched nearly the entire length of the city.[16] The chain of protesters blocked traffic for miles along one of Tehran's main boulevards.[17]

Faced with such popular mobilization for Mousavi, the government resorted to intimidation and repression. Yadollah Javani, political chief of the Revolutionary Guard, warned shortly before the voting that the Guard would crush any "revolution" against the Islamic regime by the "Green Movement."[18] The communication ministry blocked text messaging throughout the country twenty-four hours before the polls opened.[19] Tehran city crews removed any sign of political rallies the day before the voting, tearing down posters as police tried to prevent reform supporters from wearing green.[20] On election eve, authorities disconnected the three hundred landlines servicing Mousavi's headquarters and closed down websites belonging to reformists and their adherents.[21] Government agents began arresting well-known activists and dissidents.[22] Security forces occupied newspapers offices and changed the headlines of publications to ensure that their reports would be progovernment.[23]

Prominent public figures called attention to some problems in the campaign, the opposition reported. Former president Khatami claimed that all the resources—including propaganda, implementation, and supervision— were in the hands of one side and that the other side was defenseless.[24] Seyyed Hossein Mousavi Tabrizi, a cleric and head of the Association of Researchers and Teachers of Qom, charged that Ayatollah Jannati, head of the Guardian Council that supervised the elections, was not neutral and had taken the president's side.[25] Mousavi and another presidential candidate, Mehdi Karroubi, former speaker of the Majles, warned shortly before the election that there were signs of plans to interfere in the voting.[26]

On election day, June 12, voter turnout was "unprecedented," according to Interior Minister Sadeq Mahsoul.[27] Approximately 85 percent of eligible voters went to the polls, the highest rate in the history of the Islamic Republic.[28] Some voters had never before participated in the political process, dismissing it as undemocratic or ineffective. Polling places remained open until midnight, six hours later than usual, to accommodate the huge turnout.[29] Voters in warm regions of the country stood for hours in extreme heat to cast their ballots. Urban supporters of the Green Movement imaginatively displayed their candidate's signature color. Men sprayed their hair green in Tehran and flashed green ribbons wrapped around their wrists, while women wore green scarves and matching shoes to express their support.[30] Pro-Mousavi voters filled the streets even in south Tehran, a working-class area predicted to support Ahmadinejad.[31]

Observers and the opposition camp reported many irregularities in the election process. In a departure from previous elections, journalists were prevented from asking voters their candidate preference.[32] The government disrupted communication between Mousavi's headquarters and his aides in polling stations. The candidate alleged that some of his representatives were blocked from entering polling stations, and one of his top aides charged that a shortage of ballots in some polling stations in northwestern and southern Iran was deliberate.[33] In a statement to the Guardian Council, Mousavi declared that at least six major violations had occurred during voting, including the fact that many election monitors did not receive valid identification cards from the Interior Ministry. He also claimed that in many branches, ballot boxes were not inspected to ensure that they were empty before voting began. Mousavi further accused the government of dispatching fourteen thousand mobile voting booths to collect ballots where voting stations were already in operation, sometimes only ten meters away. Opposition monitors were unable to inspect these mobile booths.[34]

Repression continued during and after the voting. Antiriot troops were stationed near sensitive areas in Tehran the day after the balloting. "Police stormed the headquarters of Iran's largest reformist party, the Islamic Iran Participation Front, and arrested several top reformist leaders."[35] The Interior Ministry banned all rallies and stated that the government would not tolerate any political gathering or rallies until the final results were known.[36] University exams throughout the country were postponed from June 13 until the following month, probably to demobilize students.[37]

The manner in which the election results were announced was highly unusual. In the absence of an electronic voting system, ballots were counted by hand. Nevertheless, the state news agency, IRNA, announced a preliminary result two hours before the polls closed, naming Ahmadinejad the winner. Ahmadinejad's supporters in Tehran began celebrating at dawn.[38] The Interior Ministry announced the official results a few hours later, proclaiming Ahmadinejad's winning margin at 63 percent of the votes compared with Mousavi's 34 percent.

Another unusual aspect of the election was the swift entry of Ayatollah Khamenei and other officials into the political arena. Rather than waiting the required three days to certify election results,[39] Khamenei issued a message to state television the day after the election, congratulating Ahmadinejad on his landslide victory. The supreme leader urged the nation to unite behind the president, claiming that "the miraculous hand of God" was evident in the "great epic" results of the election.[40] Ahmadinejad's victory was a "feast that can guarantee the country's progress, national security, and lasting joy."[41] But, Khamenei cautioned, "I assume that enemies intend to eliminate the sweetness of the election with their hostile provocation."[42] The Guardian Council declared the election to be among the cleanest in the thirty-year history of the Islamic Republic.[43] Ahmadinejad celebrated his victory in a speech on June 14, mocking outraged protesters as "dirt and dust" *(khas O khashak)*.[44]

The opposition immediately rejected the election results, calling attention to irregularities. The Committee to Protect the People's Votes, a group formed by the three opposition candidates, announced that they would not accept the results.[45] Mousavi appeared at a news conference as the first election returns were released on June 12 and urged Khamenei to reject them. The next day, he took an even bolder stand, declaring, "The officially announced results of the tenth presidential election are shocking.

People who waited in long lines and witnessed the voting process, and know who they voted for, are watching in complete disbelief the unfolding of magic tricks by election officials and the state radio and television."[46] Mousavi sent an open letter to the Qom grand clerics, challenging the supreme leader's position on the election results.[47] He instructed his supporters to resist a "governance of lies and dictatorship."[48] Karroubi insisted that the only solution was to cancel the election results completely. Twenty-seven moderate clerics in the Association of Combatant Clergy declared that the vote was rigged and called for it to be annulled.[49]

The public suspected fraud for a number of reasons. People from all walks of life had mobilized on a large scale at huge opposition rallies. Residents of major cities had witnessed green paraphernalia associated with Mousavi's campaign distributed widely in neighborhoods, on streets, in schools, and at workplaces for several days before and on election day. The very large, countrywide voter turnout pointed to mobilization by the opposition. Some government officials admitted that even some soldiers in the army barracks and some members of the Revolutionary Guard had supported the opposition. According to Ali Reza Zakani, a Majles deputy, of 800 votes cast at the Iranian radio and television station, 750 were for Mousavi.[50] Important government officials, including Ali Larijani, hardline speaker of the Majles, and his brother Sadegh Larijani, a member of the Guardian Council, called Mousavi soon after the election to congratulate him, concluding from popular expression of voter preferences that he had won.[51]

The government's actions immediately following the voting compounded popular mistrust. Many citizens questioned the authorities' decision to send all ballot boxes to the capital for counting instead of counting the votes locally, in the presence of all parties. The quick declaration of victory by a sizeable margin was unusual after such an unprecedented voter turnout. The supreme leader broke with past practice by not waiting for the Guardian Council to legally certify the election results before issuing congratulatory remarks to the victor. Widespread voter complaints of election fraud were made to the council, but the government refused to establish an independent body to investigate these allegations, further eroding popular trust in the election results.

Events on election day and afterward raised further suspicions for many Iranians that the election was fraudulent. First, election results were announced by IRNA, the official news agency, two hours before polls closed in Tehran and other cities. Second, security forces began making arrests on the night of June 12 (election day) before results were announced, using the warrants that had been issued on June 9, three days before the election. The timing of these events strongly suggested that an electoral "coup" had been planned in advance, and many accused the military supporters of Ayatollah Khamenei with having been involved in rigging the election.[52] Third, the regime presented no credible evidence of Ahmadinejad's victory or of a fair, free election, leading many to conclude that no such evidence existed. Instead, the regime responded to protests with months of severe repression. Security forces arrested thousands of demonstrators, shut down at least fourteen newspapers, issued warnings to dozens of other publications, and even banned shouts of *"Allahu Akbar"* (God is great). Fourth, the regime, which had been accustomed to mobilize public support during previous crises, failed to mount a single progovernment demonstration for more than six and a half months, reinforcing popular doubts about the election results.

Finally, after the election, three high-ranking officials of the Islamic Republic revealed specific incidents that suggested improper intervention and possibly fraud in the electoral process. Roohallah Jomeie, IRNA deputy, disclosed that the president's office had pressured the official news agency to declare Ahmadinejad the winner even before polls closed. General Moshfegh, deputy director of intelligence for the Sarallah military base, and General Mohammad Ali Jaafari, commander of the Revolutionary Guard, separately revealed in closed meetings that the Guard had interfered directly in the election. (See Chapter 8.)

Popular Protests and Repertoires of Repression

The official election results outraged broad segments of the population who had voted and told others about their preferred candidate via the Internet, cell phones, and informal networks in neighborhoods, schools, and workplaces. They ignored the Revolutionary Guard's preelection warning against a velvet revolution and demanded to know "What happened to my vote?" Several hundred demonstrators gathered near the Interior Ministry the day after the election, chanting, "The government has lied to the people." Protesters set tires ablaze as antiriot police fought back with clubs and smashed cars.[53] Tehran University students demonstrated on their campuses, chanting "Death to the dictator."[54]

In reaction, thousands of antiriot police charged into the biggest concentration of protesters in Tehran, using batons and tear gas; one person was reportedly shot dead.[55] Security forces and progovernment militias damaged university dorms in Tehran, and a report noted that five students—two women and three men—were killed.[56] Four days after the elections, the leading student organization, Daftar Tahkim Vahdat, announced that seven students in Tehran and Shiraz had been killed.[57] The attacks were not restricted to campuses. Mustafa Kashani Resa was shouting political slogans when security agents hurled him from the roof of Mousavi's headquarters in Tehran, killing him.[58]

The opposition reacted swiftly to the declared election results. E-mails from the Green Movement posted on most news websites announced a silent protest march on Sunday, June 14, in Tehran and over thirty major cities.

> Tomorrow afternoon at 5, Ahmadinejad, the president elected by the Supreme Leader, will celebrate his fake victory. But Iranians who are loyal to their vote and are opposed to this coup, will support Mr. Karroubi and Mousavi, the two coalition leaders who are the winners of the election. We will march at the same time on Valiasr Street in Tehran, between Valiasr Square and Tajrish Square. We will hold green and white napkins in a sign of unity. Kurds, Azeris, Baluchis, Turkmen, Bakhtiaris, Arabs, Persians, Sunnis, Shiites, Christians, Jews, Zoroastrians, Dervishes, Baha'is—this country belongs to you. . . . If we allow this coup to prevail today, we will have to grieve for many years.[59]

Thousands marched silently in large cities across the country. The opposition called for another march the following day.

After state radio and television repeatedly broadcast the government's ban on protests, Mousavi admonished his supporters not to participate in protests without an official permit. The populace largely ignored both. The June 15 demonstration was one of the largest in modern Iranian history and exposed the yawning gulf between the populace and the rulers of the Islamic Republic. Protests erupted in every major city. Tehran's mayor estimated that city's crowd at three million.[60] A broad coalition of major segments of Iranian society came together, ranging from "the trendy, young, sunglassed ladies of north Tehran" to the poor, who allegedly supported Ahmadinejad.[61] Students, women in chadors, older adults, shopkeepers, government employees, ordinary people, and even turbaned mullahs marched to Azadi (freedom) Square. Many wore green and shouted, "Mousavi, we support you. We will die, but retrieve our votes." Others chanted, "We are Mousavi's green army," "Death to injustice *(Marg bar zolm)*," and "Tanks, guns, Basijis, you have no effect now."[62] Still others reversed the words of Ahmadinejad's dismissal of protesters who challenged the outcome of the election, proclaiming, "Dirt and dust are you, it is you who are the enemy of Iran."[63]

At the opposition's urging, residents of Tehran and large cities climbed to their rooftops after dark and shouted protests, including *"Allahu Akbar,"* a favorite slogan from the 1979 revolution. The shouts rang out at exactly 9:00 p.m., the same hour that protesters had chanted the slogan years before, in the last phase of the revolution in 1979. On both occasions, the chant's antidespotic message proclaimed that God was greater than earthly tyranny. The shouts were a reminder to others of the power of resistance against a former regime and a veiled call for another revolution.

The government introduced new, widespread repertoires of repression in an effort to head off further mass demonstrations. Police briefly placed Mousavi and Karroubi under house arrest and sealed off their headquarters in an effort to demobilize the opposition. They also arrested roughly one hundred well-known reformist figures in Tehran and detained more than one hundred prominent civic figures in Tabriz. The government also closed the university in Tabriz to demobilize students and announced across the country that the universities could not guarantee students' safety and that students must leave. Security forces and plainclothes individuals attacked students in Tehran University dormitories with various weapons, arresting and injuring students. Fifty students were unaccounted for by June 23.[64] The security forces threw some students from balconies.[65] In some cases, they buried slain protesters without notifying their families.[66]

Repression and mistreatment of students provoked strong condemnation. Students rallied and held sit-ins at universities across the country, demanding the release of fellow students, some seventy of whom had been jailed. Fifty-seven professors and lawyers issued a statement that called for the punishment of "aggressors to the holy vicinity of the university campuses and dormitories in cities across the nation."[67] The dean of Shiraz University resigned in protest,[68] as did 120 professors at prestigious Tehran University and the entire chemistry department at Sharif University.[69] Even Ali Larijani, conservative speaker of the Majles, condemned the police and militia attacks on student dormitories.

Threatened by the scale of the protests, Ayatollah Khamenei sought to calm the situation and appease the opposition. He called on the Guardian Council to "precisely consider" the complaints, even though he had already approved the election results. He also ordered state radio to repeat his statement every fifteen minutes.[70] The Guardian Council launched a review of 646 election-related complaints[71] and offered to conduct a random partial recount of 10 percent of the ballots, while rejecting demands to cancel the vote.[72] Ayatollah Ahmad Jannati, chair of the Guardian Council, warned that if they failed to discover fraud in the electoral process, Mousavi could be sentenced to up to three years in prison for libel.

The actions of some members of the Guardian Council, whose budget had increased fifteenfold under Ahmadinejad, gave the appearance that they had taken sides and favored the incumbent.[73] Not surprisingly, opposition leaders did not trust the council. Mousavi opposed a recount because some council members had campaigned for Ahmadinejad,[74] an issue that was confirmed several years later by Mohsen Esmailie, a member of the Guardian Council.[75] Former President Khatami called for an independent, competent commission to render a fair judgment. Former President Hashemi Rafsanjani, powerful head of the Assembly of Experts, sided with the opposition and refused to endorse the election results. Khatami and Rafsanjani had criticized the student protests in 1999 but now supported the people in the wake of the presidential election. Even Hadi Khamenei, the supreme leader's brother, a cleric and former Majles deputy, endorsed the appointment of an impartial committee to probe the election results and provide a full public accounting.[76]

The public continued to reject the official outcome. The Green Movement organized large demonstrations on June 16 in Tehran and other major cities, including Isfahan, Shiraz, Tabriz, Rasht, and Mashhad. Protesters wearing green marched from Valiasr to Park Way in Tehran, shouting, "Where is my vote?" "*You* are dirt and dust, *you* are the enemy of this land," and "Death to the dictator." Marchers came from all walks of life and included students, women, merchants, mullahs, and even some members of the country's elite families. Protests continued in the next few days. In one case, Faezeh Hashemi, daughter of Ayatollah Hashemi Rafsanjani, joined the march and addressed the protesters.[77] Her appearance sparked chants, "Hashemi, Mousavi, support, support" *(Hashemi, Mousavi, hemayat)*.

The government routinely threatened and repressed the protesters. The Basij attacked at night, beating, looting, and sometimes gunning down protesters they had tracked during the day.[78] Mohammad Reza Habibi, prosecutor of Isfahan province, warned that those responsible for postelection unrest could face the death penalty under Islamic law.[79] "We warn the few elements controlled by foreigners who to try to disrupt domestic security by inciting individuals to destroy and to commit arson that the Islamic penal code for such individuals waging war against God is execution."[80] In one week, the state arrested hundreds of people. On a single day, June 20, the government detained at least 457 people.[81]

Young people organized unofficial militias in some neighborhoods to defend themselves against the Basij. An unofficial "commander" took responsibility for each street and met every afternoon to prepare for the evening's battle.[82] Some protesters spread oil on the streets to upend Basij motorbikes and then beat up fallen riders. Older supporters stayed hidden indoors but hurled ashtrays, vases, and other items at the Basij.[83]

The protesters' slogans targeted the dominant conservative faction of the Islamic regime. Most revolved around issues of votes and dictatorship. Protesters in large cities, chanted, "Where is my vote?" and "Death to the dictator."[84] Some displayed large banners that read, "The epic of *Khas O khashak*" or shouted, "*You* are dirt and dust; *you* are the enemy of this land" *(Khas o khashak tu-ee, doshman-e in khak tu-ee)*. Others called, "Mousavi, take back my vote."[85]

Youths were no match for armed Basij militias, and casualties mounted. Mousavi called for a day of mourning on June 18. Hundreds of thousands of black-clad protesters bearing candles gathered in central Tehran.[86] One placard read, "Our martyred brothers, we will take back your votes," and another asked, "Why did you kill our brothers?"[87]

Ayatollah Khamenei addressed Friday prayers in Tehran the following day, one week after the election, in an effort to stem the mass protests. He noted that the election was unprecedented in the history of the Islamic Republic history, apart from the 1980 referendum. Around 85 percent of eligible voters, he declared, took part. "One can see the auspicious hand of the Lord of the Age (Twelfth Imam) behind such great events." He denied that the election was fraudulent and praised Ahmadinejad's victory as an "epic moment that became a historic moment."[88] He noted that Ahmadinejad's winning margin of eleven million votes, officially declared a landslide, was so big it could not have been falsified. "The Islamic Republic would not cheat and would not betray the vote of the people," he declared.[89] He sought to reassure the public that "the legal structures for election in our country do not leave us room for vote rigging." Khamenei admitted the existence of financial corruption but claimed that the Islamic Republic was one of the healthiest in the world.[90] The supreme leader made clear his own preference, declaring that the president's viewpoint was closer to his own. He warned the opposition to stay off the streets or risk the prospect of violence. Opposition leaders would be "responsible for bloodshed and chaos" if they did not stop the demonstrations.[91]

Khamenei's sermon and repressive measures further radicalized protesters, opposition leaders, and some members of the clergy. The popular slogans reverberating during demonstrations quickly reflected this radical shift, a development usually evident only in the final stages of revolutionary struggle. Some began chanting, "Death to Khamenei,"[92] while others targeted Khamenei's son, Mojtaba: "Die Mojtaba, so you don't become the supreme leader" *(Mojtaba bemire, rahbariroh nagiri)*.[93] Some revised revolutionary slogans from 1979: "Traitor Mahmoud, you made the people homeless, you ruined the soil of the country, you killed the country's youth, alas and regret; you put thousands into shrouds, alas and regret; death to you, death to you." Other protesters changed the slogan of the 1979 revolution and called for the formation of an Iranian republic: "Independence, Freedom, Iranian Republic."[94] Still other slogans challenged the very existence of the Islamic Republic: "Dictator, dictator, this is the last message. The green people of Iran are ready to rise up."

Mousavi, too, increasingly adopted a more critical position. The Islamic Republic must be purged of lies and dishonesty, he told his supporters and issued a warning of his own: "If this good faith and trust coming from the people is not answered by protecting their votes, or the people cannot react in a civil and peaceful way to defend their rights, there will be dangerous pathways ahead, responsibility for which lies with those who can't stand peaceful behavior."[95] Addressing a demonstration in southern Tehran, Mousavi stated that he was ready for martyrdom and called for a general strike in the event of his arrest.[96]

Such large-scale protests briefly shook the very foundations of the Islamic regime, destabilized the Islamic Republic, and produced migration and capital flight. During the conflicts, an estimated one hundred thousand Iranians left the country, according to an official in the Foreign Ministry.[97] Wealthy citizens sent millions of dollars into overseas banks.[98] Even the Revolutionary Guard transferred large sums to safe havens outside the country.[99]

Despite divisions within the elite, the conservatives in the regime were determined to repress the popular struggles. The day after Khamenei's Friday prayer sermon on June 19, a senior police officer warned that the police would "act with determination against all illegal demonstrations and protests." Security forces arrested prominent members of the polity, as well as well-known dissidents and ordinary protesters alike, although the elite were held for only a short time. Faezeh Hashemi was detained along with four other Rafsanjani family members, according to state media.[100] The government ordered doctors to report protest-related injuries to the authorities. Some of the most seriously wounded sought refuge in foreign embassies to evade arrest.[101] State media released a deliberately misleading report that Mousavi had called off an important protest.[102]

State repression expanded to demobilize the opposition. Security forces arrested and detained at least four thousand people in the two months between the election and August 13, 2009, according to a judiciary spokesperson.[103] Authorities detained at least twenty-three journalists[104] during the first week of protests and banned others from leaving their offices to report on the events.[105] The judiciary closed down the office of the Association of Iranian Journalists, which had a membership of several thousand.[106] The government shut down newspapers associated with the reformists, imprisoned a growing number of journalists, and denied some journalists the right to work in their profession. Keyvan Samimi, an editor, was arrested on June 13, one day after the elections, and sentenced to six years' imprisonment and fifteen years' ban from journalistic activities. Hamzeh Karami, editor of a website and former Revolutionary Guard commander in Tehran who had held appointments in the administrations of Rafsanjani and Khatami, was arrested on June 18, tortured, and sentenced to eleven years' incarceration.[107] Bahman Ahmadi Amuee and his wife Jila Baniyaghoub were arrested and imprisoned on June 20; he was sentenced to five years in prison.[108] Baniyaghoub was sentenced to one year in prison and prohibited from working as journalist for thirty years.[109] Masoud Bastani, a young reformist journalist, was arrested on July 5, 2009, and sentenced to six years' imprisonment for working on a reformist website.[110] Isa Saharkhiz was arrested two days after he published an article criticizing the supreme leader and was sentenced to three years' imprisonment on charges of "insulting the leadership" and "propaganda against the system." In 2011, he was sentenced an additional two years in prison for his former journalistic activities.[111]

In the meantime, the Guardian Council attempted to resolve the disputes over the votes. After reviewing hundreds of election complaints, the Guardian Council admitted that the number of votes cast in fifty cities exceeded the actual number of voters. Nevertheless, the council rejected the opposition's demand to annul the election results.[112]

In reaction, Tehran residents climbed to their rooftops on the evening following Khamenei's Friday sermon and shouted, *"Allahu Akbar"* and "Death to the dictator," in open defiance of the supreme leader and the security forces. People in major cities across the country protested the next day. Many protesters tried to assemble at Enghelab Square but were turned back by water cannon, batons, and tear gas wielded by security forces. Some demonstrators fled into nearby houses with Basij militias in plain clothes and antiriot helmets in hot pursuit.[113] More people were arrested in Tehran on June 20.

Security forces killed at least thirteen protesters, among them Neda Agha Soltan, 27, a student who was shot dead on June 20.[114] Her dying moments were posted on the Internet and seen around the world. Witnesses detained her killer and confiscated his identification card, revealing his membership in the Basij. Security forces blocked roads to the central Tehran mosque and prevented her funeral service from being held.[115]

The Islamic regime's leadership continued to threaten the protesters. The supreme leader declared that he would not yield to pressure and insisted on implementing the law.[116] The Revolutionary Guard warned protesters to "be prepared for a resolute and revolutionary confrontation with Guards, Basij and other security forces" if they continued their demonstrations.[117] Ahmad Khatami, a hardline cleric in the powerful Assembly of Experts, asserted that the judiciary would charge the leading rioters with being *mohareb* (fighters against God) and sentence them to death.[118]

In reaction to growing repression, Mehdi Karroubi called for a day of mourning on June 25 at Tehran's Behesht-e Zahra cemetery. Security forces and Basij blocked roads and intimidated families of the slain protesters to prevent them from attending the event. In the midst of intimidation and repression, protesters created a new slogan to enhance their solidarity: "Don't be afraid, don't be afraid, we are all together."

Security forces also created new repertoires of repression to demobilize protesters. They tossed some demonstrators off pedestrian bridges in Tehran to intimidate and disperse the public. When Hussein Akhtar Zand sought refuge in a building during the postelection protests in Isfahan, security forces followed and threw him from the third floor of the building.[119] The Basij carried out nighttime raids on targeted homes to arrest people shouting *"Allahu Akbar."* They destroyed property and confiscated satellite dishes to prevent people from watching foreign news. "Witnesses are telling us that Basijis are trashing entire streets and even neighborhoods as well as individual homes to stop the nightly rooftop chants," reported one observer.[120] The government levied a $500 fine on some who were arrested for shouting *"Allahu Akbar"* from the rooftops at night.[121] The regime also imposed heavy restrictions on the press, leading some 180 journalists to issue a statement that they could not continue their professional duties because of official limitations.[122] The same report revealed that senior ayatollahs in Qom were under pressure from the state to take a confrontational posture over the protests.

To prevent expansion of the protests, state repression broadened to include many organizations, associations, and professions. Repressive measures enabled the regime to gain relative control and halt the momentum of the protests by the end of June and early July. By this time, the government had arrested dozens of journalists and bloggers, hundreds of activists, and thousands of protesters. The arrest of well-known journalists, writers, and activists diminished the voice of the opposition and set the stage for the Guardian Council to certify the election on June 29 and officially declare Ahmadinejad the winner.

The repression had an impact on the politics of the reformist opposition leaders. They reduced their political activities and, for a time, avoided calling for street protests, for two main reasons. First, some in the reformist movement who did not favor major transformations were threatened by radical protesters who called for an alternative system. Second, and more importantly, many prominent reformists were themselves arrested in premeditated, coordinated raids by security forces. Leaders and activists in the Freedom Movement, the Islamic Iran Participation Front (IIPF), and the Mujahedeen of the Islamic Revolution Organization (MIRO) were incarcerated. These organizations had been a part of the Islamic regime for years (the IIPF was established in 1998, and MIRO was founded shortly after the revolution), although the latter had been repressed in the early 1980s and reestablished in 1991.

Many of those who were detained had held important government positions after the revolution, including a former vice president, cabinet members, governors, presidential advisors, and a presidential spokesperson.[123] Ebrahim Yazdi, member of the defunct Revolutionary Council, Iran's former foreign minister, and a founder and current leader of the Freedom Movement, was jailed shortly after the June election. Mohsen Mir-Damadi, former Majles deputy, head of the Islamic Iran Participation Front (the largest reformist party), and one of the student masterminds behind the 1979 U.S. embassy takeover, was also arrested. Behzad Nabavi, Iran's top negotiator during the American embassy takeover and former deputy speaker of the Majles, was also detained. He had also served as minister of heavy industries, had been a founder and leader of MIRO, and was an original member of the Komitehs that were the precursors of the Intelligence Ministry. Mustafa Tajzadeh, prominent official in President Khatami's administration, was also taken into custody. Mohammad Maleki, first chancellor of Tehran University after the revolution, was arrested and imprisoned soon after the elections, in August 2009.

Well-known artists were also targets of repression, and some were given prison sentences. Security forces arrested two prominent Iranian filmmakers as they tried to lay flowers at Neda's grave on the fortieth day of her death. One was Jafar Panahi, best known for his film *The Circle*, a work that was critical of the treatment of women under the Islamist government and banned by the regime.[124] Panahi was sentenced to six years in prison and banned for twenty years from all artistic activities, including making film, writing scripts, traveling abroad, and speaking with media.[125] Mahnaz Mohammadi, a female documentary maker, was arrested with Panahi and sentenced to five years for undermining national security and making propaganda against the Islamic Republic. She began serving her prison term in June 2014.[126]

Reports surfaced of harsh treatment of prisoners arrested during the protests. "A woman described having her hair pulled as interrogators demanded that she confess to having sex with political figures. When she was finally released, she was forced—like many others—to sign a paper saying she had never been mistreated."[127] Another report revealed that prisoners had their fingernails ripped out, were forced to lick filthy toilets, and were even beaten to death.[128]

The state increased its repression by introducing new charges against the reformists. Days before Ahmadinejad was sworn in to begin his second term, authorities opened a mass trial of more than one hundred leading reformist and opposition figures accused of conspiring with foreigners to stage a revolution through terrorism and of instigating a campaign to discredit the June presidential election. The government broadcast the trials on national television, showing humiliating confessions of the shackled detainees in which they denied the existence of election fraud and detailed foreign plots to bring down the Islamic government.[129] Two prominent reformists confessed that they had conspired to mount a protest campaign even before the presidential election and affirmed that there was no basis for accusations of election fraud. Interviewed on state television, one detainee explained to a government journalist why he had changed his views on the election: "It is only God who can change one's heart. When one is put in a situation in which one might not be alive the next day, then one can experience an evolution."[130] Prison officials telephoned family members of jailed political activists and protesters while the trials were ongoing and threatened repercussions for the detainees if the relatives gave interviews.[131] The chief prosecutor of the Revolutionary Court warned that anyone criticizing the trials would risk prosecution. Amnesty International denounced the "show trials" as a travesty of justice.[132]

Despite repression, popular protests continued, although with less frequency and intensity. Radical activists and students who had not been arrested because of a lack of ties to the reformist organizations, organized these protests. People demonstrated anew across the country, when the Guardian Council endorsed Ahmadinejad's victory, once again rejecting the endorsement of the supreme leader and the Guardian Council. When Tehran protesters tried to form a human chain and were attacked by security forces, they broke up into smaller groups and continued to demonstrate for hours, making it difficult for the police to injure, arrest, or disperse them.[133]

Unable to completely eliminate the protests, the Revolutionary Guard threatened even greater repression. General Yadollah Javani, political director of the Guard, warned, "We came up against a deep mischief during this election, a mischief that gave birth to the new divisions. During these events, the eye of the mischief was damaged, but it was not blinded. Now the eye of the mischief must be blinded and completely gouged out, and this can be done by illuminating the events behind the scenes."[134] Agents arrested Zahra Rahnavard's brother[135] and three of Ayatollah Montazeri's grandsons.[136] The National Security Council banned newspapers and news agencies from writing any news about Mousavi, Karroubi, or the tenth presidential election.[137]

Further reports revealed atrocities against jailed dissidents and political prisoners, including beatings, burning with cigarettes, and threats of execution.[138] Karroubi charged that some prisoners were tortured to death and others had been raped. "Some young male detainees were raped, while some young female detainees were raped in a way that caused serious injuries."[139] Karroubi sent a letter to Hashemi Rafsanjani, head of the Assembly of Experts, detailing the accusations: "Some detained individuals have talked about such savage rapes that have left the women victims with physical scars and ruptures in their reproductive systems. At the same time, young imprisoned boys have been raped in such atrocious ways causing them depression, physical and psychological pain, leading to their complete withdrawal from everybody."[140]

The government initially denied all charges of rape and torture. A judiciary report on September 12 described Karroubi's evidence as "fake" and recommended decisive action against all who spread lies and damaged the prestige of the system. Reports of rape of political detainees increased. Some prisoners who were raped escaped the country and related their experiences to the international media and Amnesty International.[141] A member of the Basij militia who defected to England told a television reporter of dozens of rapes of youngsters between the ages of 12 and 18.[142] Mohsen Rouholamini, son of a renowned scientist who was a senior advisor to one of the presidential candidates, died under torture in jail. As charges multiplied of torture and death in Kahrizak prison, the police and the judiciary admitted some abuse and the deaths of at least three prisoners under torture (Rouholamini, Mohammad Kamrani, and Amir Javadi Far). Even the supreme leader confirmed that "violations and crimes had been committed during post-June 12 election events, especially at the Kahrizak detention facility and on the attack on Tehran University dormitories by special police units and plain-clothed officers."[143] The prison was eventually closed down on the order of the supreme leader.[144]

State repression intensified to silence some who helped expose the Kahrizak events. Ramin Pourandarjani, 26, a doctor who examined some of the victims in prison, testified to a Majles committee that jailers tortured and raped prisoners.[145] He refused to sign death certificates, saying that the authorities wanted fake documents to cover up murder at the prison.[146] When Pourandarjani later died under mysterious circumstances, the government claimed that he had either suffered a heart attack or committed suicide. A forensic examiner identified the cause of death as drug poisoning.[147] Authorities arrested Mehdi Mahmoudian, the young journalist who had played an important role in exposing the events in Kahrizak. He was sentenced to five years in prison on the charge of assembly and collusion against the regime.[148]

To demobilize the opposition, the government began executing increasing numbers of political prisoners and hastened the execution of common criminals. Authorities executed 115 people in the fifty days following the presidential election without even announcing their crimes, according to Amnesty International.[149] The government sentenced some political prisoners and dissidents to death for opposing the regime. "A flurry of executions and death sentences in Iran has raised concern that the government is using judicially sanctioned killing to intimidate the political opposition and quell pockets of ethnic unrest," according to a *New York Times* report.[150] In an unusual move by an appeals court, Ehsan Fattahian, 27, a Kurdish political prisoner who had been sentenced to ten years in 2008 for being a member of an armed group, was sentenced to death and executed.[151] He was executed as *mohareb*, triggering widespread protests throughout Iran's Kurdistan.[152] His parents were not allowed to see his body, and authorities did not permit a public mourning service.[153] Reza Khademi, 23, arrested the day after the election, was charged with *mohareb* and sentenced to death for flying a green balloon,[154] although an appeals court later revised his sentence to twelve years in prison.[155]

New Repertoires of Protest: Anniversaries, Special Events

Students and youths invented new protest repertoires and continued to mobilize and demonstrate around the country, despite repression. Students protested on university campuses with sit-ins, through statements, and by boycotting exams, which provoked cycles of retaliatory expulsions, additional arrests, and widespread hunger strikes on campus. Other citizens defaced paper currency with political slogans, such as "Death to the dictator" and "Down with Khamenei" or "Fear the storm of dust and dirt," forcing the government to collect the bills and outlaw the activities.[156] The public used every public occasion over the subsequent months to chant political slogans against the regime, including on the anniversaries of Quds Day, the U.S. embassy takeover, Student Day, Ayatollah Montazeri's death (discussed below), and religious events such as Tasooa and Ashura. Lacking other political options such as mosques, protesters turned these state-sponsored events into antigovernment rallies and demonstrations. Citizens took advantage of every chance to mobilize and challenge the regime, as they had done for more than a century, beginning with the constitutional movement in 1905.

A prime opportunity for antiregime expression occurred on Quds Day, September 18, the official expression of solidarity with the Palestinian people and opposition to Israeli control of Jerusalem. The regime had earlier canceled some important religious events, such as the commemoration of Imam Ali's death at the mausoleum of Ayatollah Khomeini, for fear of opposition mobilization,[157] but it did not cancel the Quds march. In an effort to head off antiregime protests, Ayatollah Khamenei admonished the public to avoid divisive tactics and slogans during the event. The Revolutionary Guard threatened to crack down on displays of the opposition's green color as well as signs or slogans against any target other than Israel.

Reformists and opposition leaders Mousavi, Karroubi, and Khatami declared their plans to participate in the Quds march. Karroubi specifically noted that the "people's power will be revealed in Quds march."[158] People from diverse socioeconomic backgrounds mobilized in large cities for the march. The size of the demonstration was considerable because the regime did not ban participation, and the event was always held on Friday, the Muslim holy day. A Revolutionary Guard commander, Saeed Ghasemi, acknowledged that the number of green supporters marching in Tehran was two million.[159] The Quds march demonstrated that political repression, sexual violence, and dozens of deaths after the June election had failed to stamp out political opposition and demands for change. Marchers totally ignored official warnings against divisive slogans and targets of protests. The degree of popular opposition to the government was displayed in the huge protests during the day, the nature of the slogans, and the nightly shouts of *"Allahu Akbar"* from the rooftops.

Reports revealed that dissidents participated in protests in all major cities, including Tehran, Tabriz, Mashhad, Shiraz, Ahvaz, Rasht, Isfahan, and Kermanshah.[160] Demonstrators reiterated their earlier condemnations of the conservatives with slogans such as "Death to the dictator," "Confessions, torture will no longer work," "Cannon, tank, violations [rape] no longer work," and "Sohrab is not dead; the state is dead" (a reference to Sohrab Aarabi, who was slain in a previous demonstration). "Rape and torture will not stop us" and "Liar, liar, where is your 63 percent?" (a reference to Ahmadinejad's alleged share of June's vote). Others shouted, "I will fight, I will die, but I will take back my country," "Supreme Leader! This is the last message. The Green Movement of Iran is prepared for the uprising."[161] Some shouted slogans in solidarity with the regime's opponents: "Political prisoners must be freed," "If Karroubi [or Mousavi] gets arrested, Iran will be resurrected," and "Hail to Montazeri, hail to Saanei."

Other slogans attacked the Islamic Republic's very foundation: "Khamenei is a murderer; his leadership is revoked" *(Khamenei ghatel-e, velayatesh batel-e),* "Our heritage is Ariya; separate religion from politics" *(Nasl-e ma Ariya, deen az siyasat joda),* and "Dictator, dictator, this is the last message. The green people of Iran are ready to rise up." Some slogans exhorted protesters to act: "People, why are you sitting? Iran has become Palestine." Others harked back to a revolutionary slogan from 1979: "With God's help, victory is near; death to this deceptive government."[162] Tehran protesters spontaneously improvised when rain fell after a tear gas attack by security forces: "Peace be upon Mohammad, God is shedding tears" *(Sal-e Ala Mohammad, ashk-e khoda dar amad).*[163] Finally, some protesters shouted slogans that attacked foreign allies of the Islamic Republic, for example, "Death to Russia," and "Death to China."[164]

In response, security forces targeted members of the middle class and the intelligentsia. Over the next several months, security forces arrested hundreds of intellectuals, students, and human rights activists. Authorities summoned Tehran students who had shouted *"Allahu Akbar"* in front of the central library and in the dormitory to the disciplinary committee.[165] Saeed Mortazavi, the public prosecutor, closed down many publications and fired some two thousand journalists.[166] The regime arrested and imprisoned more than one hundred journalists by early November 2009.[167] Officials at some universities forbade displays of the color green.[168] Ayatollah Khamenei declared that questioning the election was "the biggest crime."[169] The judiciary handed down lengthy jail sentences to students, provoking widespread hunger strikes among students at Fannie College.[170] Tehran's Revolutionary Court ordered the confiscation of the Nobel Prize belonging to Shirin Ebadi, the country's only Nobel laureate, after she campaigned in Europe against government repression and violations of human rights.[171]

The people defied the government and took to the streets once again during the November 4 anniversary of the U.S. embassy takeover. In reaction, security forces posted in subways forcibly removed green armbands, bracelets, or headscarves from people heading to the protests. Despite official warnings, protesters repeated many of the same antidictatorship slogans heard in the Quds march. One new slogan called out to President Obama: "Obama, Obama, either you are with them or you are with us."[172] Authorities arrested at least four hundred protesters.[173]

The regime took measures to preempt bazaar closings and prevent shopkeepers and bazaaris from becoming politicized and joining the protesters in a broader coalition. Several months after the disputed elections, authorities arrested several prominent bazaaris, including Mohsen Dokmechi, who had been assisting families whose members were in jail; Javad Laary, a former political prisoner who had spent four years in jail in the 1980s; and Mohammad Banazadeh Amir-Khizi.[174]

Students took advantage of an opportunity to voice protests on Student Day, December 7, a day that commemorated the deaths of three students in 1953. At least two hundred students were arrested by security forces days before the event, and students were warned by university officials not to engage in antigovernment events the next day. Nevertheless, students across Iran carried out protests on the Student Day.[175] They singled out Khamenei, not Ahmadinejad, as their principal target, chanting, "Death to the dictator," and "The dictator should know he will soon be overthrown." Students took down Khamenei's portrait and chanted, "Khamenei is a murderer; his leadership is revoked." At Beheshti University, students were joined by professors; protesters chanted, "Death to the dictator."[176] Students introduced a new slogan: "Mousavi is an excuse; the target is the regime."[177] Protesting students clashed with militias, chanting, "Basiji go home; no free meal today," and "Get lost, mercenary." Other more radical slogans included: "Our curse, our shame, our incompetent leader," and "What happened to oil money? It was spent on Basiji."[178] For the first time, Tehran University students carried the Iranian flag without the symbol of the Islamic Republic.[179] Thousands of people outside Tehran University shouted, "Death to the dictator" and burned Khamenei's picture.[180] Students also burned caricatures of President Ahmadinejad.[181]

Authorities reacted swiftly in an attempt to contain the student protest. Thousands of armed Basij members stormed Tehran University for two days, firing into the air, throwing tear gas, and blocking students from leaving their campuses to join the protesters outside. Security forces surrounded other university campuses as well and tried to shield student protests from the public by covering the campus fences and shutting down cell phone networks. Their actions did little to prevent students from demonstrating. Security forces arrested more than two hundred protesters in the capital.[182] Plainclothes individuals entered the Abou Ali Sina University campus in Hamedan and hurled two protesting students, a male and a female, from the second floor of the Science building, severely injuring both.[183] The next day, female Basij militias attacked Zahra Rahnavard and prevented her from joining the student protesters.[184]

Eighty-eight professors of the renowned Technology College at Tehran University issued an open letter to the supreme leader after two days of attacks on university students. They demanded that nonuniversity personnel be banned from campus, all imprisoned students be freed, and those responsible for the attacks be brought to justice.[185] "Nighttime attacks on defenseless student dormitories and daytime assaults on students at university campuses, venues of education and learning, are not signs of strength. . . . Nor is beating up students and their mass imprisonment." The letter continued, "Unfortunately, all these (attacks) were carried out under the pretext of protecting Islam" and the position of the supreme leader.[186]

The occasion of Ayatollah Montazeri's death on December 20 likewise generated numerous collective action and protests. Thousands of mourners flooded the holy city of Qom for his funeral and chanted political slogans directed at Khamenei and Ahmadinejad: "Khamenei is a murderer; his leadership is revoked," "Traitor Mahmoud, you produced homelessness, you destroyed the soil of the country, you killed the country's youth, *Allahu Akbar;* you put thousands into shrouds, *Allahu Akbar;* death to you, death to you!" Qom protesters chanted new slogans challenging the regime's religious credentials: "Rape in prison; this too was in the Quran!" *(Tajavoz tuye zendan, inam boud tuye Quran!),* "This month is the month of blood; Yazid is overthrown," "Justice is their slogan; Kahrizak is their pride."[187] "Our leader is our shame," and "Montazeri's will: death to this dictatorship" *(Vasiyat-e Montazeri, Marg bar in dictatori).* "This is the month of blood. Seyyed Ali [Khamenei] will be overthrown."[188]

Protests spread rapidly to many parts of the country, including central Iran.[189] In Najaf Abad (Montazeri's birthplace), Isfahan, and Tehran, among other cities, security forces clashed with protesters and arrested many. The government banned gatherings at the famous Tehran Hoseinieh Ershad and prevented people from holding memorial services in mosques on the third day of the death of Ayatollah Montazeri.[190]

Sizeable protests upstaged the religious observances of Tasooa and Ashura. People mobilized and protested collectively in many cities without prompting by reformist leaders and despite government warnings. Tehran protesters seized the initiative and responded aggressively to security forces. They burned several police vehicles and motorcycles, as well as a couple of Basij stations. Protesters cornered some antiriot police, insisting that they apologize and call Khamenei a "bastard." Others confiscated police batons and helmets.[191] Demonstrators chanted antistate slogans: "Death to the principle of the rule of jurisprudence" *(Marg ba asle velayate faghih)*,[192] "Hossein, Hossein is their slogan; rape is their pride," and "Rape in prison. Is this too in the Quran?"[193] Slogans attacked both Khamenei and Ahmadinejad: "Violations [rape], crimes, death to this leadership" *(Tajavoz, jenayat, marg bar in velayat)*.[194]

Security forces and agents responded with intense repression, killing at least thirty-seven people in Tehran and injuring dozens.[195] Because Shia Islam forbids bloodshed on the day of Ashura, the regime denied killing anyone and instead blamed the deaths on the government's opponents. Seyyed Ali Habibi Mousavi, Mousavi's nephew, was killed by unidentified people.[196] Security forces removed his body from the hospital, ostensibly to investigate the terrorists they alleged had carried out the killing to discredit the regime. Plainclothes agents in automobiles struck and killed three people, including Shahram Farajzadeh Tarani, Shabnam Sohrabi, and Shahrokh Rahmani.[197] A police car ran over Tarani, 35, several times, killing him in Valiasr Square.[198] Although videos of the incident were posted on the Internet and seen all over the world, the police chief denied that the incident had occurred. A Revolutionary Court handed down a two-year prison term to a witness, Leila Tavassoli, daughter of the jailed Tehran mayor, for giving interviews to the media about the incident. Four years later, the police chief admitted that the attack had actually taken place.[199]

Authorities in Tehran arrested more than one thousand people, including Ebrahim Yazdi, a former foreign minister; Dr. Alireza Beheshti, son of one of the founders of the Islamic Republic and one of several Mousavi aides to be detained; several prominent activists and journalists, including Emadeddin Baghi, a human rights activist who had received numerous international awards; and Dr. Nooshin Ebadi, sister of Shirin Ebadi, the Nobel laureate.[200] Some people arrested during Ashura protests were given severe sentences. The regime arrested Abdolreza Ghanbari, a lecturer at Payam e Nour University, after the protests on December 27, 2009. He was charged with "enmity against God" for allegedly receiving unsolicited e-mails from an armed group to which he did not belong and sentenced to death, according to Education International.[201] The Tehran Revolutionary Court later commuted his sentence to fifteen years in prison, to be served, in part, in exile in Borazjan in the south. Agents also arrested Mohsen Daneshpour Moghadam, his wife, son, and a few friends at their home after the Ashura protests in Tehran. He and his son, Ahmad, were sentenced to death on charges of warring against God and supporting the left-wing Islamic Mojahedeen.[202]

Security forces clashed with protesters in Shiraz, Mashhad, Qom, Arak, Rasht, and Najafabad and other major cities, causing injuries and making arrests.[203] Four people were killed in Tabriz.[204] The regime arrested more than four hundred people in Isfahan,[205] including the son of Ayatollah Taheri and the brother of Abdollah Nouri and detained them for ten days.[206]

The political turmoil intensified divisions within the clerical establishment and led to further repressive measures. Grand Ayatollah Bayat Zanjani denied that *velayat-e faghieh* was a religious principle and asserted that it was not blasphemous to say so.[207] The regime responded by specifically repressing members of clergy. Unidentified persons broke windows in Ayatollah Dastgheib's mosque in Shiraz, and government agents shut off water and gas to the mosque and closed the doors. The offices of Ayatollah Dastgheib and Ayatollah Yousefi Saanai were attacked in various cities.[208] According to opposition sources, agents associated with the Revolutionary Guard were responsible for a fire and damage at Dastgheib's mosque, destroying rugs and books, and burning the Quran.[209] Qom security forces arrested Ayatollah Mohammad Taghi Khalaji, an associate of Ayatollah Montazeri, and attacked the deceased cleric's office.[210]

Threats and intimidation continued. The Guardian Council condemned the Ashura protesters and demanded punishment for rioters who burned the holy Quran, "desecrated" mosques and religious sanctuaries by clapping their hands and whistling, and attacked mourners to make happy the heart of world imperialism and the media tied to international Zionism.[211] One prominent cleric and member of the Assembly of Experts told a Tehran rally that a "bunch of calves and goats" had chanted slogans and opposed the supreme leader.[212] The Intelligence Ministry warned opponents to stop following foreign plots before it was too late.[213] Tehran's revolutionary prosecutor declared that those who set fire to vehicles and committed other crimes could be regarded as *mohareb,* and punished by execution.[214] The interior minister ordered security forces to show no mercy toward protesters and to arrest them immediately. He also noted that, based on the declaration of religious leaders, rioters were *mohareb* and their fate was clear, implying execution.[215] Friday Prayer leaders in all major cities repeatedly issued simultaneous statements declaring that Green Movement leaders were "corrupt" and associated with America and the United Kingdom. They warned that if they did not cease their protests, they would be executed as *mohareb.* The Friday Prayer leader in Shiraz, Ayatollah Imani, called for the execution of those responsible for riots. In Yazd, Ayatollah Sedoughi asked for the harshest punishment. Many quoted Ayatollah Khomeini as saying, "Those who want a republic without Islam are the enemies of Islam," according to a report by the

Guardian.[216] Other hardliners accused opposition leaders of igniting protests, labeling them "*mohareb*," a crime punishable by death.[217] The head of Iran's judiciary, Ayatollah Sadegh Larijani told judiciary officials his responsibility was no longer limited to the judiciary. "My job is highly politicised and has also to deal with national security," he said.[218]

The Islamic regime intensified its intimidation of the populace as the anniversary of the 1979 revolution approached. Khamenei's representative in the Revolutionary Guard announced that it was worth killing seventy-five thousand people to save the Islamic government.[219] Plainclothes security officers smashed the front windshield of Karroubi's car.[220]

Such warnings were underscored by unprecedented repression. Security forces arrested dissident clerics, and government agents attacked some religious leaders. The authorities posted photographs of protesters on the Internet in hopes that informants would identify them to the security forces.[221] The government arrested most of the members of the central council of the Office of Consolidation Unity, the largest student organization. They arrested Morteza Simiari and kept him in solitary confinement after he met with an EU parliamentary team in Tehran.[222] Security forces arrested numerous dissident students across the country and imposed long prison sentences, while university officials expelled many students. Authorities jailed labor leaders, journalists, human rights defenders, and women activists throughout the country. The government arrested more than a dozen Baha'is, whose religion prohibited political activity, and charged them with "directing" the unrest during Ashura.[223]

Karroubi condemned the government's intense repression of protesters, charging that even the shah had honored the holiday's ban on violence.[224] In his statement, Karroubi noted that the Islamic regime had shed people's blood on Ashura and unleashed a "barbaric" gang against the people.[225]

The regime placed an increasing number of political prisoners on the execution list, notably Kurds. The state executed 388 people in 2009, exceeded that year only by China, according to Amnesty International.[226] One source stated that seventeen Kurdish citizens were placed on the execution list.[227] Fasih Yasmani, 28, a Kurd, was executed for being a member of a Kurdish opposition organization.[228] Aziz Mohammad-Zadeh, also a Kurd, was condemned to death.[229] The regime executed eleven individuals sentenced to death for participating in postelection protests. Ayatollah Jannati praised the executions during the Friday prayer sermons at Tehran University and called for more.[230] "I thank the judiciary for executing these two men so quickly," Ayatollah Jannati said in comments broadcast on state television, "but the judiciary needs to stand firmly. Otherwise, if it shows weakness, we will suffer more. There is no room for Islamic mercy."[231] "The Koran, Islam, and the leader must be preserved; we should have no mercy towards those who commit evil; despite having Islamic kindness, Imam Ali killed thousands in one of the wars."[232] Arash Rahmanipour and Mohammad Reza Ali Zamani had been arrested before the June 12 elections, but were executed.[233] Abbas Jafari Dolatabadi, Tehran's chief prosecutor general, said in an interview that the two men had been found guilty of "planning to assassinate officials and to carry out explosions."[234]

Government forces and militias also targeted prominent members of the elite. Ahmad Alamolhoda, a member of the Assembly of Experts, demanded that Green Movement leaders repent or risk being charged as *mohareb*, enemies of God, for which the Sharia punishment was death.[235] Abbas Vaez-Tabasi, representative of the supreme leader, said on state television that opposition leaders were enemies of God and should be executed. "Those who are behind the current sedition in the country . . . are *mohareb* . . . and the law is very clear about punishment of a *mohareb*."[236] Some five hundred progovernment Basij militias and local regime loyalists surrounded a building in Qazvin that Karroubi was in and attacked it with stones. He managed to get into his car, but as the car was pulling away, it was hit by gunfire, damaging the windows.[237]

The country's intellectual elite also came under attack. Professor Masood Ali-Mohammadi, a physicist, was killed in a bomb blast in front of his house. Although authorities blamed his death on enemies of the Islamic Republic, the assassination generated an atmosphere of terror in the country. Ali-Mohammadi had engaged in some pro-Mousavi activities, supported the student movement, and was openly critical of high-ranking officials of the Islamic Republic in his classes, according to some of his students. He participated in the June 15 postelection protests along with his students and many others. He also authored a letter to the supreme leader, which was signed by eighty-eight professors, criticizing attacks on students in dormitories and on campuses. Ali-Mohammadi was on a list of scholars who had campaigned for Mousavi.[238] His name appeared among those of 420 professors who had endorsed Mousavi's candidacy for the presidency.[239] Authorities arrested him because he met with Mousavi shortly after the election. With rising repression, other academics also came under attack. A number of faculty members were dismissed, including one professor who was fired for attending the funeral of Ayatollah Montazeri.[240] Simin Behbahani, 82, one of the most prominent Iranian poets and former president of the banned Writers' Association, had been invited by the city of Paris to deliver a speech on International Women's Day on March 8, 2010. Her passport was confiscated at the airport, and authorities prevented her from leaving the country.[241]

The regime's campaign of mounting repression produced a few results. Mousavi issued a statement that appeared to retreat from some of his earlier demands. Remaining silent about the election and Ahmadinejad's fraudulent presidency, Mousavi condemned the disrespect for religious sanctities shown on Ashura (December 27, 2009) and made five general demands of the government: be accountable to the people, the Majles, and the judiciary; pass transparent and reliable election laws; release political prisoners; guarantee freedom of the press; and recognize the people's right to gather and establish political parties. The Islamic regime declared the Freedom Movement to be illegal. The Intelligence Ministry ordered their websites to be taken down.[242] The Freedom Movement, the oldest Islamic organization whose leaders ran the country in the first year of the revolution until the hostage crisis, complied and discontinued its web activities.

Anniversary of the Revolution and Repression

With the anniversary of the revolution approaching, the opposition renewed challenges against the regime. Interviewed a few days before the revolution's anniversary on February 11, Mousavi said he did not believe that the revolution had fulfilled its goals. "The majority of people believed in the beginning of the revolution that the roots of dictatorship and despotism were abolished. . . . I was one of them but now I don't have the same beliefs. You can still find the elements and roots that lead to dictatorship."[243] He criticized the culture that called the people "dirt and dust" and "calves and goats." Mousavi further declared, "Dictatorships in the name of religion are the worst kind of dictatorships."[244]

The government announced a 31 percent increase in the budgets of the Revolutionary Guard and the army at the end of January 2010 to ensure their cooperation in preventing opposition protests during the revolution's anniversary.[245] Prison officials forced political prisoners to call their families on the eve of the anniversary and plead with them not to participate in protests.[246] People were roused from their beds during midnight raids, disappeared without a word to family and friends, and were subjected to long, solitary confinement.[247] In addition to well-known reformists, the ranks of the imprisoned included artists, photographers, children's rights advocates, women's rights activists, students, and journalists. Just two days before the anniversary of the revolution, Iran had at least sixty-five journalists in prison, more than any other country in the world, according to Reporters Without Borders.[248] Agents arrested Saleh Noghrehkar, a high-ranking official in Mousavi's campaign, and the nephew of Mousavi's wife, Zahra Rahnavard.[249]

The government put on trial 250 people and sentenced some of the protesters to death. Mohammad Amin Valian, 20, a university student and member of the central council of the Islamic Association in Dameghan, was indicted as *mohareb* and sentenced to death for holding rocks in his hands and shouting, "Death to the dictator" during an Ashura protest.[250] The prosecutor, however, gave him a chance to appeal.[251] The sentence was later reversed, but the ruling intimidated Valian and other political activists. Security forces warned recently released activists and journalists that they would be rearrested if they remained in Tehran on the revolution's anniversary.[252] Government officials and the police announced that anyone caught shouting "alternative" *(enherafi)* slogans during the February 11 observance would be kept in prison well past the Persian New Year.[253] The nation's police chief, Ismail Ahmadi Moghaddam, warned against organizing protests through text messages and e-mail, saying that those systems were monitored and that "disseminating opposition plans deserved great punishment."[254] To head off popular mobilization, the government disrupted Internet access in all major cities some days in advance of the anniversary.[255]

Security forces restricted traffic around Freedom Square on the evening of February 10. The next day, authorities jammed the Internet and mobile phone networks to disrupt the opposition.[256] The Revolutionary Guard and Basij forces occupied major portions of the capital to tighten the government's control over the official ceremony in Freedom Square and block the Green Movement from seizing the moment. The government bused in large numbers of people from the provinces, fed them, and provided unusual work-related benefits to civil servants who signed up to attend the march and the rally.[257] Security forces prevented Mousavi from reaching the rally site. They also beat up Zahra Rahnavard.[258] They marked protesters for arrest with paintballs and attempted to prevent people from photographing the protests. Security forces briefly detained Zahra Eshraghi, Khomeini's granddaughter, and her husband.[259] A tear gas explosion in front of Karroubi damaged his eyesight.[260] His son Ali was arrested, and Karroubi's wife addressed an open letter to Ayatollah Khamenei, charging that her son was tortured in a mosque and threatened with sexual assault.[261]

Although the government succeeded in restricting the dissidents, the opposition still managed to demonstrate. Opposition supporters in Tehran and other major cities shouted radical slogans against the regime. Many protesters called for the complete downfall of the government, and some shouted "Death to the dictator."[262] People listening to Ahmadinejad's address could hear cries of "Death to the dictator in the background."[263] Protesters chanted slogans familiar from previous demonstrations and created new ones, such as "Referendum, referendum, this is the slogan of the people" *(Refrandom, refrandom, inast shoar-e mardom)*, "Freedom of thought is not possible under the current order" *(Azadi-ye endishe, ba in nezam nemishe)*, and "Political prisoners must be released." Protesters targeted the supreme leader, chanting, "Death to Khamenei," "Rape, crime, death to this supreme leader" *(Tajavoz, jenayat, marg bar in velayat)*, and "We didn't give our lives to compromise and won't praise the murderous leader" *(Koshteh nadadim ke sazesh konim, rahbar-e ghatel ro setayesh konim)*.[264]

To reduce the possibility of further conflicts, the supreme leader issued a fateful pronouncement in February 2010, two weeks after the revolution's thirty-first anniversary. Declaring that the opposition had lost credibility by rejecting the 2009 presidential election, Ayatollah Khamenei told the Assembly of Experts that those who were unwilling to accept the law and the vote of the majority had lost the competence to participate in the framework of the Islamic system.[265] In a subsequent speech, Khamenei called protesters and dissidents social and political "microbes."[266] Several months later, the judiciary dissolved the main reformist organizations—the Islamic Iran Participation Front and the Mojahedeen of the Islamic Revolution.[267]

In addition, the regime stepped up repression in the following months. Security forces in major cities arrested a large number of people. Repression targeted dissident students, journalists, and activists for human rights, labor, and women's rights following the anniversary of the revolution. Authorities particularly targeted students. The minister of sciences cited statistics indicating that 70 percent of people associated with universities had voted for opposition candidates for president.[268] The minister revoked the scholarships and announced the expulsion of students who had protested after the election and continued to do so despite the supreme leader's ultimatum intended to end the protests.[269] The Intelligence Ministry arrested Mitra Aali, a distinguished student and member of the National Elite Foundation, on March 10, 2010. She had worked in Karroubi's headquarters during the presidential campaign and was sentenced to six years' imprisonment.[270] College and university authorities throughout the country expelled a number of students and fired faculty and employees who were detained in jail after protesting the election. Authorities sentenced Majid Tavakoli, a prominent student leader, to more than eight years in prison and barred him from enrolling in any of the country's colleges or universities.[271] The judiciary sentenced Bahareh Hedayat, another student leader and a women's rights activist, to nine and a half years for acting against national security and insulting the supreme leader and the president.[272]

Activists and human rights organizations reported negligence toward political prisoners and prisoners of conscience. Hoda Saber, a journalist and veteran activist, was last arrested in July 2010. While in prison, he went on hunger strike, in early June 2011, to protest the death of Haleh Sahab, a fellow activist who died in a confrontation with security forces during the funeral of her father.[273] Political activists and Saber's family claimed that gross negligence resulted in a heart attack and Saber's death.[274] An increasing number of people were also charged with *moharebeh*, an offence that was imposed for a wide range of crimes, often ill defined, according to an Amnesty International report.[275] The government carried out a number of secret executions in the absence of lawyers or relatives, at times without revealing the charges, according to the UN Special Rapporteur.[276] The regime announced death sentences for six additional participants in the December 2009 Ashura demonstrations.[277] Some political prisoners were executed on minor charges. Two men arrested during the postelection demonstrations in 2009 were later put to death for filming and taking photos of the protests and allegedly having ties to the outlawed Mojahedeen Khalgh.[278]

State repression over the following months also targeted those engaged in the legal profession to render the opposition defenseless. The judiciary ordered lawyers not to grant interviews to foreign media.[279] The regime prosecuted forty-two lawyers for defending political prisoners and prisoners of conscience between election day, on June 12, 2009, and July 10, 2011.[280] Authorities charged several human rights lawyers with threatening national security and punished them severely.[281] Nasrin Sotoudeh, a prominent lawyer and female activist, was charged with "acting against national security," and "propaganda against the regime" and was sentenced to eleven years in prison and barred from practicing law or leaving the country for twenty years.[282] Some claimed that her sentence stemmed from interviews she gave to foreign news outlets, which was not a crime even in Iran.[283] Sotoudeh's husband, Reza Khandan, was summoned to court for speaking to the media about his wife's condition in jail.[284] Sotoudeh's imprisonment was reduced and she was freed, but she was barred from practicing law.

Other prominent lawyers and human rights activists were given long jail terms. Abdolfattah Soltani, winner of the Nuremberg Human Rights Award, was convicted by the judiciary for spreading antiregime propaganda and endangering national security. He was initially sentenced to eighteen years in prison and a twenty-year ban from practicing law in March 2012, although an appeals court reduced the prison sentence to thirteen years the following June.[285] Soltani's wife, Massoumeh Dehghan, was arrested and detained for six days in July 2011 on charges of traveling to Germany and receiving the Nuremberg Human Rights Award on behalf of her husband. She was charged with "participation in earning illegitimate income through accepting a human rights award." An appeals court upheld the sentence but suspended it for five years.[286] Ghassem Sholeh Saadi, a university professor, lawyer, and former Majles deputy, was arrested on charges of interviewing with various media. He was sentenced to one year in prison and banned for ten years from teaching and practicing law.[287] Mohammad Ali Dadkhah, another prominent lawyer, was sentenced to nine years and banned for ten years from practicing law and teaching.[288] Mohammad Seyfzadeh received a sentence of nine years and a ban of ten years from practicing law. He and Nobel laureate Shirin Ebadi had been among the founders of the Center for Defense of Human Rights, which defended many political prisoners.[289] Narges Mohammadi, deputy chair of the Center for Human Rights Defenders, was fired from her job in 2010 for criticizing the government.[290] She was arrested and sentenced to eleven years in prison for "assembly and collusion against national security." Mohammadi was released from prison because of neurological paralysis but was rearrested[291] in May 2015 and sentenced to ten years in prison for various charges including "assembly and collusion against national security," and "propaganda against the state."[292]

To prevent any mobilization, the regime attacked public gatherings. Security forces raided evening parties in large cities and arrested many young people. The government photographed women as evidence that they had violated strict Islamic dress codes and fined them more than $1,000 each.[293] Even ordinary nonpolitical activities came under scrutiny. The government arrested, imprisoned, and lashed young people for mingling with the opposite sex and participating in water-gun fights.[294]

The regime repressed other activities that were not overtly political. The regime disbanded a committee established by the opposition to identify and assist families of victims of violence during protests and arrested its members, sentencing some to several years in prison.[295] When the regime was threatened by a bazaar strike over taxes, progovernment militiamen stormed the Tehran bazaar and murdered a prominent trader who had given a speech urging the continuation of the strike.[296] Authorities arrested seventy Tehran fashion designers for teaching Western culture to two hundred girls. The *Wall Street Journal* reported that the designers' crime was training young women for fashion shows. Such activity, the report noted was seen as a part of the West's "soft war" against Iran. In this war, "the goals are changes in cultural customs, beliefs, ideas and the beliefs of authorities, politicians, political parties and youths."[297] The regime sentenced the mother of Koohyar Goudarzi, an imprisoned human rights activist, to twenty-three months in jail for speaking to the media about her son.[298]

Opposition Gambit: Radical Challenges

Although protests continued on a smaller scale for several months, political changes in the region provided a new opportunity for the opposition movement to mobilize. Following the 2011 democratization movements in Tunisia, Egypt, and other countries in the region, Mousavi and Karroubi seized the initiative with another attempt to revive the challenge against the regime. Ignoring the February 11 anniversary of the Iranian Revolution, they called instead for demonstrations on February 14, ostensibly in solidarity with the people of Tunisia who had overthrown their autocratic ruler and Egyptians who were struggling to do the same. On February 10, the two leaders jointly issued a critical analysis of the regime's ruling faction. Moving beyond election issues, the statement attacked the very foundation of the Islamic Republic.

> Isn't it painful that after more than thirty years after the revolution, the people are once again concerned about the return of the monarchical relationship in the name of religion? We are in a situation in which all of the people's constitutional rights and the goals of the revolution have been trampled; people's rights emphasized in the constitution have been placed in parentheses, and whatever has been in the interest of the rulers has been magnified and exaggerated; absolute obedience to power has taken on a sacred and heavenly color. . . . Governance today is entrenched, trying to mobilize support by creating the concern that without it religion will be wiped out. In reality, the most adverse factor damaging religion has been the government's own oppressive and antireligious activities.[299]

Although security forces detained many reformists and arrested a number of dissidents on February 14, many residents of large cities were able to join the demonstrations. In addition to the popular slogans of previous protests, such as "Death to dictator," demonstrators shouted some new ones: "Mubarak, Ben Ali, your turn Seyyed Ali" (Khamenei). Other protesters called for democratic change in the country: "Neither Gaza nor Lebanon! Tunisia, Egypt, and Iran!"

The Islamic regime moved preemptively to silence Mousavi and Karroubi, former prime minister and speaker of the parliament, respectively, and placed them under house arrest the day before the demonstration. Some members of the Majles even called for Mousavi and Karroubi to be tried and executed.[300] Several days passed without any information as to their whereabouts. Finally, reports circulated that the Revolutionary Guard had forcibly taken Mousavi, Karroubi, and their spouses to Heshmatieyh Prison.[301] They were returned to their homes several weeks later, where they remained under house arrest and incommunicado without being charged. Security forces subsequently removed Karroubi from his house and placed him in solitary confinement, permitting his wife to visit him occasionally. While allowing some family visits, authorities stopped payment of Mousavi's retirement pension and expropriated some of his personal belongings, including his laptop and cell phone.[302]

The Islamic regime continued to pursue and repress other opposition leaders and political activists. Authorities banned former president Mohammad Khatami from leaving the country.[303] The government arrested two other reformist leaders—Mohsen Mir-Damadi, one of the embassy takeover masterminds and a former member of the Majles, and Mustafa Tajzadeh, a former advisor to President Khatami and vice minister in the Interior Ministry. They were given prison sentences of six years each and banned for ten years from political and media activities.[304] Tehran University dismissed Mir-Damadi from his teaching position while he was in prison.[305] Mohsen Armin, a leading reformist deputy in the sixth Majles and spokesperson and a leader of the Mojahedeen of the Islamic Revolution, was sentenced to six years in prison and banned from political work and media activity for five years.[306] Ebrahim Yazdi, 80, a member of the disbanded Revolutionary Council and Iran's foreign minister in the provisional government after the 1979 revolution, as well as a leader of the Freedom Movement, was sentenced to eight years in jail.[307] Other leading reformists and dissidents who were arrested included former members of the Majles Behzad Nabavi, Mohammad Reza Khatami, former deputy foreign minister Mohsen Aminzadeh, and Dr. Mohammad Maleki of the Freedom Movement and the first chancellor of Tehran University after the revolution. Dr. Ahmad Sadr Haj Seyyed Javadi, 95—another member of the disbanded Revolutionary Council, interior minister and minister of justice in the provisional government, and deputy in the first Islamic Majles—was prohibited from leaving the country.[308]

Even the highest elite's families and relatives were not immune. The children of Hashemi Rafsanjani were also targeted for repression. Faezeh Hashemi, former member of the Majles, was charged with antiregime propaganda and participating in demonstrations and jailed for six months in 2012. Dr. Mehdi Khazali, son of Ayatollah Abolghasem Khazali, former head of the Guardian Council and a member of the Assembly of Experts, was arrested and imprisoned six times after the 2009 presidential election for criticizing the government. He was sentenced to six years but went on hunger strike in June 2014 and suffered two heart attacks.[309] The supreme leader's cousin, Sorajeddin Mir-Damadi, a reformist and a former leader of the OCU, was arrested on charges of making propaganda against the Islamic Republic and conspiring against national security. He was sentenced to six years in jail.[310]

Political repression even silenced Iran's political elite, representatives in the Majles. Ali Motahari, outspoken Majles deputy, asserted that the Majles had become a mere decoration after the 2009 presidential election.[311] Majles deputies were afraid of making statements on behalf of Mousavi and Karroubi for fear of being disqualified from running for election in the next round, as happened to over one hundred members of the sixth Majles (2000–2004), according to Motahari.[312]

The judiciary often handed out long prison terms, sometimes without due process to activists involved in collective events or intellectuals whose works were performed in public. Teachers were targeted because they repeatedly demonstrated for higher salaries and equal treatment. In 2013, a judge sentenced Mahmoud Beheshti Langroudi, spokesperson for the Teachers' Trade Union, to nine years in prison for participating in a demonstration after the 2009 presidential elections. The judge allowed Beheshti to defend his case for five minutes only, leading him to go on a hunger strike when he began serving his sentence.[313] During his hunger strike, 1,463 teachers and civil rights activists issued an open letter warning that his life was in danger and demanding his release and retrial in a competent court with a fair jury.[314] A judge sentenced Esmail Abdi, the secretary general of the Teachers Association of Iran, to ten years for "propaganda against the state," and "revealing national security secrets." The sentence was suspended for five years. Abdi was rearrested after teachers protested in April and May 2015, even though he claimed he had nothing to do with those events.[315] Abdi was sentenced to six years in prison in 2016, provoking teachers' objections.[316] Poets also came under attack for the impact of their works on the public. A court sentenced a male and a female poet, Mehdi Mousavi and Fatemeh Ekhtesari, to nine- and eleven-year jail terms, respectively, and ninety-nine lashes each for "insulting the sanctities"[317] and exchanging the traditional Iranian greeting—handshake and kiss on the cheek—forbidden in the Islamic Republic.[318]

Authorities treated political prisoners harshly. On April 17, 2014, intelligence officials, along with one hundred guards, raided Section 350 of the Evin Prison, where political prisoners were held, to conduct a search. According to media reports, the security forces, dressed in riot gear, severely injured dozens of the prisoners, causing a skull fracture and broken ribs.[319] One of the prisoners suffered a heart attack and was transferred to the intensive care unit of a hospital outside of the prison. At least thirty-two prisoners, including lawyer Abdolfattah Soltani and labor activist Behnam Ebrahimzadeh, were sent to solitary confinement, according to Amnesty International.[320] In response, some of the prisoners protested and went on a hunger strike for several days. Some of the relatives of the prisoners protested outside the prison, and others went on hunger strikes to condemn the treatment of the prisoners. Iran's justice minister and prison authorities denied any harm to any prisoners or any violation of their rights.[321]

The fate of labor dissidents was the worst. Sattar Beheshti, a blogger and worker, was arrested on October 30, 2012, in his home and charged with activities against "national security" for his Facebook entries. Beheshti died a few days after his arrest.[322] Although the government declared that he had died of stress, the forensic report showed that he had extensive internal bleeding. After his death, forty-one political prisoners who had been with him in Evin Prison for two days released a statement noting that they had seen extensive signs of torture on his body.[323] The prison doctor who had prepared a report on Beheshti's physical condition upon his transfer to Evin Prison prepared a report documenting signs of extensive torture on his body before his death.[324] The doctor was later sentenced to six months in prison.[325] Afshin Osanloo, a 40-year-old labor activist who had no history of ill health died in prison under mysterious circumstances after his brother, Mansoor, fled the country and published a *New York Times* opinion piece criticizing the regime (recounted in Chapter 5).[326]

The Islamic regime subsequently enlarged its repertoire of repression beyond widespread detention of dissident students, intellectuals, women, labor and human rights activists, and members of religious and ethnic minorities. The state restricted or banned a number of professional organizations and associations and blocked events that brought people together, such as anniversaries, memorials, funerals, cultural activities, and even some religious events. In one case, in the religious city of Mashhad, the supreme leader's representative declared musical concerts to be disrespectful of religious sanctities.[327]

Summary and Conclusions

Large-scale postelection protests lasted for twenty months, shook the foundation of the Islamic Republic, and demonstrated that the rulers had lost the support of a substantial portion of the Iranian people. They created new repertoires to challenge the regime and made it difficult for the security forces to demobilize the protesters. While the conflicts erupted in response to the presidential elections, the protesters were quickly radicalized and demanded an end to the Islamic Republic. They charged the regime with various violations and called for the establishment of an Iranian republic to replace the Islamic Republic.

The regime countered with widespread repression, targeting all major organizations for the purpose of demobilizing the opposition. The state also devised new repertoires of repression. Authorities arrested and detained at least four thousand people in the eight weeks after the elections, according to a judiciary spokesperson.[328] At the same time, "long-standing human rights issues, including restrictions on freedom of expression and association, religious and gender-based discrimination, and the frequent use of the death penalty, including on juvenile offenders, continued unabated."[329] Executions in Iran increased during 2009, surpassed in number only by China. In the eight weeks between the June 12 election and Ahmadinejad's August reinauguration, the government executed 112 people, according to Amnesty International.[330] The judiciary, the Revolutionary Guard, the Basij militia, and the Ministry of Intelligence were responsible for serious human rights violations, according to Human Rights Watch.[331]

Despite massive repression, the movement persisted, albeit at a lower intensity. The spread of regional democratic struggles provided an opportunity for the opposition leaders to issue a critical statement, challenging the core of the Islamic Republic. The leaders of the Green Movement called for a solidarity gathering in Tehran, pointing to the shortcomings of the Islamic Republic's political system and deviations from revolutionary ideals. Their statement in the context of events in Tunisia and Egypt threatened the Islamic regime.

In reaction to the spread of democratization movements in the region, the regime took harsh action to repress the movement and put an end to the protests. The supreme leader ordered the dissolution of the reformist parties, declaring that they had no right to participate in the political process. The ruling clergy attacked Islamic organizations that had been a part of the polity for three decades, including the Mosharekat, the Mojahedeen Enghelab-e Eslami, the Freedom Movement, and Melli Mazhabi. This blow, directed at some of the Islamic regime's closest, longtime revolutionary allies and supporters—some of whom had previously occupied some of the most important positions in the political structure of the Islamic Republic—dramatically limited the scope of an already-exclusive polity. State repression succeeded in excluding the reformists, who had been a principal faction of the Islamic regime and had played a crucial role in the formation and maintenance of the Islamic Republic. By expelling the reformists, the rulers signaled that they did not intend to reform or modify the political system or grant the democratic rights people had fought for in the 1979 revolution. The move marked one of the most significant turning points in the history of the Islamic regime.

❧ IV ❧

IRRECONCILABLE CONFLICTS

CHAPTER EIGHT

Why the Movement Failed

T HE GREEN MOVEMENT shook the foundation of the Islamic Republic like no other event in the thirty years since the revolution. The movement unfolded so rapidly that it quickly resembled the last phase of the 1979 revolution, mobilizing a substantial segment of Iran's urban population. Despite repression, the movement succeeded in sustaining protests for twenty months. More importantly, the conflicts and confrontations radicalized a considerable portion of the public, which demanded fundamental changes in the social and political system once the supreme leader declared his support for President Ahmadinejad and dismissed allegations of election fraud. The protesters' slogans revealed that a substantial portion of the public believed that they had no legal recourse and could no longer resolve their conflicts within the framework of the Islamic Republic.

Yet, despite the Green Movement's calls for fundamental change, none of the leading reformists—including Mousavi, Karroubi, and others—called for the overthrow of the Islamic regime.[1] The postelection conflicts also radicalized some reformers who were repressed by the state. The movement's popularity revealed underlying weaknesses in the Islamic regime. During the conflicts, the rulers of the Islamic Republic realized for the first time that they had lost the support of a substantial portion of Iran's population. The regime was unable to mount a single protest in its favor for more than six and a half months.

To maintain power, the Islamic regime resorted to large-scale repression, which further antagonized the people and narrowed its popular support. More importantly, as the regime attempted to repress the protesters after the election, it lost the support of portions of the Revolutionary Guard, a vital constituency in the Islamic polity. Nevertheless, state repression ultimately succeeded in defeating the challengers because the movement failed to forge a broad, nationwide coalition capable of disrupting the social, economic, and political processes to bring about democratic transformation.

Shaking the Foundation

President Ahmadinejad during his first term pursued policies that adversely affected major segments of the population and generated intense conflict. He advocated social justice and policies to gain the support of the poor, but many of his policies were repressive and adversely affected portions of the population. Although his economic policies served some segments, the country's economy suffered due to rising corruption, stagflation, and international sanctions. As a result, broad segments of the population mobilized to vote in the 2009 presidential elections. Conservative forces became alarmed by the rising mobilization of the public in the final days of the campaign. They did not favor the return of reformists to power and viewed them, including former prime minister Mousavi, as counterrevolutionaries. Conservatives argued that reformists did not share the values of the Islamic Revolution and would undermine the Islamic nature of the system if they were allowed to gain power. The most active forces in the effort to block reformists were the president's office and the Revolutionary Guard.

The office of the president heavily pressured IRNA, the Islamic Republic News Agency, to declare Ahmadinejad as the winner of the election. The office released a bulletin in the waning hours of election day announcing that Ahmadinejad had received 90 percent of the vote in small towns and rural areas, despite the fact that polls were still open. The president's office issued another bulletin an hour later announcing that Ahmadinejad had won the election with more than 60 percent of the votes. The office threatened Roohallah Jomeie, deputy head of IRNA, who refused to broadcast the bulletin. Jomeie left his office around 10 p.m. in protest, arguing that such an announcement should come either from the Interior Ministry or the Guardian Council. Within minutes, IRNA broadcast the official announcement that Ahmadinejad was declared the winner with more than 60 percent of the votes, although voting continued for about two more hours.[2, 3]

The Revolutionary Guard also became actively involved in the election process and played an important role in its outcome. An audio recording of General Moshfegh, deputy director of intelligence for the Sarallah military base, revealed that the Guard had planned to intervene in the election process long before the opposition declared their candidates. The recording disclosed how the Guard eavesdropped on the internal discussions of the opposition campaigns and interfered with the work of election monitors, thereby enabling the regime to declare Ahmadinejad the victor. Moshfegh's revelations prompted seven opposition leaders to file a lawsuit against the commanders of the Revolutionary Guard.[4]

General Mohammad Ali Jaafari, commander of the Revolutionary Guard, revealed in a videotaped, closed meeting a number of important points about the Guard's intervention to alter the election's outcome.[5] Addressing the senior commanders of the Guard and Ali Saeedi, the supreme leader's representative in the Revolutionary Guard, Jaafari articulated the Guard's specific concerns. He noted that the sensitivity of the presidential election was clear to all. He continued that during the election, the revolutionaries' concern and red line were that those who opposed the revolution and its values would return to power. Those forces "found an opportunity and penetrated governance" when Khatami was elected in 1997. According to Jaafari, the reason reformists insisted that the Guard not interfere during and after the election was to enable the reformists to carry out their plot without interference from the Guard or the Basij. He asserted, "This slope was worrisome, and everyone analyzed that if the trend continued, the election would go to a second round; and in the second round, the outcome would be unpredictable." Jaafari reminded the audience that, shortly after the election, the supreme leader made a speech demanding an end to all protests, including peaceful ones. Finally, Jaafari identified two critical decisions by the security forces and the Guard that disrupted the opposition: to carry out rapid, widespread arrests of the activists, analysts, and reform leaders, and to disrupt the phones, mobile networks, and Internet communication used by reformists to mobilize and protest.[6]

The public postelection pronouncements of the rulers of the Islamic Republic demonstrated how seriously they regarded the threat of the Green Movement and its alarming character. Months after the election, Supreme Leader Ayatollah Khamenei admitted that "the sedition was a great challenge."[7] He criticized the opposition for damaging the system and bringing it to the "edge of the cliff."[8] In response to calls that Mousavi, Karroubi, and Rahnavard be released from house arrest, Khamenei noted that their crime was great and that if the imam had been alive, he would have treated them more severely. He said that, had they been put on trial, their punishment would have been harsher. "We have treated them with kindness," Khamenei said.[9]

Similarly, in a public speech, General Jaafari declared that during the sedition, "the Islamic system went nearly to the border of overthrow." He added that in the recent events, all the domestic reformists and their external supporters had capitalized to achieve victory and regain power. It was by the people's astuteness and the leadership of the supreme leader, he said, that this huge conspiracy was neutralized.[10] Ayatollah Jannati, head of the Guardian Council, commented that the country would have been destroyed during the 2009 sedition had it not been for the supreme leader's perceptiveness and tact. The enemy had been confident that the revolution and the Islamic Republic would be terminated, but God didn't want that.[11]

Officials of the Islamic Republic acknowledged divisions in the armed forces and difficulties of repressing the opposition and ending the protests. General Ataollah Salehi noted that portraits of the sedition's leaders were hanging in garrisons.[12] General Jaafari admitted publicly that "the post-election protests were more dangerous for the revolution and Islam than the eight-year war against Iraq."[13] He added that during the sedition, the credibility of the Islamic system had been undermined and that it would take years to eradicate its negative impact.[14] Mohammad Jaafar Asadi, a senior officer in the Revolutionary Guard, commented that defending against the 2009 protests was considerably more difficult than defending against Iraqi aggression during the eight-year war.[15]

The Islamic Republic's leaders were greatly alarmed by the decline of support for the regime within their most important constituency—namely, the Revolutionary Guard—in the aftermath of the 2009 election and conflicts. During these conflicts, the Revolutionary Guard's rank and file was not unified, and many members were unwilling to repress the protesters. Possibly, some Guard members dissented against their leaders because of the Guard's alleged interference in the outcome of the election, as General Jaafari indicated in his video. Clerics representing the supreme leader in the Revolutionary Guard and a Guard commander confirmed that the regime's support base during the conflicts had narrowed dramatically. Even with the challengers' lack of a broad nationwide coalition, the regime had difficulty repressing their protests for several months. Seyyed Amrollah Mohammadi, a cleric and the supreme leader's representative in the Revolutionary Guard, stated in an interview published by the Islamic Republic's official news agency that during the postelection conflicts, "many of our own waivered; the Revolutionary Guard was the only entity that fully supported the supreme leader to the end."[16] According to

Mohammad Hajizadeh, many of their forces "deviated and lost their way because they had not gained perfect insight."[17] Ali Saeedi, Khamenei's representative in the Revolutionary Guard, complained at a national gathering of Guard commanders that even some commanders had remained silent during the conflicts.[18] "Some of our commanders had sealed their mouths," Saeedi noted.[19]

General Jaafari went further and acknowledged that the schism and opposition within the Revolutionary Guard forced the regime to rely on the Basij, the Revolutionary Guard's paramilitary division. He noted that the "presence of the Basij and their support for the supreme leader put an end to the conspiracies. Had the Basij not existed, we don't know what might have happened, and it is possible that the seditionists might have achieved their goals."[20] Ali Fazli, another Revolutionary Guard commander, revealed that "due to inadequate forces to repress protesters in Tehran, all the Basijis from the province of Tehran and even some from other provinces had to be recruited to put down the rebellion."[21]

Despite some inconsistencies, these statements illustrate the regime's situation in repressing the protesters during the postelection conflicts. Segments of the Revolutionary Guard refused to carry out the repressive policies, thereby undermining the regime's most important base of support. According to a dissident general in the Revolutionary Guard, the regime replaced several dozen Guard generals and senior Basij personnel for refusing to use violence against protesters.[22] An Iranian dissident source reported that ten commanders of the Revolutionary Guard from the Iran-Iraq war died in less than a year.[23] Four commanders died on four consecutive days. Another commander, Ahmad Sodagar, who died a few weeks after the four, requested in his will that his body be autopsied and that his coffin be inscribed with the words "fate of the person who lived honestly."[24]

The rulers of the Islamic Republic had expected to have the backing of large segments of the population. They were surprised to see that so many people remained silent during the protests and confrontations. Saeedi, the supreme leader's representative in the Revolutionary Guard, noted in a public gathering that those who chose silence and watched the events made a great mistake. He emphasized that past mistakes should not be allowed to be repeated. "Two hundred years from now we will be history, and we will be judged; therefore, the divine trust that was gifted to Islam and the revolution must be protected and maintained."[25]

The rapid mobilization, scale of protests, and swift radicalization of protesters so eroded the regime's social base of support that it was unable to mount a single progovernment demonstration, despite having done so repeatedly over the previous thirty years. The regime finally assembled rallies to support the supreme leader in a few major cities on December 30, 2009, more than six and a half months after the postelection protests began. Organizers provided free buses, metro rides, and food for the attendees of a "spontaneous" rally.[26] The government gave civil servants the day off to attend the rallies [27] and bused school children to the event. [28] Some factories closed for workers to attend the rallies.[29] Some companies also provided buses to transport employees to the rallies.[30] Authorities printed placards and flags for the event.[31] Organizers in Tehran held the demonstration in Revolution Square, rather than the larger Freedom Square, site of the largest events such as the anniversary of the revolution.[32]

In contrast, the opposition had no difficulty organizing huge protests in major cities, particularly at the beginning of the conflicts before repression intensified. A comparative analysis of the size of the protests in 1979 and 2009 illustrates the capacity of the opposition to mobilize large numbers of people. The opposition took approximately one year to assemble demonstrations as large as one million people in Tehran during the anti-shah protests. The Islamic regime's opponents needed just three days to mobilize more than three million people in Tehran on June 15, 2009. Furthermore, unlike the early protests of 1979, which did not have a revolutionary character, the 2009 protests quickly surged beyond the election outcome, factional disputes, and calls for reform to slogans and demands that attacked the very existence of the Islamic state. The protests following the 2009 election and demands for fundamental change had the potential to ignite a revolutionary situation. They sounded an alarm for the rulers of the Islamic Republic.

Given the state's difficulties in mobilizing public support, dealing with the Green Movement, and repressing the opposition, some members of the polity expressed concerns about possible future threats. Ayatollah Haeri Shirazi, an assistant to the supreme leader and former Friday prayer leader of Shiraz, addressed an open letter to Mousavi and Karroubi, who remained under house arrest. "With your insistence," he said, "the sedition of the 2009 election will remain as fire under the ashes, and the system cannot remain indifferent toward it. Removal of the sedition is putting out the torch, but putting out the torch is different from putting out the candle. Your admission of error will put out the candle. The enemies insist on keeping the candle lit so that at an appropriate time they can relight the torch. Your insistence is the same as keeping the candle lit, and your admission of error is putting it out. Now, you are the only ones that can undertake this great action; thus, do not neglect its great reward."[33] Similarly, Justice Minister Mustafa Pour-Mohammadi was concerned about the future activities of the leaders of the movement and their political endeavors. He stated that if Mousavi and Karroubi were to declare that "they are law abiding and would not disturb the peace of the country, they would be forgiven."[34]

Causes of the Movement's Failure

Despite shaking the foundations of the Islamic Republic, the postelection protests eventually failed. Protesters could not sustain their movement once repression largely demobilized demonstrators and challengers. This outcome can be attributed to four main factors: insufficient leadership and lack of preparation, a disjunction between leadership and protesters, limited solidarity structures, and the failure to consolidate and form a broad, disruptive coalition.

First, the reform movement's leadership exhibited shortcomings from the beginning, notably in its initial tendency to follow events, not lead them. Mousavi failed to use his position during the early stages of the conflicts to direct protesters, devise new tactics, or expand the capacity of the collective actors to challenge the system. The leaders missed an early opportunity to command the largest following in Iran's political history. Mousavi initially attempted to prevent protesters from taking to the streets on June 15, on the grounds that the event did not have an official permit. He appeared at the rally only after they defied his exhortations. Reformist opposition leaders ceased to call for street demonstrations following several rounds of protests, out of fear of greater state repression. The leaders of the Green Movement stopped convening protests because they did not want to put the country through a shock and were concerned about the lives of Iranians, including the lives of security forces that were engaged in repressive activities, according to Ardeshir Amir Arjomand, Mousavi's advisor.[35] The leaders also ceased to call for protests, possibly concerned that demonstrators were becoming radicalized and threatened the reformists.

Tactically, the leaders of the movement were unprepared to counter state repression. Despite knowing the history of the Islamic Republic, the leaders failed to devise contingency plans to deal with disruptions in the Internet and their communications systems. They left their key activists unprotected against the first wave of arrests that began the day after the election.

Mousavi and Karroubi assumed greater leadership roles in the final stage of the conflicts and issued more critical statements, which led to their imprisonment. By then, however, security forces had gained the upper hand and arrested thousands of people, including many well-known activists who were given long-term sentences. Throughout hardship in custody,

Mousavi and Karroubi continued to insist that the election results were fraudulent. Both men refused officials' suggestions that they would be released if they repented, and chose instead to remain in confinement despite multiple health problems. Karroubi, a man in his seventies, endured solitary confinement for about three years with no access to sunshine or fresh air and underwent several surgeries. When placed under house arrest to continue his detention, he refused to repent because, according to his son, he did not believe in earthly gods to repent to.[36] Instead, Karroubi expressed his willingness to be tried before a jury composed of regime supporters, but he demanded mass media coverage.[37]

A second factor contributing to the outcome was the disjuncture between the movement's leadership, which pursued a path of reform within the legal framework of the Islamic system, and popular protesters, who quickly embraced radical change and shouted slogans against the regime. Demonstrators even called for an Iranian, not an Islamic, republic. "Mousavi told Iranians they should not, however, be seeking to change the Islamic regime."[38] As protesters became increasingly radicalized, Mousavi urged his supporters to protest through legal channels only and remain faithful to the "sacred system of the Islamic Republic."[39] He blamed the repressive violence in the early stages of the conflicts on the radical slogans of some protesters.[40] He also had a message to those who sought the downfall of Iran's Islamic regime: "It is up to you," he wrote, "to distance yourself from them, and do not allow them to misuse the current situation."[41] Other reformist leaders, too, discouraged demonstrators from voicing radical slogans or demanding fundamental change as conflicts intensified and protesters became radicalized. Some reformists even maintained that regime agent provocateurs had concocted radical slogans to provoke state repression. In the end, neither Mousavi nor Karroubi nor any other leading reformist called for the overthrow of the Islamic regime.

This disjuncture within the movement weakened the opposition and prevented it from consolidating. The leaders' attempts to rein in the secular and more radical forces had negative consequences for the opposition as a whole. The two camps never reconciled their positions and, as a result, failed to consolidate behind a unified program. As repression intensified, the number of protesters declined. Some secular and radical activists may have withdrawn from the protests because they were unwilling to pay a heavy cost for a movement reluctant to challenge the Islamic Republic's existing framework. Conversely, some reformist protesters may have backed away from the movement because they were discouraged by its rapid radicalization.

Third, the movement's solidarity structures were limited by the characteristics of its supporters, in part because the leaders of the movement
failed to broaden the nature of the conflicts, address the economic shortcomings of the Islamic Republic, or mobilize the working classes. Little
detailed data are available about the backgrounds and characteristics of
the thousands of protesters imprisoned during the year following the election. The Iranian human rights organization, *hra-news.net*, provided some
data on 2,582 individuals arrested during that period. Excluding prisoners
of conscience, such as Baha'is, Christians, and Sunnis, who were not
involved in the political protests, the data for the remaining 2,394 detainees
revealed that the vast majority had no political affiliation.[42] Of those whose
political affiliation was known, 3.67 percent were members of the five legal
political organizations that participated in the election (Mosharekat,
Mousavi campaign, Karroubi campaign, Mojahedeen Enghelab-e Eslami,
and Kargozaran). If all politically affiliated detainees are included, the
percentage rises to 5.9 percent. Protesters' lack of strong solidarity structures and preexisting ties to reformist organizations help explain why
many rapidly became radicalized and demanded fundamental change
despite reformist leaders' reluctance to do so. Ironically, the regime viewed
organized constituencies such as the reformist political organizations to be
a more significant threat, and efforts to destroy them intensified. Detainees
with strong ties to reformist organizations remained in custody, despite
their more moderate ideological views. In contrast, many detainees who
lacked ties to reformist organizations were eventually released by the
regime, although their views were very radical, and some were rearrested
later.

Finally, the movement succeeded in mobilizing some segments of Iranian
society to act collectively, but failed to attract others. The government provided no statistics, but data provided by the Iranian human rights organization revealed some information about 112 people slain during the postelection conflicts.[43] There were many victims in a few weeks of protests,
including a conspicuous number of young people. Of forty-four victims
whose ages were given, 13.6 percent were below the age of 20; 56.8 percent were between 20 and 29; 20.5 percent were between 30 and 39; 6.8
percent were between 40 and 49; and 2.3 percent were over 50 years old.

Several large, important constituencies were well represented among the
protesters. Students and women were among the most active participants
in the struggles. Concentrated mainly in large cities, the country's student
population had expanded by 2009 to more than 3.5 million, facilitating
their mobilization and collective action. With access to the Internet and

social media at the universities, students played an important role in broadcasting opposition activities and innovating new repertoires such as writing slogans on bank notes and posting them on Facebook, YouTube, and Twitter. While some students belonged to the major, legal reformist political organizations, the vast majority of students and women had no preexisting ties. They mobilized in reaction to the disputed 2009 presidential election. Because they lacked preexisting ties, their political activities were not shaped by reformist organizations. Many students and women became confrontational during the postelection protests, quickly radicalized, and demanded fundamental changes in the Islamic Republic. Students' radicalization and confrontation placed them among the principal targets of repressive violence. They comprised 50 percent of those slain and 11.86 percent of those jailed during the protests.[44]

Students were demobilized following the disputed elections. The universities, historically the conscience of the nation and citadels of freedom, were silenced. Student organizations were shut down, their publications were banned, and their social, cultural, and political activities were blocked. Many students arrested in the aftermath of the election were kept in prison, and countless others were "starred" or marked for disciplinary action, suspension, or dismissal.[45] As of November 2010, more than seventy students were still in prison and hundreds had been expelled from the universities.[46] Mohsen Rahamani, a university student, was sentenced to seven years for holding a picture of Mousavi in an election campaign event for Hassan Rouhani in 2013. He was charged with insulting the supreme leader and founder of the Islamic Republic.[47] Payman Morovati, a student activist, was shot to death in front of his house on December 18, 2015. Intelligence officers and security agents warned the family not to publicize the killing, according to Radio France Internationale Persian service.[48]

Repressive measures further reduced university autonomy and reinforced decisions made by outside entities. After the 2009 disputed presidential elections, Ayatollah Khamenei expressed concerns about teaching Western social sciences that contradicted the Quran and religious principles. Immediately, President Ahmadinejad notified all universities that a new council under the direction of the Cultural Revolution Council would begin purging academic institutions of materialist and Western ideologies. In the autumn of 2009, the Supreme Council formed a new authority headed by Haddad Adel to carry out the task.[49]

State repression severely affected the lives of students in academic institutions. Repressive forces intervened extensively in academic institutions and, for a while, silenced student dissent. At the conclusion of Ahmadinejad's term as president, students lamented the "ruination" of the universities during his eight-year presidency.[50] Reza Faraji Dana, President Rouhani's minister of science who defended students' rights to protest, acknowledged that sometimes students in the Tehran University dormitory were too terrified to complain about even simple matters related to student affairs.[51]

Despite relentless repression and lengthy jail sentences, student political activities and protests remained a serious threat to the Islamic regime. The supreme leader met with hundreds of faculty members five years after the disputed election and noted that the field of humanities should be based on spiritual and Islamic worldviews. He also emphasized that the universities and higher education must be depoliticized and should not become locations for the activities of political clubs.[52] He publicly exhorted the minister of science to prevent disturbances of the "calm environment of the universities."[53]

Women, many of whom were also students, were more actively involved in the postelection protests than they had been in the 1979 revolution. They actively chanted radical slogans and hurled rocks at security forces on some occasions,[54] and they often led the chants of radical slogans such as "Death to the Dictator," reported Roger Cohen from Tehran.[55] Young women were seen hurling stones and confronting police and security forces for the first time in Iranian history.[56] Women sometimes berated as "cowards" the male demonstrators who fled Basiji attacks.[57] During Quds protests in September 2009, a young female student commented, "The cheating, the raping, the killing and the torture drive you mad. I've come to express my hatred for Ahmadinejad and his protector, that so-called Great Leader of the Revolution."[58] An older woman declared, "They have raped, murdered and tortured our youth after stealing the election. May God's wrath come down on them."[59]

Women's active participation in the conflicts, confrontations, and radicalization made them among the leading victims of state repression. Women comprised 11.6 percent of those killed during the protests following the election and nearly 13 percent of those imprisoned. Of those women who were in jail, 25 percent had husbands who were also incarcerated for political reasons. Another 41 percent of imprisoned women had other family members who were also imprisoned for political reasons.[60] Female victims of repression such as Neda became the face of the movement and vivid symbols of women's victimization and struggles.

Conservative forces reacted strongly against women's radicalization and mobilization during the antigovernment protests. The supreme leader declared that gender equality was a Western concept and unacceptable in Islam. He noted that anyone who considered the problem of women separate from the problem of family would be engaging in disorder.[61] Ayatollah

Khamenei reversed Iran's family planning policy and called for doubling the country's population to 150 million.[62] "Given the importance of population size in sovereign might and economic progress . . . firm, quick and efficient steps must be taken to offset the steep fall in birthrate of recent years," he wrote on his website.[63] Authorities imposed new restrictions upon women. Iranian women, who had outnumbered and outperformed men for more than a decade, faced adverse decisions at universities.[64] In 2012, thirty-six universities and colleges stopped admitting women in seventy-seven fields[65] and reduced female admission in higher education by 11,500 between 2012 and 2014.[66] Authorities closed down women's studies departments in some major universities, including Tehran University.[67] Conservative forces spoke increasingly of the need to segregate genders in public spaces.[68] The majority of cities barred women from playing music in concerts following the 2009 election.[69]

Other collectivities concentrated in large cities were also active in the protests. Highly educated professionals, such as journalists, university professors, lawyers, and doctors were important groups that participated in the postelection protests. Broad segments of Iran's intellectuals began to defect following the 1979 revolution. Journalists, dissident intellectuals, academics, lawyers, and doctors were among the first to support struggles for democracy. They published critical statements condemning government repression, joined student protesters, addressed campus rallies about the causes of the conflicts, and participated in the 2009 protests. A few professors were arrested and imprisoned, and many were dismissed or forced to retire.

Like students and women, many highly educated professionals lacked preexisting ties to reformist political organizations. Only some of the professionals belonged to these organizations. Like students and women, professionals were located primarily in major Iranian cities. Professionals represented almost 22 percent of those slain during the protests. Altogether, 138 professionals were arrested during the protests following the 2009 election. They comprised nearly 70 percent of all detainees who were employed and whose occupation was included in the data sample made available by the human rights activists in *hra-news.net*.

In contrast, some important collectivities were largely absent from the demonstrations and protests. Aside from the highest religious leaders, or sources of emulation, many of whom criticized the government and the election results (discussed in Chapter 9), the vast majority of Shiite clergy did not support the opposition or join the protests. Only seven members of the clerical community were arrested during the twelve months of postelection protests. Most clerics and Friday Prayer leaders did not participate in the protests or support the people. Historically, the clergy had possessed independent financial resources from religious taxes. As a result, their politics at times contradicted state policies. After the revolution, mosques lost their autonomy, came under strict state control, and were no longer available to mobilize or launch collective action. Empowered by the Islamic constitution, the vast majority of the Shiite clergy became beneficiaries of the state, and their politics underwent a shift. In the Islamic Republic, clergy gained new economic resources from the state and also depended on the state for their positions and livelihood. Many also ended up working for the state bureaucracy. Not surprisingly, the majority of clergy pursued politics that largely supported the state.

Other major social classes, including bazaar merchants, shopkeepers, and industrial workers, were likewise largely absent as collectivities in the postelection protests, although individuals joined the demonstrations in large cities. Government repression of liberal bazaar organizations after the revolution significantly transformed bazaar politics, weakening the capacity of bazaars for collective action. The liberal Society of Merchants, Guilds, and Artisans of the Tehran Bazaar, which had fought for democracy for decades and played an important role during the revolutionary struggles, was banned and severely repressed by the Islamic government. The Islamic regime also imprisoned, murdered, and executed some well-known bazaar activists, including Ali Asghar Zehtabchi, Ahmad Javaherian, and Karim Dastmalchi, who had supported the liberal-nationalists and dissident organizations. Mahmoud Manian, a bazaar activist and well-known leader of the liberal National Front, was killed in 1994 in a suspicious car accident after earlier attempts on his life had failed.

With the repression of liberal merchants, the Islamic state facilitated the rise of a conservative organization within the bazaar. Its leading members were a small group of pro-Khomeini bazaaris who received permits and resources to operate their organization and promote their cause. Although these bazaaris had modest resources prior to the revolution, they quickly prospered once the Islamic Republic was established. They were organized in the Coalition of Islamic Societies, the Tehran bazaar's only active business organization. As cronies of the Islamic regime, they used their state connections to control important sectors of Iran's economy and amass vast fortunes.

The coalition adopted antidemocratic positions during major political conflicts. It swiftly condemned student protests in July 1999 and accused most of the demonstrators' slogans of attacking the "sanctities" of the system and the foundation of the Islamic Revolution. "The slogans have all been illegal, making the counterrevolution and oppressive America happy." The same statement criticized the interior minister for failing to take a firm stand against the protesters or provide security for the public.[70] The coalition likewise followed the ruling clergy's definition of the protests as sedition. The leader of the organization, Hassan Habibi, repeatedly criticized the protests that erupted following the 2009 presidential election. In an interview, he remarked that the sedition used the electoral mechanism to overthrow Islamic order. "As long as we insist on preserving the values of the Islamic Revolution, we must be prepared for the fact that conspiracies do not end," he noted.[71] The organization's general secretary condemned reformist challenges to the state and opposed lifting the restrictions and the house arrest of Mousavi and Karroubi, arguing that the reformist leaders' "sins could not be forgiven."[72]

Although bazaaris as a class did not join the 2009 protests, not all of them supported Ahmadinejad. Segments of the bazaars in major cities had gone on strike in 2008 to protest Ahmadinejad's tax policies. According to one report from Tehran, about 70 to 80 percent of the bazaaris sympathized with Mousavi after the 2009 elections.[73] In some cities, a number of bazaaris closed their shops during the protests, and some participated in the protests. A 69-year-old merchant told a reporter, "I came to show solidarity with the youth of my country. The regime is destroying Islam and Iran."[74] In cities such as Mahabad and Orumieh many shopkeepers were arrested because they shut down their stores during protests. Some self-employed entrepreneurs were arrested, and others were killed, comprising 10 percent of those slain during the protests.

The regime took preemptive measures to halt bazaar closings and prevent shopkeepers and bazaaris from becoming politicized and joining the protesters in a broader coalition. Before the end of 2009, the regime arrested several well-known bazaaris, including Javad Laary, Mohammad Banazadeh Amir-Khizi, and Mohsen Dokmechi. Dokmechi died while in prison.[75] In another preemptive action, progovernment militiamen and police officers stormed the Tehran bazaar, leaving a prominent merchant dead. They arrested a member of the textile merchant guild who had given a speech urging the continuation of the bazaar strike that had been organized against government tax policies. Although temperatures were normal, the government then declared two days of national holiday citing excessive heat, in an attempt to encourage the people to leave the capital and blunt opposition protests.[76] The repressive measures likely played an important role in preventing bazaaris from mobilizing and joining the political protests.

After the Green Movement had been demobilized, Tehran bazaaris shuttered their businesses again and took to the streets in 2012 to protest government economic policies that depreciated Iran's currency.[77] During their protests, bazaaris' slogans resembled those of the Green Movement, such as "Mahmoud traitor, you ruined the country."[78] Other slogans included "Death to the dictator," "Ahmadi be warned, we are the people, not rabble," "Death to the government that deceives the people," and "Mahmoud, shame on you, leave politics."[79] Bazaaris reopened their businesses only under pressure by security forces, according to a dissident report.[80]

Industrial workers did not join the political struggles in 2009 nor initiate any strikes as they had done in the final stage of the 1979 revolution. Economic grievances were completely absent from the slogans during the protests. Green Movement failed to broaden the scope of the conflicts by including the grievances of the working classes.

Industrial workers were certainly adversely affected by the country's economic decline, which became severe after the Green Movement was largely repressed and demobilized. State subsidies for fuel and basic foods, which had helped the less well-off segments of the population, were terminated at the end of 2010, negatively affecting the working class. Stagflation resulting from a combination of state policies and the intensification of Western sanctions appeared largely after the movement had been repressed.

More importantly, Iran's industrial working class lacked the solidarity structures to act as a class and join the Green Movement following the 2009 elections. Between 70 percent and 90 percent of workers worked on a temporary contractual basis and had no job security. These temporary workers received no protection from labor laws and could not develop strong, nationwide solidarity structures to mobilize for collective action.

Repression was another factor precluding industrial workers from participating in political protests. Iran's working class has mobilized primarily when political repression was low. Industrial workers joined the revolutionary struggles in the fall of 1978 when political repression declined. Intensified state repression beginning in 2005 under Ahmadinejad adversely impacted workers' capacity to mobilize for collective action. The secretary of the Isfahan Labor House, Asghar Breshan, complained to reporters that labor organizations had never been so intensely repressed as during Ahmadinejad's presidency. Breshan also noted that Ahmadinejad's government intended to extirpate all labor organizations.[81] He complained bitterly about intense government repression, which had reached a peak in postrevolutionary Iran during Ahmadinejad's rule.[82] Mansoor Osanloo, a prominent labor leader, remarked that even contemplating organizing union meetings or engaging in strikes could have "devastating consequences."[83]

Hence, Iranian workers did not join the protests collectively because, unlike the situation in 1978, state repression did not decline in 2009. Political repression against workers increased both prior to and after the 2009 presidential election. In the weeks prior to the 2009 election, the Islamic government arrested 150 labor leaders and activists during Tehran's May Day celebration. Security forces even arrested Mehdi Farahi Shandeez, cousin of Ahmadinejad's wife and a supporter of worker rights and the labor movement. He was kept in solitary confinement for months.[84]

To be sure, individual workers in major cities joined the 2009 protests, and some were killed.[85] Workers slain during the protests accounted for more than 18 percent of the deaths for which occupations were known. Workers continued to be a target of state repression after the election, and dozens were arrested.[86] Reza Shahabi, the treasurer of the Syndicate of Workers of the Tehran and Suburbs Bus Company, was arrested in June 2010 and sentenced to six years. Behnam Ebrahimzadeh of the Committee to Pursue the Establishment of Workers' Organizations and a children's rights advocate, was arrested in the same month and sentenced to twenty years in prison (later reduced to five years) on what Amnesty International called spurious charges.[87] Shahrokh Zamani, a labor leader in Tabriz, was arrested for "participating in the organization of an unlawful group opposing the state . . . with the aim of disrupting national security by way of workers' strikes and armed rebellion," "assembly and collusion to further illegal activities," and "propaganda against the regime."[88] Zamani died in custody after being denied medical care.[89] Two other workers, Sattar Beheshti and Afshin Osanloo, died in prison in 2012 and 2013, respectively, discussed in Chapters 5 and 7.

The state's decision to continue to repress industrial workers following the presidential election suggests that a significant number were hostile to the regime. The dissolution of independent labor unions, restrictions on even Islamic labor associations, and the continuing detention of labor leaders further suggest that the regime was aware of the threat posed to the state by these groups and lacked confidence in its support base among the industrial workforce.

The differential impact of two major social classes on the revolution and the postelection conflict of 2009 offers a clear, dramatic contrast. Unlike their actions in 1979, bazaaris and workers failed to protest as collectivities to disrupt the economy through bazaar shutdowns or industrial strikes. They took no steps to disrupt the production or distribution of goods and services or, most critically, halt oil exports, the lifeblood of the regime. Had such disruptive actions occurred in combination with the political crisis, they would have signaled instability and, possibly, a realignment of the contending forces. Instead, the absence of such actions contributed to the defeat of the protesters and challengers.

The 2009 protests resembled the uprising of 1963, when protests erupted in several major cities in reaction against the arrest of Ayatollah Khomeini. Both conflicts failed to disrupt the economy and society or bring about political change. The 2009 protests differed from those of 1963 because millions of Iranians did turn out to engage in collective action in major cities across the country. Unlike the 1963 protests, which lasted only three days, the 2009 conflicts continued for twenty months and resembled in intensity the end stage of the 1979 revolution. But the 2009 protests lacked the breadth of the revolutionary protests, which rocked more than 170 cities during the final phase.[90] The 2009 protests were confined mainly to large cities. Tehran alone accounted for approximately 80 percent of all arrests. Other protest centers included Tabriz, Orumieh, Sanandaj, Ahvaz, Shiraz, Isfahan, Zanjan, Ahavz, and Ghazvin. But most small and medium-sized cities were not affected by the protests.

In the absence of a national coalition encompassing all major classes and collectivities, the government succeeded in controlling its security and paramilitary forces through close supervision to prevent defections and insubordination. Had the opposition formed a broad coalition and extended its protests across the entire country, the regime's hierarchy would have had greater difficulty in controlling its coercive forces. Thinly dispersed around the country and in contact with the protesting civilian population, these forces would have been vulnerable to insubordination and defections, and the outcome might have been very different.

Summary and Conclusions

Large-scale protests and rapid radicalization of protesters briefly shook the core of the Islamic Republic and demonstrated widespread opposition to the regime's conservative faction. Despite the declining number of protesters over time, challengers sustained their protests for twenty months. In contrast, the regime failed to mount a single progovernment demonstration for more than six and a half months following the election, confirming its narrow base of support. The regime's inability to mobilize the Revolutionary Guard and its reliance instead on the Basij to repress the protesters further demonstrated the erosion of the regime's own power base and how near the system had come to the cliff's edge.

The Green Movement failed because of weaknesses in its leadership, a disjuncture between leaders and protesters, and its failure to consolidate into a broad, disruptive coalition that could effectively usher in democracy.

The movement's leaders were slow to lead the protesters in disruptive events and missed an initial opportunity to lead the largest following in Iran's recent history. A disjuncture developed between leaders that seemed committed to the Islamic Republic and radicalized street protesters that called for large-scale transformation, including the formation of an Iranian republic in place of an Islamic republic.

In time, the movement's leaders, Mousavi and Karroubi, issued more critical statements in response to the elite's intransigence and new opportunities provided by the overthrow of nearby regimes. By then, however, repressive forces had arrested and imprisoned thousands of people in Tehran and several other major cities that were rocked by protests. Ultimately, the movement was defeated because it failed to consolidate and forge a nationwide coalition of all major social classes and collectivities to isolate the state and counter the power of repression. People in most small and medium-sized cities failed to mobilize in protest against the regime. As collectivities, bazaaris and industrial workers did not join the protests or disrupt the economic structure and trading networks. These shortcomings enabled the state to deploy security and the coercive forces to crush the opposition. But the underlying conflicts were far from over.

CHAPTER NINE

Irreconcilable Conflicts and Endless Repression

S TATE REPRESSION OF the Green Movement, which conservatives called "sedition," had crucial consequences. It radicalized many in both factions of the regime, with each side leveling accusations against the other. Those in the opposition charged the leaders with dictatorship, citing a lack of democratic freedoms, continued violations of constitutional rights, and failure to fulfill the promises of the revolution. Some also called for an end to the Islamic Republic, while others pushed for fundamental changes, including separation of the clergy from the state. Regime supporters accused the opposition camp of foreign influence and demanded punishment and continuous repression. With rising polarization within Iran and declining popular support for the Islamic regime, the ruling clerical elite and their allies repeatedly harkened back to the ideological claim that the Islamic order's legitimacy was rooted in Shiite Islam, not in the people, a view at variance with Iran's constitution, which stressed popular sovereignty. Some members of the elite believed that the Islamic Republic must be defended even if it was supported by only a small minority. At the same time, many conservative leaders expressed concern that the Green Movement would survive and reemerge in the future. Finally, the ruling elite announced unprecedented powers for the supreme leader, exalting his position, sanctifying him, and invoking autonomy and divine support.

These contradictions and conflicts illustrated the gulf between the irreconcilable ideologies of the elite factions. Although state repression ended the protests and silenced the challengers, it became increasingly clear that the elite in the two camps defended ideologies that were fundamentally incompatible: one demanded freedom and democratic rights; the other insisted on divine legitimacy, the ruler's absolute power, and citizens' duty to obey God's government rooted in the Prophet's teachings.

Dissident and Reformist Reactions to Repression

Despite failing to bring about reforms, a number of reformists and moderate political activists continued to issue radical political statements that reinforced the irreconcilability of the conflicts between the factions. They condemned the government for suppressing the people's will, criticized the supreme leader, and implicitly praised some aspects of the prerevolutionary monarchy.

Abolfazl Ghadyani, a member of the reformist Mojahedeen Enghelab-e Eslami who was imprisoned for four years during the monarchy, issued a number of statements from his cell in the notorious Evin Prison, arguing that the Islamic Revolution had deviated from its original goals. He claimed that the despotism of the *velayat-e faghieh* (guardianship of the jurist, commonly referred to as the supreme leader) produced a situation of lawlessness that prevented the reform movement from removing antidemocratic laws. Absolutist power, Ghadyani argued, could only be tamed by the power of the people.[1] When authorities charged Ghadyani with new crimes following his statements, he refused to appear before the judge to hear the charges. He was forcibly removed from the prison hospital and taken to court, where he accused the judge and the court of illegitimacy and charged the government with committing a crime by taking him to court. "Be sure that because of this one day, you will be put on trial," he said. When the judge told him that his new crime was insulting the supreme leader and spreading propaganda against the Islamic order, he replied: "The greatest propagandist against the Islamic Republic is Mr. Khamenei. It was he who called the Iranian people microbes. It is he who has destroyed the country, and it has been during his leadership that three billion dollars have been embezzled." Ghadyani told the judge that Mr. Khamenei was now the idol *(Taghout)*, a term Khomeini had used to refer to the shah. "I have not spent fifty years of my life in struggle so that he could rule without accountability," he declared.[2] In another statement, this time to the head of the judiciary, Ghadyani compared the Islamic Republic's treatment of the families of political prisoners to that of the previous regime.

As a political prisoner in the former regime, I declare that your prosecutors' treatment of the families of political prisoners, approved by you, make the shah's SAVAK, with all their torture, look good. Despite their corruption and oppression, the previous regime did not disrespect the families of the prisoners and did not generate difficulties for wives and children. Unfortunately, this is an eternal disgrace, for this religious despotism will do anything and use any inhuman means to achieve their goals. This demonstrates the peak of moral decline of the power-holders.[3]

Mustafa Tajzadeh, a reformist former deputy interior minister under President Khatami, and confined in solitary confinement in Evin Prison, wrote a number of critical statements. In a letter to the supreme leader, Tajzadeh decried the fact that in Iran the clergy "commanded" the election.

In today's world, free elections are unavoidable, and if you do not voluntarily accept this, sooner or later you will be obliged to. It is unfortunate that thoughtlessness will put us in the severe situation of Syria. It is even more regrettable that during the shah's time obedience to him was sufficient, but today they demand belief in the supreme leader; otherwise people are not allowed to participate in elections.[4]

Tajzadeh argued that "Despotism and slavery are despotism and slavery. Whether the form is *velayee* [jurisprudence] or monarchist does not alter much its antagonism to freedom."[5] When Ayatollah Khamenei demanded that opposition leaders apologize for mistakenly calling the 2009 presidential election fraudulent, Tajzadeh countered that the supreme leader was the one who owed the people an apology. "Those people should apologize to the Iranian people for having brought Iran to this deplorable and virtually bankrupt situation," he wrote from his jail cell.[6]

Throughout his imprisonment, Tajzadeh remained committed to promoting people's democratic rights. In a letter addressed to his reformist colleagues, he stressed that reformists should always keep flying the flag and defending people's basic rights and liberties. Criticizing authoritarian tendencies in the conservative camp, Tajzadeh declared that he subscribed to the slogan "Long live my enemy!" He stated that the conservatives' slogan "Opponents of the leadership are opponents of the Prophet" had never been and would never become his slogan.[7] In another letter to Ayatollah Khamenei, he declared, "I do not recognize any right more incontrovertible and basic than people's right to determine their own destiny; nor do I recognize any governmental position or status as sacred, free from error, or above criticism from citizens."[8]

Tajzadeh wrote to the supreme leader, characterizing Iran's political and judicial systems as apartheid and maintained that "attempts at establishing a system with a unified voice and style in the country, along with the denial of rights and freedoms for critics, not only violates the constitution, but it also requires dualistic measures that privatize people's public rights; only a specific number have civil and political rights and immunities, while defenders of all aspects of the constitution who oppose absolutist and personalistic rule are deprived of rights and security."[9] Regarding renewed attacks against the United States, he argued that "Death to America" was the sword of obstructionists determined to use it against people's democratic rights. "Please don't say that this analysis is pessimistic. It would be enough for you to show only one case in which radical, anti–White House slogans were accompanied by the opening of political space." He ended the letter with a warning that the era of government based on a single religious or secular voice had come to an end.[10]

Mohsen Mir-Damadi, secretary general of the Islamic Iran Participation Front and one of the masterminds of the embassy takeover, also criticized the Islamic regime from Evin Prison. He called for the formation of a broad, powerful political party to advance democracy. Absent such an organization, he argued, democratic forces might not be able to achieve their goals. Even as dictatorship is defeated, authoritarian forces may reassert themselves, he warned. "This is a regrettable fact that has been repeated several times so far; parts of those forces that initially fought against the despotic regime reproduced the same system once they gained power and were stricken by the same problems they had fought against." Mir-Damadi further argued that the goals and ideals of the revolution had been forgotten, particularly those that pertained to people's rights promised in the constitution. He maintained that the system was supposed to be republican, which meant ascendancy of "the people's vote." In practice, however, a minority imposed its will on the majority. The new system was also supposed to be Islamic, which meant inclusive and absorbing all segments of the population. Instead, the opposite occurred as repression increasingly was used to control the public. Mir-Damadi argued that the Islamic system's constitution guaranteed political freedom for people to express their views. "But today, the country's prisons and prisoners speak of a different bitter reality." Finally, Mir-Damadi noted that "we were supposed to fulfill our promises and offer a novel system so that others would emulate us; but the way we behaved, even our former allies and the supporters of our revolution avoid us."[11]

Dr. Mohammad Maleki, first chancellor of Tehran University after the revolution and longtime member of the Freedom Movement, who earlier had been arrested, tortured, and imprisoned for years, also spoke out against state repression after the 2009 election. At 76 and sick, Maleki was rearrested in August 2009 and held for ninety-one days; after his release, he wrote to the prosecutor of the Islamic Revolutionary Court in Tehran:

> You and your cabal in the judiciary and the minister of information and other security organs have demonstrated that you are enemies of freedom and do not accept any criticism or opposition from anyone. And you are not afraid of lying and producing charges against anyone who thinks differently. How long do you think you, your bosses, and other despots can continue your criminal activities? . . . Mr. Prosecutor, I know that you, your judges, and the judiciary are nobodies and take orders from above and obey the orders. But be aware that tomorrow you will have to answer and be accountable. Observe the history and learn from the history of others. Stop it. For thirty-three years, you have burned our beloved country. Look at your surroundings; do you see anything but corruption, theft, lies, addiction, and hostilities? Be sure that the spring of freedom of the Iranian people is near and that the regrets of tyrannical rulers are late.[12]

In a subsequent open letter entitled "Stop Demanding Death, Long Live Freedom," Maleki went further than most analysts in the country and blamed Khomeini for the Islamic Republic's problems. He noted, "Mr. Khomeini came to Iran with a pack of beautiful words that incorporated the people's principal demands and deceived the people with his promises . . . and built a foundation of lies and hypocrisy." Maleki criticized the regime's repressive policies after the revolution, including the executions of military leaders in "ridiculous courts" that lacked due process of law, and violent interventions and massacres in Kurdistan, Gonbad, and Gharena. He asked rhetorically, "Were the new rulers sitting in place of God or the Prophet?" Finally, Maleki noted that Khamenei's gift to the Iranian people was Ahmadinejad's government, which produced eight years of complete lies, hypocrisy, and deception, including ridiculous claims such as "Iran is the freest country in the world" and "The Hidden Imam has chosen the deputies and the ministers."[13]

In an open letter on the anniversary of the Islamic Republic's formation, Maleki said that thirty-five years earlier, "we went to the polls, and because of our ignorance, naïveté, and thinking that an 80-year-old cleric would not lie and would remain true to his words and promises, voted yes for the Islamic Republic. With this action, we lit a fire that is continuing to burn a nation." Maleki went on to enumerate many violent events, including the hostage crisis and the war that the Iranian people had not voted for when they approved the referendum of the Islamic Republic. Specifically, he noted, people did not vote to repress Iran's ethnic minorities, promote a single party—the hezbollah, a single leader, Ruhollah (referring to Khomeini)—to terrorize the country, fight against those who thought differently, or drown the nation in violence and bloodshed so that Khomeini and the Islamic Republican Party could impose their premeditated programs to control and dominate the country. Nor did people vote for Khomeini to declare a coup in the name of a cultural revolution against the universities, arresting, imprisoning, torturing, and executing more than sixty thousand students and faculty so that the leaders would no longer need to worry about the universities. The letter continued, "We did not vote so that Khomeini could carry out the massacre of thousands of political prisoners in 1988, killing tens of thousands of freedom-demanding men and women who fought for the ideals of the revolution and opposed Khomeini's despotism." Maleki expressed his willingness to be put on trial—by people who had not voted for the Islamic Republic—for his share in what occurred under Islamic rule. But first, "I ask that Mr. Khamenei confess to his responsibility for everything that has happened in the past thirty-five years and ask the Iranian people to accept his resignation because he lacks competence to lead the country; and Khamenei should announce his readiness to stand for trial in a people's court supervised by international human rights organizations."[14]

Even moderate former president Mohammad Khatami criticized the Islamic Republic's repressive tendencies and the conservative clergy's ideological claims. He maintained that the revolution had come to eradicate despotism so that "people could determine their own destiny." He noted that in addition to people's sovereignty, the Islamic Republic must have freedom, security, and morality and provide social justice.[15] In contrast to conservative clerics who denigrated people's rights in the Islamic Republic, Khatami asserted that in an Islamic republic, power belonged to the people; the government represented the people and was accountable to them, and the people had supervision over the government.[16] More importantly, he spoke out against fascism and fascist tendencies. In a speech to university students, he declared that those who advocate freedom want it for everyone, even for the fascists. Fascists, in contrast, want freedom only for themselves, not everyone else, and do not tolerate others. "Methods used have been fascist, fabrication of lies, falsification and distortion of the revolution, monopolistic control, resorting to violence, and elimination of all other tendencies; these have been the principal traits of this trend."[17] Khatami's statements led the Supreme National Security Council to issue an edict prohibiting the media from publishing his picture and other material related to him, according to Gholam Hussein Mohseni Ejei, spokesperson for the judiciary.[18]

Political opposition and polarization also engulfed Ayatollah Khomeini's descendants. One grandson, Hassan Khomeini, a midranking cleric in charge of Khomeini's mausoleum, sided with the reformists. He met with Mousavi after the 2009 presidential election and called for the election results to be discarded. In the years that followed, he adopted a different outlook than that of the conservative government. He stated publicly that governing was a trust and that no group should monopolize it or declare it had the right to impose its will. He also mentioned that no one had the right to monopolize the revolution. He asked, "When the constitution has specified people's rights, how can a group decide to exert influence, exclude people, or arrest them?"[19] Where Ayatollah Khamenei insisted on calm in the universities,[20] Hassan Khomeini urged university students to speak out. Meeting with Tehran University students, he noted that student movements were alarm bells that "must shout the basic ideals of the society and not censor themselves."[21] Seyyed Ali Khomeini, another grandson and also a cleric, declared that Islam must be compatible with the times. In a public gathering, he noted, "When we speak of independence and an Islamic government, we do not mean the Taliban state."[22] He also noted that Islam must be compatible with existing conditions and advised against attempting to impose Islam on the youth through harsh language because such an approach would be counterproductive.[23]

While many of Khomeini's grandchildren publicly supported the reformist faction during the postelection conflicts, Hossein Khomeini, the oldest grandson, sounded the most radical. After the presidential election, he spoke from his residence in Iraq of the need to overthrow the Islamic regime. "Now we have had twenty-five years of a failed Islamic Revolution in Iran, and the people do not want an Islamic regime anymore," he told Christopher Hitchens.[24] He favored separating religion and the state and even welcomed an American invasion of Iran to free Iranians.

Mehdi Karroubi, too, from his cell in solitary confinement under the Intelligence Ministry building, issued sharply worded statements that surpassed his previous criticism of the government. For the first time, he characterized the Islamic regime as despotic and dictatorial. He sent a message carried by his wife to newly elected Iranian President Rouhani. He urged the president to "appreciate and protect the people's votes and wishes." He continued, "Be sure to enforce the people's rights enshrined in the third chapter of the constitution, because under a system that is not accountable to the rule of law and does not believe in human rights, where despotism and dictatorship are institutionalized, the voice of powerless people will not be heard."[25] In another message through his son, Karroubi charged that "after Khomeini's death, the power-holders sacrificed the republican aspect of the system in the interest of factional and personal interests." He also claimed that the Islamic Republic "engineered all the elections." In the case of a few healthy elections, he said, the power-holders simply lost control.[26]

Some relatives of Ayatollah Khamenei also issued critical analyses and statements about the country's political situation. The supreme leader's younger brother, Hadi Khamenei, a midranking cleric and former member of the parliament whose newspaper, *Hayat-e No*, was shut down after the 2009 presidential election, criticized political repression and the absence of freedom of expression and the press. He declared that the goals of the revolution had not been fulfilled.[27] Meeting with Karroubi's wife, he noted with regret that Karroubi was still in solitary confinement, "a strange confinement that no one in the Islamic regime is willing to accept responsibility for." He expressed bewilderment regarding existing political conditions, noting that no one could have predicted such days. Khamenei further declared, "Some think that power and glory last forever. But, as the Quran states, power and wealth are not everlasting. What last forever are actions and behavior."[28] In a meeting with reformist youths in Mashhad, he made some of his most radical assertions about the structure of the Islamic system. Regarding the clergy's role in the Islamic regime, Khamenei stated that some theologians, notably Akhound Khorasani, were against clerical rule and argued that government should not be in the hands of any particular group because governments had ups and downs and were sometimes involved in oppression, corruption, theft, and treason. If clergy remained in charge of the government, they would be held responsible, and people would become pessimistic and lose confidence in religion. While he favored an Islamic system that followed Islamic principles, he rejected state religion. The clergy, he said, does not have to rule the country to make it an Islamic system. It would be sufficient to have Islamic laws or laws that did not contradict Islam.[29]

Ayatollah Khamenei's uncle, Seyyed Hussein Mir-Damadi, a former university faculty member, also issued a statement critical of the country's political situation. He noted, "We have witnessed a great deal of oppression of various social classes." He criticized the highest religious leaders' silence about the five years of house arrest of Ayatollah Montazeri before his death and the current house arrest of Mousavi, Karroubi, and Zehra Rahnavard. He reminded religious leaders of a slogan during the revolution: "The silence of any Muslim is a betrayal of the Quran." Mir-Damadi noted that many citizens were arrested and imprisoned for merely criticizing the previous head of the state, while today many of the high-ranking officials of the Islamic regime make the same criticisms, but remain free. Mir-Damadi's statement supported Ali Motahari's defense of Mousavi and Karroubi and his criticism of Jannati, who declared that the Green Movement leaders' punishments should have been execution.[30]

When his son was arrested and imprisoned after returning to Iran, Mir-Damadi issued another statement, warning the supreme leader about excessive repressive measures. He reminded his nephew that the SAVAK experience during the monarchy demonstrated that repression and sophisticated tortures not only did not save the regime, but unified the revolutionaries and led to the overthrow of the monarchy. Mir-Damadi noted that the supreme leader unjustly imprisoned and tortured people by placing political prisoners in solitary confinement. He also told his nephew that power tended to corrupt and recommended the release of all political prisoners and those under house arrest.[31] In an interview, Mir-Damadi told *Kaleme*, "With utmost regret [I must say that] the lack of tolerance of criticism has placed our revolution on the path of dictatorship."[32]

The postelection conflicts and protests led to divisions in the conservative camp and affected their political views. Mohammad Nurizad, self-styled "devotee" of the supreme leader and a critic of reformists, reversed his political orientation after the 2009 election and urged Khamenei to apologize to the people for the bloody crackdown on the opposition. After serving jail time and enduring torture, Nurizad excoriated the repressive nature of the Islamic regime. The Islamic Republic was a failed experiment, he maintained, because it had not fulfilled its promises more than thirty years after the revolution. Nurizad regretted the 1979 revolution in a posting on his website, arguing that Iranians would have been better off socially, economically, and politically without the disruption of the revolution. "If we had not had a revolution, the hands of the clergy would not have been stained with the blood of the people." Additionally, the people would be more accepting of the clergy and seminaries and accord them higher status. Nurizad asserted that even God, Islam, the prophets, and the imams, too, would be more accepted by the people without the experience of the revolution. "The revolution drove the people away from God and religion, generating resentment against sanctities and religion," Nurizad asserted.[33]

Nurizad publicly disobeyed an injunction by the Islamic rulers prohibiting Muslims from interacting with Baha'is. He visited the home of a 4-year-old Baha'i boy being raised by his grandmother because both of his parents had been imprisoned. They were teachers of physics, chemistry, and psychology at the Baha'i institute for higher learning, established after Baha'i students were expelled from Iran's universities and colleges. Nurizad apologized for the regime's persecution of the Baha'is. He drank water, ate fruit offered him in the boy's home, and kissed the boy's feet,[34] in a remarkable rejection of the Islamic regime's official policy that Baha'is were untouchable.

The supreme leader issued a new fatwa shortly thereafter, declaring that people should avoid any social interaction with the "misguided" Baha'i sect.[35] Nurizad responded on his blog by describing the Islamic Revolution, too, as a sect. This sect, he wrote, began killing people from its establishment in 1979 and, in a prolonged "marathon," has continued to murder its opponents. "If you like, I can personally take you to the individual and collective graves of the dissidents so that you know that from the beginning, this sect has been [more] greedy in drinking blood than inhaling oxygen."[36] He noted that the sect expropriated public assets, censored and imprisoned dissidents, reduced Majles deputies to a herd of "goats," and monopolized power. The sect's military and security agents killed as many people as they could, stole their assets, and engaged in smuggling. He accused the sect's leader of distributing plundered assets to whomever he pleased, losing some in the nuclear gamble, and filling the pockets of the murderer Assad. This sect, Nurizad observed, valued only its ideological allies while destroying and imprisoning anyone who deviated to the slightest degree from the sect's leader. He concluded his statement with an ironic question directed to Ayatollah Khamenei: "Now, can you tell us if we are permitted to engage in social interaction with this sect?"[37]

Ali Motahari, a moderate conservative Majles deputy and son of a martyred founder of the Islamic Republic, became an outspoken critic of state policies regarding political and ideological matters. Motahari repeatedly disagreed with other conservatives on political issues. Unlike conservatives who refrained from criticizing the supreme leader, Motahari maintained that people have the right to criticize and that the supreme leader should respond. Motahari himself at times contradicted the supreme leader's views. When Ayatollah Khamenei insisted that Mousavi and Karroubi apologize for falsely claiming that the election was fraudulent, Motahari called for their release because they were guilty only of criticizing the government. At least, he argued, Mousavi and Karroubi should be allowed to defend themselves and repeatedly demanded that the government allow them to present their claims about the 2009 election and let the people judge for themselves. Their continued punishment without trial or court order was legally and logically unacceptable.[38] Responding to conservatives who claimed that Mousavi and Karroubi were treated with kindness, Motahari argued that it was wrong to place people under house arrest without a legal order or trial and then tell them that their captors were kind to them.[39] He went further and declared that house arrest without a trial was oppressive and that "the oppressed must be defended."[40] Unlike other conservatives who labeled the postelection protesters "seditionists," Motahari rejected the claim and maintained that protesters had different views and should not be called seditionists.[41] He also rejected a former intelligence minister's comment that Mousavi and Karroubi were *mohareb,* stating that the minister's label was incorrect.[42] Motahari even alleged that Jannati, the Guardian Council secretary, was afraid of a public trial of Mousavi and Karroubi.[43]

Motahari further criticized political repression in the Islamic Republic. He objected to the arrest of many activists and reformists a few days before the 2009 presidential election, calling them interference in the election. He criticized the postelection repression for creating an atmosphere of "fear and horror that led even some of the highest religious leaders to prefer silence."[44] He maintained that the revolution was for justice, freedom of expression, and political independence. Motahari argued that it had been wrong to eliminate opponents during Imam Khomeini's tenure and afterward.[45] He noted that even Majles deputies were afraid of institutions such as the Guardian Council and the Ministry of Intelligence and that their hands were tied in the atmosphere created by those institutions. The deputies worried about saying certain things that might disqualify them during the next round of elections.[46] Motahari asserted that the Majles had become a mere decoration after the 2009 presidential election,[47] and also criticized the country's judiciary system.

Motahari charged that the security forces overstepped their boundaries and interfered in political and judicial matters. He declared that "the Revolutionary Guard and the Basij were directly involved in the election and announced everywhere that the leader wanted so and so to get elected, and this was effective."[48] He asserted later that the Revolutionary Guard intervened in economic and political matters and merged them with its military powers. By doing so, Motahari stated, the Guard had become similar to a political party and rendered itself vulnerable.[49]

Motahari disagreed with conservative clergy who claimed that the Islamic regime was God's government and did not require the people's approval to gain legitimacy. He asserted that the Islamic Republic needed two dimensions: an Islamic government and the people's approval. Without the people's approval, the Islamic regime would not be possible, and no qualified individual could establish an Islamic government.[50] Motahari also disagreed with the predominant conservative interpretation of the status of the supreme leader. The supreme leader did not rule like a king, he declared, and was different from the innocent imam (who received divine revelations). Instead, the supreme leader's supervisory role derived from his knowledge of Islam and justice, and served to ensure that society did not deviate from the Islamic path, "just as a doctor specializes in a field of medicine."[51]

Motahari's outspoken views provoked some governmental agencies and officials to respond. The Intelligence Ministry placed listening devices in his office. Motahari declared that soldiers of the Imam of the Age (the Hidden Imam) who would do anything to maintain order were, in reality, "soldiers of Satan."[52] Another Majles deputy declared that Motahari was either an agent of MI6 or under the influence of spy agencies.[53] The judiciary declared that Motahari's claim that it lacked independence was a crime of insult and defamation and summoned him to appear in court. Motahari countered by claiming parliamentary immunity and characterized their actions as smelling of despotism and intended to intimidate other critics.[54] When Motahari condemned the house arrest of Green Movement leaders in a speech in the Majles, conservative deputies shouted slogans such as "Death to seditionists" and physically attacked him, preventing him from finishing and slightly injuring his left hand.[55] One deputy even snatched Motahari's speech and ripped it up.[56] When Motahari traveled to Shiraz for a speech at the university, a group of men on motorcycles attacked his car and injured his face and left eye. He took refuge in a police station and was forced to return to Tehran.[57]

At least two major collectivities also criticized conditions in the country. The Islamic Association of Teachers of Iran demanded that President Rouhani defend and enforce the constitution, specifically Articles 32 to 37 that delineated people's civil rights. The teachers demanded that the house arrests of Mousavi, Karroubi, and Rahnavard be lifted and others be released from prison. No one should be arrested outside the framework of the constitution, they argued, and no one should be found guilty unless proven in a court of law. The association also supported the reform movement, former president Khatami's guidance, and Motahari's efforts to defend the rights of the oppressed. The teachers' statement condemned repression of political parties and professional associations, insisted that the constitutional rights of ethnic groups and minorities be enforced, and called for social justice. Lastly, the teachers demanded that government combat corruption and pursue those in the previous administration who had looted the treasury.[58]

The women's branch of the Islamic Iran Participation Front also issued a statement on the thirty-sixth anniversary of the revolution and demanded the release of the Green Movement leaders and other political prisoners. The women argued that the Islamic Republic was supposed to establish independence, freedom, and popular sovereignty based on divine faith; that the constitution was meant to safeguard the rights of the people; and that the country was responsible for providing security, trust, and justice. "We were not supposed to have conditions in which our daughters and women worry about acid thrown on their faces in the alleys and streets." The statement claimed that everyone was supposed to have equal opportunity and that women were meant to participate in the destiny of the country and not be limited to less than 5 percent of the seats in the legislative branch. Finally, the statement noted, "Everyone is supposed to enjoy the country's development. Poverty, corruption, and inequality are not supposed to endanger the foundations and institutions of society, and corruption and political exploitation should not force increasing portions of the people of the country, and especially women, into poverty."[59]

The Independent Clergy's Reactions to the Presidential Election and Repression

Despite the state's eventual success in demobilizing protesters and silencing challengers, the postelection conflicts demonstrated that it had lost the support of important members of Iran's elite. The conflicts fragmented and polarized Iran's political system. The following declarations and statements by members of the elite, mostly the high-ranking clergy, illustrate the depth of both democratic and authoritarian tendencies that developed after the revolution. The statements also demonstrate the nature of the divisions and irreconcilability of the conflicts within the Islamic Republic.

After the 2009 election, the majority of high-ranking clerics either supported the people and their struggles or remained silent. Hussein Nouri Hamedani was the only one of twelve grand ayatollahs who congratulated Ahmadinejad on his victory, and he later regretted doing so.[60] Six other grand ayatollahs took critical positions. Grand Ayatollahs Assadollah Bayat Zanjani, Makarem-Shirazi, and Haeri Shirazi either rejected or criticized the election results.[61] Grand Ayatollah Hossein Ali Montazeri categorically condemned government repression and rejected the election results. Ayatollah Montazeri, the most senior and important religious leader in Iran at the time, declared early on, "A political system based on force, oppression, changing people's votes, killing, closure, arresting and using Stalinist and medieval torture, creating repression, censorship of newspapers, interruption of the means of mass communications, jailing the enlightened and the elite of society for false reasons, and forcing them to make false confessions in jail, is condemned and illegitimate."[62] Montazeri denounced Ahmadinejad's government and pronounced the Islamic Republic neither Islamic nor a republic. Grand Ayatollah Yousef Saanei, too, rejected the election results and supported peaceful, popular protests.[63] Saanei repeatedly defended the people's sovereignty in an Islamic republic and asserted that instituting Islamic social values and economics without the people's support only results in "oppression, despotism, and rejection of religion [Islam]."[64] Grand Ayatollah Mousavi Ardebili, former attorney general of the revolution, went further: "I am afraid that all of us, former and current officials of the country, must apologize to the people, more so those of us that wear the cloak of spiritual leaders."[65]

Grand Ayatollah Seyyed Ali Mohammad Dastgheib, member of the Assembly of Experts, argued that the constitution was not properly observed during the presidential election or afterward. He called for an emergency meeting of the assembly in a direct challenge to the supreme leader.[66] In various statements, he defended Mousavi and Karroubi when they were placed under house arrest and solitary confinement. He even maintained that Ayatollah Jannati, head of the Guardian Council, should repent because charges against Mousavi and Karroubi were unproven and constituted great sins.[67] In a statement on the thirty-fifth anniversary of the revolution, Dastgheib criticized the politicization of the Revolutionary Guard, the Basij, the judiciary, and the Intelligence Ministry, and their intervention in politics. He stated that the country's radio and television broadcasting system should not be tied to a specific person or a specific faction. *Supreme leader* did not mean despotism, he maintained. Dastgheib pointed out that "the past eight years witnessed the plunder and looting of people's property, the blockade of the seminary and the university, the flight of brains from the country, the rejection of religion by the youth, the exposure of corruption and prostitution, and the irrelevance of the Majles and the judiciary." Once again, he urged that the regime respond to the demands of the people, release all political prisoners, and end the house arrest of Mousavi, his wife, Rahnavard, and Karroubi.[68] In a letter to the Guardian Council and the Assembly of Experts, he criticized the way elections were held in the country and how authorities helped elect Ahmadinejad to the presidency for two terms. Dastgheib maintained that the outcome was the election of a president who was not qualified to lead the country. In the end, political repression expanded, committed and qualified people were imprisoned or placed under house arrest, corruption widened, the country's treasury was emptied, and the economy was paralyzed.[69] Dastgheib was disqualified in 2016 from running for his seat in the Assembly of Experts.

Ayatollah Seyyed Hussein Mousavi Tabrizi, whose son was arrested during the 2009 conflicts, supported the people and the Green Movement, declaring, "Greed has robbed the opponents of reform of their power of political analysis."[70] He further argued that an Islamic system could not be established on dictatorship but must be based on the will of the people. Ayatollah Mousavi Tabrizi challenged the institution of the supreme leader and went so far as to assert that "the issue of the leadership of a senior cleric referred to as 'velayat-e faghieh' in the Islamic Republic constitution can very well be put to a referendum, and even the late leader of the 1979 revolution, Ayatollah Khomeini, would have agreed with such a referendum."[71] He also rejected the constitutionality of the Guardian Council's vetting of candidates running for office and argued that it had not been a part of the constitution. He maintained that although the revolution had achieved political independence, the people's goals of freedom and an Islamic republic—a country run on a democratic basis—had not materialized. Even those who had struggled for the Islamic Revolution were unable to speak freely, he said. Mousavi Tabrizi criticized the division within the Islamic Republic between first- and second-class citizens.[72]

Grand Ayatollah Bayat Zanjani described the conflicts in Iran as a confrontation between two ideologies. "One side is defending the Islamic Republic while the other side does not believe in the republic at all and interprets the 'Islamic' part the way it likes." He added that he defended an establishment that has justice, freedom, respect for peoples' votes and their rights and all the Islamic Revolution slogans within it.[73] Over the following years, Bayat Zanjani repeatedly supported the Green Movement leaders who had been placed under house arrest. Calling for their release, he criticized the country's establishment: "In today's society, neither morality nor religious principles and values have maintained their place."[74]

Other influential ayatollahs and religious organizations also condemned the process and outcome of the 2009 presidential election and supported the people's movement. Ayatollah Jalaleddin Taheri, former Friday prayer leader of Isfahan, declared the presidential election to be invalid and Ahmadinejad's presidency "illegitimate."[75] The proreform Assembly of Qom Seminary Scholars and Researchers also rejected the election results and denounced the government as illegitimate.[76] In a subsequent statement, the organization referred to the conservative faction as a minority that opposed change and criticized them for labeling the postelection protests as sedition: "The minority that is intolerant of any changes . . . speaks of sedition and through official media labels the 2009 protests as sedition." Most unfortunate, the statement continued, was the fact that this group used religion as a tool and discussed these issues in the name of and from the point of view of religion.[77]

The reformist Association of Combatant Clergy called the election result fraudulent and demanded it be annulled. They noted that if election fraud became routine, it would adversely affect the republican character of the system and erode the people's trust and confidence. The statement also declared that the Association and other supporters of Mousavi would not abandon him.[78] The Association of Combatant Clergy issued another statement several years later, asserting that popular sovereignty was the advantage produced by the Islamic Revolution. The statement maintained that, in Khomeini's view, the principle of *velayat-e faghieh,* the supreme leader, was not incompatible with popular sovereignty. The association argued that Khomeini always emphasized the vote of the people. He insisted on a referendum to establish the Islamic system and then asked people to vote on the Islamic constitution. The association noted that Khomeini even demanded that people vote for the religious experts that would choose the *velayat-e faghieh.* Finally, the statement requested the supreme leader's government to fulfill its promises, move away from the repressive atmosphere, and provide freedom for the media, universities, and society. It asked the president to obtain the supreme leader's consent to lift house arrests and pressures against collectivities and forces.[79]

The Ruling Elite's Reaction to Conflicts and the Erosion of Support

The ruling clergy faced major challenges after the 2009 election. They could not ignore declining social support and public alienation. The elite saw that people shunned religious observances and increasingly engaged in passive resistance, despite repeated attempts to shore up popular participation in activities to support the Islamic regime. They reacted to the conflicts and the erosion of social support by becoming more intransigent, further polarizing the political system and underscoring the irreconcilability of the conflicts.

The clerical elite advanced a three-pronged agenda. First, they alleged foreign involvement in the postelection protests and continued to implement repressive measures against dissidents, including former elites and the family of the founder of the Islamic Republic. Second, and more importantly, they repeatedly insisted that the people had no role in providing legitimacy for the Islamic Republic. Third, they exalted and sanctified the supreme leader's position and status to a degree unprecedented in Shiite Islam. From the perspective of democratic forces and political activists, such claims contradicted the parts of Iran's constitution that emphasized people's democratic rights.

The dominant conservatives targeted reformist elites, who had vigorously pursued anti-Western politics, insinuating they were now directed by those same external powers. Javad Karimi Ghoddousi, a Majles deputy, claimed that Ayatollah Khamenei charged that the postelection protests and the sedition had been in the making for thirty years, guided by a special center. Ghoddousi went further and claimed that one arm of the sedition was located in a center outside of the country. He alleged that Hashemi, Khatami, Mousavi, and Karroubi were directed by that center and implied Western government involvement in the reformist camp. Ghoddousi also claimed that a previous Majles investigation had produced evidence demonstrating that "seditionists had asked NATO to attack Iran militarily if it became necessary."[80] Heydar Moslehi, former intelligence minister and Revolutionary Guard advisor, noted that the postelection sedition was an international coup to overthrow the Islamic Republic and involved the Gulf countries, Europe, and the United States. The United States was responsible for dishonoring the image of the Islamic regime, and all European countries were involved in various activities against the regime.[81] Ayatollah Jannati, head of the Guardian Council, repeated the allegation of American ties to the leaders of the "sedition" and declared that they should be ashamed for being supported by the United States. "Their crime was thousands of times more serious than those of armed robbers and rapists," he noted.[82] Mohsen Rafighdoust, former minister of the Revolutionary Guard, also asserted that the sedition was directed by outside forces, specifically the United States and Israel. Calls from the U.S. State Department to release the sedition's leaders proved that Mousavi and Karroubi were foreign agents.[83] Jaafar Shajooni, conservative cleric and former prison investigator for opponents of the Islamic Republic, went further in an interview and accused Mousavi and Karroubi of committing treason in the 2009 elections and accumulating vast sums, "billions," through connection with foreigners.[84]

Similar allegations were made about other prominent figures, such as Ayatollah Hashemi Rafsanjani, one of the founders of the Islamic Republic. Ayatollah Mohammad Khamenei, the older brother of the supreme leader, stated that the enemies of the Islamic Republic, supported by Rafsanjani, had chosen Mousavi for the 2009 presidential elections. He alleged that American think tanks had changed their tactics shortly before Iran's 2013 presidential elections and picked someone who could garner the largest number of votes and whose views were closer to theirs, namely, Hashemi Rafsanjani.[85] Mohammad Khamenei repeated similar remarks in another interview, asserting that "Hashemi's clique had long been in contact with the United States."[86]

As politics became more radicalized, the ruling clergy extended their repressive posture against the postelection protests and the Green Movement's leaders. Many ruling elites argued that the "sedition" had caused great harm to the revolution and the nation and should not be forgiven. When reformists requested pardons for their leaders, the supreme leader's office issued a poster declaring that the sedition was a great, "unforgiveable" sin that could not be tolerated or ignored.[87] The country's police chief, Esmail Ahmadi Moghadam, agreed that the sedition's leaders could not be forgiven and accused them of making charges they could not prove, plunging the country into turmoil for eight months, and tarnishing the country's prestige.[88] Saeedi, Khamenei's representative in the Revolutionary Guard, went a step further, maintaining, "The people do not allow us to forgive Mousavi and Karroubi. . . . These two gentlemen caused the greatest damages against a great, divine revolution. . . . The punishment of the two individuals would have been much greater. It is just the situation of the country and the Islamic kindness that required such a punishment."[89] Other members of the ruling elite called on Mousavi and Karroubi to repent and apologize, which both refused to do. Ayatollah Jannati, head of the Guardian Council and Tehran's Friday prayer leader, condemned Mousavi and Karroubi for their lack of remorse. "If it weren't for Islamic compassion, they would have been executed," he said.[90] Ayatollah Sadegh Larijani, head of the judiciary, accused those involved in the sedition of acting in concert with the country's enemies. He declared, "Your oppression against the order and the people will never be forgotten."[91]

When supporters of Mousavi and Karroubi asked for their release after one thousand days of detention, Mehdi Taeb, a conservative cleric and commander of Amar, a paramilitary organization, defended their detention and asserted that the Islamic Republic's sentence of house arrest actually protected Mousavi and Karroubi from those who might attempt to murder them.[92] Mohseni Ejei, a cleric and speaker of the judiciary, declared that after the 2009 election, "individuals and certain tendencies caused great damage to the people and the country, including destroying private and public properties and burning mosques. They committed immense tyranny against the people and the system." He maintained that the system had treated the leaders with great leniency, adding, "Perhaps we were negligent in not treating them more severely."[93]

Other members of the elite took a harder line and called for their execution. Heydar Moslehi, a cleric, advisor to Ayatollah Khamenei, and former intelligence minister, made a number of critical statements, calling Mousavi and Karroubi "corrupt on earth," blaming them for the deaths of the protesters, and demanding their execution.[94] Similarly, Alrireza Khosravi, a Majles deputy, declared that those engaged in the sedition deserved the "hangman's rope."[95] The Basij commander, Mohammad Reza Naghdi, labeled the leaders of the protesters "corrupt on earth," an offense punishable by death. He asserted that Mousavi and Karroubi had lied to the people and caused the deaths of many young Iranians. He stated that their crimes could not be forgiven by the people and called on the government and the judiciary to punish Mousavi and Karroubi "so that others who would commit treason learn from their fate."[96] Ghasem Ravanbakhsh, an outspoken cleric and seminary teacher, went further and declared that Mousavi and Karroubi were *mohareb,* enemies of God, and should be executed. He volunteered to execute them by placing the executioner's rope around their necks himself.[97]

Some officials singled out other members of the elite and called for their repression. General Masoud Jazayeri, deputy commander of the Iranian armed forces' chiefs of staff, attacked others, including Hashemi Rafsanjani and former reformist president Mohammad Khatami. He told Fars News that two members of the sedition should have been detained but were not, alluding to Rafsanjani and Khatami. He noted that they were still free to organize, warning, "The Intelligence Ministry should be very careful about the new sedition."[98] A number of Majles deputies denounced cabinet members who met with former president Khatami during the Persian New Year. Ayatollah Alamolhoda, Friday prayer leader of Mashhad, asked cabinet members who were followers of the supreme leader not to meet with Khatami.[99]

More importantly, in the aftermath of the 2009 election, right-wing forces attacked members of the Islamic Republic's founding family. In an unprecedented event, proregime forces disrupted a speech by his grandson, Hassan Khomeini, on June 5, 2010, the anniversary of Khomeini's arrest in June 1963, which Islamic clergy regarded as the beginning of the Islamic Revolution that eventually toppled the monarchy. Hardliners chanted, "Death to Mousavi" and shouted slogans supporting Supreme Leader Ayatollah Khamenei. During Rouhani's presidency, right-wing entities again attacked Hassan Khomeini, and insisted on removing his name from a list of conference speakers convened at Boroujerd University to interpret the views of Ayatollah Khomeini. The university was forced to cancel the entire event.[100]

Attacks were leveled against other members of Khomeini's family. When many of Khomeini's relatives, including Hassan Khomeini, sided with the reformists and called for the election results to be discarded, conservatives criticized their views. A conservative cleric went so far as to charge that all of Khomeini's relatives were counterrevolutionaries.[101] Shajooni from the conservative Society of Combatant Clergy declared that many of Khomeini's relatives did not deserve to be descendants of the imam. He argued that Ayatollah Khomeini had strong views on the United States, music, and women's veils, but some of his relatives expressed opinions that contradicted those of the deceased supreme leader. Shajooni was apparently referring to Zahra Eshraghi, Khomeini's granddaughter, a reformist who publicly stated that she enjoyed the singing of banned female singers (Hayedeh and Mahasti) from the monarchist period and called for reform in women's dress code. Shajooni noted that an in-law of Zehra Eshraghi had been imprisoned for counterrevolutionary crimes and suggested that other relatives of Khomeini should be also imprisoned.[102]

Despite their allegations against the reformists and the Green Movement, the actions of the Islamic Republic's rulers demonstrated that they lacked popular support and were concerned about future popular protests. Responding to questions about putting imprisoned Green Movement leaders on trial, Justice Minister Mustafa Pour-Mohammadi responded that the regime had "wisely decided to prevent another sedition." If Mousavi and Karroubi declare that they are law-abiding and would not disturb the peace of the country, they would be forgiven, he said.[103]

Many conservative leaders expressed concerns about a future revival of the Green Movement. Mohammad Bagheri Bonabi, a cleric and Majles deputy from Bonab stated during a public Majles session, "I believe that at least one generation in our country will be under the direct influence of the 2009 sedition."[104] Ghasem Yaghoubi, Friday prayer leader of Kashmar, warned in an interview that the sedition was like "fire under the ashes" and that everyone should be watchful so that the country would not again face difficulties.[105] Mohammad Nabi Habibi, head of the Islamic Coalition Society, stated that fire still existed under the ashes and warned that if seditionists gained power, it was clear what might happen.[106] Ayatollah Ahmad Khatami, a member of the Assembly of Experts and Friday prayer leader of Tehran, noted that the sedition would not dry up as long as its leaders continued their grudge match and insisted on false claims.[107] Haidar Moslehi, a cleric and former intelligence minister and Revolutionary Guard advisor, warned the Hezbollah and the Basij "to be watchful and to act with astuteness because the sedition has not died down, and seditionists are looking for opportunities to strike at the foundation of the revolution."[108] Mohammad Javad Larijani, head of the Human Rights Council at the judiciary, condemned the 2009 "sedition" at a public gathering and asserted, "Iranian people, the revolution, and the Islamic Republic of Iran are constantly facing sedition; seditions are never-ending."[109]

The highest leaders of the Islamic Republic called for vigilance against the Green Movement. Ayatollah Khamenei advised President Rouhani and his cabinet more than five years after the election disputes, "The problem of sedition and seditionists is one of the important problems and a red line," and thus, cabinet ministers should maintain their distance from it and remain resolute.[110] Addressing a gathering of Friday prayer leaders, Ayatollah Jannati expressed the concerns of the supreme leader about the sedition. He noted that the supreme leader had warned more than two hundred times about the sedition as the red line.[111]

Distrusting the people, the radicalized clerics discounted their role in legitimizing the Islamic Republic and ignored the fact that it was a product of a broad revolutionary coalition and a popular referendum. Instead, they asserted that the Islamic Republic's legitimacy derived from the Twelfth Imam, not from the will of the people. Saeedi, a cleric and Khamenei's representative in the Revolutionary Guard, confirmed the view that the Islamic government's legitimacy did not emerge from the vote and views of the people.[112] He reiterated that opposition to the God-given structure of the Islamic order was unacceptable.[113] Similarly, Ayatollah Sedegh Larijani, the powerful head of the judiciary, noted that the legitimacy of the Islamic government did not depend on the vote of the people.[114] Ahmad Khatami, Tehran's Friday prayer leader and a member of the executive committee of the Assembly of Experts, declared, "People have no role in the legitimacy of the supreme leader, because the supreme leader receives his legitimacy from God."[115] Many other prominent theologians, like Ayatollahs Mohammad Yazdi and Mesabh Yazdi, argued that the *velayat-e faghieh* received legitimacy not from the people, but from God, the Prophet, and the imams.[116]

Because the ruling clergy recognized that the majority of Iranians did not share their political ideology, they discounted any role of the majority in determining the fate of the Islamic regime. Ayatollah Mesbah Yazdi, a member of the Assembly of Experts, had little regard for liberal culture, which followed the votes of the majority. The standard in Islamic society, he insisted, must be God's consent. "In materialist schools of thought, the legitimacy of the government rests on the demands of the people; but if we live with such an approach in an Islamic society, after a while, we will be no different from unbelievers."[117] Ayatollah Jannati, head of the powerful Guardian Council, dismissed majority rule in deciding the fate of the Islamic regime, declaring, "Servants of God are obligated to preserve the Islamic order even if they are in the minority."[118] Saeedi, Ayatollah Khamenei's representative in the Revolutionary Guard, stated that the belief that the legitimacy of a religious government was based on the people's vote was a "deviation."[119] He labeled the Islamic Republic a divine trust and urged that the divine trust that was gifted to Islam and the revolution be protected and maintained. He noted that divine leaders played a role in the background, victory, and establishment of the revolution.[120]

Finally, the ruling elite exalted and sanctified the status of the *velayat-e faghieh* to a degree unprecedented in Shiite Islam, according to dissident theologians.[121] The rulers urged everyone to obey and follow the leader because maintaining the Islamic system was the most important duty, according to Mohammad Golpaygani, a cleric and head of the supreme leader's office.[122] Ayatollah Mohammad Yazdi, the new head of the powerful Assembly of Experts, declared in 2015 that the *velayat-e faghieh* was appointed by the Imam of the Age (Hidden Imam), not chosen by the people; the people are the principal support of the jurist, the supreme leader.[123] Abdollah Haj Sadeghi, a cleric and Khamenei's representative in the Revolutionary Guard, noted at a public gathering in Qom that "when you accompany God's guardian, you must accept that the guardianship is the expression or emanation of monotheism, and therefore there should be no question; we should just submit to the guardianship of the jurist and comply with his commands."[124] In another event, he declared, "Guardianship of the jurist is the same as God's guardianship, and disobedience to the jurist is tantamount to polytheism."[125] Kazem Sadighi, Friday prayer leader of Tehran, stated in a religious gathering in Mashhad that the jurist's rule is a manifestation of the rule of God. The only one above the supreme leader is God.[126] Saeedi, the supreme leader's representative in the Revolutionary Guard, noted that the rule of the jurist is the same as the rule of the Prophet: "The authority of the jurist in administering the government is the same as that of the Prophet; and following the jurist is the same as following the Prophet."[127]

Some members of the ruling elite put forward innovative assertions about the nature of the supreme leader. Seyyed Mohammad Shahcheraghi, Friday prayer leader and the supreme leader's representative in Semnan province, made the novel claim that "undoubtedly the supreme leader is chosen by the 'Imam of the Age' [the Twelfth Imam], and the Assembly of Experts only discovers the individual through careful examination."[128] Ayatollah Mohammad Yazdi, head of the Society of Qom Seminary, said that the supreme leader never makes any mistakes. "Even if he makes a decision that is 100 percent against the Islamic nation, it is the duty of the Imam of the Age to guide him in any way possible."[129] Ayatollah Mesbah Yazdi, a member of the powerful Assembly of Experts, concluded that the legitimacy of the entire Islamic system was rooted in the *velayat-e faghieh,* that the innocent Twelfth Imam provided legitimacy for the supreme leader, and that anyone who did not believe in the supreme leader was a pagan.[130] On another occasion, Yazdi claimed that Imam Husain had selected the supreme leader as his representative 1,400 years ago and that everyone must obey him. He also confirmed that the "supreme leader never makes mistakes."[131] Similarly, Grand Ayatollah Hussein Nouri Hamedani noted that the Islamic order was based on *velayat* and had the approval of imams who strived to establish such an order.[132]

In yet another statement, Ali Mesbah Yazdi, a cleric and a seminary teacher, asserted that the people regarded the supreme leader as a superior being who was an intermediary between themselves and God.[133] Ahmad Khatami declared, "We do not consider the supreme leader to be merely a political leader; he is also the deputy of the Hidden Imam."[134] Ali Saeedi went further and told reporters, "The supreme leader's decrees are equal to the commands of the prophets."[135] He also declared that "disobeying the orders of the supreme leader is equivalent to opposing the orders of God and the Imam of the Age."[136] Similarly, Hussein Firoozabadi, armed forces chief of staff, proclaimed that *velayat* "is the same as God manifested in prophecy, and the result of prophecy is *velayat*."[137] Ayatollah Ali Movahedi Kermani, a member of the Assembly of Experts and Tehran's Friday prayer leader, declared in a sermon that the most important quality for presidents and other elected officials was "obedience to the supreme leader."[138] Ayatollah Alavi Gorgani stated that obedience to the *vali faghieh* was obedience to the *emam zaman* (Imam of the Age), a religious duty, and that everyone had to move in that path.[139] Mohammad Mohammadi Golpaygani, the supreme leader's chief of staff, warned that "today anyone who expresses any cynicism toward the imam and the leadership will be dealt with in this world because of their ingratitude toward this blessing."[140] Ayatollah Mahdavi Kani, head of the Assembly of Experts before his death, repeatedly insisted that supporting Ayatollah Khamenei and obeying him was obligatory for the people of Iran.[141] Finally, Grand Ayatollah Makarem Shirazi declared that one reason for the success of the supreme leader was his communication with the Hidden Imam in Jamkaran Mosque.[142]

Summary and Conclusions

The election dispute and subsequent government repression of the Green Movement polarized the political system and radicalized many in both factions of the regime. The elites in both camps made irreconcilable claims and defended ideologies that were fundamentally incompatible. Challengers criticized dictatorial rule and violations of people's constitutional rights, and demanded freedom and democratic rights. Conservatives insisted on divine legitimacy, the ruler's absolute powers, and citizens' duty to obey the Islamic order and government rooted in the Prophet's teachings.

Some Green Movement activists and prominent conservatives issued statements even more extreme than those of the presidential campaign— including Khomeini's grandson, who declared the failure of the Islamic

Revolution, and Hadi Khamenei, the supreme leader's brother, who advocated separating the clergy from the state. Some dissidents even called for Khamenei's resignation on the grounds of incompetence. Some former conservatives, such as Mohammad Nurizad and Ali Motahari, criticized the ruling elite. Nurizad went further and engaged in actions unprecedented and prohibited in the Islamic Republic.

The postelection conflicts exposed the erosion of popular support for the ruling faction of the Islamic regime. The expulsion of the reformists from the polity further eroded the Islamic regime's power base because reformists had provided legitimacy for the regime. They helped maintain the system by offering hope to the Iranian people that the system could be reformed to fulfill the promises of the revolution without fundamental change. Their repression and expulsion represented a significant turning point in the Islamic Republic's history because it undermined both the system's legitimacy and the claim that change was possible through reform without disruptive revolutionary upheaval.

The disputed election and repression also polarized the people and the rulers, who moved in separate directions, defending ideologies that were fundamentally irreconcilable. The people increasingly rejected the foundation of the Islamic Republic and clerical rule by shunning religious events, forgoing obligatory daily prayers, and shouting radical slogans during protests. On the other hand, the radicalized elite in the regime reacted in extreme fashion and dismissed altogether the people's role as the basis of the legitimacy of the Islamic system. In contrast with dissidents who called for Khamenei to resign because of incompetence, the radicalized clerical elite sanctified the Islamic order and the status of the supreme leader. One prominent cleric, Ayatollah Jannati, head of the Guardian Council, went so far as to claim that servants of God had to fight to preserve the Islamic order, even though they might be in the minority. Despite the effectiveness of repression in demobilizing the Green Movement, a number of the leaders of the conservative camp expressed concern that the Green Movement might survive and reemerge. Thus, the gulf between the conservatives and the people widened further.

These developments demonstrated the ideological shift from 1979 to 2009, the depth of the challenge posed by popular vote, and the limits to which conservatives went to preserve the Islamic state. During the revolutionary struggles, the rulers of the Islamic regime promised political freedom but ultimately denied basic social and political freedoms to virtually all citizens, thereby rendering them powerless. At the same time, the ruling clergy empowered the supreme leader to a degree unprecedented in the country's history. While the ruling strata did not view this development as monopolizing power, some opponents and critics characterized it as a new form of despotism that negated Article 3, Section 6 of the constitution, which defined the goal of the state as "the elimination of all forms of despotism and autocracy and all attempts to monopolize power." The clergy also promised that the Islamic Republic would serve the interests of the downtrodden but shifted to serve the Islamic order that ruled the country.

From the reformists' perspective, the conservative elite's ideological claims both differed from Khomeini's statements and contravened important clauses in the constitution. The shift directly negated Ayatollah Khomeini's earlier pronouncements, made upon returning to Iran, that every nation must determine its own destiny and that the present generation had no right to decide the destiny of their descendants.[143] This ideological shift denied rights to the people, as the rulers claimed that the people could not determine the legitimacy of the regime. It also departed from constitutional guarantees of people's rights and redefined opposition to the regime "as enmity against God." The Islamic regime's rulers, in essence, negated Article 56 of the country's constitution, which declared that God "has made man the master of his own social destiny. No one can deprive man of this divine right, nor subordinate it to the vested interests of a particular individual or group."[144]

In sum, the incompatible ideological claims by the dissidents and the ruling clergy in the Islamic Republic generated irreconcilable conflicts and endless repression. In the absence of serious reforms and lack of democratic rights, these conflicts render the Islamic state vulnerable to challenge and attack. Indeed, these contradictions, along with other structural features of the Islamic Republic, set the stage for a future round of conflict.

CHAPTER TEN

The Path Forward

DEMOCRATIZATION—empowering the civilian population vis-à-vis the state—in highly authoritarian and antidemocratic regimes is a complex, contentious process involving multiple conflicts and actors. Historically, disparate challengers have taken the lead in promoting democracy, often resorting to noninstitutional insurgency. Routes to democracy differ, as do the structural variables that influence them. The complexity of the process has made it difficult for social scientists to develop a universally applicable theory to analyze salient factors that determine routes to democratization and fully explain why certain actors rise to prominence at different times. Broadly speaking, democratization can proceed through either reform or revolution. In the reform route, democratic challengers proceed with reforms but tend to keep political elites in power. In the revolutionary route, democratic challengers disrupt the institutional mechanisms and forcibly remove the political elites or compel them to resign. In the reform route the dimensions of the conflicts are limited and reconcilable, while in the revolutionary route the conflicts remain multidimensional and are often irreconcilable. In other words, a high level of cohesion between state and society contributes to democratization through reform; in contrast, a low level of cohesion between the state and society channels democratization through a revolutionary route. In both routes, democratic challengers may forge broad coalitions, explicitly or implicitly, to force the power-holders to democratize. A number of structural and process-based variables affect the dynamics of democratization.

The research benefitted from a comparative analysis of other highly authoritarian Asian countries. Although Iran's theocracy has been unique in modern history, Iran's experience with failed democratization was far from unique in developing countries. An analysis of the critical variables in Iran's failure to democratize, augmented by comparisons with other Asian countries such as South Korea and Indonesia, illuminated the dilemma of democratization facing highly authoritarian regimes in developing countries. This research examined Iran's political conflicts over several decades. The work collected and analyzed primary data on contentious political events in Iran for the 1977–1979 revolutionary conflicts through the post-2009 election conflicts. The analysis synthesized several critical structural and process variables, including the nature of the state and its relation to the economy and society; the nature of economic development; elite ideology, convergence of conflicts, and available exit options; and alliances and the likelihood of consolidation and coalition formation.

Taken together, these variables help determine whether the likely route to democratization will proceed through reform or revolution. The variables suggest that it is highly unlikely for Iran to democratize through reform due to multiple, complex contradictions and irreconcilable conflicts.

Despite repeated attempts at democratization for more than a century, Iran has been ruled by highly authoritarian regimes with sizeable resources, which enabled them to keep the unruly in check. Iran experienced two major revolutionary struggles and a nationalist movement during the twentieth century, but democratization has remained out of reach. Authoritarian rulers eliminated or repressed challengers, weakened or rendered political parties irrelevant, and strictly controlled civil society. The 1979 revolution established a theocracy that none of the major collectivities had called for during the revolutionary struggles. The theocracy has denied popular demands for freedom and democracy. Challenging the theocracy, a faction of Iran's elite initiated a short-lived reform movement in the waning years of the twentieth century. Blocked by the ruling conservative faction, moderate reformists attempted to regain power in the 2009 presidential election. They were denied victory, igniting popular protests that increasingly assumed a revolutionary character. In the end, the conservative faction decisively repressed the reformers and choked off the popular movement for democratization.

Alternative Routes to Democracy

In highly authoritarian and repressive states like the Philippines, South Korea, Indonesia, Tunisia, and Egypt, noninstitutional, disruptive collective action proved to be the most important factor in the democratization process. Such states blocked political reform and refused to undertake gradual, peaceful transformations. In these regimes, the opposition was likely to be repressed in the name of national security or as an imperative of economic development. To democratize these regimes, democratic challengers were forced to launch large-scale disruptive activities involving broad coalitions of diverse segments of the population.

Whether democratization proceeds through reform or revolution has been a complex question that depends on both structural and process-related variables. In South Korea, the moderate opposition launched a concerted effort to democratize in the mid-1980s and succeeded in mobilizing a large segment of the population. Faced with widespread mobilization, the South Korean military regime agreed to negotiate with the opposition and democratize through reform. In contrast, in the Philippines, Indonesia, Tunisia, and Egypt, the opposition could not negotiate with the state to democratize, and intra-elite divisions were insignificant in achieving democracy through reform. In these cases, irreconcilable conflicts led to polarization, eroded cohesion between the state and society, and produced political revolutions. Democratic forces had to remove their governments from power in order to democratize those countries.

To understand the determinants of the alternative routes to democratization—that is, reform or revolution—the present study focused on *structural variables* such as state structure, state ideology, and state intervention in cultural arenas; the level of state intervention in capital accumulation; and the characteristics of economic development, including levels of inequality and corruption. The study also examined *process-related variables,* including repression, mobilization, exit options, convergence of conflicts, the likelihood of coalition formation, and the influence of external factors. In combination, the two sets of variables mapped out a novel, comprehensive analysis that may be useful to understand the alternative routes to democratization and suggest Iran's likely path to democracy.

Virtually all of the Islamic Republic's economic, political, social, cultural, and ideological spheres and structures have generated irreconcilable conflicts. None of the multiple contradictions and conflicts have been resolved, but instead protests have been suppressed through state repression. Repression has led to exclusion, reduced the social base of support for the regime, and diminished cohesion between the state and society, making it increasingly difficult to find common ground. Repression and polarization have activated more Iranians than ever before to fight for democratic rights. Comparative and historical analyses have demonstrated that prolonged repression, exclusion, and polarization tend to marginalize the moderate forces and radicalize increasing portions of the population, preparing conditions for a disruptive, revolutionary route to democracy.

State Structure To varying degrees, undemocratic states in developing countries formed exclusive polities with the majority of the population having little or no access to the states and their rulers. These states often possessed independent resources, made significant decisions without public input or consultation, and were not accountable to the general populace. Such undemocratic states frequently relied on the military and a coercive apparatus to repress their people. These repressive policies effectively blocked the rise of autonomous social and political organizations and allowed the populace few social or political rights. More importantly, such undemocratic, authoritarian regimes often repressed or rendered irrelevant the moderate opposition and left little room for compromise and change. At the same time, state repression undermined popular support for these regimes, rendering them vulnerable to challenge and attack by opposition and democratic forces. Repressing and weakening the moderate opposition also radicalized segments of the opposition, particularly students and intellectuals, thereby favoring revolutionary transformation in the long run.

Where exclusive, authoritarian states did not completely repress the moderate opposition, they were able to avoid revolutionary transformations. South Korean military rulers repressed the moderate opposition during the country's rapid economic development of the 1960s and 1970s, but did not completely destroy them. Instead, in the mid-1980s, the military changed its policy toward the moderate opposition, reduced repression, and permitted it to mobilize and press for democratization. As a result, the military enabled the moderate opposition to play a leading role in democratizing through reform. Under pressure, the military agreed to the opposition's demands and introduced constitutional changes that paved the route for democratization through reform.

The Islamic Republic established an exclusive state that empowered the clergy, centralized power, created categorical inequalities, excluded its former revolutionary allies from the polity, and repressed its opponents. Despite promises of freedom and democracy during the revolutionary struggles, the Islamic regime's leaders rejected democracy and enshrined in the constitution vast, unprecedented powers and privileges for the clergy. The clergy was empowered with extensive rights and privileges, while the vast majority of the population was assigned numerous obligations and no actual power.

The process excluded moderates, the liberal Freedom Movement and the National Front, which had been the clergy's coalition partners during the revolutionary struggles and formed the provisional government after the revolution. The clerical rulers also removed from power Bani-Sadr, the first president, and expelled his allies from the polity in 1981. Threatened by rising conflicts and unable to fulfill the revolutionary promises, Khomeini justified the use of repression, declaring that maintaining the Islamic Republic was one of the most important religious obligations and that, protecting Islam necessitated even spying and lying. Khomeini's pronouncements laid the foundation for endless repression.

After Khomeini's death, the regime's rulers imposed additional educational and ideological qualifications for candidates to elective office, facilitating the election of clerics while restricting civilian access to state power. The Guardian Council routinely disqualified candidates on the basis of insufficient commitment to the constitution of the Islamic Republic or the supreme leader. The Islamic Republic continued to narrow the polity and exclude those who did not follow the theocratic hierarchy. When a reformist faction emerged in the 1990s and attempted to expand the scope of the polity, conservatives blocked any real change. Conservatives in the Guardian Council disqualified more than eighty sitting reformist members of the Majles in 2004 and prevented them from running for reelection, claiming that they lacked sufficient commitment to the constitution and the supreme leader. The council even disqualified Zahra Eshraghi, the granddaughter of Ayatollah Khomeini.

In the aftermath of the 2009 presidential election, the ruling clergy expelled the two major reformist political organizations, the Islamic Iran Participation Front and the Mojahedeen Enghelab-e Eslami, which had largely supported the regime during the first three decades of the Islamic Republic. In the most recent wave of conflicts, the Islamic Republic's rulers expelled from the polity Mousavi, Khomeini's prime minister for eight years, and Karroubi, former Majles speaker, and placed them under house arrest. Some members of the elite even insinuated that former presidents Hashemi Rafsanjani and Mohammad Khatami should be arrested as well.

The formation of an exclusive state inevitably led to heavy reliance on repression. The coercive apparatus did not initially wield significant power within the state, but it became an important tool to expel former revolutionary allies and challengers, repress the unruly, and eliminate thousands of secular and Islamic leftists in the Islamic Republic's early years. While the shah's regime was responsible for the deaths of nearly three thousand people during the revolutionary struggles, the Islamic Republic killed at least three times as many between 1981 and 1985. The Islamic regime executed about five thousand political prisoners and prisoners of conscience in the summer of 1988. In addition, the repressive forces were responsible for the deaths of prominent members of the polity—Foreign Minister Sadegh Ghotbzadeh, Health Minister Kazem Sami, Labor Minister Dariush Forouhar—and even, allegedly, Ayatollah Khomeini's son, Ahmad.

The Islamic state relied on the coercive apparatus to alter the results of the 2009 presidential election. An audio recording of General Moshfegh and video of General Jaafari, commander of the Revolutionary Guard, corroborated the opposition's charge that the Guard determined in advance to block the reformists' ascendancy to power. The commander of the Guard declared that a reformist return to power was a red light for the Revolutionary Guard and unacceptable. General Jaafari also noted that "This slope was a worrisome one, and everyone anticipated that if the trend continued, the election would go to a second round; and in the second round, the outcome would be unpredictable." Jaafari's speech disclosed the Guard's premeditated disruption of the Internet, mobile phones, and landlines, as well as other communication by reformists. The video demonstrated that the wave of arrests and imprisonment of reformists on the night of the election had been preplanned to demobilize the opposition before protests intensified. The president's office also pressured Roohallah Jomeie, deputy head of IRNA, to declare Ahmadinejad the winner of the election as voting continued.

The irregularities sparked large-scale protests and repression. Large segments of the population, particularly students and women, protested against the Islamic regime. Many became radicalized and demanded fundamental changes. When they called for freedom and popular sovereignty, which were enshrined in the constitution, the ruling elite rejected their demands, claiming that the Islamic system was a divine trust sent by God through the Prophet. The exclusion of the vast majority of the population from the polity and the repression of moderate reformists polarized the political system and reduced the likelihood of reform and compromise.

Repression targeted organizations, including the Freedom Movement, Islamic student associations, the Office of Consolidation Unity, women, labor, and human rights activists. The state even arrested lawyers who only defended human rights activists, prisoners of conscience, and political prisoners. Political repression intimidated Majles deputies, who were afraid of making statements on behalf of Mousavi and Karroubi for fear of being disqualified from running for election in the next round.

Three decades after the revolution, the Islamic Republic had become highly exclusive, generating potentially grave implications for its future. Of the original twenty-one members of the Revolutionary Council, only two were still in the polity and fully supportive of the ruling conservative faction: Supreme Leader Ayatollah Khamenei and Ayatollah Mahdavi Kani, the head of the Assembly of Experts. Most others who had held powerful elected or appointed positions in the Islamic Republic in the first decade of the revolution had become critical of the regime or joined the opposition.

The rise of the exclusive state and its reliance on repression had significant consequences. First, centralizing power and granting special privileges to the clergy generated new conflicts. Forming an Islamic state excluded the vast majority of the people from the polity and violated the revolutionary promises. Khomeini's declaration that defending the Islamic system was the highest imperative and required even spying and lying undermined trust in the rulers. Second, relying on repression expanded the power of the Revolutionary Guard to the point where it rendered the government powerless, as discussed in Chapter 4. Third, carrying out these policies contributed to the irreconcilability of the conflicts, polarized the political system, and reduced cohesion between the state and society.

Centralization of power, continuation of the exclusive polity—which reached new heights in the aftermath of the 2009 presidential election—and political repression make it highly unlikely that Iran's democratization will proceed through reform. Unlike exclusive states dependent on powerful individuals, the Islamic Republic has relied on the clergy, a category that was empowered after the revolution. The clergy developed a vested interest in preserving the system beyond the rule of specific leaders. Thus, the rulers have made it difficult to reform the system. It is highly likely that Iran's future democratization will only proceed through a disruptive route. Persistent irreconcilable conflicts, eroding cohesion between the state and society, and relentless repression will, in the long run, further impel democratic forces to challenge the state and attempt to democratize the polity. The scope of the changes and the intransigence of the rulers suggest that democratization may only be possible through a disruptive, large-scale transformation.

State Ideology State ideology and its orientation toward democracy, e.g., empowering civilian population vis-à-vis the state, affect the route to democratization. Generally speaking, authoritarian states that did not reject democracy on ideological grounds were more prone to grant some rights to a moderate-democratic opposition, thereby providing an opening for a reformist route to democracy. South Korea's military rulers never rejected democracy in principle. The regime's repression radicalized the student movement but did not completely destroy the moderate opposition. Reduced state repression in the mid-1980s facilitated democratization by enabling the moderate opposition to develop nationwide networks, defend the rights of the radical students, and press for democratic rights. The moderate opposition initially lacked widespread social support but gradually developed into an autonomous, democratic opposition able to mobilize the middle class and attract radical, leftist students into an implicit coalition against the military. This democratic coalition successfully used disruptive collective action and widespread protests to force the military to accept constitutional changes and political reforms in June 1987.

In contrast, in authoritarian states that rejected democracy in principle on ideological grounds, democratization was more likely to proceed along a revolutionary route. Ideologically driven, antidemocratic states tended to become unaccountable and highly autonomous of the underlying population. Such regimes institutionalized large power disparities and severely repressed the moderate opposition or rendered it ineffective. As a result, the political system became polarized and created opportunities for the emergence of radical challengers and their hegemony within the opposition.

Suharto and his military allies in Indonesia created a political system rooted in a nondemocratic ideology that rendered the moderate, democratic opposition ineffective and irrelevant for thirty-two years. The government interfered in the internal organization of moderate political organizations, prevented any autonomous activities, and even dictated the external activities and political platforms of opposition parties. Once conflicts erupted, the moderate opposition was incapable of leading the struggle for democratization. Unlike South Korean moderates who organized many nationwide protests against the military government, the Indonesian opposition was unable to mount even a single major protest by the end of Suharto's rule. Absent a viable, autonomous moderate opposition, Indonesian students—the most militant, radical elements of society—spearheaded the struggle for democratization, joined by the unemployed and urban poor. The moderate opposition and even some elements of the regime eventually followed the radical students' lead and called for Suharto's ouster. Students who demanded his removal refused to consider negotiation or compromise and prevailed in the end, forcing him from power.

Despite some democratic features of Iran's constitution, the Islamic Republic evolved into one of the most antidemocratic political systems of the world. State ideology shifted from the revolutionary ideals of independence, freedom, and promises to serve the destitute *(mostazafin)* to declarations of divine roots and rejection of the people's role in conferring legitimacy to the system. The rulers of the Islamic Republic introduced absolutist principles, empowered the clergy, rejected compromise and reform, and denied popular sovereignty. With the revolution, the dominant clergy acquired a high level of autonomy from the population, established an unequal power relationship, and no longer ruled in the name of the people. This new ideology clashed with democratic ideals of popular sovereignty and human freedom, reduced cohesion between the state and society, and generated irreconcilable conflict.

Khomeini and his clerical allies made no mention of a theocratic ideology during the revolutionary struggles. On the contrary, they repeatedly invoked the promise of political freedom and real democracy. Khomeini specifically called for independence from foreign powers, political freedom, and an end to corruption and the pillaging of national resources. Once in power, he altered his ideological pronouncements. In response to the rising influence of leftist and socialist organizations, Khomeini modified his political stance to gain the support of the working classes and weaken the leftist challengers by emphasizing that the Islamic regime would serve the interests of the oppressed and the downtrodden. As the regime resorted to greater repression against mounting leftist and liberal challenges, Khomeini pressed for a theocracy, which violated the principle and promise of political freedom, popular sovereignty, and basic democratic rights. By declaring the Islamic regime to be divine and its preservation to be a paramount obligation, Khomeini himself set the stage for irreconcilable conflicts. When Khomeini and his followers pronounced any opposition or rebellion to be *mohareb*, enmity against God, and punishable by death, they opened the door to endless repression.

In the aftermath of the 2009 presidential election, the Islamic state no longer ruled in the name of the people and rejected popular sovereignty. The Islamic regime's ideology evolved after Ayatollah Khomeini's death, widening the power disparity between the rulers and the ruled. As the Islamic Republic's rulers lost social support following the 2009 election, they articulated a more extremist ideology and contradicted Article 56 of the constitution, which declared that God "has made man the master of his own social destiny." Instead, they asserted that the regime's legitimacy derived from divine sources, notably the Twelfth Imam, thereby sanctifying the Islamic order. Some noted that the Islamic Republic was a divine trust and that it had to be protected and maintained. Other clergy argued that the servants of God were obliged to preserve the Islamic order even if they were in a minority.

The radicalized elite also exalted the position of the supreme leader and made claims that were unprecedented in Shiite Islam. These claims included that the supreme leader was the deputy of the Hidden Imam; that his success was due to his contact with the Hidden Imam; that the supreme leader's decrees were equal to the prophets' commands; that disobeying the supreme leader was equivalent to opposing the orders of God and the Imam of the Age; that the absolutist *faghieh* never made mistakes; and that Islam without the jurist would be an "incomplete blessing."

These ideological pronouncements had two crucial consequences. By sanctifying the status of the supreme leader, they further decreased the ruler's accountability to the public. Secondly, they were harbingers of repressive measures to come. Anyone who challenged the system had to be eliminated. Groups and collectivities that opposed the foundations of the theocracy should not be allowed to gain political power. The clergy and the leaders of the Guard viewed reformists as counterrevolutionaries who should not have access to power, as revealed by the video of General Jaafari. To counter popular demands for democracy, the rulers were forced to rely on the coercive apparatus, repressing dissidents and human rights activists and rejecting compromise or reform.

To reformists and democratic challengers these ideological claims contradicted the values of the revolution and the principle popular sovereignty, enshrined in the Islamic Republic's constitution. From a democratic point of view, the Islamic Republic's rulers laid claim to a monopoly of power that could not be challenged by the people. Some dissidents and reformists rejected these claims as tantamount to despotism. They demanded freedom and democratic rights, the rule of law, and popular sovereignty. Others called for more fundamental changes. Some even argued that it was better for the clergy to stop ruling the state. Hussein Khomeini, Ayatollah Khomeini's grandson, called for an end to the existing system.

The divisions in Iranian politics reduced cohesion between the state and society, producing an irreconcilable conflict with significant future consequences. The exclusive polity, the categorical inequality, and discarding the people's role in determining the legitimacy of the Islamic regime will have serious consequences for democratization and the Islamic Republic itself. Upholding antidemocratic ideology and failing to respond to popular demands for democracy can only lead to greater polarization and radicalization. Prolonged exclusion and repression will likely only further radicalize the populace and the opposition. Exclusion and repression will increase the likelihood that the people will reject the imposition of categorical inequality and antidemocratic ideology.

Refusal to find common ground due to ideological incompatibility will have serious political consequences, precluding a reformist route to democracy. Continued repression of the moderate opposition will likely prevent democratization through a reformist route and instead pave the way for a revolutionary path to democracy. In the long run, the huge power disparity between the rulers and the ruled (the vast majority of the people) will further polarize the Islamic Republic and render it susceptible to disruptive, revolutionary political processes.

Intervention in Social-Cultural Arenas Authoritarian regimes generally do not interfere in social and cultural activities of the populace and thus democratization could proceed through a reformist path. The absence of state intervention in the social and cultural life of the citizens relegates these activities to the private sphere and thus reduces the likelihood that the state will become the target of conflict emanating from social issues. In contrast, high levels of state intervention in social and cultural matters transfer decision making from the private to the public, political arena, tending to expand the scope of the conflicts, politicize these phenomena, and polarize the people against the rulers. In this situation, state power expands at the expense of people's rights to determine the most personal, private aspects of their identities. In the long run, politicization and polarization inevitably render the state and the system vulnerable to contention, challenge, and attack, increasing the likelihood of a revolutionary path to democratization.

South Korean military rulers from the early 1960s to 1987 left social and cultural affairs to the private sphere. The South Korean government did intervene in a limited way to prohibit hotel weddings and extravagance at funerals, with the goal of promoting savings and capital accumulation, but it did not impose strict social and cultural codes of conduct. Consequently, such matters did not become politicized or contentious during the democratization struggles of the mid-1980s. The opposition maintained its focus on political issues and successfully forced the military to accept constitutional change. As a result, South Korean democratization succeeded through reform and did not involve the overthrow of the government.

In contrast, state intervention in social and cultural spheres in the Islamic Republic of Iran has been high by any measure and likely to influence the route to future democratization. The ruling clergy insisted on using state power to ensure Islamic behavior even though none of the major collectivities demanded social and cultural transformations during the revolutionary struggles. The regime maintained that social and cultural changes were the cornerstone of the Islamic Republic, and those in power spent substantial resources to Islamize the population. High levels of state intervention expanded the scale of the conflicts, politicized numerous social and cultural practices that formerly resided in the private sphere, and contracted the scope of freedom Iranians enjoyed prior to the revolution. The Islamic state regulated virtually all aspects of culture and society, including the arts and intellectual activities, to ensure that they were compatible with Islamic principles. The state severely restricted personal freedom and liberties by legislating morality and regulating dress, appearance, dancing, drinking alcohol, listening to music, and even walking dogs in public spaces. Ancient Persian festivals were discouraged or prohibited, among them the traditional fire festival that preceded Persian New Year.

State intervention in social and cultural activities led to passive resistance, generated irreconcilable conflicts, and polarized major segments of the population, particularly the youth, against the Islamic Republic. Resistance and defiance included refusing to observe recommended cultural practices regarding drinking alcohol, covering women's hair, entertainment, and other activities. Resistance also included more serious offenses such as indifference to mosque attendance, failure to say obligatory daily prayers, and even conversion to other religions. In reaction against gender policies, women launched a movement to assert their democratic rights and protest government restrictions. They defied the regime's imposition of the hejab at every opportunity, despite arrest and fines. The people celebrated the fire festival on a huge scale. Youths increasingly engaged in premarital sexual activities, and growing numbers of couples in large cities chose to live together without getting married. People listened to Persian and foreign music that was prohibited, watched satellite television stations, and consumed alcohol on a large scale. Some Iranians publicly insulted the clergy and even attacked them. A growing number of Shiite Muslims chose to convert to other religions, provoking state persecution of religious minorities and converts. Iranians resisted a compulsory path to paradise.

Popular resistance to social and cultural prohibitions forced the rulers to introduce new repressive measures to enforce Islamic practices. The regime enacted legislation in 2014 that permitted the Revolutionary Guard and the Basij to enforce virtue and prevent vice in public spaces, thereby militarizing cultural activities. The Majles Research Center warned against this intensification, noting that the people might not cooperate or comply with the new legislation, which would lead to greater polarization.

Continued state intervention in social and cultural spheres will likely intensify the conflicts, further radicalize the population—particularly youths and women—and channel the movement for democracy through a disruptive, revolutionary route that will require an overhaul of state structures and ideology.

State Intervention in the Economy Low levels of state intervention in capital accumulation permit market forces to determine the process of production and depoliticize important economic processes. Where abstract, depoliticized market forces determine the nature of production and distribution, class conflict will be confined within the civil society, leaving the state insulated from social and political conflicts. In this scenario, democratization movements tend to assume a reformist character. In contrast, high levels of state intervention tend to empower the government and politicize capital accumulation and market forces. Class conflict, too, may become politicized and target the state. More importantly, social conflict may assume a political character and render the state vulnerable to challenge and revolution. As a result, democratization struggles may take on a revolutionary character and directly attack the state.

For example, South Korea democratized in the 1980s through a reformist route in part because of low levels of state intervention in capital accumulation. State intervention had been relatively high in the 1960s and 1970s but declined due to the privatization of banks and state enterprises. South Korea had one of the lowest levels of state intervention among developing countries in the 1980s. Nor was the military engaged in operating large-scale economic enterprises. By the time democratization struggles intensified in the mid-1980s, private conglomerates, known as chaebols, dominated the economy. Economic conflicts and issues did not play a significant role, except those raised by radical students who eventually abandoned their revolutionary demands in 1987 and joined the moderate opposition in pressing for democratization through political reform.

In contrast, high levels of state and military intervention in the economy and capital accumulation have several consequences. High intervention strengthened the position of the state and the military in Indonesia and Egypt against the civilian population and undermined democratic institutions. State intervention in capital accumulation increased inequalities of income and wealth, generated widespread corruption in both states, and adversely affected their entire populations. Suharto was widely regarded as the most corrupt politician in the world during the last decade of his rule. High levels of state intervention in the economy and capital accumulation undermined market mechanisms, politicized inequalities, and propagated corruption, increasing the state's vulnerability to attack once the economic situation deteriorated—in 1998 in Indonesia and in 2010 in Egypt. The public blamed the states for the economic crises in those countries and attacked the rulers, who could not escape responsibility for economic mismanagement. These conflicts reduced cohesion between the state and society, and eventually became irreconcilable. Popular struggles forced both Suharto and Mubarak to abandon power.

More specifically, democratization in Indonesia proceeded through a revolutionary route in 1998, due in part to the fact that the hyperactive Indonesian state intervened extensively in the economy. State intervention was made possible by rising oil revenues, foreign aid, and international borrowing. Indonesia's public share of fixed capital expenditure from 1978 to 1980 was more than twice that of South Korea. Although state resources and intervention declined in the 1980s due to reduced oil revenues, the state remained Indonesia's single largest economic actor in the 1990s. The assets of state enterprises surpassed those of the rapidly expanding conglomerates by 1995. The militaries of Indonesia and Egypt owned economic assets and conducted economic activities and capital accumulation on their own.

In contrast to South Korea, state intervention in capital accumulation in Iran has been very high, rendering the Islamic regime vulnerable to challenge and attack. State intervention expanded following the monarchy's ouster in oil-rich Iran. The Islamic government nationalized all banks, expropriated the assets of the royal family and wealthy capitalists who fled, and became the country's largest industrialist, banker, and employer. Like Indonesia and Egypt, Iran's high state intervention in the economy brought about correspondingly high intervention in capital accumulation by the coercive apparatus. State reliance on the Revolutionary Guard for repression enhanced the Guard's opportunity to accumulate capital. As the state attempted to reduce intervention in the economy, the Guard stepped in to purchase newly auctioned enterprises. As a result, the Guard became a major economic actor and the first armed bourgeoisie in Iran's history, controlling a substantial portion of the country's economy. Benefitting from its ties to the state, the Guard competed unfairly with the private sector and won a large number of contracts during Ahmadinejad's rule.

Economic intervention by the Islamic regime and the military has politicized economic conflicts and generated antagonism between the state and some businesses. The high level of state intervention undermined the market mechanism and led businesses to blame the state and the Guard for economic difficulties. High intervention also adversely affected the working classes and rendered the regime vulnerable to challenge. While military ownership of economic assets produced a key ally for the rulers in the upper echelon of the Guard, it promoted repressive conditions and undermined democratic rights. Iran's high levels of state (and military) intervention in the economy and the politicization of economic conflicts make democratization through reform unlikely. Like Indonesia and Egypt, Iran's democratization is more likely to occur through a revolutionary path.

Economic Development Economic development, measured by per capita income and level of human capital, can improve the populace's standard of living and provide a large middle class and a skilled working class with stable employment. Successful economic development produces a more egalitarian distribution of wealth and income and reduces polarization. Moreover, economic development reduces corruption and cronyism and the impact of these grievances in the political arena. Economic development expands the social base of support for the system and increases popular trust in the state. Successful economic development can also strengthen the position of moderate and reformist challengers and pave the way for a reformist route to democracy.

In contrast, failed economic development may result in stagnation or deterioration of the standard of living. Failed development may render the society vulnerable to economic crises, reduce the social base of support for the state, and lead to polarization of the state and society. Failed development may increase disparities in the distribution of income and wealth and expand corruption and cronyism. Moreover, failed economic development may intensify distributional conflicts, produce greater polarization, and radicalize disadvantaged collectivities. It may also lead the power elite to exert their political power to gain greater access to economic resources, thereby politicizing privilege. These conditions may prevent rulers and challengers from finding common ground and compromise in the political arena. The resulting conflicts render the state vulnerable to challenge and attack, especially where state intervention is high and the government is a major actor in the economy. Thus, the failure of economic development may pave the way for a revolutionary route to democratization and the forcible removal of power-holders.

South Korea provides an example of successful economic development where democratization proceeded through a reformist path. By the mid-1980s, South Korea had developed a successful industrial economy, surpassing that of Iran. South Korea's per capita GDP ranking climbed from 111th in 1970 to 60th in 1987 when the country democratized. By this time, the country had developed a sizeable middle class and a skilled industrial labor force and was exporting industrial goods to the United States, Europe, and Japan. These developments raised the population's standard of living and greatly improved their education. Economic success was accompanied by a relatively egalitarian distribution of income in comparison with other developing countries. As a result, most industrial workers refrained from joining socialist students that attempted to bring about a radical revolution in the 1980s. Similarly, the middle class's political conflicts were reformist in nature and did not demand fundamental transformation during the democratization struggles. Consequently, South Korea democratized through a reformist path.

Indonesia, in contrast, never equaled South Korea's economic success. The government failed to carry out land reform to reduce agrarian inequalities, and much of the country's population still lived in the countryside by the late 1990s. Indonesia's industrial expansion was limited, its manufacturing labor force was small compared to South Korea, and its economy remained dependent on the export of raw material, notably oil. The distribution of wealth and income was highly unequal, with the bulk going to Suharto, his allies, and Chinese expatriates. Indonesia's Gini coefficient was much higher than that of South Korea. Economic failure in the late 1990s generated sudden, massive poverty and hardship among the working class and the urban poor, who had benefitted little from development. Corruption was widespread as Suharto and allies had used state power to accumulate great wealth. These conditions produced highly disruptive actions and attacks by burning and looting directed against wealth and power, which contributed to the eventual removal of Suharto from power.

Iran's economic development suffered after the revolution due to mismanagement, capital flight, war, sanctions, and continuing brain drain. The rulers failed to fulfill the revolutionary promises. Iran's economic development resembled that of Indonesia, not South Korea, making it more likely that Iran's democratization would proceed through a revolutionary route rather than one of reform. Like Indonesia, Iran did not undergo industrial transformation, and its economy remained highly dependent on a single commodity. The country's reliance on the world oil market has led to the economy's vulnerability to world financial downturns. Iran's GDP growth rate declined from 7.84 percent in 2007 to 0.83 percent in 2008 as a result of reduced oil sales. Intense Western sanctions exacerbated Iran's high level of dependence on oil and its economic vulnerability, and Iran's growth rate plunged from 3.2 percent in 2011 to −5.4 percent in 2012. Furthermore, state intervention in the economy and capital allocation and accumulation expanded after the revolution and undermined the market mechanism. Iran's economy also suffered from a monopolistic grip on resources—not by private chaebols as in South Korea, but by the state, the clergy, and the Revolutionary Guard. These monopolies have undermined competition and hindered Iran's economic development. Unlike the chaebols, which succeeded in innovating, producing, and exporting industrial goods, Iran's monopolies were unable to capture a place for themselves in the world market. Still worse, the Guard remained unaccountable to the government, despite undertaking the largest development projects, sometimes without bids. When the Guard reneged on its responsibilities and refused to complete its contract at Gheshm Island, President Rouhani's chief advisor admitted that the state could do nothing because the Guard was more powerful than the government.

State intervention, monopolistic control, and mismanagement undermined Iran's economic performance after the revolution. Unlike South Korea, Iran's economic development failed to raise the standard of living, a key demand of protesters during the revolutionary struggles. Iran's per capita GDP was slightly higher than South Korea's in 1979, but by 2009, it was less than a third of South Korea's. In 1976, just before the crisis that led to the revolution, Iran's per capita GDP was ranked fifty-fourth in the world. By 2009, despite a massive rise in oil revenues during Ahmadinejad's first term (2005–2009), Iran's per capita GDP ranking had dropped to ninety-fifth. Still worse, the Iranian standard of living declined for years after the revolution. Iran's real per capita GDP (in 2005 US$) peaked in 1976 at $13,329 and declined to $9,644 in 1978. Thirty years later, in 2009, it reached $9,421, slightly below the 1978 level and well below the 1976 peak. Deteriorating economic conditions undermined public confidence in the rulers' capacity to fulfill the revolutionary demands and their promises to improve people's standards of living.

Inequality and Corruption The leaders of the Islamic Republic, in particular Ayatollah Khomeini, promised to eliminate high levels of inequality, concentration of wealth, corruption, and cronyism. Nearly four decades after the revolution, these promises had not materialized. Iran's income inequality declined somewhat after the revolution. Iran's Gini coefficient, the measure of income inequality, in 2009 was .41, still higher than South Korea's during that country's period of rapid development, between 1975 and 1988. The decline in Iran's Gini coefficient was due in large part to the expropriation of the assets of the royal family and the top echelon of the capitalist class. But the expropriated assets were not distributed to the people. Instead, they went directly to the clergy, their foundations, and the state, and were thus removed from the equation, giving the appearance of greater social equality. Furthermore, the erosion of the income of the middle class probably contributed to the decline of the Gini in 2009.

However, after the 2009 election, income inequality and people's livelihood worsened. Income inequality began to rise again when Ahmadinejad
eliminated subsidies for fuel, utilities, and basic food items, as the Majles
Research Center reported in 2014. Another report by the Ministry of
Economics announced that the discontinuation of subsidies in 2010
reduced the purchasing power of the population by 25 percent and
adversely affected the poor. Finally, among urban Iranian families, average
annual income was slightly lower than their annual expenses in 2013, the
last year of Ahmadinejad's presidency, according to the Statistical Center
of Iran.

The larger problems in Iran have been the high level of concentration of
wealth—which the Gini coefficient does not reveal—and the politicization
of economic privilege and its potential consequences. While a substantial
portion of the population lived below the poverty line, five to six million
Iranians had become so rich that their wealth was not dissimilar to that of
wealthy people in countries such as the United States, according to Ali
Rabiei, Iran's labor minister under President Rouhani. The accumulation
of wealth in Iran has had a decidedly political dimension, as the control of
wealth became associated with state power and access to the government.
Revolutionary expropriations enabled the clergy to amass substantial
resources. The supreme leader alone controlled more resources than the
combined wealth of the shah and the top echelon of the capitalist class
prior to the revolution. He gained control of additional assets of monarchists in the decades following the revolution. The concentration of such
resources polarized the social structure and politicized the accumulation of
wealth and inequalities. These developments in turn rendered the state
vulnerable to challenge and attacks.

Another aspect of Iran's inequalities revolved around the issues of corruption and cronyism, which provided additional measures of inequality.
In spite of Ayatollah Khomeini's promises to end these practices, corruption and cronyism played an unprecedented role in Iran's economy, state,
and society and affected the distribution of wealth and income. Reports
have implicated virtually all the Islamic Republic's ruling elite and families.
Corruption and cronyism were rampant in Iran's state and financial institutions, as recent trials and sentences have revealed. Access to the country's banks and financial institutions, mostly state owned, also was critical
in the concentration of wealth. The bulk of the country's banking assets
during Ahmadinejad's presidency were allocated to a small portion of the
population. While powerful and privileged businesses, such as the
Revolutionary Guard, used their power and access to state resources to

accumulate vast fortunes, a substantial portion of the population suffered from poverty and a declining standard of living.

The high level of concentration of wealth and widespread corruption and cronyism demonstrate that the regime has not fulfilled its promises. These developments undermine the Islamic Republic's legitimacy and erode trust in the system, as many in society view the state as serving particular, rather than national, interests. In a national survey, more than 77 percent of Iranian citizens expressed an intense injustice over economic disparities. Even Supreme Leader Ayatollah Khamenei remarked on the regime's failure to achieve economic justice.

The failure of economic development and high levels of inequality in wealth and income, along with corruption and cronyism, have historically contributed to polarization of the political system and undermined state legitimacy. Continuing this pattern of economic development in Iran will inevitably exacerbate polarization between the state and society and undermine the Islamic Republic's legitimacy. Stagnating standards of living, high levels of corruption and cronyism, continued and rising inequalities, particularly after the elimination of subsidies in 2010, and the polarization of wealth will reduce the likelihood of finding common ground in Iran's political arena. The persistence of these conditions, including conflicting interests, will make it increasingly difficult for contenders to find common interests and compromise in the political sphere. In the absence of a reversal in policies and practices, these conditions and variables make it unlikely that Iran's democratization will proceed through a reformist path. Instead, continuation of these conditions may prepare the way for a disruptive, revolutionary route to democracy.

Mobilization Channels Challengers and rulers face different options for mobilization. Challengers may mobilize for democracy through reformist or revolutionary paths, while the ruling elite can respond through reform or repression. Where the ruling elite accedes to demands for reform, challengers tend to pursue the reformist route to democratization. Conversely, where elites resort to repression to block democratization through reform, challengers are more likely to pursue a revolutionary route to democratization. When repeated attempts to achieve democratization through reform end in failure, challengers may redirect their actions toward a revolutionary path. The capacity of challengers and the extent of state vulnerability may also affect the democratization route. The lower the capacity of challengers to mobilize, the greater the likelihood that they will pursue a reformist route. Conversely, the greater the capacity of challengers and the greater the state's vulnerability, the greater the likelihood that democratic forces will pursue a revolutionary path to democracy.

South Korea and Indonesia followed two different paths. In South Korea, the military regime reduced repression of the moderate opposition and permitted them to mobilize and participate in national elections. Eventually, radical students abandoned years of struggle for their goal of a socialist revolution and joined with the moderate opposition to press for democratic reforms. As popular mobilization expanded, an implicit coalition of students, the middle class, and the moderate opposition forced the military to reform the political system and change the electoral system. The military was thus able to avoid a revolution and maintain power for several more years until they lost elections. In Indonesia, Suharto refused to agree to any reforms for more than three decades. He blocked the moderate opposition's efforts to mobilize and participate in free and fair elections. Indonesian students, the most active and radical elements of the opposition, acted in contrast to their South Korean counterparts by abandoning attempts to reform the system and demanding Suharto's removal from power. He was eventually forced out by an implicit coalition of students and the urban poor, who suffered from economic grievances and political repression.

Iran's political development has been primarily characterized by reform efforts and government repression. In the 1990s, students and moderate forces mobilized to reform the system, but regime conservatives responded by blocking all efforts to change the theocracy. As a consequence, most students involved in the democratization movement became radicalized and abandoned the reformist route to democracy. After the 2009 presidential election, the Islamic regime responded with repression and eventually banned the reformists from the polity, rendering them irrelevant. If the reformist option continues to be repressed, the likelihood increases that segments of the reformist opposition will radicalize and seek democratization through noninstitutional, disruptive collective action—i.e., a revolutionary route.

Exit Options The occupations and economic condition of the elite or power-holders and the availability to them of exit options may also affect the route to democratization. If the power elite's occupations and economic well-being are secure, they may be willing to accept democratization through reforms. Likewise, if the power-holders are confident of regaining political power in a free and fair election, they may agree to abandon power and accept democratization. Conversely, if the elites lack secure occupations, independent economic means, or political popularity, they may resist democratization and block institutional change.

The occupational and economic position of the ruling elite had differing impacts on the route to democratization. The military background of the ruling elites in both South Korea and Indonesia appeared to have little impact on the route to democratization in those countries. Theoretically, both sets of rulers could have agreed to relinquish power and return to their military careers, but instead, they resisted democratization and political change for years. However, the economic position of both elites did influence the different routes to democratization in the two countries. Although South Korean leaders engaged in some corrupt practices, the military did not create its own economic empires or control large economic enterprises for their own interests. Under pressure, they eventually agreed to reform and institutionalize democratic practices. In contrast, Suharto and his allies in Indonesia assembled vast economic empires using state power to enrich themselves through widespread corruption and cronyism. Suharto relied on the political system to protect his wealth and refused to relinquish power or accept political reform. In the end, he had no viable exit option and was forced from office through noninstitutional, disruptive collective action.

In Iran, the clergy used their control over the mosques to gain political and economic power, an outcome that no one had demanded or expected during the revolutionary struggles. The clergy theoretically could have avoided taking power once the Islamic Republic was established and exercised the option of returning to their mosques and the occupations for which they trained. Instead, the clergy promised freedom but used their social position to seize power after the 1979 revolution and gain control over huge economic resources.

Broken promises and the introduction of theocratic rule dramatically diminished the clergy's image and prestige. Respect and trust for the clergy declined as early as the 1980s, long before Khomeini's death. Disrespect and insults toward the clergy increased, according to their own reports. Some women reportedly refused to marry clerics, and some people physically attacked individual clerics. The political participation of clergy in Majles declined sharply. The proportion of clerics elected to the Majles dropped from 60.7 percent of deputies in the first Majles in 1980, to 5.5 percent in 2016.

A significant gulf has emerged between the Iranian people and their clerical rulers. For a substantial portion of the population, the betrayal of the 1979 revolution and the government's failure to provide democratic reforms seriously undermined the clergy's social status. Many citizens and intellectuals regard the clerical rulers as antidemocratic and wielding political power only to enrich themselves, their families, and their cronies. In contrast to the popular will, the ruling clergy emphasized their divine mission and imperative to rule the country following the 2009 election. The Islamic regime's rulers have derived their legitimacy from divine will rather than the people.

Thus, the ruling clergy will have no interest in democratic transformation. They have little to gain and much to lose by agreeing to democratize the political system and broadening the polity. Democratization would undermine their economic position and political power. Interested in maintaining their privileges, the ruling elite has opposed democratic change, which would likely result in the loss of economic privileges and political power. The clergy would be unlikely to regain power through fair and free elections, nor would unelected officials—including the supreme leader, the Guardian Council, and the Expediency Council—be likely to regain power if they accepted democratic changes. It appears highly unlikely that the clergy will voluntarily relinquish power and permit democratic changes through reforms. As a result, Iran's democratization is likely to be achieved only by means of a disruptive, revolutionary route.

Convergence of Conflicts Where conflicts over social, economic, and political issues remain isolated and discrete, power-holders and challengers may be able to find common ground, agree on gradual political reforms, and avoid disruptive, revolutionary outcomes. For example, where state intervention in capital accumulation is low and economic development is successful—producing low levels of inequality and corruption—economic concerns may be relatively minor or even absent in conflicts between an authoritarian state and its challengers. Similarly, low state intervention in social and cultural spheres reduces the scope of the conflicts. As a result, challengers may focus on a relatively narrow set of political conflicts in their demands to democratize through reforms.

In contrast, convergence of multiple conflicts may bring democratization through a disruptive, revolutionary path. Where multiple conflicts converge, they expand the breadth and depth of the grievances. Where the state intervenes heavily in the economic, social, and cultural spheres, convergence of conflicts polarizes the social system, reduces cohesion between state and society, and renders the political system vulnerable to revolutionary challenge and attack. Convergence of multiple conflicts that focus on the political system requires continuous state repression. Additionally, exposure to multiple conflicts adversely affects broad segments of the population, making it difficult to disentangle the conflicts and resolve each issue piecemeal. Convergence of multiple conflicts complicates the argument made by moderate challengers that change is possible, and that some aspects of the system are functional and should be preserved. More importantly, the intersection of conflicts tends to radicalize large segments of the population, leading them to demand fundamental transformation. Thus, convergence of large-scale conflicts increases the likelihood of a disruptive, revolutionary route to democratization.

In South Korea, state intervention in the social and cultural spheres was limited, and state intervention in the economy had declined by the early 1980s before democratization conflicts reemerged. Social, economic, and political conflicts did not converge around the state and, as a result, the middle class and the industrial workforce failed to support radical students' demands for fundamental social and economic transformation. Because the economic position of the middle class improved along with successful development, they had little interest in radical change. In the absence of multiple conflicts, the moderate opposition was able to focus on the single issue of constitutional change and successfully pressed for a moderate reform agenda to achieve democratization.

In Indonesia, in contrast, economic and political conflicts converged, making it more difficult for Suharto's regime to resolve them through gradual reform. State intervention in the economy and capital accumulation was high and generated a high level of concentration of wealth and rising inequalities, with Suharto and his allies controlling the largest share of the Indonesian economy through corruption and cronyism. Economic development failed to substantially improve conditions for the vast majority of the population. Eventually, the urban poor in major cities mobilized and attacked economic targets, causing widespread damage, economic losses, and the departure of wealth-holders. Their collective actions augmented the protests by students and segments of the middle class targeting the state. Because Suharto adamantly refused to agree to reforms or democracy, even in principle, the intersection of these multiple conflicts severely disrupted the institutional political processes and forced Suharto from power, preparing the system for the establishment of democratic institutions.

In Iran, convergence of multiple conflicts has reached a relatively high level and rendered the Islamic regime vulnerable to challenge. It has resulted in erosion of social cohesion and polarization of society against the state, forcing it to resort to continuous repression to contain the conflicts. The exclusive nature of the state and the clergy's rejection of democracy in principle have generated opposition, as most of those interested in political participation or gaining power have been excluded from the polity. High levels of state intervention in capital accumulation have undermined the market mechanism, politicized distributional conflicts, and adversely affected broad segments of the population. In addition, state economic policies, corruption, concentration of wealth, and inequalities in the distribution of resources have had negative consequences for major classes and collectivities, which blame the state for their problems. State intervention in social and cultural spheres has politicized issues that formerly were determined by the people, based on traditional customs and perspectives. The imposition of morality codes, multiple codes of conduct in various spheres of life, gender discrimination, and religious persecution have expanded social conflict against the state. More importantly, the intersection of political, ideological, and social-cultural conflicts has politicized substantial segments of the population as virtually all conflicts converge against the state—the main entity intervening in public and private spheres alike.

The convergence of multiple conflicts has generated opposition to conservative forces within the ruling elite. Despite huge government expenditures to encourage people to observe traditional Islamic practices such as obligatory prayers, 86 percent of students and 75 percent of the public in general did not say daily prayers, according to a poll in 2000. A 2002 poll in Tehran found that only 6.2 percent of respondents declared themselves satisfied with the current state of affairs, while 48.9 percent favored "reform," and 44.9 percent favored "fundamental change." In a national survey, almost nine out of ten favored directly electing and replacing the supreme leader. Only 8 percent said that they would vote for the conservatives (discussed in Chapter 1).

Despite a relatively high level of convergence, a number of factors prevented the opposition from consolidating following the 2009 presidential election. Iran's short-term economic performance was one reason for the failure of consolidation. Iran's economy did not experience a sudden decline or crisis in 2009. Such an occurrence would have increased the likelihood of consolidation. Sanctions produced an economic decline that adversely affected major segments of the population, but it occurred after the protests had already been largely repressed.

Moreover, a broad coalition failed to emerge because the working class and bazaaris did not join the protests. The urban working class were unable to mobilize on a large scale. They lacked nationwide, independent organizations and were severely repressed. Unlike 1978, when repression declined and workers mobilized, the postelection conflicts brought an increase in repression, as the deaths of two imprisoned workers, Sattar Beheshti and Afshin Osanloo illustrated. While bazaaris had grievances against the government and closed down after the 2009 elections, they did not coordinate their business shutdowns with the political protests. Repression and the dissolution of liberal organizations in the bazaar, arrests of several bazaaris, and the murder of a prominent merchant, discussed in Chapter 8, were significant in preventing bazaaris from joining the political protests. The absence of workers and bazaaris hindered the consolidation and formation of a broad coalition.

Future convergence of social, economic, and political conflicts may render the Islamic regime vulnerable to challenge and attack. The intersection of multiple conflicts may prevent a gradual, piecemeal resolution of problems. The relatively high level of state involvement in so many aspects of Iranian society has forced the state to rely on continuous repression to maintain power. This repression and the failure to reform are likely to further politicize, polarize, and mobilize various collectivities, encouraging the formation of broad coalitions to target the state. In the absence of serious changes, the result in the long run is likely to be a movement to transform the political system through a disruptive, revolutionary route.

External Conflicts External pressures and conflicts may impact the route to democratization by influencing the interests, capacities, and opportunities of the state and major social and political actors. External conflicts, including wars, tend to promote national cohesion, enhance the position of the coercive organs within the state, and enable the regime to repress its opponents and undermine democratic rights. States that are economically and politically dependent on more powerful countries are particularly vulnerable to external pressures.

Both South Korea and Indonesia were dependent on the United States economically, politically, and militarily during their democratization struggles. The U.S. government, with the partial exception of the Kennedy administration, long supported authoritarian rule in South Korea, tolerating and even backing military repression, including the massacre of civilians in Kwangju in 1980. During the intense democratization struggles of the mid-1980s, democratic challengers received no support from the United States until the final stages, when the Reagan administration privately pressured the military rulers to move toward democracy. Similarly, the United States made no attempt to promote democracy in Indonesia during the Cold War but instead, supported the military coup in 1965 that removed President Sukarno from power and resulted in the massacre of Indonesian communists. In the midst of a major economic crisis in Indonesia in 1998, the United States shifted its policy, implicitly supporting the opposition and encouraging change. The change in U.S. policy isolated Suharto and contributed to his removal.

On the other hand, governments sometimes can use external conflicts to shore up their own base of support. Leaders in South Korea and Iran attempted to bolster social cohesion by promoting either nationalism (South Korea) or defense of the revolution and Islam (Iran). Both governments harshly repressed internal challengers and democratic movements. To some extent, external attacks and enhanced solidarity deflected internal challenges to regimes in both countries and diminished prospects for democratization. In South Korea, the government massacred its opponents during and after the Korean War. Successive South Korean governments passed laws that not only severely punished communist sympathizers, but also repressed the moderate opposition in the name of national security. In Iran, the government repressed political opposition and banned labor strikes during the hostage crisis and the Iran-Iraq war. The war ended in a stalemate, not technically a defeat for Iran. The Islamic regime reacted to armed challenge from the Islamic Mojahedeen by executing thousands of political prisoners.

It would be misleading to blame the failure of democracy in Iran on external conflicts such as the American hostage crisis and the Iran-Iraq war. Ayatollah Khomeini intended to establish a theocracy in Iran as early as the 1970s, although he never publicly announced his intentions. On the very day the Iranian people approved the referendum establishing the Islamic Republic, less than two months after the shah's ouster, Khomeini labeled the new regime "God's government" and repeatedly threatened harsh punishment for those who opposed it. He obtained the approval of Iran's theocratic constitution several months later, on December 3, 1979. The theocracy was in place shortly after the embassy takeover and months before the Iran-Iraq war.

However, the Islamic regime repeatedly used external conflicts with Iraq and the United States to promote national cohesion, repress opposition, and solidify its own power. During the Iran-Iraq war, the clergy strengthened the power of the Revolutionary Guard and expanded the role of the coercive apparatuses. The Islamic regime manipulated popular opposition to the United States for its own ends. During the U.S. embassy takeover, the regime took the unprecedented steps of closing down the country's universities and colleges for at least two years and banning all labor strikes. The clergy removed the liberal provisional government from power and eventually repressed and excluded the moderates from the polity. In the following decades, Iran's hardliners repeatedly invoked U.S. sanctions as a pretext for repressing the democratic opposition, characterizing the opposition as allies of the United States who attempted to undermine the security and stability of the country.

Invoking national security and attempting to generate external and international crises may have limits. The Islamic regime may not always be able to rely on provoking external conflicts in order to repress popular democratic demands. Although the government repeatedly used anti-Israeli and anti-American rhetoric during Ahmadinejad's first term, the attempt to generate national unity was unsuccessful, as the 2009 postelection political protests demonstrated.

Iran's Democratization Trajectory

Which route might Iran's democratization take: reform or revolution? The question has been debated in intellectual and political circles for some time. Dissident elites and privileged collectivities may prefer social reforms because they can maintain their privileges by avoiding disruptive, unpredictable revolutions. Intellectuals and organizations that advocate reform argue that democratization through reform avoids the cost of revolution and that revolutions produce more centralized states, not democratic outcomes. On the other hand, proponents of democratization through revolution and radical change make the case that reformists overlook the human cost of undemocratic regimes, which impose a heavy toll in human suffering and the restriction of liberty and freedom. Critics also point out that authoritarian regimes engage in widespread corruption and pillage, hindering economic development. They claim that an authoritarian system erects mounting obstacles to democracy and that piecemeal changes through reform take a long time and may not go far enough to establish democratic institutions.

Human cost is extremely important, and the goal of democratization is to reduce it. However, the choice between reform and revolution may depend, instead, on the nature of the conflicts, the historical possibilities, and the available options. The conditions and variables examined in this work point conclusively in one direction—that is, that a route to Iran's democratization through reform is not available. The Islamic Republic has generated multiple conflicts that continually reduce social cohesion and undermine reforms. The denial of democratic freedoms promised during the revolutionary conflicts, the narrowing of the polity, relatively high levels of economic inequality and polarization of wealth, widespread corruption and cronyism, and erosion of social support for the regime are likely to intensify in the future and produce large-scale conflicts that would make unlikely a transition to democracy through gradual reforms. If these conditions and conflicts persist, Iranians may have but one option remaining to democratize their political system. As of this writing, that option may be a revolution.

The postelection conflicts revealed the irreconcilability between the opposition and conservatives ruling the country. On the one hand, reformists demanded greater political freedom and civil and democratic rights. Dissidents expressed dissatisfaction over dictatorial practices, the absence of democratic freedoms, and the failure of the revolution. Some critics went further and called for fundamental changes, including an end to the Islamic Republic and separating the clergy from the state. In contrast, conservatives in power emphasized divine support and guidance for the supreme leader, and the duty of all to obey the leader and rulers. Conservatives often invoked the sanctity of the Islamic order and maintained that the people had no role in providing legitimacy for the system. Ayatollah Jannati, the head of the Guardian Council, declared that even if they were in a minority, the servants of God were obligated to preserve the Islamic Republic. Ayatollah Saeedi noted that the Islamic Republic was a divine trust gifted to Islam and the revolution and must be protected and maintained. He and other conservative leaders also called for the repression of dissidents and reformist leaders, who, they alleged, represented foreign interests and powers.

The events of the past few decades have revealed the difficulties and problems of reforming Iran's political system. The option of reform failed during the eight years President Khatami was in power because rulers of the Islamic Republic consistently blocked any serious reform of the system. Although he was committed to the constitution of the Islamic Republic, President Khatami also supported the rule of law, freedom of the press, greater social and political freedom, tolerance for opposing political views, and greater democracy through a stronger civil society. Khatami and his reformist allies attempted to check the power of the armed forces under the control of the supreme leader but failed when the Expediency Council, which arbitrates legislative disputes, rejected the bill. Khatami and his allies also attempted to empower civilians by providing greater civil liberties and freedom of the press, but their efforts failed to have lasting impact. Reformists failed in the face of the strength of the Islamic Republic's undemocratic institutions.

The conflicts, protests, and repression following the 2009 election moved Iran further away from the possibility of democratizing through a reformist route. Political repression and the banning of major reformist organizations had profound consequences for Iranian society and politics as it became increasingly clear that the contending social forces and the elites had irreconcilable ideologies. The continuing imprisonment of hundreds of political activists, students, journalists, and lawyers, as well as the house arrest of the Green Movement's leaders, illustrate the concerns of the ruling elite over the future of the Islamic Republic.

A sizeable segment of the populace spoke out in the aftermath of the 2009 presidential election. They joined the debate and publicly expressed their political and ideological preferences. Their protests and the repression that followed further radicalized them and revealed hidden conflicts within the Iranian state and society. Popular slogans and demands demonstrated that the public and the rulers had an irreconcilable dispute that could not be resolved through limited change. While the people demanded freedom and democratic rights, the rulers demanded obedience to the Islamic order and the clergy. In the end, repression prevailed, and the people lost these struggles as they had lost the battles during President Khatami's time in office. Nevertheless, repeated failures and prolonged exclusion will, in the long run, reduce cohesion between the state and society and eventually radicalize the people. As noted earlier, the persistence of these conditions will render the Islamic Republic vulnerable to greater challenges and attacks in the next round of conflicts.

The 2009 postelection conflicts hastened the erosion of the regime's social base of support. Supreme Leader Ayatollah Khamenei himself acknowledged that these conflicts brought the system to the "edge of the cliff." Similarly, General Jaafari, commander of the Revolutionary Guard, noted that the "sedition" brought the system to the border of overthrow. Other officials observed that many of the regime's former backers had withdrawn their support by the time protests erupted, which explained why the regime was unable to mount a single demonstration in its support for more than six months after the election. Some officials acknowledged that the regime could not even depend on the Revolutionary Guard to end the protests. Guard members were not united; many commanders opposed Guard intervention in political conflicts and the repression of the Green Movement. Statements by some elites revealed that the regime was forced to turn to the paramilitary Basij to repress protesters. The absence of protests in medium-sized and small cities and the failure of bazaaris and workers to join the demonstrations, enabled the coercive forces and the dominant conservative faction to end the challenges that shook the Islamic Republic's foundation.

Yet, several years after the repression of the protesters and challengers, officials of the Islamic Republic expressed concerns that the sedition was not over and that conflicts might reemerge. They called for vigilance against the reemergence of the Green Movement and kept Mousavi and Karroubi in confinement years after the conflicts were repressed. Refusing to put Mousavi and Karroubi on trial, the rulers tacitly acknowledged the threat posed by the Green Movement's leaders' possible revelations about the disputed election and the lack of freedom in the country. Similarly, the regime's relentless repression and detention of hundreds of political prisoners, lawyers, and human rights activists signified the rulers' apprehension about the erosion of support by substantial portions of the population and further instability.

Despite the loss of social support and concerns over the eruption of sedition, the Islamic Republic's rulers have repeatedly resisted any changes that might weaken their rule and empower the people. In the early 1980s, the regime resorted to repression to eliminate liberals from power. In the late 1990s, conservative forces blocked the reformists from carrying out any serious changes after they won the presidential and parliamentary elections with broad popular support. In 2009, the conservative leaders, together with the Revolutionary Guard, prevented reformists from retaking power in the presidential election—as confirmed in General Jaafari's video. Ultimately, the conservatives dissolved the two major reformist organizations, rendering them irrelevant, at least for the short run.

However, repression and failure to introduce serious change will almost certainly further undermine social support for the Islamic Republic. The variables examined in this analysis confirm the politicization and polarization of Iranian politics and social structure. Such politicization and polarization will likely produce further radicalization, reduce the possibility of compromise, and impede the search for common ground. Politicization and polarization demonstrate that theocracy and democracy are fundamentally incompatible. While theocracy defends absolute, divine principles, democracy advocates the empowerment of the people. For Iranians to achieve democracy, they would need to replace the theocratic constitution, which assigns categorical privileges and powers and validates wide disparities in political power. As past events have demonstrated, such a change is unlikely to occur through a reformist path. Successful democratization in Iran would more likely require a disruptive revolutionary route.

The rulers of the Islamic Republic have two theoretical options to forestall a disruptive revolution. They must introduce serious reforms to reverse the declining social base of support. They could fundamentally reform the system and grant the freedoms promised during the revolutionary struggles and the rights enshrined in the constitution. They could fulfill the popular, revolutionary demands for greater social and economic justice. Reforming the system might strengthen their position and preserve the Islamic Republic, albeit at the expense of reducing the clerical rulers' powers. Fundamental reform might also split the opposition camp, separating radical forces that prefer fundamental alterations in the system from the reformists, and thereby prevent the formation of a coalition. Such an option risks fracturing the ruling clergy. Its more conservative faction might refuse on the grounds that such reforms would alter the nature of the Islamic Republic and challenge the sanctity of the supreme leader and the Islamic Republic. Alternatively, the rulers could continue the exclusive and repressive policies they have followed for more than thirty years and attempt to preserve the current structures and relationships. Endless repression might enable them to maintain their power and privileges in the short run but will likely render the Islamic regime even more vulnerable to future challenge and attack.

In the absence of serious changes in the polity, reformists also have two options. They might become radicalized and more critical of the Islamic Republic and adopt the platform of more radical forces that have struggled for democratic transformations, as some reformists and a few conservatives did following the 2009 presidential elections. Greater radicalization would place the reformists more in line with popular demands and closer to the struggle for real democracy—that is, removing categorical inequalities and empowering the people vis-à-vis the theocratic state. Reformists could use their organizational capabilities to mobilize broader segments of the population in the next round of conflicts. Alternatively, the reformists might continue within the framework of the Islamic Republic and their current platform. However, regime intransigence might increasingly render the reformists irrelevant to Iran's democratization and political future. Should they fail to take a more radical stand, reformists risk losing the support of increasing portions of the population, which might abandon the reformist platform as inadequate and ineffective to resolve the Islamic Republic's contradictions and antidemocratic features.

Absent democratic changes in the system, the political crisis is bound to grow and produce two antagonistic poles. On the one side, the ruling clergy would have to resort to greater repressive measures to preserve the Islamic Republic. On the other, substantial segments of the population are likely to mobilize again and oppose the existing system. The people will inevitably demand democratic changes in the polity and the dismantling of categorical inequalities enshrined in the constitution. Democratic forces, currently demobilized, are certain to resurface and press for democratization as internal social, economic, and political contradictions converge.

In sum, the Islamic Republic has generated multiple, irreconcilable conflicts—rooted in the core of the theocracy—that are too extensive to be reformed. The Islamic Republic's rulers have systematically downgraded the people's role in the state and rejected democratic transformation. While the timing of an eruption is difficult to predict, the variables presented here strongly suggest that Iran's democratization will likely proceed through a disruptive, revolutionary path.

Iran's democratization would depend on the capacity of challengers to mobilize a broad, nationwide coalition of major social classes and collectivities to disrupt social, economic, and political structures and effect genuine transformation, as demonstrated by the preceding comparative and historical analyses. Rare as they are, broad coalitions are more likely to form when multiple contradictions and conflicts converge to consolidate the opposition and disrupt the social structure. Consolidation and disruptive collective action can potentially isolate antidemocratic regimes, neutralize repressive forces, instigate military insubordination, and bring about democratic transformation.

Iranians' struggles for democracy have been persistent and protracted. Iranians mobilized for Constitutional Revolution in 1905 but failed due to internal and external forces. They fought for democracy in the early 1950s, only to be frustrated by a CIA-backed military coup. Iranians rose up again against authoritarian rule in 1979, when revolutionary leaders promised democratic rights but instead established a theocracy. Thousands died resisting the theocracy during the first decade of the Islamic Republic. Iranian students mobilized nationwide in two rounds of protests in 1999 and 2003, challenging the core of the Islamic theocracy. Iranians launched the Green Movement in 2009, shaking the foundation of the Islamic regime with their demands for social and political rights and democratic institutions. More than one hundred persons were slain during the protests. Iranians defied the forces that denied them personal, social, and cultural freedoms. Many Iranians engaged in passive resistance to reject the social and cultural practices imposed by the theocracy. Countless Iranians were arrested, jailed, fined, lashed, and some were violated. Iranians, like all victims of social and historical processes, continued to resist domination and exploitation. Their struggle has yet to reach its climax.

Notes

1. Iran's Dilemma

1. The wave of democratization movements in the Arab Spring followed Iran's Green Movement. Some activists in the Arab Spring have also pointed to some actual inspiration from the Green Movement. See Charles Kurzman. "The Arab Spring: Ideals of the Iranian Green Movement, Methods of the Iranian Revolution." *International Journal of Middle East Studies* 44 (2012): 162.

2. Data sources included primarily official and semiofficial sites, official sources in the Islamic Republic, including *irna.ir, isna.ir, ilna.ir, mehrnew.com, farsnews.com; international sources, the bbc.co.uk/persian, Deutsche Welle (dw.de/farsi), radiofarda; the New York Times, Washington Post, Associated Press, and Reuters*; and Internet reports that covered the 2009 presidential election.

3. "Seyyed mohammad reza khatami: in system bedoon taghier dar siasat nemitavand edameh masir dahad," October 8, 2012, *kaleme.com.*

4. "Eslah talabi be manaye bar andazi nist," January 30, 2014, *baharnews.ir.*

5. "Hadi khameneie: natavanestim be ahdaf enghelab berasim," February 1, 2014, *dw.com/fa-ir.*

6. "Ziba kalam: esraiel ra be rasmiat mishenasam," January 31, 2014, *farsnews.com.*

7. "Mohem tarin khatar pish rouye jomhouri eslami fesad eghtesadi ast," January 6, 2016, *tasnimnews.com.*

8. Ruhollah Khomeini. *Sahifeh-e Nour.* Tehran: Ministry of Islamic Guidance, 1983a, 4: 252.

9. Soroush Irfani. *Revolutionary Islam in Iran: Popular Liberation or Religious Dictatorship?* London: Zed, 1983: 199.

10. Interview with Mohammad Shanehchi, chief aide to Ayatollah Taleghani, April 1998.

11. "Marge mashkook ayatollah seyyed mahmoud taleghani," September 4, 2013, *radiozamaneh.com.*

12. Personal interview with former president Abolhassan Bani-Sadr, January 18, 2011.

13. In a meeting with the supreme leader, Rafsanjani told Ayatollah Khamenei that it would be a disgrace for the system forever if anything happened to those under house arrest. "It would be better to free those under house arrest, and under the present condition this is a serious demand of the people." November 17, 2013, *bbc.com/Persian.*

14. Thomas Erdbring, "Trying unlikely comeback, Iran ex-president strikes chord with public," May 17, 2013, *nytimes.com.*

15. "Rafsanjani: ghabool nadarm ke sepah be raghibi dar malekiat tabdil shaved," January 23, 2014, *dw.com/fa-ir.*

16. "Hashemi Rafsanjani: dowlat hasht saleh Ahmadinejad mesle maraz harri bood," June 21, 2015, *tasnimnews.com.*

17. "Ayatollah hashemi: migooyand tahrim ha be nafa mast, pedar mardom ra dar avardeh, che tor be nafa mast?" June 16, 2014, *entekhab.ir.*

18. "Gorouhi baraye entekhab rahbari dar sourat pishamad hadese taaien shodeh ast," December 13, 2015, *ilna.ir.*

19. Alan Cowell, "Hard-liners ruling Iran gain ally in key post," March 8, 2011, *nytimes.com.*

20. "Faezeh hashemi baraye tanbih be zendan enferadi ferestadeh shod," December 31, 2012, *bbc.com/Persian.*

21. "Mehdi Hashemi be zendan raft," August 9, 2015, *bbc.com/Persian.*

22. Seed Kamali Dehghan, "Iran election: Rafsanjani blocked from running for president," May 21, 2013, *theguardian.com.*

23. The individuals included former president Ayatollah Hashemi Rafsanjani, Mir Hussein Mousavi (former prime minister), Ayatollah Abdolkarim Mousavi Ardebili (head of the judiciary), Ayatollah Saanei and Mohammad Mousavi Khoiniha (public prosecutors), Mohammad Reza Tavassoli (Khomeini's representative in government meetings), Abdollah Nouri (Khomeini's representative in the Revolutionary Guard), Mohammad Ali Rahmani (commander of the paramilitary Basij), Tahmaseb Mazaheri (head of Mostazafan va Janbazan Foundation), Mehdi Karroubi (head of Martyr Foundation), Mohammad Hashemi (head of radio and television), Mahmoud Doaie (Khomeini's representative at *Ettelaat* newspaper), and Mohammad Khatami (Khomeini's representative at *Kayhan* newspaper).

24. On the politics of these leaders, see Hussein Bastani, "Parvandeh yek tasfieh: moatamedan ayatollah khomeini che sarneveshti yaftand," February 12, 2015, *bbc.com/Persian.*

25. Michael Slackman, "In Iran, from heroes to state enemies," November 30, 2009, *nytimes.com.*

26. "Estekhdam 23 lisans va foghe lisans dar shahrdari khorram abad," July 8, 2015, *irna.ir.*

27. Saeed Kamali Dehghan, "Iranian pair face death penalty after third alcohol offense," June 26, 2012, *theguardian.com*.

28. Alex Efty, June 13, 1979, *Associated Press*.

29. Paul Martin, "Laughing is a crime," August 6, 1979, *Newsweek*.

30. "Iran proposed penal code retains stoning," June 3, 2013, *hrw.org*.

31. "Four in Iran executed by stoning," July 4, 1980, *nytimes.com*.

32. Philip Dopoulos, July 23, 1979, *Associated Press*.

33. Scheherezade Faramarzi, "Parliament codifies moral behavior," August 27, 1981, *Associated Press*.

34. Neil MacFarquhar, "Dog lovers of Iran, beware of growling ayatollahs," August 24, 2001, *nytimes.com*.

35. "Raadan khabar dad/bar khord baa sag gardani, zanan khiabani, va mankan nama ha," April 28, 2013, *khabaronline.ir*.

36. Ian Black, "Dainty dish defies the rulers' wrath," April 5, 1994, *The Guardian*.

37. Jerome Socolovsky, "Iran's parliament approves satellite TV ban," January 1, 1995, *Associated Press*.

38. "Mardom be ehteram ghanoon, anten haye ashkar mahvareh ra jam konand," March 1, 2011, *khabaronline.ir*.

39. "Nazar Ayatollah Abdollah Javadi Amoli dar bareh chahr shanbe souri," March 12, 2014, *tabnak.ir*.

40. "Chahr shanbeh akhar sal zolm be mardom iran ast," March 18, 2014, *tasnim.com*.

41. "Chahar shanbeh souri az nazar marajea taghlid," March 6, 2010, *tabnak.ir*.

42. "Se basiji mottahm be ghatle behnood ramazani az etteham ghatle amd tabrae shodand," September 8, 2015, *sahamnews.org*.

43. Dorothy Gilliam, "The optimism of a holy man in exile," November 15, 1978, *Washington Post*.

44. "Emam Khomeini: chador baraye zanan ejbari nist," January 21, 1979, *Kayhan*.

45. "Gender inequality and discrimination: The case of Iranian women," March 8, 2013, *iranhrdc.org*.

46. Ibid.

47. Mitra Shojaie, "Haghe safar; haghi gerah khordeh ba ghaymomiat mard bar zan," September 23, 2015, *dw.com/fa.ir*.

48. "Iranian women fight controversial polygamy bill," November 30, 2011, *amnesty.org*.

49. Scheherezade Faramarzi, "Parliament outlaws alcohol, music and pornography," August 27, 1981, *Associated Press*.

50. Thomas Erdbrink, "Iranian authorities step up arrests of women for immodest dress," June 2, 2010, *washingtonpost.com*.

51. "Radaan: hejab zanan dar hengam ranandegi jori bashad ke maamoran betavanand onha ra shenasaee konand," August 28, 2011, *khabaronline.ir*.

52. Kay Armin Serjoie, "Young Iranians stay home in fear of acid attacks," October 23, 2014, *time.com*.

53. "Marge zan ghorbani asid pasha dar bimarestan," April 14, 2015, *baharnews.ir*.

54. "Global Gender Gap Report 2015," *reports.weforum.org.*
55. "Saham zanan az advar noh ganeh majles che boodeh ast," May 1, 2013, *isna.ir.*
56. United Nations Development Programme, Human Development Report 2010: 157, *undp.org.*
57. "Iranian women fight controversial polygamy bill," November 30, 2011, *amnesty.org.*
58. "Rahbari az shellik doshman be ghalbe javanan negaranand," March 11, 2014, *farsnews.com.*
59. "Hokoomat vazife dard mardom ra be behesht bebarad, hata be zoor shallagh," May 30, 2014, *bbc.com/Persian.*
60. "Ba hameh ghodrat jeloye kesani ke manea behesht raftan mardom shavand khahim istad," May 30, 2014, *mehrnews.com.*
61. "Nemi tavan motmaen bood ke farzandan ma manand ma enghelabi bashand," October 16, 2014, *mehrnews.com.*
62. "Nategh nouri: dar 37 sale gozashteh dar khayli az masael sair ghah gharaie dashtim," June 30, 2016, *isna.ir.*
63. "Moteassefane emrooz na jomhuri ast na eslami!" December 21, 2014, *jamaran.ir.*
64. Elaine Scilino, "Chaotic protests reign in Tehran; vigilantes active," July 14, 1999, *nytimes.com.*
65. "Most of the wanted students escape police dragnet," June 30, 1985, *Korea Times.*
66. "Helicopters used to break up resistance: Students hurl fire bombs, set barricades," November 1, 1986, *Korea Times.*
67. Niles Lathem, "Iran threatens dissidents with death," July 15, 1999, *nypost .com.*
68. Khomeini 1983a, 7: 58.
69. Khomeini, *Sahifeh-e Nour.* Tehran: Ministry of Islamic Guidance, 1991, 7: 288–290.
70. "Nimee az masajed dar toole sal faaliati nadarand," December 5, 2009, *alef.ir.*
71. "57000 majed dar had jomhuri eslami nist," September 6, 2015, *farsnews .com.*
72. "Mardom az barkhi maz habiyoun naa omid shodeh and," July 13, 2015, *ilna.ir.*
73. "Modir howzeh haye elmieh: si hezar masjed iran bedoon rouhani ast," June 4, 2012, *bbc.com/Persian.*
74. "Khanevadeh ha yeki az farzandan khod ra vaghfe emam zaman konand," November 2, 2013, *digarban.com.*
75. Khomeini 1991, 7: 288–290.
76. "Nameh sar goshadeh sadegh ziba kalam be ali motahari," May 16, 2015, *khabaronline.ir.*
77. "Drugs and prostitution soar in Iran," July 6, 2000, *bbc.com.*
78. "Namaz jamaat dar tamam madares bar gozar mishavad," September 4, 2014, *irna.ir.*

79. "Gharaati: tanha panj dar sad mardom zakat mi dahand," September 17, 2014, *tabnak.ir.*

80. "Habs va shallagh mojazat rouzeh khari dar malae aam," June 7, 2013, *farsnews.com.*

81. "Dastgiri pansad rouzeh khar dar shiraz," June 30, 2015, *tabnak.ir.*

82. "Jozieyat Dastgiri rouzeh kharan dar hotele shahriar Tabriz," June 23, 2015, *farsnew.com.*

83. "Amare rouzeh kharan dastgir shodeh az 660 gozasht," July 1, 2015, *dw.com/fa.*

84. "Farmandeh entezami sirjan: bar khord baa 32 nafar ke dar malea aam rouzeh khari kardehand," July 4, 2015, *hra-news.org.*

85. "Dastgiri dah nafar dar neka be jorm rouzeh khari," July 5, 2015, *ghatreh .com.*

86. "98 nafar atbaa biganeh va 228 rouzeh khar dar mahmoudabad dastgir shodand," July 4, 2015, *mehrnews.com.*

87. "Shallagh khoran 207 nafar be ettehaam rouzeh khari dar malaa aam dar shahr haye mokhtalef," August 6, 2014, *iranhumanrights.org.*

88. "Amar markaz pazhouhesh haye majles az ham jens garaie dar madares iran," August 8, 2014, *radiofarda.com* (http://www.radiofarda.com/article printview/26521371.html).

89. "80 dar sad dokhtaran irani doost pesar darand," October 27, 2013, *jamejamonline.ir.*

90. "Amar tekan dahandeh majles az ravabet jensi dar iran," August 9, 2014, *tabnak.ir.*

91. "Enteghad Mohammadi Golpaygani as ezdevaje sefid," November 30, 2014, *isna.ir.*

92. "Hoshdar vezarate behdasht dar mored amar sooa masraf alko dar iran," May 14, 2012, *bbc.com/Persian.*

93. "Masraf salaneh 60 melyoun litr mashroubat alkoli dar iran," January 2, 2016, *radiofarda.com.*

94. "Islam and alcohol: Tipsy taboo," August 18, 2012, *economist.com.*

95. "Negarani tolid konandegan alkoli nesbat be estefadeh az towlidateshan dar tehayeh mashroobat alkoli," October 5, 2014, *icana.ir.*

96. "Masraf salaneh 420 melyoun litr alkol dar keshvar," July 21, 2015, *fararu .com.*

97. "Davazdah milliard dollar kharj mashroub irani ha," December 9, 2014, *roozonline.com.*

98. "Ghachagh yek milliard dolari mashroubat alkoli be keshvar," January 3, 2016, *isna.ir.*

99. "Nameh kar khane daran be majles: alkol ma be mashroub tabdil mishavad," May 14, 2012, *bbc.co.uk/Persian.*

100. "Shajooni: tarhe amniyat akhlaghi bayad be ravesh aghelaneh va dini anjam shaved," April 19, 2016, *isna.ir.*

101. "Voroud rouzaneh 115 kamyoun 10 toni mashroubat alkoli be keshvar," July 22, 2015, *farsnews.com.*

102. "Hoshdar yek masool: paye alkol be madares ham baz shod!" October 3, 2015, *isna.ir.*

103. "Chand dar sad danesh amoozan sigar va ghalyun mikeshand va mashroob alkoli masraf mikonand," October 31, 2012, *khabaronline.ir.*
104. "Gozareshi tekan dahandeh az barkhi no javanan tehrani," November 29, 2014, *isna.ir.*
105. "Avvalin clinic dowlati tark alkol dar iran rah andazi shod," August 1, 2014, *bbc.com/Persian.*
106. "Rah andazi 150 markaz tark eatiad alkol dar keshvar," January 3, 2016, *shahrvand-newspaper.ir.*
107. Saeed Kamali Dehghan, "Iranian pair face death penalty after third alcohol offence," June 25, 2012, *theguardian.com.*
108. "Ejraye hokme 99 zarbeh shallagh baraye tamaam hazeran dar yek party shabaneh dar ghazvin," May 26, 2016, *bbc.com/Persian.*
109. "Hokme Marg baraye no kishan masihi va vahshat az gostareshe taghier din," May 24, 2012, *ir.voanews.com.*
110. "Tahajjor va efrat tanha donyaye mardom ke ghabl har chiz din mardom ra az beyn mi barad," February 25, 2015, *jamaran.ir.*
111. "Kelisahaye khanegi va tablighe masihiyat," April 19, 2010, *shia-news.com.*
112. "Che kesani Javanan mosalman ra az masajed be kelisahaye khanegi mi barand?" October 3, 2010, *asriran.com.*
113. "Rosd bahaiyat va masihiyat dar shargh keshvar," August 17, 2011, *khabaronline.ir.*
114. "Roshd gorouhhaye zalleh dar roustaha negaran konnandah ast,"August 16, 2011, *farsnews.com.*
115. "Dar khast faalaan siasi baraye bar khord ghoveh ghazaieh ba khoshunat aleyhe bahaian," March 13, 2014, *bbc.com/Persian.*
116. "Ba hozour Jamie az faalaan madani, marasem salgard baz dashte modiran jameah bahai bar gozar shod," May 16, 2014, *sahamnews.org.*
117. "Enteghad yek rouhani shia dar iran az nahveh bar khord ba bahaian," September 5, 2013, *bbc.com/Persian.*
118. "Deljooyee yek rouhani shia az bahaian ba taghdim yek asar honari," March 13, 2014, *hra-news.org.*
119. "Ayatollah masoumi tehrani ba ersal hedieh va nameh be baytoladl az bahaian deljooyee kard," retrieved October 3, 2015, iranwire.com/news /56/5818.
120. "Farman hasht maddeh ie emam motaraghghi tarin hoghoughe shahr vandi ast," December 16, 2014, *farsnews.com.*
121. "Hoghoghe shahr vandi be ravayate ayat ollah mousavi boroujerdi," December 17, 2014, *rahesabz.net.*
122. "Naghde aarae mousavi bojnourdi dar bareh bahaiat, be ghalam Mohsen kadivar," December 23, 2014, *iranhumanrights.org.*
123. "Vakenesh ha be didar faezeh hashemi baa modiran baha'i," May 14, 2016, *bbc.com/Persian.*
124. "Ravayate faezeh hashemi va nasrin Sotoudeh az didar ba zendani baha'i," May 13, 2016, *iranwire.com.*
125. Fereshteh Ghazi, "Faezeh hashemi dar goftegoo baa youro news: khalafi nakardeham va pashiman nistam," May 15, 2016, *Persian.euronews.com.*

126. "Aghideh nemi tavand mabnaye jorme hoghoughi ya maasiyat dini bashad," May 21, 2016, *zeitoons.com*.
127. "Nimei az masajed dar toole sal faaliyati nadarand," December 5, 2009, *alef.ir*.
128. "Tarhi ke booye baz shodan shekaf ejtemaie ra midahad," September 7, 2015, *tabrizefarda.com*.
129. "Chand daghigheh azadi yavashaki dar eateraz be hejab," May 10, 2014, *dw.de/fa.ir*.
130. "Saport zanan irani; mowzooa porsesh az vazir keshvar dar majles," June 24, 2014, *dw.com/fa.ir*.
131. "Towghif khod roye 40 hezar bad hejab," December 15, 2015, *farsnews .com*.
132. "Azme melli baraye gostaresh hejab eijad nashodeh ast," July 11, 2014, *irna.ir*.
133. "Dou million nafar moatad ba asib haye faravan dar keshvar vojood darad," September 2, 2014, *tasnimnews.com*.
134. "Moaven ghovveh Ghazaieh: az bad hejabi be samt bi hejabi mi ravim," June 21, 2016, *dw.com/fa-ir*.
135. "Makeup speaks volumes for women," June 24, 2014, *nydailynews.com*.
136. "Vezarate behdashte iran: haftomin keshvar por masraf lavazem arayeshi donya hastim," December 6, 2014, *bbc.com/Persian*.
137. Najmeh Bozorgmehr, "Iran's women continue to defy hardliners: There is widespread dissatisfaction among the under-35s," January 15, 2005, *Financial Times* (London).
138. "Iranians defy hard-liners to mark festival of fire," March 17, 2015, *ap.org*.
139. Seed Kamali Dehghan, "Iran's festival of fire—and fury," March 18, 2009, *theguardian.com*.
140. "Barkhi Chehreh amrika ra bazak mikonand," March 13, 2015, *mehrnews.com*.
141. "Bar paie tajammoa dar chahar shanbeh akhar sal mamnooa," February 22, 2015, *isna.ir*.
142. "Iranians defy hard-liners to mark festival of fire," March 17, 2015, *Associated Press*.
143. "Orzhance iran: dar marasem chahar shanbe souri emsal se nafar koshte shodand," March 18, 2015, *bbc.com/Persian*.
144. "Dou melion nafar moatad ba asib haye faravan dar keshvar vojood darad," September 2, 2014, *tasnimnews.com*.
145. "Rouhani: mobarezeh ba mahvareh dar poshte baam taasir gozar nabood," May 17, 2014, *khabaronline.ir*.
146. "Vaghti 71 dar sad mardom mahvareh negah mi konand, che mitavan kard," September 18, 2013, *tabnak.ir*.
147. "Vazir ershad: har ja dish haye mahvareh ra jam kardim, do rooz baad nasb kardand," February 8, 2015, *khabaronline.ir*.
148. "Anten haye boshghabi dar sadabad jam shod," August 27, 2014, *irna.ir*.
149. "Jam avari 270 hezar mahvareh dar tehran," December 30, 2015, *tasnimnews .com*.
150. "Mokhateban barkhi shabake haye seda va sima az teadad kar konanash kamtarand," December 19, 2015, *dw.com/fa.ir*.

151. "Iran: Happy video dancers sentenced to 91 lashes and jail," September 19, 2014, *bbc.com*.

152. "Effective factors in deterioration of the role of religion under the present condition of Iran," October 28, 2000, *payvand.com*.

153. Misagh Parsa. *Social Origins of the Iranian Revolution*. New Brunswick: Rutgers University Press, 1989: 288.

154. Mansour Osanloo, president of the Syndicate of Workers of the Tehran and Suburbs Bus Company, personal communication, November 22, 2014.

155. Robin Wright. *The Last Great Revolution: Turmoil and Transformation in Iran*. New York: Vintage, 2001: 53.

156. "Mohtashemi-pour: sali yek melion naft raygan be asad dadim," July 22, 2012, *baztabonline.com*.

157. "Pasokh 'be man che' mantegh eslam nist," November 8, 2014, *rasanews.ir*.

158. "Arrests follow acid attacks on Iranian women," October 20, 2014, *nytimes .com*.

159. "Zarb va shatm rouhani amr be maaroof tavasot dokhtaran bad hejab," September 17, 2012, *mehrnews.com*.

160. "Ali khalili janbaz nahi az monker daavat hagh ra labaiyk goft," March 25, 2014, *alef.ir*.

161. "Zarb va shatm rouhani amr be maaroof tavasote dokhtaran bad hejab," September 17, 2012, *mehrnews.com*.

162. "Hamleh be yek talebeh khorram abadi ba ghameh va chagoo," October 25, 2014, *khabaronline.ir*.

163. "Zarb va jarhe vahshiyaneh rouhani javan dar eslamshahr," May 17, 2016, *jamnews.ir*.

164. "Namehe estefaye tarikhi ayatollah taheri be mellat va pasokh rahbari," June 2, 2012, *rahesabz.net*.

165. Doctor Rahami spoke in a public Ahura mourning ceremony at the office of the grand ayatollah on December 14, 2014. "Marasem arbaien hoseini ba hozour aza daran eba abdollah ol hossein v aba sokhanrani hojat ole slam val moslemin doctor mohsen rahami dar daftar marjaa alighadr ayat ollah ol ozma saanei khorasan razavi (mashhad moghaddas) bar gozar shod," December 14, 2014, *saanei.org*.

166. Thomas Freidman, "Iran by the numbers," June 23, 2002, *nytimes.com*.

167. Robin Wright, "Survey says Iranians favor free election of top leader," March 9, 2008, *washingtonpost.com*.

168. Yuval Porat, "Iranians have democratic values," May 13, 2012, *wsj.com*.

169. "Kahesh dah barabari teadad rouhaniyoun dar majles dahom nesbat be majles avval," May 1, 2016, *radiofarda.com*.

170. "Bayanieh hambastegi baraye demokrasi va hoghoogh bashar dar iran dar bareh entekhabat majles dahom," November 30, 2015, *jebhe.net*.

171. "Ayat ollah Yazdi: vali motlagh faghieh hich gah eshtebah nemi konad," July 21, 2011, *aftabnews.ir*.

172. "Eslam menhaye vali neamate na tamam ast," December 3, 2015, *isna.ir*.

173. "Vazayef amr be maaroof va nahy az monker," April 12, 2015, *fararu .com*.

174. "Shuraye negahban tarhe amre be maaroof majles ra rad kard," January 3, 2015, *bbc.com.Persian.*

175. "Tasvib bakhsh haye digari az tarhe hemayat az ameran be maaroof," February 1, 2015, *radiofarda.com.*

176. "Gershad, aplikaysheni baraye dowr zaden gasht ershad," February 9, 2016, *bbc.com/Persian.*

177. "New App that Detects Morality Police Is Instant Hit in Iran," February 9, 2016, *iranhumanrights.org.*

178. "Didar rais jomhur va aazaye hayat dowlat ba rahbare enghelab," August 27, 2014 *khamenei.ir.*

179. "Jannati: onha ke khahan rafe hasr hastand dark siasi nadarand," October 17, 2014, *bbc.com/Persian.*

180. "Hokm saran fetne efsad fel arz va baghi bar nezam eslami ast," December 20, 2014, *mehrnews.com.*

181. "Amoly Larijani: Naghse ghovevehe ghazaieh dar bar khord ba fetne hashtado hasht ghabel defa ast," December 31, 2014, *isna.ir.*

182. "Vokalaye mottahaman amniyati dar iran az in pas mored taied rais ghovveh ghazaieh bashand," June 23, 2015, *bbc.com/Persian.*

183. "Eateraz khanevadeh haye zendanian siasi be feshar haye mamoran amniyati," July 7, 2015, *bbc.com/Persian.*

184. "Enteghad molavi abdolhamid az takhribe namaz khaneh ahle sonnat dar tehran," July 31, 2015, *bbc.com/Persian.*

185. "Mowzooa adame bar gozari konsert be daneshgah ha eblagh shod," August 26, 2015, *mehrnews.com.*

186. "Az se hezar eslah talab 30 nafar taied shod," January 17, 2016, *ilna.ir.*

187. "Namayandeh majles: barkhi aemeh jamaat be dalil adam eltezam be eslam rad salahiyat shodeh and," January 27, 2016, *radiofarda.com.*

188. "Ealaam asami rad salahiyat shodeh ha va ehraz salahiyat neshodeh haye khebregan," January 26, 2016, *tabnak.ir.*

189. "Gorouhy az daneshgahain iran: adam bar gozari entekhabat ghair raghabi va naa adelaneh bar anjam aan arjaieyat darad," February 9, 2016, *bbc.com /Persian.*

2. Alternative Routes to Democracy: Synthesizing Structures and Processes

1. John Lie. *Han Unbounded: The Political Economy of South Korea.* Stanford: Stanford University Press, 1998: 149.

2. Samuel Huntington. *The Third Wave. Democratization in the Late Twentieth Century.* Norman: University of Oklahoma Press, 1991: 37.

3. "Ahmad khatami be rouhani: jaddeh jehannam ra saf nekonid," May 27, 2014, *bbc.com/Persian.*

4. "Jameahe bedoun rahbar be birahe keshideh mishavad," May 29, 2014, *mehrnews.com.*

5. "Raies jomhour: be zoor nemitavanim behesht ra be mardom tahmil konim/ hadde dava haye siasi bayed negah dashte shaved," May 24, 2014, *isna.ir.*

6. "Hokoomat vazifeh darad mardom ra be behest bebarad, hatta be zoor shallagh," May 30, 2014, *bbc.com/Persian*.

7. Jeff Goodwin. *No Other Way Out: States and Revolutionary Movements, 1945–1991*. Cambridge: Cambridge University Press, 2001.

8. Timothy McDaniel. *Autocracy, Modernization, and Revolution in Russia and Iran*. Princeton: Princeton University Press, 1991: 6; Dietrich Rueschemeyer, Evelyne Stephens, and John Stephens. *Capitalist Development and Democracy*. Chicago: University of Chicago Press, 1992: 40–68.

9. John Foran. *Taking Power: On the Origins of Third World Revolutions*. Cambridge: Cambridge University, 2005: 25; Jeff Goodwin. "Toward a New Sociology of Revolutions." *Theory and Society* 23 (1994): 731–766; R. Snyder. "Paths out of Sultanic Regimes: Combining Structural and Voluntaristic Perspectives." In *Sultanic Regimes*, edited by Houchang Chehabi and Juan Linz. Baltimore: Johns Hopkins University Press, 1998: 56.

10. Chung-Hee Park (Leon Sinder). *The Country, the Revolution, and I*. Seoul: Hollym Corp., 1963: 177–178.

11. Eugene C. I. Kim. "Transition from Military Rule: The Case of South Korea." *Armed Forces and Society* 1 (3), (1975): 304.

12. Park 1963: 17.

13. Park 1963: 97.

14. R. E. Elson. *Suharto: A Political Biography*. Cambridge: Cambridge University Press, 2008: 189.

15. Edward Aspinall. *Opposing Suharto: Compromise, Resistance and Regime Change in Indonesia*. Stanford: Stanford University Press, 2005: 116.

16. Misagh Parsa. "Economic Development and Political Transformation: A Comparative Analysis of the United States, Russia, Nicaragua, and Iran." *Theory and Society* 14 (1985): 623–675.

17. Misagh Parsa. *States, Ideologies, and Social Revolutions: A Comparative Analysis of Iran, Nicaragua, and the Philippines*. Cambridge: Cambridge University Press, 2000: chap. 1; Dietrich Rueschemeyer and Peter Evans. "The State and Economic Transformation: Toward an Analysis of the Conditions Underlying Effective Intervention." In *Bringing the State Back In*, edited by Peter Evans, Dietrich Rueschemeyer, and Theda Skocpol. Cambridge: Cambridge University Press, 1985: 69.

18. Harold Crouch. *The Army and Politics in Indonesia*. Ithaca: Cornell University Press, 1988: 275.

19. Shana Marshall and Joshua Stacher. "Egypt's General and Transnational Capital." *MERIP Reports* 262 (Spring 2012): *merip.org*.

20. Parsa 2000: 16.

21. Parsa 2000: 16.

22. Michael Vatikiotis. *Indonesian Politics under Suharto*. London: Routledge, 1993: 37.

23. Theodore Friend. *Indonesian Destinies*. Cambridge: Belknap, 2003: 169.

24. Seymour Lipset, Kyoung-Ryung Seong, and John Charles Torres. "A Comparative Analysis of the Social Requisites of Democracy." *International Social Science Journal* 45 (1993): 155–175.

25. Rueschemeyer, Stephens, and Stephens 1992: 40–68.
26. On the relationship between economic development, inequality, and democracy, see Kenneth A. Bollen and Robert W. Jackman. "Political Democracy and Size Distribution of Income." *American Sociological Review* 50 (1985): 438–457; and Edward N. Muller. "Economic Determinants of Democracy." *American Sociological Review* 60 (1995): 966–982.
27. Muller 1995: 966.
28. Rober Wade. *Governing the Market*. Princeton: Princeton University Press, 1990: 34–35.
29. Huntington 1991: 115–121.
30. Parsa 2000: 62–65.
31. Parsa, 2000: 239.
32. Parsa 2000: 197.
33. Stephen Haggard and Robert R. Kaufman. *The Political Economy of Democratic Transitions*. Princeton: Princeton University Press, 1995: 7–8 and 29–30.

3. Ideologies, Revolution, and the Formation of a Theocracy

1. Theda Skocpol. "Rentier State and Shi'a Islam in the Iranian Revolution." *Theory and Society* 11 (1982): 265–283.
2. Misagh Parsa. "Ideology and Political Action in the Iranian Revolution." *Comparative Studies of South Asia, Africa, and the Middle East* 31 (2011): 53–68, 54.
3. Ruhollah Khomeini. *Sahifeh-e Nour*. Tehran: Ministry of Islamic Guidance, 1983a: 1, 359.
4. These figures appear in a written statement by students at the Madraseh-e Faizieh Qom (in the possession of the author).
5. Misagh Parsa. *States, Ideologies, and Social Revolutions: A Comparative Analysis of Iran, Nicaragua, and the Philippines*. Cambridge: Cambridge University Press, 2000: 94.
6. Assadollah Alam. *The Shah and I: The Confidential Diary of Iran's Royal Court, 1969–1977*. London: I. B. Tauris, 1991: 488.
7. Azadeh Kian. "The Politics of the New Middle Class in Iran and Egypt from the Nineteenth Century until 1979." Unpublished PhD dissertation, University of California, Los Angeles, 1993: 465.
8. Misagh Parsa. "State, Class, and Ideology in the Iranian Revolution." *Comparative Studies of South Asia, Africa, and the Middle East* 29 (2009): 3–17, 12–13.
9. Ervand Abrahamian. *The Iranian Mojahedin*. New Haven: Yale University Press, 1989: 128.
10. Parsa 2000: 105.
11. Parsa 1989: 266.
12. James Dorsey, "Power struggle in Iran becomes more intense," December 19, 1980, *Christian Science Monitor*.
13. "Ashnaie ba tarikhcheh showraye aali enghelab farhangi," August 8, 2008, *hamshahrionline.ir*.

14. "Asami va moshakasat bakhshi az shohadaye enghelab novin iran," September 6, 1985, *Mojahed* #219.

15. Parsa 2009: 11.

16. Asef Bayat. "Revolution without Movement, Movement without Revolution: Comparing Islamic Activism in Iran and Egypt." *Comparative Studies in Society and History* 40 (1), (1998): 136–169, 150.

17. Interview with Assef Bayat (April 1998), who participated in both sets of events.

18. Parsa 1989: 286.

19. Hossein Bashiriyeh. *The State and the Revolution in Iran, 1962–1982.* New York: St. Martin's Press, 1984: 61; Farideh Farhi. *States and Urban-Based Revolutions: Iran and Nicaragua.* Urbana: University of Illinois Press, 1990: 92; Skocpol 1982: 271–273.

20. Lebaschi 1983, Tape 3:15, Iranian Oral History Collection, Houghton Library, Harvard University.

21. Interviews with Abolghassem Lebaschi (February 1997) and Mohammad Shanehchi (April 1998).

22. Lebaschi 1983, Tape 1:9, Iranian Oral History Collection, Houghton Library, Harvard University.

23. Kennett Love, "Mosaddegh quits Tehran hideout; is held for trial," August 21, 1953, *New York Times*; Kennett Love, "Tanks stand guard in Iran's capital; shah is due today, August 22, 1953, *New York Times*.

24. Robert C. Dotty, "New regime in Iran opens war on reds; prince is arrested," August 25, 1953, *New York Times*.

25. Parsa 1989: 193.

26. Hooshang Chehabi. *Iranian Politics and Religious Modernism: The Liberation Movement of Iran under the shah and Khomeini.* Ithaca: Cornell University Press, 1990: 131.

27. Parsa 1989: 97.

28. Parsa 1989: 97.

29. Parsa 1989: 193.

30. Leonard Binder. *Iran: Political Development in a Changing Society.* Berkeley: University of California Press, 1962: 295.

31. Interviews with Abolghassem Lebaschi (February 1997) and Mohammad Shanehchi (April 1998).

32. Lebaschi 1983, Tape 3:5 and 15, Iranian Oral History Collection, Houghton Library, Harvard University.

33. For example, after the massacre of Qom, Azerbaijanis in the Tehran bazaar issued a public statement supporting the SMGATB's mobilization and closures. Parsa 1989: 111.

34. Parsa 1989: 109.

35. "Akhbar," December 1, 1977, *Zamimeh Khabar Nameh* 8: 12–13.

36. "Ettelaieh," December 1, 1977, *Zamimeh Khabar Nameh* 8: 9–11.

37. Parsa 2000: 210.

38. Parsa 2000: 210.

39. Parsa 2000: 210.

40. Parsa 2011: 59.
41. Parsa 1989: 114.
42. Parsa 2000: 213.
43. Personal interview with Mohammad Shanehchi, a leading bazaar activist, Paris, April, 1998.
44. Parsa 1989: 276.
45. Parsa 1989: 276.
46. Parsa 1989: 277.
47. Lebaschi 1983, Tape 3:18, Iranian Oral History Collection, Houghton Library, Harvard University.
48. Parsa 1989: 281.
49. "Asami va moshakasat bakhshi az shohadaye enghelab novin iran," September 6, 1985, *Mojahed* #219.
50. "Two Tehran bazaar merchants are among 22 executed in Iran," July 14, 1981, *nytimes.com*.
51. Asef Bayat. *Workers and Revolution in Iran*. London: Zed, 1987: 91.
52. Jonathon C. Randal, "Protests are forcing cutbacks in Iran," October 25, 1978, *Washington Post*.
53. Parsa 2000: 168–169.
54. Parsa 2000: 169.
55. Ed Blanche, "Ahwaz, Iran," November 12, 1978, *Associated Press*.
56. Jonathan C. Randal, "Khomeini followers struggle for control in oil fields," February 26, 1979, *Washington Post*.
57. Yousef M. Ibrahim, "Despite army's presence, Iranian oil town is challenging the shah," November 19, 1978, *New York Times*.
58. Ervand Abrahamian. "Iran in Revolution: The Opposition Forces." *MERIP Reports* (March–April, 1979): 3.
59. Parsa 2000: 172.
60. Personal interview with Yadollah Khosrow-Shahi, a former member of the oil workers' council, March 1999.
61. Mehdi Bazargan. *Enghelab-e Iran Dar Dou Harkat*. Tehran: Mazaheri, 1984: 37–38.
62. Ervand Abrahamian. *Iran between Two Revolutions*. Princeton: Princeton University Press, 1982: 448–449.
63. Parsa 1989: 292.
64. Ahmad Khomeini, "Hameh rouhaniyoun ra be yek chashm negah nakonid," September 23, 1979, *Ettelaat*.
65. Parsa 2000: 140.
66. Khomeini 1983a, 1: 437.
67. Ahmad Salamatian, 1983, 23–26, Iranian Oral History Collection, Houghton Library, Harvard University.
68. Ahmad Salamatian, interview by author, May 30, 2008.
69. Behrooz Moazami. *State, Religion, and Revolution in Iran, 1796 to the Present*. New York: Palgrave Macmillan, 2013: 125.
70. Ruhollah Khomeini. "Talieh enghelab eslami," *Setad-e Enghelab-e Farhangi*, 1983b: 3–4.

71. Khomeini 1983a, 4: 252.
72. Khomeini 1983a, 2: 62–63.
73. Khomeini 1983b: 30.
74. Khomeini 1983b: 21.
75. Khomeini 1983b: 49.
76. "Emam khomeini: dar hokoumat eslami dictatory vojood nadarad," January 23, 1979, *Kayhan.*
77. Otto C. Doelling, January 29, 1979, *Associated Press.*
78. Khomeini 1983b: 85.
79. "Shoar haye komo nisti dar rah paymaie jomeh mana shod," January 18, 1979, *Kayhan.*
80. "Eslam din azadi ast, azadi kesi ra salb nemi konad," January 24, 1979, *Kayhan.*
81. Khomeini 1983a, 6: 21.
82. Khomeini 1983a, 5: 98.
83. Khomeini 1983a, 5: 238.
84. "Ejazeh towteah dadeh ne mishavad, amma azadi ghalam va bayan va aghideh baraye hameh hast," February 28, 1979, *Kayhan.*
85. "Ekhtenagh dafn shodeh va digar baz nakhahad gasht," April 16, 1979, *Ettelaat.*
86. Khomeini 1983a, 1: 436.
87. Khomeini 1983b: 41.
88. Khomeini 1983b: 30.
89. "Emam: rouhaniyoun nabayad rais jomhour shavand," December 30, 1979, *Kayhan.*
90. Personal interview with Mr. Tahmaseb Pour, a former clerical student, February 1999.
91. Ervand Abrahamian. *Khomeinism: Essays on the Islamic Republic.* Berkeley: University of California Press, 1993: 30.
92. Abrahamian 1993: 54.
93. Khomeini 1983a, 15: 62 and 220.
94. Khomeini 1983a, 15: 149–150.
95. "Payam be monasebat 22 Bahman va salgard-e piroozi enghelab eslami dar bareh jang, daneshgah-ha, vazayef ghovaye se ganeh, resaneh haye gorouhi, va tashakkor az mellat," February 11, 1984, sahifeh emam, vol. 19, section 5, *jamaran.ir.*
96. "Shekast napaziri mellat iran va lozoom hoshyari mellat dar moghabel tow-te-eh-ha," sahifeh emam, vol. 15, section 7, *jamaran.ir.*
97. Asghar Schirazi. *The Constitution of Iran: Politics and the State in the Islamic Republic.* London/New York: I.B.Tauris, 1997: 35.
98. "Vezarat amr be maaroof va nahy az monker eijad mishavad," March 3, 1979, *Kayhan.*
99. Khomeini 1983a, 10: 27
100. Parsa 1989: 256, 292
101. Mahmood Monshipoori. "Civil Society, Velayat-e faqih, and Rule of Law." *Journal of Iranian Research and Analysis* 15 (1999): 106–110, 106.

102. "Iran budget extends reach over religious bodies," December 20, 2000, *reuters.com*.

103. Khomeini 1983a, 5: 234.

104. Khomeini, 1983a, 9: 101.

105. Khomeini 1983a, 9: 246.

106. Khomeini 1983a, 6: 71.

107. Khomeini 1983a, 5:127.

108. "Vezarat amr be maaroof va nahy az monker eijad mishavad," March 3, 1979, *Kayhan*.

109. Khomeini 1983a, 10: 50.

110. Abrahamian 1993: 71.

111. Khomeini 1983a, 5: 120.

112. "Vezarat amr be maaroof va nahy az monker eijad mishavad," March 3, 1979, *Kayhan*.

113. Richard Tomkins, March 1, 1979, *Associated Press*.

114. Thomas Kent, April 19, 1979, *Associated Press*.

115. Khomeini 1983a, 5: 120.

116. Amir Farshad Ebrahimi, leader of an Islamic vigilante group, discussed his links to hardline Iranian politicians on videotape, according to news reports. The taped confessions named several senior members of the government and alleged that they used his group to attack their opponents. Ebrahimi was subsequently sentenced to two years' imprisonment after the video surfaced. See "Iran: Human Rights Developments," World Report 2001, *hrw.org*.

117. Parsa 1989: 285–286.

118. "Press freedom march broken up in Tehran," August 10, 1979, *Washington Post*.

119. Philip Dopoulos, August 12, 1979, *Associated Press*.

120. "Emam, resaneh va matbooat," June 4, 2015, *irna.ir*.

121. "Ayare majles ideh al eslah talaban dar sanjeh andisheh emam," June 29, 2015, *farsnews.com*.

122. William Branigin, "Leading Iranian newspaper shuts after attack by Khomeini," May 13, 1979, *Washington Post*.

123. August 10, 1979, *Washington Post*.

124. William Branigin, "Moslem militants seen moving on Iran's press," May 16, 1979, *Washington Post*.

125. Houshang Asadi, "The day the shah left," January 24, 2013, *wsj.com*.

126. Philip Dopoulos, August 12, 1979, *Associated Press*.

127. "22 nashryieh towtea gar ke sal 58 taatil shodand," August 20, 2015, *khabaronline.ir*.

128. Philip Dopoulos, August 21, 1979, *Associated Press*.

129. "Baz khani tarikh/rouzi ke kayhan va ettelaat mosadereh shodand," September 11, 2012, *parsine.com*.

130. Asghar Schirazi. *The Constitution of Iran: Politics and the State in the Islamic Republic*. London: I. B. Tauris, 1997: 135.

131. Ibid.

132. Iran's largest opposition newspaper ordered closed, April 8, 1981, *nytimes.com.*

133. "Towteahe ahzab va gorouh haye faased," August 18, 1979, farsi.rouhollah .ir/library/sahifeh; and "Moze giri maghamate vaght dar bareh eadam haye dahe 60," September 12, 2013, *bbc.com/Persian.*

134. "Towteahe ahzab va gorouh haye faased," August 18, 1979, farsi.rouhollah .ir/library/sahifeh; and September 12, 2013, *bbc.com/Persian.*

135. William Branigin, "Kurdish rebellion poses severe challenge to Khomeini," August 30, 1979, *Washington Post.*

136. "Nameh sar goshadeh hayat ejraie jebhe demokratik melli," June 3, 1979, *iranrights.org.*

137. Parvin Paidar. *Women and the Political Process in Twentieth-Century Iran.* Cambridge: Cambridge University Press, 1997: 229.

138. August 23, 1979, *New York Times.*

139. "Kurds vow 'all-out war' on Iran's Islamic government," August 26, 1979, *Washington Post.*

140. Philip Dopoulos, August 21, 1979, *Associated Press.*

141. William Branigin, "Kurdish rebellion poses severe challenge to Khomeini," August 30, 1979, *Washington Post.*

142. Dopoulos, August 21, 1979, *Associated Press.*

143. Branigin, August 30, 1979, *Washington Post.*

144. Fereshteh Emamy, August 22, 1979, *Associated Press.*

145. "Marsedeh Mohseni: eadam haye bedoun mohakemeh aghaz dowran shoome 34 saleh regime hakem ast," May 29, 2013, *iranhrc.org.*

146. Alexander G. Higgins, "Khomeini supporters, opponents clash in Tabriz," January 10, 1980, *Associated Press.*

147. Jonathan C. Randal, "Iranian troops move to end Tabriz battle," December 10, 1979, *Washington Post.*

148. Michael Weisskopf, "11 Executed in Iranian crackdown," January 13, 1980, *Washington Post.*

149. "Chera emam jebhe melli ra mortad ealaam kard," June 15, 2014, *farsnews .com.*

150. Semira N. Nikou, "Timeline of Iran's political events," *iranprimer.usip.org.*

151. Abbas William Sami, "The changing landscape of party politics in Iran—a case study," April 3, 2006, *payvand.com.*

152. "Barakat defa-a moghadas dar kalam emam khomeini," September 28, 2014, *imam-khomeini.ir/fa.*

153. Moazami 2013: 133.

154. Masood Behnood, "Bisto panjomin salgard habs abbas amir entezam," December 17, 2004, *bbc.com/Persian.*

155. "Iran's longest-serving political prisoner sent back to jail," April 27, 2003, *Agence France-Presse.*

156. "Iran's longest-held political prisoner receives prestigious human rights award," November 12, 2012, *payvand.com.*

157. Ervand Abrahamian. *The Iranian Mojahedin.* New Haven: Yale University Press, 1989: 198.

158. Ibid., 201–202.

159. Ibid., 201–202.
160. Soroush Irfani. *Revolutionary Islam in Iran: Popular Liberation or Religious Dictatorship?* London: Zed, 1983: 198.
161. Bayram Sinkaya. *The Revolutionary Guard in Iranian Politics: Elites and Shifting Relations.* London: Routledge, 2015: 89.
162. "Iran demonstrators want Bani-Sadr ousted and tried," June 12, 1981, *nytimes.com*.
163. "Khomeini strips Bani-Sadr of office, leaving Iran's clergy in full control," June 23, 1981, *nytimes.com*.
164. Khomeini 1983a, 16: 211.
165. Scheherezade Faramarzi, "Iran cracks down on monarchists," August 26, 1981, *Associated Press*.
166. June 23, 1981, *nytimes.com*.
167. "Asami va moshakasat bakhshi az shohadaye enghelab novin iran," September 6, 1985, *Mojahed* #219.
168. Ibid.
169. "Two Tehran bazaar merchants are among 22 executed in Iran," July 14, 1981, *nytimes.com*.
170. Tom Baldwin, September 20, 1981, *Associated Press*.
171. Ibid.
172. Ervand Abrahamian. *Tortured Confessions: Prisons and Public Recantations in Modern Iran.* Berkeley: University of California Press, 1999: 129.
173. September 20, 1981, *Associated Press*.
174. Parsa 2000: 250.
175. Shaul Bakhash. *The Reign of the Ayatollahs: Iran and the Islamic Revolution.* New York: Basic Books, 1984: 221.
176. Abrahamian 1999: 215.
177. "Iran still seeks to erase the 1988 prison massacre from memories, 25 years on," August 29, 2013, *amnesty.org*.
178. "Iran tribunal judgment," February 5, 2013, *irantribunal.com*.
179. "Ghotbzadeh, ex-foreign minister, executed in Iran," September 16, 1982, *Reuters*.
180. Hazhir Teimorian, "Murdered ex-minister was victim of Iran power feud; Dr Kazem Sami," November 30, 1988, *Times* (London).
181. Anwar Farouqi, "Dissidents claim Iran executions party of political purge," November 28, 1988, *Associated Press*.
182. Scheherezade Daneshku, "Why Iran is carrying out purge of the clergy," December 12, 1988, *Financial Times* (London).
183. "Khomeini dissolves party following dissension reports," June 2, 1987, *United Press International*.
184. Irfani 1983: 199; Shanehchi 1983, Tape 2:23, Iranian Oral History Collection, Houghton Library, Harvard University.
185. Interview with Mohammad Shanehchi, chief aide to Ayatollah Mahmoud Taleghani (April 1998).
186. Jalal Yaghoobi, "Ayatollah Shriatmadri, marjae taghlidi ke dar hasr dar gozasht," April 6, 2014, *bbc.com/Persian*.

187. "Ayat ollah Hassan ghomi, marjae montaghed velayat dar gozasht," June 13, 2007, *radiofarda.com.*
188. "Marajea taghlidi ke dar hasr khanegi boodand," July 10, 2014, *shia -online.ir.*
189. "Ayat ollah haj seyyed mohammad shirazi," *rasaam.net.*
190. "Human rights violations against Shi'a religious leaders and their followers," June 1997, *Amnesty International.*
191. Ibid.
192. John Kifner, "Aide to Khomeini heir apparent is reported executed in Tehran," September 29, 1987, *nytimes.com.*
193. "Leading Iranian dissident calls for freedom from house arrest," November 17, 1999, *Agence France-Presse.*
194. For different estimates, see the works of Ervand Abrahamian: 2009 and Ahmad Ashraf and Ali Banuazizi. "The State, Classes, and Modes of Mobilization in the Iranian Revolution." *State, Culture, and Society* 1 (1985): 3–40.

4. Politicization of the Economy and Declining Performance

1. "Mesalam dar bareh ghorme sabzi va abgoosht be maanye aghab boodan teknolozhi dar iran bood," November 13, 2014, *farsnews.com.*
2. "120 daghigheh monazereh dagh allah karam va ziba kalam dar khabar online piramoon mozooat mohem siasi va farhangi," May 5, 2015, *khabaronlin.ir.*
3. "Rotbeh avval iran dar saderat servat ensani momtaz," August 21, 2014, *fararu.com.*
4. "Iran dar saderate servat ensani dar rotbehe momtaz avval shod," August 21, 2014, *sharghdaily.com.*
5. "Hazineh salaneh mohajerat nokbegan, az kole boodjeh keshvar bishtar ast," May 24, 2014, *irna.ir.*
6. "Mohajerat chehel dar sad nokhbegan dar barkhi reste ha," April 19, 2014, *isna.ir.*
7. Ibid.
8. "Yeki digar az nokhbegan pezeshki keshvar in hafteh az keshvar kharej mishavad," May 4, 2014, *farsnews.com.*
9. "Khorouje Salaneh 150 miliard dolar az keshvar baa mohajerat," August 21, 2014, *sharghdaily.com.*
10. "Maryam mirzaKhani: zibayee riaziat ra be sabr dar miyabad," August 14, 2014, *bbc.com/Persian.*
11. "Salaneh sado panjah hezar nokhbeh az iran kharej mishavand," January 7, 2014, *bbc.com/Persian.*
12. "Hazineh salaneh . . . ," May 24, 2014, *irna.ir.*
13. "Dar khast rahbar iran az nokhbegan baraye mandan dar iran," October 17, 2015, *bbc.com/Persian.*
14. "Rouhani: keshvar ba shoar darmani va goftar darmani dorost nemi shaved," May 18, 2014, *alef.ir.*
15. "Siasat haye kolli jamieyat tavasot rahbar moazam enghelab eblagh shod," May 20, 2014, *farsnews.com.*

16. "Daavat rouhani az iranian moghim kharej az keshvar: dar iran sar maye gozari konid," September 27, 2015, *alef.ir.*

17. "Dowlat az hozour Iranian kharej az keshvar baraye towsea ostan ha esteghbal mikonad," December 2, 2014, *irna.ir.*

18. "Pishnehad sar maye gozari dou milliard dolari iranian ghair moghim dar sanayea danesh bonyan parvar," September 28, 2015, *isna.ir.*

19. Paul Klebnikov, "Millionaire mullahs," July 21, 2003, *forbes.com.*

20. Farhad Nomani and Sohrab Behdad. *Class and Labor in Iran: Did the Revolution Matter?* Syracuse, NY: Syracuse University Press, 2006: 100.

21. "8.5 melyoun karmand hoghough be gir dowlat/ pajah dar sad karmandan zir lisans hastand," January 27, 2015, *mehrnews.com.*

22. Nomani and Behdad 2006: 89.

23. "8.5 melyoun . . . ," January 27, 2015, *mehrnews.com.*

24. "Panjah dar sad khanvarhaye keshvar hoghough begir dowlat hastand," August 16, 2014, *mehrnews.com.*

25. "Vazir eghtesad: tanha 17 dar sad va gozari ha be bakhsh khosousi vagheie bood," November 5, 2013, *irna.ir.*

26. "Enhesar che bar sar eghtesad iran avardeh ast," January 5, 2014, *fararu.com.*

27. "Ahmadi nejad dar poushesh ejraye asle 44 malekiat ha ra be basteganash va gozar kard," January 23, 2015, *ilna.ir.*

28. "Ehyaye vaghf yeki az bozorg tarin barkat enghelab eslami boodeh ast," January 13, 2016, *mehrnews.com.*

29. "Yek sevom masahat iran vaghf ast," November 3, 2011, *farsnews.com.*

30. "Edamehe vaakenesh masoolan owghaf be namayandegan majles," October 15, 2014, *irna.ir.*

31. "Enteghad az adam bar khord masoolan iran baa emam zadeh haye be doon shajareh," January 3, 2013, *bbc.com/Persian.*

32. "Bar rasi shekayat marboot be sazman owghaf," December 30, 2012, *tabnak.ir.*

33. "Bar rasi shekayat az sazman owghaf dar jaleseh emrooz komesyoun asl navad," February 12, 2013, *tasnim.ir.*

34. "Bar rasi shekayat marboot be sazman owghaf dar komesyoun asl navad," December 30, 2012, *ican.ir.*

35. "Bar rasi shekayat az sazman owghaf dar jaleseh emrooz komesyoun asl navad," February 12, 2013, *tasnim.ir.*

36. "Vaghti ke majlesi ha owghaf ra be zamin khari mottaham mikonand," September 25, 2014, *tabnak.ir.*

37. "Sabre majles dar bareh amalkard sazman owghaf rou be payan ast," September 23, 2014, *irna.ir.*

38. "Bar rasi shekayat az sazman owghaf dar jaleseh emrooz komesyoun asl navad," February 12, 2013, *tasnim.ir.*

39. "Sabre majles dar bareh amalkard sazman owghaf rou be payan ast," September 23, 2014, *irna.ir.*

40. "Mowghoofat va amakeni ke mashmool maliat nemi shavand," January 22, 2016, *mehrnews.com.*

41. "Moaven rouhani: aastan ghods va gharar gaah ha bayad maliat be pardazand," February 14, 2016, *dw.com/fa-ir.*

42. "Ekhtelaf nazar ahali roustaye marz baan arak baa edareh kolle owghaf va omoor kheyrieh ostan markazi," April 30, 2008, *jamejamonline.ir.*

43. "Shahri ke hameh sakenan aun ejareh neshin shodand," July 4, 2015, *mehrnews.com.*

44. Nomani and Behdad 2006: 45.

45. Yeganeh Torbati, Steve Stecklow, and Babak Dehghanpisheh, "Special Report: To expand Khamenei's grip on the economy, Iran stretched its laws," November 13, 2013, *reuters.com.*

46. Babak Dehghanpisheh and Steve Stecklow, "Special Report: Khamenei's conglomerates thrived as sanctions squeezed Iran," November 12, 2013, *reuters.com.*

47. Steve Stecklow, Babak Dehghanipisheh, and Yeganeh Torbati, "Khamenei controls massive financial empire built on property seizures," November 11, 2013, *reuters.com.*

48. Majid Mohammadi, "Velayate faghieh salaneh cheghadr baraye shahrvandan irani kharj dar bar darad?" July 19, 2010, *Iranianuk.com.*

49. "Emperatoori mali rahbari," February 28, 2013, *Ofogh,* VOA, http://ir.voanews.com/media/video/1612715.html?z=0&zp=4.

50. Klebnikov, July 21, 2003, *forbes.com.*

51. "Rahbari goftand ke dekhalat khebregan dar joziat ra nemi pazirand," Februay 18, 2012, *bbc.com/Persian,* http://www.bbc.com/Persian/iran/2012/02/120218_l39_khobregan_khamenei_supervision.shtml.

52. Behrooz Karouni, "41 dar sadi ke maliat nemi pardazand, nahad haye zir nazar rahbari hastand," December 5, 2011, *radiofarda.com.*

53. Wilfried Buchta. *Who Rules Iran? The Structure of Power in the Islamic Republic.* Washington, DC: The Washington Institute, 2000: 73.

54. "Safaie Frahani: eghtesad bayad az dast bonyad ha va nehad ha kharej shavad," June 9, 2014, *khabaronline.ir.*

55. Ibid.

56. Klebnikov, July 21, 2003, *forbes.com.*

57. Ibid.

58. Mehdi Khalaji, "Politics and the Clergy," October 2015, *iranprimer.usip.org.*

59. "Safheh akhar: naser makarem shirazi ra behtar beshnasid," November 20, 2015, *ir.voanews.com.*

60. "Marjaie ke digar morgh ne mikhorad," July 23, 2012, *irangreenvoice.com.*

61. Mohammad Nurizad, "Nameh bist sheshom mohammad nouri zad be rahbari," October 5, 2012, *nurizad.info/blog.*

62. "Nameh estefaye tarikhi ayatollah taheri be mellat va pasokh rahbari," June 2, 2012, *rahesabz.net.*

63. "Marasem arbaien hoseini ba hozour aza daran eba abdollah ol hossein v aba sokhanrani hojat ole slam val moslemin doctor mohsen rahami dar daftar marjaa alighadr ayat ollah ol ozma saanei khorasan razavi (mashhad moghaddas) bar gozar shod," December 14, 2014, *saanei.org.*

64. Kim Murphy, "Iran's $12-billion enforcers: from road building to laser eye surgery, the Revolutionary Guard dominates the economy," August 26, 2007, *latimes.com.*

65. Kim Murphy, "Iran's $12-billion enforcers: From road building to laser eye surgery, the Revolutionary Guard dominates the economy," August 26, 2007, *latimes.com*.

66. "Che taadad pasdar dar gharar gah sazandegi khatam mashgool be kar hastand," October 11, 2014, *farsnews.com*.

67. Michael Slackman, "Hard-line force extends grip over a splintered Iran," July 20, 2009, *nytimes.com*.

68. "Iran's Revolutionary Guard: Showing who is the boss," August 27, 2009, *economist.com*.

69. "Tafahom bist hezar miliardi sepah va shahr dari," July 8, 2014, *isna.ir*.

70. Maryam Kashani, "Va gozari ghair ghanooni; chehar melyoun haktar zamin khar," September 11, 2014, *roosonline.com*.

71. "Baaz gasht bish az 7000 miliard toman be baytolmal baa rafa tasarof arazi melli," May 31, 2015, *isna.ir*.

72. "Zoor gharar gah khatam ziad ast," September 21, 2014, *ilna.ir*.

73. "Barkhi afrad benam mapna va khatam ol anbia naft mi froshand," September 22, 2014, *ilna.ir*.

74. Behrooz Mina, "Rich kids of the revolution," October 11, 2014, *iranwire.com*.

75. Kaveh Omidvar, "Sandali larzan vezarat naft iran," August 12, 2013, *bbc .com/Persian*.

76. "Dard sar haye siasatmadare miliarder," March 4, 2013, *asriran.com*.

77. "Chand sekans az sadegh mahsouli; farmandeh milyarder jebhe paidari," March 2, 2013, *namehnews.ir*.

78. Muhammad Sahimi, "Ahmadinejad's security cabinet," August 20, 2009, *pbs .org*.

79. "Billionaire general to replace Kordan," November 10, 2008, *roozonline.com*.

80. Philip Sherwell, "Iranian Guards amass secret fortunes," August 19, 2007, *telegraph.co.uk*.

81. Ibid.

82. Kaveh Omidvar, "Vavaseh haye nafti ahmadi nejad dar hayat khalvat dowlat," June 6, 2011, *bbc.com/Persian*.

83. "Chand sekans az sadegh mahsouli; farmandeh milyarder jebhe paidari," March 2, 2013, *namehnews.ir*.

84. Ibid.

85. "Hashemi Rafsanjani: sepah be kamtar az kol keshvar raazi nist," *sahamnews .org*, April 16, 2013.

86. "Hashtad dar sad projeh haye omrani dar dast nehad haye hakemiati ast," *ilna.ir, January* 18, 2015, *ilna.ir*.

87. "Rouhani: vaghti tofang, pool, va resane dar ekhtiar yek nehad bashad, fesad mi avarad," December 8, 2014, *bbc.com/Persian*.

88. "Nobakht: ne mikhahim sepah be bakhsh khosossi raghabat konad," May 21, 2014, *isna.ir*.

89. "Amadeh komak be dowlat hastiem, bar gozari jalasat sepah baa dowlati ha," September 18, 2013, *hamshahrionline.ir*.

90. "Aamadeh komak be dowlat hastim; bar gozari jalasat sepah baa dowlati ha," September 18, 2013, *hamshahrionline.ir*.

91. "Moaven rouhani: aastan ghods va gharar gaah ha bayad maliat be pardazand," February 14, 2016, *dw.com/fa-ir.*
92. Mina, October 11, 2014, *iranwire.com.*
93. "Moghayese servat asgar oladi va babak zanjani," (February 28, 2013, *isna.ir.*
94. "Corruption Perception Index 2009," http://www.transparency.org/research /cpi/cpi_2009.
95. "Fesad dar yek sal 34 miliard dolar baraye eghtesad iran hazineh dashteh ast," December 18, 2011, *mehrnews.com.*
96. "Jomleh tarikhi rahbar dar bareh mobarezeh ba fesad," April 28, 2015, *tabnak.ir.*
97. "Khamenei declares war on corruption in Iran," June 29, 1997, *Agence France-Presse.*
98. Najmeh Bozorgmehr, "Khamenei pledge on Iranian corruption," October 3, 2011, *FT.com.*
99. "Iran leader calls for real steps against corruption," April 29, 2015, *bbc.com.*
100. "Bayad ba fesad mobareze konim va molaheze hich kas ra nakonim," December 8, 2014, *tasninews.com.*
101. "Mashrouh gofto gouye tafsili fars ba ahmad tavakkoli, talash rant kharan baraye nefooz," March 11, 2014, *farsnews.com.*
102. "Fesad khorehie ast ke kashvar ra az pishraft baz midarad," July 8, 2014, *isna.ir.*
103. "Mohseni ejeie:mojrie aloodeh nemitavand ba fesad mobreze konad," January 7, 2013, *tabnak.ir.*
104. "Tars az shok ejtemaie, dalil efsha nashodan mafased eghtesadi," May 27, 2014, *tabnak.ir.*
105. "Eddehie dar sotooh balaye mamlekat servat haye kalan mamlekat ra be andonezi, emarat, torkiyeh, va oroopa mi barand," April 15, 2016, *entekhab .ir.*
106. "Dast yabi ahmadi nejad be asnad variz yek milliard va sheshsad million yuro variz nafti be hesab mojtaba khamenei," February 28, 2012, *rahesabz .net.*
107. Mohammad Nurizad, "Namehe bisto sheshom mohammad nourizad be rahbari," October 5, 2012, *nurizad.info.*
108. "Nourizad migooyad asnadi az pool dadan shahram jazayeri be mojtaba khameneie dar ekhtiar darad," November 6, 2012, *alarabiya.net.*
109. "Torture victims first battle Ottawa for right to sue other countries," December 3, 2003, *cbc.ca.*
110. Hassan Zarea Zadeh Ardeshir, "Bouzari: heshemi raaye dadgah ra jeddi neggreft," May 6, 2012, *radiofarda.com.*
111. Kambiz Foroohar, "Rafsanjanis are Iran's power brokers for investors (Update 2)," September 11, 2003, *bloomberg.com.*
112. Ahmad Tavakoli, "Astat oil bish az panj million dolar be Mehdi hashemi roshveh dadeh ast," February 3, 2015, *bbc.com/Persian.*
113. "Mehdi Hashemi be zendan raft," August 9, 2015, *bbc.com/Persian.*
114. "Ekhtesasi bamdad khabar; enteshar asnad mahremaneh zamin khari bradaran larijani," June 16, 2012, *bamdadkhabar.com.*

115. "Akharin vazieyat parvandeh javad larijani," April 21, 2013, *mehrnews .com*.
116. "Shafaf shodan parvandeh iran-marin servis be salamat eghtesadi-siasi keshvar komak mikonad," October 29, 2002, *iran-transportation.com*.
117. "Hamsar modir amel iran marin servis tavaghof mozayedeh amval vay ra khastar shod," January 20, 2004, *isna.ir*.
118. "Aya taklif parvandeh takhallof 320 miliard tomani ahmadi nejad rowshan khahad shod?" November 4, 2014, *aftabnews.ir*.
119. "Miliard ha dolar pool naft har gez be khazane baz nemigardad," February 9, 2013, *tadbirkhabar.com*.
120. "Pool naft iran dar jib 63 nafar!" April 21, 2014, *khordadnews.ir*.
121. "Yaad avari zanjireh takhallofat modiran dowlate gozashteh," February 1, 2014, *khabaronline.ir*.
122. "Yad avari zanjireh takhallofat modiran dowlate gozashteh," February 1, 2014, *khabaronline.ir*.
123. "Divan mohasebat az tozihat vazarat eghresad ghana nashod," May 18, 2009, *jahannews.com*.
124. "Pay giri towzia ghair ghanooni pool tavasot dowlat iran ghabl az entekhabat 88," May 25, 2011, *bbc.co/Persian*.
125. "Defaa dowlat az towziea saham edalat pish az entekhabat riasat jomhuri," October 16, 2011, *bbc.com/Persian*.
126. "Chegooneh 250 nafar saham 45 melion irani ra dar enhesar greftand," October 12, 2014, *irna.ir*.
127. "Ahmadinejad dar poshesh ejraye asl 44 malekiat ha ra be basteganash vagozar kard," January 23, 2015, *ilna.ir*.
128. "Maajaraye sekke haye dowlat nohom," September 1, 2015, *ana.ir*.
129. "Morteza bank: komak 9 miliard tomani ahmadi nejad be sazmani motaal-legh be nazdikanash," May 17, 2014, *radiofarda.com*.
130. "Jozieyat yek ekhtelas dar dowlat ghabl," August 12, 2014, *isna.ir*.
131. "Enteghal bi baz gasht 22 milion dolar nafti be dobay va estanbol," January 18, 2015, *irna.ir*.
132. "Jahangiri: 22 miliard dolar nafti be estanbol va dobay montaghel shodeh ast," January 18, 205, *bbc.com/Persian*.
133. "Jahangiri: kesani bayad sharmendeh bashand ke 22 miliard dolar pool mamlekat ra be bahaneh taadol ghaymat arz dar dobay va estanbol baa ghaymat apien be kharejiha foroukhtand," February 15, 2016, *asriran.com*.
134. "Jahangiri: kesani bayad sharmendeh bashand ke 22 miliard dolar pool mamlekat ra be bahaneh taadol ghaymat arz dar dobay va estanbol baa ghaymat apien be kharejiha foroukhtand," February 15, 2016, *asriran.com*.
135. "Khod row ha va khaneh haee ke ahmadi nejad pas ne midahad," May 28, 2014, *etedal.ir*.
136. "Rabiee: khaneh 106 miliard tomani ra 30 liliard toman foroukhtand," December 8, 2014, *khabaronline.ir*.
137. Thomas Erdbrink, "Top Iranian banker flees amid embezzlement scandal," September 28, 2011, *washingtonpost.com*.
138. Ibid.

139. "Baraye ekhtelas se hezar miliardi afrad ba nefoozi dar se ghoveh ajir shodeh boodand," December 10, 2013, *bbc.com/Persian.*

140. "Ejei: dar parvandeh se hezar milliard tomani moaven ghoveh ghazaieh ham that taaghib ghrar geraft," May 21, 2014, *bbc.com/Persian.*

141. Monavar Khalaj, "Iran sentences bank fraudsters to death," July 30, 2012, *ft.com.*

142. Ibid.

143. "Eadam shod ta ekhtelas kesh nayabad," May 24, 2014, *kaleme.com.*

144. "Vazir eghtesad iran az kashfe fesad hezar milliard tomani khabar dad," December 6, 2014, *bbc.com/Persian.*

145. "Efshaye abad tazei az takhalof hezaran miliard tomani modiran ahmadi nejad," December 9, 2014, *dw.de/fa-ir.*

146. "Hadayaye saeed mortazavi be namayandegan majles manea residegi be parvandeh ou," April 12, 2014, *dw.de/fa-ir.*

147. "Tajammoa kar garan va baz neshastegan moghabel majles," December 24, 2013, *tabnak.ir.*

148. "Parvandeh namayandegan hedyeh begir rouye miz heyat nezarat," May 24, 2013, *irna.ir.*

149. "Pavandeh ghadis sazi ahmadi nejad baraye frar az takhallofat," August 28, 2014, *icana.ir.*

150. "Jozieyat rant tekan dahandeh dar dowlat ahmadi nejad/ haft hezar milliard sood se sarraf ba hamkari bank markazi," September 30, 2014, *entekhab.ir.*

151. "Akharin vaziat haft hezar miliardi," October 1, 2014, *tabnak.ir.*

152. "700 pavandeh takhallof dowlat ahmadi nejad bar rasi mishavand," October 6, 2014, *Persian.aawast.com.*

153. "Iranian billionaire Babak Zanjani arrested," December 30, 2013, *bbc.com.*

154. "Dadsetan tehran ealam kard: babak zanjani, bozorgtarin parvandeh eghtesadi dastgah ghaza baad az enghelab," May 7, 2014, *khabaronline.ir.*

155. "Zangeneh: ba emzaye vozaraye dowlat ghabl 2.7 miliard dolar ra be babak zanjani dadand," August 12, 2014, *bbc.com/Persian.*

156. "Paye 4 vazir ahmadi nejad dar parvandeh babak zanjani gier ast," September 28, 2014, *entekhab.ir.*

157. "Iran Sentences Tycoon to Death for Corruption," March 6, 2016, *nytimes .com.*

158. "Khial ham dastan penhan assodeh shod: mahkoomiyat babak zanjani be eaadam," March 6, 2016, *kaleme.com.*

159. "Afrad baa nefooz baa eaadam zanjani az band ghanoon motavari neshavand," March 6, 2016, *icana.ir.*

160. Arash Karami, "Iran counts $22 billion in Forex abuses under Ahmadinejad," August 27, 2014, *al-monitor.com.*

161. "Takahllof 400 milion dolari dar varedat ghataat hava paymaee," November 5, 2014, *ilna.ir.*

162. "Gozareshi dar bareh majaraye dakal gomshodeh," July 6, 2015, *hamshahrionlin.ir.*

163. "Zangeneh az yek dakal nafti gom shodeh digar khabar dad," October 15, 2015, *bbc.com/Persian.*

164. "Ahmadinejad's VP out on bail confirms prosecutor," January 5, 2014, *iranpulse.al-monitor.com.*
165. "Yad avari: Mohammad Reza Rahimi dar hale geraftan neshan darjeh yek khedmat az ahmadi nejad," January 1, 2015, *aftabnews.ir.*
166. "Mohammad Reza Rahimi be panj sal va 91 rooz habs va pardakht se milliard va 850 milion toman mahkoom shod," January 21, 2015, *isna.ir.*
167. "Baghaie be khatere 300 milion baz dasht shod east," June 20, 2015, *fararu .com.*
168. "Efsha gari haye tazeh dar bareh parvandeh baghaie," July 11, 2015, *isna.ir.*
169. "Hamid Baghaie, moaven raiese jomhur sabegh iran az zendan azad shod," January 18, 2016, *bbc.com/Persian.*
170. "Majid Ansari: Khatami bish az moddaian emrooz tabea rahbar bood," February 24, 2013, *ebrat.ir;* and "Ansari: bad ekhlaghi haye gostardeh tahdid bozorgi ast," February 23, 2013, *baharnews.ir.*
171. "Dowlat Ahmadinejad aloodeh tarin dowlat baad az enghelab bood," March 9, 2015, *farsnews.com.*
172. "Rouhani: eddeie be naam istadegi barabar aabar ghodrat ha mardom ra gharat kardand," May 13, 2014, *fararu.com.*
173. "Zangeneh: baa emzaye vozaraye dowlat ghabl 2.7 miliard dolar be zanjani dadand," August 12, 2014, *bbc.co.uk/Persian.*
174. "Ali Motahari: 3000 miliard ekhtelas bedoon ham ahangi baa dowlat emkan pazir nist," May 16, 2014, *entekhab.ir.*
175. "Vazir keshvar: poole kasif va ghachagh siasat iran ra aaloodeh kardeh ast," February 21, 2015, *bbc.co.uk/Persian.*
176. "Tahrim ejlas khebregan az sooye ayatollah dastgheib: chera be takhallofat 84 ta 92 residegi nemi konand," *rahesabz.net.*
177. "Ayat ollah dastgheib az aazaye majles khebregan khast ta bar zir majmooeh rahbari nezarat konand," March 8, 2015, *sahamnews.org.*
178. "Fehrest maghamat molzem be ealam daraie ha ealam shod," May 24, 2014, *alef.ir.*
179. "Dowlat Ahmadi nejad amel gosast eslah talaban va osoul garayane moatadel bood," December 16, 2014, *ilna.ir.*
180. "Enteghad jahan giri az resane-ie shodan asnad serri keshvar," December 16, 2014, *isna.ir.*
181. "Jahangiri: Bozorg tarin fesad haye gharn dar dowreh gozashte ettefagh oftad," February 2, 2015, *irna.ir.*
182. "Fesad asli tarin roykard eghtesadi dowlat ahmadi nejad," June 29, 2015, *etedaal.ir.*
183. "Doktor reza eslami dar goft va goo ba fararu bar rasi kard haraje madrak!" December 8, 2015, *fararu.com.*
184. "Aghaaz moghabele baa kharid va foroush payan nameh," June 17, 2014, *yjc.ir.*
185. "Hazineh 17 melyouni yek taghallob va daneshjooyan kaghazi," February 17, 2016, *tabnak.ir.*
186. "Fazel mousavi: Ahmadi nejad be onvan sar parast vezarat ettelaat be parvandeh haie dast yaft," June 15, 2016, *khabaronline.ir.*

187. Mojgan Modarres Oloom, "Post haye dowlati dar ghabzeh bastegan Ahmadinejad," June 9, 2009, *roozonline.com.*

188. "Voroud edehie agh zadeh dar gharar dad haye nafti mowjeb fesad shodeh ast," May 20, 2014, *farsnews.com.*

189. "Janjal hoghough ha dar iran," July 3, 2016, *bbc.com/persian.*

190. "Edeh ie be donbal ehtekar va bloke shodan pool ha hastand," December 14, 2012, *ilna.ir.*

191. "Bedehy 80 hezar milliard tomani 30 nafar be bankha," December 17, 2014, *farsnews.com.*

192. "Ezharate rabiei dar bareh afzayesh zanan biveh, faghr va eatiad dar keshvar," May 8, 2016, *ilna.ir.*

193. "Yek chahrom naghdinegi iran dar dast 600 nafar ast," July 26, 2014, *bbc.com/Persian.*

194. "Motalebate moavvagh bank haye iran: 82 hezar milliard toman," May 5, 2014, *bbc.com/Persian.*

195. "Omdeh atrafian va khanevadeh haye masoolan va vozaraye dowlat ghabl ghair ghanooni estekhdam shodand," July 16, 2014, *hamshahrionline.ir.*

196. "Efshaye joziat 450 hezar estekhdam family, bisavad, madrak rahnamayee, diplom va zir diplom dar dowlat ahmadi nejad," July 17, 2014, *aftabnews.ir.*

197. "Estekhdam 499 hezar nafar bedoon mojavez ghanooni dar dowlat ghabl," January 29, 2015, *isna.ir.*

198. July 17, 2014, *aftabnews.ir.*

199. Ibid.

200. "3000 daneshjooy doktora, konkoor nadadeh ghabool shodand," January 10, 2014, *tabnak.ir.*

201. "Madarek mofsedeh modiriyate jasbi ra dar maareze ghezavate afkar omoomi gharar mi daham," May 11, 2008, *farsnews.com;* and "Dar monazereh piramoun modiriyat jasbi dar daneshgah azad rokh daad," May 13, 2008, *hamseda.ir.*

202. "Boursieh haye cheragh khamoosh," May 26, 2014, *sharghdaily.ir.*

203. "Dah zan va showhar va panzdah khahar va bradar dar list boursieh haye ghair ghanooni dowlat ahmadi nejad," June 23, 2014, *aftabnews.ir.*

204. "Jahangiri: agar 10 vazir oloum ham taghier yaband, boursieh ha ra paygiri mikonim," August 24, 2014, *irna.ir.*

205. "Ayatollah khamenei az janjal dar mored boursieh haye ghair ghanooni enteghad kard," July 5, 2015, *bbc.com/Persian.*

206. "Vazir oloom iran: faghat 36 daneshjoo dar pavandeh boursieh ghair ghanooni moshkel darand," August 8, 2015, *bbc.com/Persian.*

207. "Aref behtarin gozineh baraye riasat Majles ast," May 24, 2016, *farsnews.com.*

208. "Daad khast baraye kamran daneshjoo va 16 masool vezarat oloom dar parvandeh boursieh ha," June 19, 2016, *khabaronline.ir.*

209. "Per capita GDP at current prices-US dollar," *data.un.org.*

210. Mohammad Jahan-Parvar. "The Cost of a Revolution." *Social Science Research Network,* September 2012, *papers.ssrn.com.*

211. Figures for Iran's per capita GDP are extracted from Penn World Tables data

bank, maintained by the University of Pennsylvania: https://pwt.sas.upenn
.edu/php_site/pwt_index.php.

212. "Enteghad shadeed tayyeb nia az tavarrom maskan," August 5, 2014, *merhnews.com.*

213. Milad Mohammadi, "Dar amad saraneh irani ha, aghab tar az 4 dahe pish," December 10, 2015, *eghtesadnews.com.*

214. Saeed Kamali Dehgah, "Iran's currency hits all-time low as Western sanctions take their toll," October 1, 2012, *theguardian.com.*

215. "Gozaresh bizines monitor az sanayea khod row sazi iran: aya var shekaste mishavand?" June 4, 2014, *khabaronline.ir.*

216. Behdad, Sohrab. "Foreign Exchange Gap, Structural Constraints, and the Political Economy of Exchange Rate Determination in Iran." *International Journal of Middle East Studies* 20 (1988): 1–21.

217. "Khorooj sar mayea 150 brabar afzayesh yafte ast," September 17, 2014, *mizanonline.ir.*

218. "Khorooj 600 miliard dolar sar mayea az keshvar," September 20, 2013, *tabnak.ir.*

219. "Fighting Climate Change," 2007/2008: 285–286, *undp.org.*

220. "Dar saderat va mobadelat jahani adadi nistim," January 2, 2015, *dw.com /fa-ir.*

221. "Markaz amar iran roshd eghtesadi sal gozashte iran ra manfi 5.4 dar sad ealam kard," September 15, 2013, *bbc.com/Persian.*

222. Akbar Torkan and Hamed Farnam, *Modiriat Manabe Nafti va Taamin-e Mali Projeh Haye Nafti.* Tehran: Center for Strategic Research, 2012.

223. "Gozaresh az bedeheye dowlat ahmadi nejad be bank ha," June 26, 2015, *entekhab.ir.*

224. "Ahmadi nejad Iranian ra ya bikar kard ya bedehkar," July 31, 2011, *bbc .com/Persian.*

225. "Hoshdar eghtesad danan dar mored vaziat eghtesadi iran," February 24, 2013, *bbc.com/Persian.*

226. "Dar khast 43 eaghtesad dan az ahmadi nejad," February 24, 2013, *khabaronline.ir.*

227. "Gozaresh maydani az vazieyat zendegi mardom dar sakhteman haye maskan mehr," May 31, 2014, *khabaronline.ir.*

228. "Sad ha hezar vahed maskan mehr, ab, bargh va gaz nadarand," August 22, 2014, *bbc.com/Persian.*

229. "Sad ha hezar vahed maskan mehr, ab, bargh va gaz nadarand," August 22, 2014, *bbc.com/Persian.*

230. "Tayyeb nia: bedehye doalat 250 hezar milliard toman ast," July 31, 2014, *radiofarda.com.*

231. "Sisat haye ahmadi nejad edamehe taadil eghtesadi ast," May 5, 2013, *eghtesadeiranonline.com.*

232. "Taatili kar khane ha dar sourat edamehe varedat bi ravieh," August 5, 2013, *tasnimnews.com.*

233. "Yek metr par chehe chini, bikari yek kargar irani," March 13, 2013, *tabnak .ir.*

234. "Amar tekan dahande taatily vahed haye sanati," July 11, 2014, *isna.ir.*
235. "Motavaghghef boodan faaliat 14 hezar shahrak sanati va bikari 112 hezar nafar," July 12, 2014, *irna.ir.*
236. "Amar tekan dahande taatily vahed haye sanati," July 11, 2014, *isna.ir.*
237. "Vahed haye sanati negarane var shekastegi," June 27, 2014, *khabar online.ir.*
238. "Sanaye dasti dar dou sal payani dowlat dahom zamin gir shod," September 21, 2014, *irna.ir.*
239. Kazem Alamdari, "Payamad haye solteh rouhaniat bar daneshgah," April 23, 2014, *iran-emrooz.net.*
240. Hossein Shamsian, "Be javanan takieh konid," May 14, 2014, *kayhan.ir.*
241. "Vaghti ahmadi nejad be sib zamini ham rahm nemi konad," May 12, 2014, *entekhab.ir.*
242. "Siasat haye ahmadi nejad edameh taadil eghtesadi," May 5, 2013, *eghtesadeiranonline.com.*
243. "Afzayesh 17 barabari hashieh neshini dar toole se dahe," March 5, 2015, *icana.ir.*
244. "Arazi keshavarzi borj mi shavand; keshavarzan bikar," May 19, 2014, *ilna.ir.*
245. "1643 abadi semnan khali az saken and," September 20, 2014, *isna.ir.*
246. Sohrab Ahmari, "The Iranian regime and workers' rights," May 1, 2014, *wsj.com.*
247. "Feghdan amniyat shoghli angizehe faaliat kar garan ra kaahesh dadeh ast," April 6, 2014, *ilna.ir.*
248. "Asle ghanoon asasi dar mored mozd kar garan ejra nashodeh ast," June 14, 2014, *ilna.ir.*
249. "Tashakkolat senfi kar gari hich haami nadarand," May 9, 2014, *ilna.ir.*
250. "Osool ghanoon asasi dar mored mozd kar garan ejra nashodeh ast," June 14, 2014, *ilnair.*
251. "Rakood 19 mahe kahesh bi kari belakhareh shekast," January 5, 2014, *mahernews.com.*
252. "Taatili bish az 40 dar sad kar khanejat foolad," November 23, 2013, *ilna.ir.*
253. "Motavaghghef boodan 14 hezar shahrak sanati va bi kari 112 hezar nafar," November 25, 2014, *isna.ir.*
254. "Rakood 19 . . . ," January 5, 2014, *mahernews.com.*
255. "Moghayese karnameh eghtesadi ahmadi nejad va rouhani," June 15, 2014, *entekhab.ir.*
256. "Moghayese hasht sale dowlat ahmadi nejad va yek sale dowlat rouhani," June 10, 2014, *khabaronline.ir.*
257. "Joziat gozaresh vizhe raies jomhur az eshteghal," August 10, 2014, *mehrnews.com.*
258. "Ekhraj yek million kargar ghrar dadi dar sal jari," December 1, 2012, *entekhab.ir.*
259. "70 dar sad az kargaran keshvar ghrar dadi va paymani hastand," April 27, 2014, *ilna.ir.*
260. "Parvandeh estekhdam dar iran bygani shod," June 8, 2014, *mehrnews.com.*
261. "93 dar sad az kargaran iran be ghrar dad moveghat kar mikonand," August 30, 2014, *ilna.ir.*

262. "Kargaranan irani hodoud yek million toman kasri boodje darand," November 11, 2014, *dw.com/fa.-ir.*
263. "Moghayese kar nameh eghtesadi ahmadi nejad va rouhani," June 15, 2014, *entekhab.ir.*
264. "90 dar sad jamea keshvar zir khat faghr zendegi mikonand," August 7, 2014, *ilna.ir.*
265. "Eateraz dou hezar kargar be vazieyat eghtesadi keshvar," June 17, 2012, *bamdadkhabar.com.*
266. "Dovvomin tumar emzaie kargaran iran," September 22, 2012, *bbc.co.uk /Persian.*
267. "Ersal sevvomin tumar eaterazi kargaran be vazir kar," December 18, 2012, *ilna.ir.*
268. "Tajdid nazar nakonid, charkhe towlid ra mi khabanim," March 18, 2014, *akbar-rooz.com.*
269. "Enteghad shadeed tayyeb nia az tavarrom maskan," August 5, 2014, *merhnews.com.*
270. Salehi-Isfahani. "Poverty, Inequality, and Populist Politics in Iran." *Journal of Economic Inequality* 7 (2009): 13.
271. Salehi-Isfahani 2009: 13–18.
272. "10 melion irani zir khat motlagh, 30 melion zir khat faghr nesbi," May 28, 2010, *aftabnews.ir.*
273. Shekofeh Habibzadeh, "Shekl giri madoon tabaghe dar manategh bar khordar," August 3, 2014, *sharghdaily.ir.*
274. "Amaar jadeed dowlat az vazieyat yarane begiran," October 27, 2014, *mehrnews.ir.*
275. "Hoshdar 2 vazir nesbat be gostaresh faghr va bikari dar iran," October 19, 2013, *hamshahrionline.ir.*
276. Shekofeh Habibzadeh, "Shekl giri madoon dabaghe dar manategh bar khordar," August 3, 2014, *sharghdaily.ir.*
277. "Dar amad pezeshkan, yek dar sad dar amad bongah daran ast," October 29, 2012, *sinanews.ir.*
278. Robert Tait, "Iran cracks down on teachers' pay protest," March 16, 2007, *theguardian.com.*
279. "Se cheharom moalleman keshvar zir khat faghr gharar darand," May 7, 2014, *mehrnews.com.*
280. "Estekhdam 23 lisans va foghe lisans dar shahr dari khorram abad," July 8, 2015, *irna.ir.*
281. "Ghalibaf: tehran 15 hezar karton khab darad," October 20, 2014, *irna.ir.*
282. "Karton khabi 200 hezar nafar dar mantaghehe 12 tehran," November 2, 2015, *iribnews.ir.*
283. "Chera teadad faregh ot tahsilan bikar bala ast," November 3, 2013, *eghtesadonline.com.*
284. "Kahesh 2 milion nafari chand shoghleh dar se mah," January 20, 2014, *khabaronline.ir.*
285. Thomas Erdbrink, "Iran's rich eat ice cream covered in gold as poor struggle to survive," August 6, 2011, *washingtonpost.com.*

286. Joby Warrick, "Food prices, inflation rise sharply in Iran," October 5, 2012, *washingtonpost.com.*
287. Marcus George and Zahra Hosseinian, "Unemployment mounts as Iran's economy falters," September 19, 2012, *reuters.com.*
288. "Yaraneh naghdi, khanvar haye kam dar amad ra faghir kard," May 23, 2014, *bbc.co.uk/Persian.*
289. "Vezarat eghtesad: mardom iran baad az dar yaft yaraneh, faghir tar shodand va sanat var shekaste!" July 4, 2014, *qudsonline.ir.*
290. Houshang Amirahmadi. *Revolution and Economic Transition: The Iranian Experience.* Albany: State University of New York Press, 1990: 199–202.
291. Salehi-Isfahani 2009: 20.
292. Markaz Amar Iran, "Towzia dar amad dar khane vaar haye shahry, roustaee, va kol keshvar, 1380–1391," *amar.org* (http://www.amar.org.ir/Portals/0 /Files/reports/income_1380–90.pdf).
293. "Sheyoua tahavoa avar va joon amiz masraf garaie/12 dar sad mardom gorosne and," February 2, 2013, *isna.ir.*
294. "Servat har sal adelane tar towzia mi sahvad!" March 7, 2013, *isna.ir.*
295. "Foghara va servat mandan irani che ghadr hazineh mikonand," October 31, 2014, *bbc.com/Persian.*
296. "Jolan dadan javanhaye sar mast ghoror servat ba khod row haye geran ghaymat az mazaher na amni dar jamea and," *alef.ir,* April 26, 2014.
297. Hossein Bashiriyeh, "Anomic Society and Authoritarian Polity: Post-Khatami State Structure in Iran," Wilson Center, Occasional Paper Series, 2004: 14.
298. Erdbrink, August 6, 2011, *washingtonpost.com.*
299. Steve Crabtree, "Half Iranians lack adequate money for food, shelter," July 1, 2013, *gallup.com.*
300. "73 melyoun irani baraye dar yaft yaraneh naghdi sabt nam kardand," April 23, *bbc.com/Persian.*
301. "Top cleric says Iran's poor forced to sell their children," January 13, 2001, *gulfnews.com.*
302. "Eghtesad moghavemati ba bi orzegi va ekhtelas mohaghegh nemishavad," April 26, 2014, *mehrnews.com.*
303. "Vazifeh dowlat mobarezeh ba faghr va faseleh tabaghati ast," May 31, 2014, *kayhan.ir.*
304. Khomeini 1983a, 10: 50.
305. Afshin Molavi, "Economic ills fuel Iranian dissent," July 8, 2003, *washingtonpost.com.*
306. Erdbrink, August 6, 2011, *washingtonpost.com.*

5. Failure to Reform and a Return to Repression

1. "Bohran afarinan az dowlat Khatami ta ahmadinejad," November 30, 2005, *aftabnews.ir.*
2. "Speech on birth anniversary of Imam Mahdi," October 22, 2002, *english .khamenei.ir.*
3. "Khatami endorsed for second term," August 3, 2001, *gulfnews.com.*

4. Michael Slackman, "A cleric steeped in ways of power," September 9, 2006, *nytimes.com.*

5. Borzou Dargahi, "Iran's supreme leader demands support of clerics," October 30, 2010, *latimes.com.*

6. Schirazi 1997: 77.

7. "Iranian clerics reaffirm absolute powers of leader," January 13, 2000, *reuters.com.*

8. "Iranian leader says his authority is indisputable," January 26, 2000, *Associated Press.*

9. "Nezarat khebregan bar rahbari ghair ghanooni ast," December 14, 2015, *isna.ir.*

10. "Khata haye farhangi va vazife haye dowlat," July 26, 2014, *farsnews.com.*

11. "Didar raies jomhour va aazaye heyat dowlat ba rahbar enghela," July 14, 2014, *khamenei.ir.*

12. "Mokhalefan din, sadeh zisti ra bahanehie baraye koobidan eslam gharar dadehand," July 17, 2014, *farsnews.com.*

13. "Masooliyat yaftan rant kharan vaza mamlekat ra khoob nemi konad," July 18, 2014, *farsnews.com.*

14. "Iranian youth shun religion, prayers after entering school," December 31, 2000, *irna.ir.*

15. "Mesbah Yazdi, kami az eslam va kami az farhang amrekaie migirand va migooyand eatedal mikonim," May 1, 2014, *entekhab.ir.*

16. "Donya parasti dar farhang eslami mored nekohesh ast," July 2, 2014, *farsnews.com.*

17. "Hokoomat vazife dard mardom ra be behesht bebarad, hata be zoor shallagh," May 30, 2014, *bbc.com/Persian.*

18. "Enteghad emam jomeh mashhad az owzaa farhangi," September 18, 2012, *tabnak.ir.*

19. "Baa hameh ghodrat jeloye kesani ke manea behesht raftan mardom shavand khahim istad," May 30, 2014, *mehrnews.com.*

20. "Bar khord ba boursiyeh ha mesdagh nofooz ast/basij; motia tarin nehad nesbat be faramin rahbar enghelab," November 28, 2015, *tanimnews.com.*

21. "Iran budget extends reach over religious bodies," December 20, 2000, *reuters.com.*

22. "Az dowlat boodjeh mi girim vali mostaghel hastim," December 22, 2009, *asriran.com.*

23. "Dav talaban namayandegi majles bayad fough lisans bashand," December 20, 2006, *asriran.com.*

24. "Ekhtelaf osool garayan mardom enghelabi ra dochar tazalzol mi konad," February 20, 2012, *hamshahrionline.ir.*

25. "Movahhedi Kermani: bar gozidegan entekhabat khebregan bayad motia rahbar bashand," February 20, 2015, *bbc.com/Persian.*

26. Said Arjomand, *After Khomeini: Iran under His Successors.* Oxford: Oxford University Press, 2009: 43–44.

27. "Setad entekhabat: agar rad salahiyat ha taghier nakonad dar barkhi hozeh ha reghabat nist," January 21, 2016, *radiofarda.com.*

28. Helia Ighani and Garrett Nada, "Khomeini's rebel grandchildren," May 29, 2013, *iranprimer.usip.org.*
29. "Iran enshrines new Islamic penal code," July 9, 1996, *Agence France-Presse.*
30. "Iran Report: October 12, 2005," October 12, 2005, *rferl.org.*
31. "Sar lashgar jaafari: be mokhalefan faaliyat siasi sepah tavajjoh nadarim, kar khod ra mi konim," December 11, 2013, *bbc.com/Persian.*
32. "Sar lashgar jaafari: az ebteda gharar nebood sepah, nirouye nezami bashad," September 1, 2015, *bbc.com/Persian.*
33. "Khomeini abolishes Iran's ruling party," June 2, 1987, *Associated Press.*
34. Ali Mohammadi. "Government within the Government: Roots of Attack on Students." *Journal of Iranian Research and Analysis* 15 (1999): 63–73.
35. Morteza Kazemian, "Baz khani hasht dowreh entekhaba majles dar jomhuri eslami," December 23, 2011, *bbc.com/Persian.*
36. Ibid.
37. "Che gooneh showraye negahban nehadi ghodrat saz shod," May 16, 2009, *bbc.com/Persian.*
38. Nazila Fathi, "Former hostage taker now takes on the mullahs," November 5, 2002, *nytimes.com.*
39. John F. Burns, "Iranian's career: From hostage-taker to reformer," October 13, 1999, *nytimes.com.*
40. Douglas Jehl, "Iran closes a leading newspaper and arrests top editors," September 18, 1998, *nytimes.com.*
41. "Ma nevisandeh iem," January 9, 2014, *bbc.co/Persian.*
42. Robin Wright, "Silencing ideas: The crisis within Iran's theocracy," December 31, 1995, *latimes.com.*
43. Jehl, September 18, 1998, *nytimes.com.*
44. "Powerful Islamic association calls for free speech guarantees," December 1, 1996, *ap.org.*
45. Hazhir Temourian, "Iran bans Baywatch with purge on Satan's dishes," April 23, 1995, *Sunday Times* (London).
46. Heila Ighani and Garrett Nada, "Khomeini's rebel grandchildren rock the vote," May 31, 2013, *atimes.com.*
47. Neil MacFarquhar, "A Khomeini breaks with his lineage to back U.S.," August 6, 2003, *nytimes.com.*
48. Pam O'Toole, "Iran's rulers should call referendum," August 7, 2003, *bbc.com.*
49. "Khomeini's kin seeks action on Iran," September 27, 2003, *bbc.co.uk.*
50. John F. Burns, "Its voters have spoken. Now meet Iran's gunmen," March 19, 2000, *nytimes.com.*
51. Anwar Faruqi, "Human rights group calls for independent autopsy on writer," November 30, 1994, *Associated Press.*
52. Muhammad Sahimi, "The chain murders: Killing dissidents and intellectuals, 1988–1998," January 5, 2011, *pbs.org.*
53. "Saeed emami: fallahian be man dastoor hazf seyyed ahmad khomeini ra dad," March 16, 2012, *rahesabz.net.*
54. "Iran: Iranian Writers' Association (IWA), its nature, its chairman in 1996, whether members have been executed, and attitude toward the Iranian government," May 1, 1998, *refworld.org.*

55. "Human Rights Watch World Report 1998: Iran, Human Rights Developments," 1998, *hrw.org.*
56. Mehdi Moslem. *Factional Politics in Post-Khomeini Iran.* Syracuse, NY: Syracuse University Press, 2002: 250–251.
57. "Hashemi: sale 1376 jeloye taghallob ra gareftam," May 24, 2015, *baharnews.ir.*
58. Elaine Sciolino, "Mullah who charmed Iranians cannot change status quo," February 1, 1998, *nytimes.com.*
59. Ibid.
60. Genevive Abdo, "Katami was never a rebel and has no cause, critic charges: Iran's weary would-be reformer," February 1, 1998, *nytimes.com.*
61. Paul Taylor, "Khatami says Iranians expect too much reform," September 7, 2000, *reuters.com.*
62. Sciolino, February 1, 1998, *nytimes.com.*
63. Douglas Jehl, "Iranians warily await reforms they voted for," October 11, 1997, *nytimes.com.*
64. "Iran not yet delivered from dictatorship: Khatami," November 30, 2000, *Agence France-Presse.*
65. Afshin Molavi, "In Iran, one-act play sparks cultural drama," September 30, 1999, *washingtonpost.com.*
66. "Top reformer presses foes on Iran anniversary," February 11, 2001, *reuters.com.*
67. Douglas Jehl, "Iranians assert rogue officers slew dissidents," January 6, 1999, *nytimes.com.*
68. Scott Peterson, "Iranian revelations as press tests new freedoms," June 29, 1998, *csmonitor.com.*
69. Michael Eisenstadt, "Iran's revolutionary commander sends a warning," May 7, 1998, *washingtoninstitute.org.*
70. Burns, October 13, 1999, *nytimes.com.*
71. Jehl, January 6, 1999, *nytimes.com.*
72. "Iran security chief says ordered dissident killings," December 31, 2000, *reuters.com.*
73. "Iranian killers spared death penalty," January 29, 2003, *bbc.com.*
74. Sahimi, "The chain murders," 2011 *pbs.org.*
75. Jonathan Lyons, "Iran traces source of mystery murders," August 4, 1999, *reuters.com.*
76. "Matne kamel nameh farmandehan sepah be khatami," June 11, 2005, *aftabnews.ir.*
77. Amir Namdar, "Naghshe abdollah nouri dar sakhtar siasi iran," May 11, 2002, *bbc.com/Persian.*
78. Howard Schneider, "Cleric's defense puts the system on trial," November 21, 1999, *washingtonpost.com.*
79. John F. Burns, "Court silences Iran reformist with jail term," November 28, 1999, *nytimes.com.*
80. "Iran's heroic voice of freedom," December 3, 1999, *Toronto Star.*
81. Burns, November 28, 1999, *nytimes.com.*
82. Ibid.
83. "Leading reformist Nouri pardoned in Iran," November 5, 2002, *reuters.com.*

84. Douglas Jehl, "Iran's leader asks for unity after release of his moderate ally," April 17, 1998, *nytimes.com.*
85. Douglas Jehl, "Tehran mayor's trial begins and the strains are showing," June 12, 1998, *nytimes.com.*
86. John Daniszewski, "Tehran's reformist mayor sentenced to 5 years jail," June 24, 1998, *latimes.com.*
87. "Iran's liberal culture minister is out, dealing blow to reform," December 15, 2000, *nytimes.ir.*
88. "Iranian lawmaker on trial in security case," November 8, 2000, *Associated Press.*
89. Molly Moore and John Ward Anderson, "Iran sentences 8 dissidents: Conservative judiciary sets back Khatami's reform effort," January 14, 2001, *washingtonpost.com.*
90. Vickie Maximova, "Iran's conservatives go on the offensive," June 2, 1999, *bbc.com.*
91. "Conviction of Iranian lawyers condemned," September 29, 2000, *bbc.com.*
92. Afshin Valinejad, "Iran's first reformist-dominated parliament in two decades opens," May 27, 2000, *Associated Press.*
93. "Iran's MPs refuse privileges for supreme leader," February 3, 2001, *Reuters.*
94. "Khatami says democracy 'a must for Iran,'" February 15, 2001, *Reuters.*
95. "Kar nameh Majles sheshom-bakhshe nakhost: dar majles sheshom che gozasht," July 29, 2004, *hamshahrionline.ir.*
96. Jonathon Lyons, "Iran's supreme leader quashes press reform bill," August 7, 2000, *reuters.com.*
97. "Anbooh roydad haee ke dar chahr sal gozashteh dar majles sheshom gozashteh ast," May 27, 2004, *bbc.com/Persian.*
98. "Their last chance," January 15, 2004, *economist.com.* Another source stated that the Guardian Council vetoed close to 36 percent of the bills approved by the sixth Majles: "Che gooneh showraye negahban nehadi ghodrat saz shod," May 16, 2009, *bbc.com/Persian.*
99. Larl Vick, "The appearance of change in Iran," January 15, 2004, *washingtonpost.com.*
100. "Freedom of the Press," 2005, *freedomhouse.org.*
101. "Kar nameh Majles sheshom-bakhshe nakhost: dar majles sheshom che gozasht," July 29, 2004, *hamshahrionline.ir.*
102. "Enemies of the Press 2001," May 3, 2001, *cpj.org.*
103. "21 journalists held, making Iran the biggest prison for journalists in the Middle East," August 1, 2003, *en.rsf.org.*
104. "Iranian authorities responsible for Siamak Pourzand's death," May 2, 2011, *rsf.org.*
105. Nazila Fathi, "Iran acquittal in death case is challenged," July 26, 2004, *nytimes.com.*
106. "Iranian MPs demand end to crackdown against writers," February 1, 2003, *Agence France-Presse.*
107. Jim Muir, "Iran cleric escapes death sentence," May 20, 2001, *bbc.com.*
108. Personal interview with Mr. Yousefi Eshkevari, July 21, 2013.
109. Moore and Anderson, January 14, 2001, *washingtonpost.com.*

110. Robin Wright, "Iranian dissident Akbar Ganji, at liberty to speak his mind, at least until he goes back home," August 14, 2006, *washingtonpost.com*.

111. "Khatami: Shooting will unite people," March 12, 2000, *bbc.com*.

112. "Iran's liberal culture minister is out," December 15, 2000, *nytimes.com*.

113. Jim Muir, "Iranian leader denounces unrest," November 22, 2002, *bbc.com*.

114. "Iranian appeals court further eases sentence of dissident Aghajari: Lawyer," March 9, 2005, *afp.com*.

115. Amy Waldman, "Iran intensifies crackdown on opposition," December 8, 2001, *nytimes.com*.

116. Ibid.

117. Ibid.

118. Nazila Fathi, "Court disbands Iranian party, sentencing 33 members to jail," July 29, 2002, *nytimes.com*.

119. Ibid.

120. "Iranian dissident confesses," June 4, 2001, *bbc.com*.

121. Roger Hardy, "Row deepens over jailed Iranian MP," December 31, 2001, *bbc.com*.

122. "Khatami's brother accused of libel," April 5, 2000, *bbc.com*.

123. "Iran court sentences MP to a year in jail," June 29, 2001, *gulfnews.com*.

124. Nazila Fathi, "Iranian pardoned after reformists walk out," January 16, 2002, *nytimes.com*.

125. Ibid.

126. "Iranian MPs walk out of parliament, as does speaker Karroubi," January 15, 2002, *irna.ir*.

127. "Kar nameh Majles sheshom-bakhshe nakhost: dar majles sheshom che gozasht," July 29, 2004, *hamshahrionline.ir*.

128. Personal interview with Fatemah Haghighatjoo, Boston, MA, June 14, 2010.

129. Jim Muir, "Cleric denounces Iran chaos," July 10, 2002, *bbc.com*.

130. "Nameh estefaye tarikhi ayatollah taheri be mellat va pasokh rahbari," June 2, 2012, *rahesabz.net*.

131. "Matne nameh sar goshadeh 127 namayandeh majles be rahbar iran," May 25, 2003, *bbc.com/Persian*.

132. Morteza Kazemian, "Baz khani hasht dowreh entekhabat majles dar jomhuri eslami," December 23, 2011, *bbc.com/Persian*.

133. Elaine Sciolino, "Governed by God; in Iran, a quiet but fierce struggle for change," February 15, 2004, *nytimes.com*.

134. Nazila Fathi, "One-third of Iranian parliament quits," February 2, 2004, *nytimes.com*.

135. Ibid.

136. Dan De Luce, "Iran's top leader betraying revolution," February 17, 2004, *theguardian.com*.

137. Hossein Bastani, "Shesh sal pas az tahasson majles sheshom," February 5, 2010, *bbc.com/Persian*.

138. Nazila Fathi, "Nobel laureate in Iran joins boycott of elections," February 17, 2004, *nytimes.com*.

139. "Texts adopted: European Parliament resolution on Iran," February 12, 2004, *europarl.europa.eu*.

140. "Rooydad haye mohem majles dar sal 82," May 27, 2004, *bbc.com/Persian*.

141. Ibid.

142. Ibid.

143. "9 dowreh entekhabat majles showraye eslami dar yek negah," January 13, 2016, *farsnews.com*.

144. Kim Murphy, "Iran's $12-billion enforcers," August 26, 2007, *latimes.com*.

145. Students constituted the single largest category, representing 44 percent of the total number of signatories. Of the signers whose occupational background was reported, 3.6 percent were merchants, a little over 7 percent were workers, and the overwhelming majority came from the modern middle class—that is, professors, engineers, doctors, lawyers, and journalists. Some of the prominent signatories included: Ali Afshari, Mansoor Osanloo, Abbas Amir-Entezam, Simin Behbahani, Fariborz Rais-Dana, Naser Zarafshan, Akbar Atri, Hadi Kahal-Zadeh, Bahareh Hedayat, Abdolfattah Soltani, Soraj Eddin Mir-Damadi, Mohammad Maliki, Shahrokh Zamani, Ali Akbar Mousavi Khoeniha, Hossein Shah Hosseini, Fatemeh Haghighatjoo, and Parviz Vajavand. Many were arrested and imprisoned following the disputed 2009 presidential election. See "Bayanieh gorouhi az azad andishan, nevisandgan, faalan siasi, daneshjooie va kar gari iran," May 15, 2005, *iran-emrooz.net*.

146. Ali Gheissari and Kaveh-Cyrus Sanandaji. "New Conservative Politics and Electoral Behavior in Iran." In *Contemporary Iran: Economy, Society, Politics*, edited by Ali Gheissari. Oxford: Oxford University Press, 2009: 275.

147. "Mizan mosharekat dar 10 dowreh entekhabat riasat jomhuri cheghadr bood?" June 13, 2013, *khabaronline.ir*.

148. Sadegh Saba, "Taghallob dar entekhabat riasat jomhouri, mozooie ke nezam ra raha ne mikonad," July 11, 2005, *bbc.com/Persian*.

149. "Nezamian hami rahbar, mottaham be mohandesi entekhabat," May 15, 2013, *dw.com/fa.ir*.

150. Michael Slackman, "Iran moderate says hard-liners rigged election," June 19, 2005, *nytimes.com*.

151. Sadegh Saba, "Taghallob dar entekhabat riasat jomhouri, mosooie ke nezam ra raham ne mikonad," July 11, 2005, *bbc.com/Persian*.

152. Ibid.

153. "Na gofteh haye hashemi az entekhabat 84," March 16, 2014, *isna.ir*.

154. Murphy, August 26, 2007, *latimes.com*.

155. Mojgan Modarres Oloom, "Post haye dowlati dar ghabzeh basyegan ahmadi nejad," June 9, 2009, *roozonline.com*.

156. "Dar khast rafea mahdoudiat be ja maandeh az dowran ahmadi nejad baraye voroud be aramgah mosaddegh," March 1, 2016, *bbc.com/Persian*.

157. "Iran: Women's rights defenders defy repression," February 2008, *amnesty.org*.

158. "Iranian mob attacks ex-president Mohammad Khatami on anniversary of Islamic revolution," February 10, 2009, *telegraph.co.uk*.

159. "Iran executes two over post-election unrest," January 28, 2010, *bbc.com*.

160. "Wife and mother of illegally exiled political prisoner die in car crash after prison visit," December 18, 2013, *iranhumanrights.org*.

161. "Iran: Investigate death of political prisoner," March 19, 2009, *hrw.org*.
162. "Sar nevasht sazandegan film haye toghifi dowreh ahmadi nejad," October 14, 2013, *aftabnews.ir*.
163. "UN to Iran: Stop jamming broadcasts," March 25, 2010, *voanews.com*.
164. "Iran declares ban on Western music," December 20, 2005, *theguardian.com*.
165. "Dowlat ahmadi nejad ba ahali mousighi taamol nadasht," September 8, 2013, *ilna.ir*.
166. Ali Sheikholeslami, "Iran bars music in private schools, may impose moral code for universities," June 1, 2010, *bloomberg.com*.
167. Anju Chopra, "Iran's illegal rappers want cultural freedom," January 28, 2008, *independent.co.uk*.
168. "Iran has banned a Ramadan song by Shajarian," August 4, 2011, *bbc.co.uk*.
169. "Mohammad Reza Shajarian: sharayet monaseb bashad, concert ham mi daham," September 7, 2013, *isna.ir*.
170. Robin Wright, "Iran curtails freedom in throwback to 1979," June 16, 2007, *washingtonpost.com*.
171. "Azme melli baraye gostaresh hejab eijad nashodeh ast," July 11, 2014, *irna.ir*.
172. Sheikholeslami, June 1, 2010, *bloomberg.com*.
173. Thomas Erdbrink, "Iranian authorities step up arrests of women for immodest dress," June 2, 2010, *washingtonpost.com*.
174. "Seyo panj sal hejab ejbari va naghze hoghoughe zanan," March 8, 2013, *radiozamaneh.com*.
175. Erdbrink, June 2, 2010, *washingtonpost.com*.
176. Neil MacFarquhar, "Iran cracks down on dissent," June 24, 2007, *nytimes .com*.
177. "Iran shuts 'Western' barber shops," August 23, 2007, *bbc.com*.
178. "Bakhshnameh mamnoueiyat keravat va popyoun eblagh shod," April 29, 2007, *asriran.com*.
179. "Iran: Police assault women's rights demonstrators," June 14, 2006, *hrw.org*.
180. "Iranian women fight controversial polygamy bill," November 30, 2011, *amnesty.org*.
181. "Belakhareh taklif tarhe mamnooiyat sag gardani che shod," April 4, 2012, *khabaronline.ir*.
182. "Sag haye negoon bakht ra ham be kahrizak bordand," April 16, 2013, *baharnews.ir*.
183. Frances Harrison, "Fears as Iran professors retire," June 22, 2006, *bbc.com*.
184. Seyyed Mohammad Khatami, "Azadi shart danaee ast," March 10, 2014, *khatami.ir*.
185. "Araye heyat omoomi divan edalat edari," July 1, 2013, *divan-edalat.com*.
186. "Vazeyat anjoman daneshgah amir kabir," September 3, 2006, *aftabnews.ir*.
187. Robert Tait, "Student rebels in Iran expelled and earmarked for army," March 2, 2007, *theguardian.com*.
188. Hooman Azizi, "Anjoman eslami daneshgah shahroud monhal shod," July 22, 2007, *roozonline.com*.
189. "Students in Iran face growing clampdown as academic year begins," September 21, 2012, *amnestyusa.org*.

190. "Bahareh Hedayat," Amnesty International, http://www.amnestyusa.org /our-work/cases/iran-bahareh-hedayat.
191. "Mahroumiat sad ha daneshjooye montaghed," December 7, 2010, *dw.com /fa-ir.*
192. "Mahkoomiyat mohammad yousef rashidi be yek sal habs taaziri," May 19, 2010, *hra-news.org.*
193. "Gozaresh hasht sal naghze hagh tehsil dar iran: bish az 1000 daneshjoo az tehsil mahroom shodand," June 8, 2013, *rahesabz.net.*
194. Elise Auerbach, "Student activist Aia Nabavi marks another birthday in prison," December 20, 2011, *blog.amnstyusa.org.*
195. "Majid Dorri pas az panj sal azad shod," December 7, 2014, *rahesabz.net.*
196. "Ettelaieh: bish az se hafte az baz dasht amir gholi gozasht," December 24, 2014, *chrr.biz.*
197. "Mahkoomiyat amir amir gholi be 21 sal habs taaziri," February 16, 2016, *sahamnews.org.*
198. "Amir amir gholi, faal chap gara be haft sal va nim habs mahkoom shod," February 18, 2016, *bbc.com/Persian.*
199. "Yazdan Mohammad Baygi az edameh tehsil dar maghtaa doctora mahroom shod," September 19, 2012, *hra-news.org.*
200. "Iran should stop student bans," October 20, 2006, *bbc.com.*
201. Saied Golkar. "Cultural Engineering under Authoritarian Regimes: Islamization of Universities in Postrevolutionary Iran." *Digest of Middle East Studies* 21 (2012): 1–23, 12.
202. "Eateraz ha be ghair ghanooni khandan daftar tahkim vahdat," February 1, 2009, *dw.com/fa-ir.*
203. "Ejraye hokm zendan mitra aali, daneshjooye kar shenasi arshad daneshgah sheriff," July 27, 2012, *bamdadkhabar.*
204. "Vazieyat negaran konandeh mehdi sajedi far dar zendan evin," October 10, 2014, *hra-news.org.*
205. "Retrial granted for Omid Kokabee, raising hope for release," October 13, 2014, *iranhumanrights.org.*
206. Michele Catanzaro, "Iranian says he was jailed for refusing to engage in military research," April 26, 2013, *nature.com.*
207. "Nahad haye kar gari hich gah be sheddat dowran ahmadi nejad mahdood neshodeh boodand," November 21, 2013, *ilna.ir.*
208. Mansour Osanloo, "Brazil should support the struggle of Iranian trade unionists," March 22, 2014, *iranhumanrights.org.*
209. Mansour Osanloo, "Reading Marx in Tehran," June 13, 2013, *nytimes.com.*
210. "Negahdari mehdi shandeez dar miyan zendanian aaddi band 8 zendan evin," June 25, 2013, *kaleme.com.*
211. "Goftegoo ba mehdi shandeez zendani siasi," November 30, 2014, *hra-news .net.*
212. "Trade unionist given six-year prison sentence," May 9, 2012, *amnestyusa .org.*
213. Robert Tait, "Iran cracks down on teachers' pay protest," March 16, 2007, *theguardian.com.*

214. "Iran: EI condemns arrest of over 300 teachers," March 16, 2007, *ei-ie.org.*
215. "Iranian activists stand up for dozens of detained teachers," September 26, 2012, *iranhumanrights.org.*
216. "Held in solitary confinement, imprisoned teacher unaware of mother's death," June 6, 2011, *iranhumanrights.org.*
217. "Imprisoned teacher sentenced to three more years in prison after completing six," September 24, 2015, *iranhumanrights.org.*
218. "Union champions detained Iranian teacher," July 19, 2012, *radiozamaneh .com.*
219. "Baz dasht alireza akhavan faal kargari," June 4, 2010, *hra-news.net.*
220. "Dabir kole sazman moalleman iran baz dasht shod," April 19, 2015, *smi-edu.com.*
221. "Kanoon senfi moalleman iran khastar azadi moalleman dar band," July 30, 2013, *rahesabz.net.*
222. "Moalleman moatarez: khahan azadi bi ghaid va shart hamkaran zendani khod hastim," March 2, 2015, *rahesabz.net.*
223. "Abdofattah Soltani lawyer at the bar of Tehran, detained incommunicado at the Evin Prison since July 30, 2005," March 7, 2006, *idhae.org.*
224. "Shahr norenberg ba mardomm iran ealam hambastegi kard," October 5, 2009, *dw.com/fa-ir.*
225. "Abdolfattah soltani be tahamol 18 sal zendan mahkoom shod," March 4, 2012, *dw.com/fa-ir.*
226. "Abdolfattah soltani be tahammol 18 sal zendan va tabied mahkoom shod," March 4, 2012, *bbc.com/Persian.*
227. "Taatili dah ha nashriyeh az sale 85," March 3, 2010, *new.parlemannews .net.*
228. "Vojood list siyah matbooat dar zaman ahmadi nejad," November 25, 2013, *dw.com/fa.ir.*
229. "While pointing finger at Bahrain, Iran uses culture ministry to interrogate journalists," May 23, 2012, *rsf.org.*
230. "Faezeh Hashemi: Matbooat aghab gard kardeh and," February 24, 2014, *isna.ir.*
231. "Oft 9 hezar noskhe ie miyangin tiraje ketab," August 7, 2014, *fararu.com.*
232. "Jelo giri az enteshar ghoran dar edareh ketab ahmadi nejad," November 21, 2013, *ilna.ir.*
233. "Hossein derkhsah mored afve rahbar iran gharar gereft," November 20, 2012, *bbc.com/Persian.*
234. "Dou nameh az vahid asghari zendani mahkoom be marg," Novmeber 2, 2012, *hra-news.org.*
235. Saeed Kamai Dehghan, "Fears grow for Iranian blogger on hunger strike," August 28, 2013, *theguardian.com.*
236. "Canadian resident sentenced to death in Iran," December 6, 2010, *cbc.ca.*
237. "Saeed Malekpour's death sentence commuted to life because he repented," August 29, 2013.
238. "Kurdish MP accuses Iran's regime of repression, murders," November 28, 2000, *Agence France-Presse.*

239. Saeed Kamali Dehghan, "Iran poised to execute student accused of being Kurd terrorist," December 25, 2010, *theguardian.com*.

240. "Habibollah Latiffi's death sentence stopped by leadership pardon," September 2, 2015, *hra-news.org*.

241. "This urgent action might save a life," May 30, 2008, *amnesty.se*.

242. "Death penalty/torture and ill-treatment!" May 30, 2010, *amnesty.se*.

243. "Mohammad sadegh Kaboodvand, faal kord zendani be molaghat farzand bimarash bordeh shod," February 19, 2012, *bbc.com*.

244. "Iran: Kurdish woman losing sight in Iranian prison: Zeynab Jalalian," June 16, 2014, *amnesty.org*.

245. "Sodoor 175 sal habs baraye 13 nafar taye dou sal," November 29, 2011, *hra-news.net*.

246. "Mard kohansal 103 sale be etteham ertebat ba ahzab kordi dar zendan makoo be sar mibarad," April 2, 2013, *iranhumanrights.org*.

247. "Mahroumiyat az tadris bisto panj moallem kord va mahroumiyat az tehsil gorohe az pezeshkan kord," October 30, 2012, *rahsabz.net*.

248. "Bist va panj moallem kord az tadris mahroom shodand," October 30, 2012, *mellimazhabi.com*.

249. "Chahar faal arab irani eadam shodand," December 4, 2013, *bbc.com /Persian*.

250. "Mojazat khanevadeh ha baad az eadam faalan arab irani," July 31, 2014, *bbc.com/Persian*.

251. "Bar rasi hoghoughi hokme 45 sal zendan baraye panj tan az faalin madani va siasi azarbijan," May 16, 2013, *hra-news.org*.

252. Unid Niayesh, "Tens of Azerbaijanis civil activists arrested in Iran," February 21, 2014, *en.trend.az/azerbijan*.

253. "Jannati: ghair mosalmana, hayvanati hastand ke rouye zamin micharand va fesad mikonan," November 21, 2005, *gooya.com*.

254. "Mesbah yazdi: nagooiem baha'I va yahudi, va mosalman farghi nadarand," May 9, 2014, *dw.com/fa-ir*.

255. "Masihiyat dar iran: jorm siasi-amniyati," June 23, 2012, *ir.voanews.com*.

256. "A faith denied: The persecution of the Baha'is of Iran," *iranhrdc.org*.

257. "Seven Baha'i leaders given harsh prison sentences," amnestyusa.org, http:// www.amnestyusa.org/our-work/countries/middle-east-and-north-africa/iran /Seven-Bahai-Leaders-Given-Harsh-Prison-Sentence

258. "We are ordered to crush you," 2012, *amnesty.org*.

259. "Bazdasht modiran daneshgah bahaian dar iran," May 23, 2011, *bbc.com /Persian*.

260. "Silenced, expelled, imprisoned: Repression of students and academics in Iran," 2014, *amnesty.org*.

261. "A lesson in exclusion—Iran's harsh treatment of student activists," September 23, 2013, *amnesty.org*.

262. "Ozve team melli jodo az haghe tehsil va sherkat dar mosabeghat mahroom shod," March 16, 2012, *hra-news.net*.

263. "Silenced, expelled, imprisoned," 2014, *amnesty.org*.

264. "Najes shemordan na mosalman va nejasat roubi az eslam," September 21, 2012, *ir.voa.com.*
265. "Taharat-ahkam kafer," April 10, 2014, *Khamenei.ir.*
266. "World Report 2015: Iran," *hrw.org.*
267. "Emam jomahe rafsanjan khastar ekhraj bahaian az in shahr shod," December 4, 2014, *bbc.com/Persian.*
268. "Baha'i victim of land confiscation by Iranian government speaks out," May 6, 2016, *iranhumanrights.org.*
269. "Sad ha bahaie iran: maraja shia ba azar bahaian mokhalefat konand," March 11, 2014, *dw.com/fa-ir.*
270. "Ghatle yek shahrvand bahai dar Bandar abbas," August 26, 2013, *bbc.com /Persian.*
271. "Masihiyat dar iran: jorm siasi-amniyati," June 23, 2012, *ir.voanews.com.*
272. Ibid.
273. Ibid.
274. Alasdair Palmer, "Hanged for being a Christian in Iran," October 11, 2008, *telegraph.co.uk.*
275. "Masihiyat dar iran," June 23, 2012, *ir.voanews.com.*
276. "Hokme marg baraye no-kishan masihi va vahshat az gostaresh taghier din," March 5, 2011, *i.rvoanews.com.*
277. "Afzayesh enteghad haye bayn olmelali az ehtemal eadam yousef nadir khani," September 30, 2011, *bbc.com/Persian.*
278. "Masihiyat dar iran . . . ," June 23, 2012, *ir.voanews.com.*
279. "Sedoor hokm 18 sal habs va tabied baraye se keshish masihi," October 19, 2014, *hra-news.net.*
280. "Iran: 50 Christians temporarily arrested in Christmas raid," January 2, 2013, *wezeradio.com.*
281. "Mahkoomiat zendan baraye keshish avanesian," December 18, 2013, *roozonline.com.*
282. "Iranian pastor threatened, tortured for converting Muslims," March 8, 2010, *worldwatchmonitor.org.*
283. "Masihiyat dar iran . . . ," June 23, 2012, *ir.voanews.com.*
284. "Ghadimi tarin kelisaye protestan tavasot vezarat ettelaat tatil va yek keshish be zendan evin montaghel shod," June 1, 2013, *peykeiran.com.*
285. "Agar ma kafarim chera dar majles hozour darim," December 30, 2015, *sharghdaily.ir.*
286. "Masihiyat dar iran . . . ," June 23, 2012, *ir.voanews.com.*
287. "Zartoshtian iran zir feshar baz joie va tahdid haye vezarat ettelaat," December 9, 2013, *dw.com/fa-ir.*
288. "Hoseinieh daravish gonabadi esfahan takhrib shod," February 18, 2009, *bbc.com//Persian.*
289. "Dadgah tajdid nazar ghom, hokm aghaye amir ali mohammadi labbaf ra taied kard," October 30, 2008, *majzooban.org.*
290. "Dastgiri gostardeh daravish dar jaryan tajammoa eaterazi dar barabar daad setani tehran," March 8, 2014, *bbc.com/Persian.*

291. "Fazaye amniyati va baz dasht sad ha darvish be donbal tajammoa dar tehran," March 8, 2014, *radiofarda.com.*
292. "Kasra Nouri, crime: Journalism," September 19, 2014, *iranwire.com.*
293. "Ekhraj darvishan gonabadi az sazman haye dowlati edame darad," April 11, 2014, *majzooban.org.*
294. "Radde salahiyat shoghli yek darvish gonabadi saken Bandar abbas," April 14, 2014, *majzooban.org.*
295. "Laghve gharar dad kar shenas projeh hefazat az youz palang asiaee be dalil darvish boodan," May 3, 2014, *majzooban.org.*
296. "Dar khast payravan ahl hagh az rahbar iran baraye baz negari dar ghanoon asasi," March 20, 2015, *bbc.com/Persian.*
297. "Polumb yek namaz khaneh ahl sonnat dar tehran," February 8, 2011, *bbc .com/Persian.*
298. "Dowlat rouhani va bim va omid haye aghalliat haye dini dar iran," February 7, 2014, *dw.com/fa-ir.*
299. "Even on death row, Sunni prisoners mistreated for religious beliefs," June 5, 2013, *iranhumanrights.org.*
300. "Sunni prisoners in danger of execution after confessions broadcast on state-run media," February 19, 2014, *sunniprisonersiran.com.*
301. "Sale 92, sali bad baraye aghalliat haye mazhabi dar iran," March 16, 2014, *dw.com/fa-ir.*
302. "You have already executed one of my sons, don't execute another," February 27, 2014, *hra-news.net/en.*
303. "Olama khastar bar khord jeddi ba eghdamat zangirehie efratiyoun hastand/ shah ham ba maraja ingooneh rafter nakard," July 24, 2013, *kaleme.com.*
304. "Iran: Shi'a religious leaders as victims of human rights violations," June 3, 1997, *amnesty.org.*
305. Ibid.
306. "Baz dasht dahha tan moghalledan va haamiyan ayat ollah alozma seyyed sadegh shirazi," December 24, 2012, *rahesabz.net.*
307. Ibid.
308. "Ayatollah Sayed Hossein Kazemeyni Boroujerdi, aged 50, Shi'a cleric," September 11, 2008, *amnesty.org.*
309. "Jailed cleric seriously ill, denied treatment," April 2, 2014, *amnestyusa.org.*
310. "Dissident cleric serving additional year in prison for calling Khomeini a populist," September 11, 2013, *iranhumanrights.org.*
311. Fereshteh Ghazi, "Mohsen amir aslani chera va be che ettehami eadam shod," September 25, 2014, *roozonline.com.*
312. "Divan aali keshvar eaadam Mohsen amir aslani ra ghair ghanooni danesteh bood," September 28, 2014, *hra-news.net.*
313. "Mohsen amir aslani be entteham jarayem aghidati eadam shod," September 24, 2014, *bbc.com/Persian.*
314. "Iran executions send chilling message," March 30, 2010, *amnesty.org.*
315. "Sadegh larijani: mokhalefat ba eaadam, mokhalefat ba eslam ast," December 12, 2013, *bbc.com/Persian.*

316. Ian Black, "Iran executes Kurdish activist," November 11, 2009, *theguardian .com*.

317. The list included: Zahra Kazemi, Akbar Mohammadi, Mohammad Rajabi Sani, Valiollah Mahdavi, Zahra Baniyaghoub, Ebrahim Lotfollahi, Hossein Heshmat Saran, Kaveh Azizpour, Abdulreza Rajabi, Hashem Ramazani, Omid Mirsayafi, Amir Javidfar, Mohammad Kamrani, Mohsen Ruhulamini, Ramin Aghazadeh Ghahremani, Mohsen Dokmehchi, and Hassan Nahid. Hoda Saber died on a hunger strike while in detention (see "List of 18 Iranain political prisoners who perished between 2003 and 2011, June 21, 2011," *Irangreenvoice.com*). Sattar Beheshti, a young blogger and worker, died under torture in Evin Prison on November 6, 2012. Afshin Osanloo died in June 2013.

318. "Canadian journalist 'beaten to death,'" July 16, 2003, *bbc.com*.

319. "Ravayate pedar yek zendani siasi be nam arash arkan, az marge farzandash," November 17, 2011, *hra-news.org*.

320. "Marge dovvomin zendani siasi mahboos dar zendan rejaie shahr," June 5, 2012, *hra-news.org*.

321. "Madare shahid ramin aghazadeh ghahremani: nachar be dadan rezayat shodim," February 21, 2012, *rahesabz*.net.

322. "Pezeshkan mostaghel zendanian siasi ra moayeneh konand," October 29, 2012, *bbc.co.uk/Persian*.

323. "Zendanian siasi daar iran az hoghough yek zendani aaddi ham mahroom hastand," October 18, 2012, *melimazhabi.com*.

324. "Iran: Political prisoners denied visits, care," October 31, 2012, *hrw.org*.

325. "Iran: Sakharov prize winner and other detainees denied visits and medical care," October 31, 2012, *amnestyusa.org*.

6. Students: Vanguard of Struggles for Democracy

1. Misagh Parsa. *States, Ideologies, and Social Revolutions: A Comparative Analysis of Iran, Nicaragua, and the Philippines.* Cambridge: Cambridge University Press, 2000: 94.

2. In preparing this chapter, I interviewed the following student leaders and activists: Reza Mohajerinejad, Manouochehr Mohammad, Ali Afshari, Akbar Atri, Rouzbeh Farahanipour, Hadi Kahal-zadeh, Amir Hussein Mahdavi, and Hamid Alizadeh.

3. Parsa 2000: 97.

4. Khomeini 1983a, 1: 434–437.

5. Khomeini 1983a, 7: 58.

6. Khomeini 1991, 7: 288–290.

7. James Dorsey, "Power struggle in Iran becomes more intense," December 19, 1980, *Christian Science Monitor*.

8. "Ashnaie ba tarikhcheh showraye aali enghelab farhangi," August 8, 2008, *hamshahrionline.ir*.

9. Ibid.

10. "Silenced, expelled, imprisoned: Repression of students and academics in Iran," 2014, *amnestyusa.org.*

11. Shaul Bakhash. *The Reign of the Ayatollahs: Iran and the Islamic Revolution.* New York: Basic Books, 1984: 112.

12. "Asami va moshakasat bakhshi az shohadaye enghelab novin iran," September 6, 1985, *Mojahed* #219.

13. "Ashnaie ba tarikhcheh showraye aali enghelab farhangi," August 8, 2008, *hamshahrionline.ir.*

14. Nader Habibi. "Allocation of Educational and Occupational Opportunities in the Islamic Republic of Iran: A Case Study in the Political Screening of Human Capital." *Iranian Studies* (1989): 31.

15. Ali Akbar Mahdi. "The student movement in the Islamic Republic of Iran." *Journal of Iranian Research and Analysis* 15 (1999): 5–32.

16. Habibi 1989: 19, 27.

17. Muhammad Sahimi, "The chain murders," December 14, 2009, *pbs.org.*

18. "Khorouje Salaneh 150 miliard dolar az keshvar be mohajerat," August 21, 2014, *sharghdaily.com.*

19. Mahdi 1999: 5.

20. "Iranian cleric alarmed by youth role in unrest," July 28, 1999, *Reuters.*

21. "Drugs and prostitution soar in Iran," July 6, 2000, *bbc.com.*

22. "Iranian youth shun religion, prayers after entering school," December 31, 2000, *irna.ir.*

23. Mahdi 1999: 14.

24. "Chera taadad faregh ottahsilan bikar bala ast," November 3, 2013, *eghtesadonline.com.*

25. Mahdi 1999: 11.

26. "Vaghti hashemi dar triboon namaz jomeh be daneshjooyan hamleh kard," May 20, 2013, *mobareze.ir.*

27. Ibid.

28. Akbar Atri, personal interview, November 24, 2015.

29. Ali Afshari, "Sayre tahavolate daftare tahkim vahdat," *aliafshari.com.*

30. Mahdi 1999: 12.

31. Personal interview with Ali Afshari, one of the prominent leaders of the OCU, October 12, 2007, and November 23, 2015.

32. Manuchehr Mohammadi, personal interview, February 2007 and November 24, 2015.

33. Mohjerinejad, personal communication, February 2001.

34. Ibid.

35. The organizations included: Union of the Islamic Associations of University Students and Alumni, National Union of Students and Alumni of Iran, Islamic Union of Free Islamic University, National Organization of Students and Alumni of Iran, Organization of Student Defenders of Freedom, Organization of the Intellectual Muslim Students and Alumni, and Student Center for Defense of Political Prisoners.

36. "Powerful Islamic association calls for free speech guarantees," December 1, 1996, *Associated Press.*

37. Val Mohadam. "The Student Protest and the Social Movement for Reform in Iran: Sociological Reflections." *Journal of Iranian Research and Analysis* 15 (2), 1999: 97–105.

38. "Office of Iranian student group vandalized, director beaten," November 15, 1997, *Agence France-Presse.*

39. Robin Wright, "Youth again in the vanguard, students are still the cutting edge of revolution, but now they want democracy," August 9, 1998, *Toronto Star.*

40. "Several injured as fundamentalists attack pro-Khatami students," May 25, 1998, *afp.com.*

41. "Yek mamlekat, yek dowlat, aan ham be raaye mellat," March 18, 1998, *Kar.*

42. Wright, August 9, 1998, *Toronto Star.*

43. "Hezarn nafar dar marasem salgard dar gozasht doctor mosaddegh sherkat kardand," March 18, 1998, *Kar.*

44. "Iranian students stage protest against beatings," February 14, 1999, *Associated Press.*

45. "Freed Tehran mayor denies allegations of corruption," April 17, 1998, *latimes.com.*

46. "Hundreds of Iranian students rally in Tehran," March 7, 1999, *Agence France-Presse.*

47. Heshmatollahollah Tabarzadi, personal interview, January 10, 2016.

48. Mahdi 1999: 15.

49. Mahdi 1999: 18.

50. "Conservative Iranian students want moderate minister impeached," March 9, 1998, *Agence France-Presse.*

51. Mahdi 1999: 15–16.

52. "Director of Iranian paper arrested," June 19, 1999, *Agence France-Presse.*

53. "Fear for safety/torture," November 18, 1999, *amnesty.org.*

54. "Iranian students stage protest against beatings," February 14, 1999, *Associated Press.*

55. "Rooznameh salaam va kooye daneshgah Tehran," July 9, 2014, *shafaf.ir.*

56. Elaine Sciolino, "Iran protests spread to 18 cities; police crack down at university," July 13, 1999, *nytimes.com.*

57. "Shot protestor prosecuted and convicted after his death: Ezzatollah Ebrahimnejad," July 22, 2001, *iranrights.org.*

58. Geneive Abdo, "Tehran police on trial over student," February 29, 2000, *theguardian.com.*

59. Afshin Valinejad, "Students narrate beatings in landmark trial of ex-police chief," February 29, 2000, *Associated Press.*

60. Abdo, February 29, 2000, *theguardian.com.*

61. "Fajeah daneshgah dar tarazooye ghanoon," July 20, *Payam-e Hajar.*

62. Sciolino, July 13, 1999, *nytimes.com.*

63. "Iranian leaders vow to end protest," July 12, 1999, *Bath Chronicle.*

64. "One shot dead in student protests in Tabriz," July 12, 1999, *Agence France-Presse.*

65. "Iranian students tell of shootings, savage beatings in provinces," August 3, 1999, *Agence France-Presse.*

66. Geneive Abdo, "Iranian police fire on protestors," July 14, 1999, *The Guardian.*
67. July 13, 1999, *irna.ir.*
68. Douglas Jehl, "Despite police dismissals, Iran protest is angriest yet," July 12, 1999, *nytimes.com.*
69. Robin Wright, "Fertile times for revolt," July 21, 1999, *Sydney Morning Herald (Australia).*
70. Charles Kurzman. "Student Protests and Stability of Gridlok in Khatami Iran." *Journal of Iranian Research and Analysis* 15 (1999): 76–82, 79.
71. Kurzman 1999: 79.
72. Ibid.
73. Ibid.
74. "Showraye shahr Tehran hadeseh kooye daneshgah ra mahkoom kard," July 11, 1999, *Neshat.*
75. Ibid.
76. Behzad Yaghmaian. *Social Change in Iran: An Eyewitness Account of Dissent, Defiance, and New Movements for Rights.* Albany: State University of New York Press, 2002: 40.
77. "Gozaresh vizheh az dar giri haye khoonin dar khabgah daneshgah tehran," July 10, 1999, *Neshat.*
78. "Baz khani fajeaheh kooye daneshgah va naa arami haye khiabani pas az aan," June 7, 2012, *kaleme.com.*
79. "Baz khani fajeahe kooye daneshgah va naa arami haye khiabani pas az aan," June 7, 2012, *kaleme.com.*
80. "Fajeah daneshgah dar tarazooye ghanoon," July 20, 1999, *Payam-e Hajar.*
81. "Gozaresh chahromin rooze naa arami dar kooye daneshgah Tehran," July 12, 1999, *Neshat.*
82. "Gozaresh Ekhtesasi khordad az tajammoa eateraz amiz dar koye daneshgah," July 12, 1999, *Khordad.*
83. Ibid.
84. Ibid.
85. Jehl, July 12, 1999, *nytimes.com.*
86. "Gozaresh chahromin . . . ," July 12, 1999, *Neshat.*
87. "Gozaresh Ekhtesasi . . . ," July 12, 1999, *Khordad.*
88. "Aazaye heyat modireh daneshgah Tehran tahdid be estefa kardand," July 11, 1999, *Neshat.*
89. Ibid.
90. "Mehdi Karroubi: hemayat konandegn va tahrik konandegan gorouh haye feshar bayad shenasaie shavand," July 12, 1999, *Khordad.*
91. "Gozaresh chahromin . . . ," July 12, 1999, *Neshat.*
92. "Fajeah daneshgah dar tarazooye ghanoon," July 20, *Payam-e Hajar.*
93. Ibid.
94. "Tashahkkolha, ahzab, gorouh haye daneshjooie va shaksiat haye siasi, hamleh be daneshgah ra mahkoom kardand," July 12, 1999, *Neshat.*
95. The organizations included: Association of Combatant Clergy, Office of Consolidation Unity, Islamic Iran Participation Front Party, Servants of

Construction Party, Association of Forces Following the Imam's Path, Organization of the Mojahedeen of Islamic Revolution, Association of Qom Seminary Instructors and Researchers, Labor House, Islamic Labor Party, Islamic Association of Iranian Teachers, Islamic Association of University Lecturers, Islamic Association of Iran's Medical Community, Islamic Association of Iranian Engineers, Association of the Periodic Representatives of the Majles, and Islamic Association of Graduates from the Indian Subcontinent.

96. "Rooz nameh negaran iran pas farda ghalam ha ra zamin migozarand," July 12, 1999, *Neshat.*

97. "Fajeah daneshgah dar tarazooye ghanoon," July 20, 1999, *Payam-e Hajar.*

98. Jonathan Lyons, "Iran pro-democracy students left isolated," July 14, 1999, *Reuters.*

99. Geneive Abdo, "Khatami abandons student protesters, Iran's pro-democracy activists left stunned, confused as president sides with hard-liners," July 15, 1999, *Globe and Mail* (Canada).

100. Elaine Sciolino, "Chaotic protests reign in Tehran; vigilantes active," July 14, 1999, *nytimes.com.*

101. Cyrus Bina. "The hot summer of defiance: Student protests in Iran." *Journal of Iranian Research and Analysis* 15 (1999): 47–60, 53.

102. Jonathan Lyons, "Students defiant against hardliners," July 14, 1999, *Courier Mail* (Queensland, Australia).

103. "Fanatics help security forces crush Tehran street protests," July 14, 1999, *Daily Mail* (London).

104. Sciolino, "Chaotic protests reign," July 14, 1999, *nytimes.com.*

105. "Fajeah daneshgah dar tarazooye ghanoon," July 20 .*Payam-e Hajar.*

106. "Angry Iranian students lash out at Khatami," July 15, 1999, *afp.com.*

107. Elaine Sciolino, "Iran protests spread to 18 cities; police crack down at university," July 14, 1999, *nytimes.com.*

108. "Khamenei orders clampdown, hundreds of thousands attend rally," July 14, 1999, *Agence France-Presse.*

109. Jonathan Lyons, "Supreme leader says U.S. sought new coup in Iran," July 30, 1999, *Reuters.*

110. Sciolino, "Iran protests spread to 18 cities," July 14, 1999, *nytimes.com.*

111. "Khatami vows to put down student protests in Iran," July 13, 1999, *Agence France-Presse.*

112. "Khamenei orders clampdown, hundreds of thousands attend rally," July 14, 1999, *Agence France-Presse.*

113. Niles Latham, "Iran threatens dissidents with death," July 15, 1999, *nypost.com.*

114. Ibid.

115. "Intelligence ministry calls on Iranians to turn in protestors," July 15, 1999, *afp.com.*

116. Abdo, July 15, 1999, *Globe and Mail* (Canada).

117. "Iran arrests an alleged leader of protests," July 18, 1999, *Associated Press.*

118. Ibid.

119. Fereshteh Ghazi, "Panzdahomin salgard hamleh be kooye daneshgah," July 10, 2014, *liga-iran.de/fa.*

120. "Madare saied zinali: masoolan ghol dadeh and pas az 14 sal sar nevesht pesaram ra be man begooyand," July 9, 2013, *bbc.com/Persian.*

121. "14 sal bi khabari az saeed zinali," October 29, 2012, *kaleme.com.*

122. "Iran arrests leading pro-reform lawyers," June 28, 2000, *Agence France-Presse.*

123. Personal communication with Roozbeh Farahanipour, November 22, 2015.

124. "Student on death row claims he was tortured," March 1, 2000, *Agence France-Presse.*

125. "Iranian dies after hunger strike," July 31, 2006, *bbc.com.*

126. Scott Shane and Michael R. Gordon, "Dissident's tale of epic escape from Iran's vise," July 13, 2008, *nytimes.com.*

127. Ibid.

128. Dan De luce, "Kidnapped, jailed and beaten . . . over a bloodied T-shirt," April 3, 2004, *Observer.*

129. Shane and Gordon, July 13, 2008, *nytimes.com.*

130. Personal interview with Hamid Alizadeh, January 18, 2016.

131. Farzad Hamidi was involved in the secular student movement. Personal interview with Manouchehr Mohammadi, November 24, 2015.

132. "Entegahd yek faal daneshjooie dar hozoor rahbar jomhuri eslami," July 30, 2013, *hra-news.org.*

133. "Iranian injured in dormitory attack dies," July 31, 1999, *Reuters.*

134. "Gozaresh vizhe az dar giri haye khoonin dar khabgah daneshgah tehran," July 10, 1999, *Neshat.*

135. Jonathan Lyons, "Iran students say roots of unrest at home," July 20, 1999, *Reuters.*

136. Jonathan Lyons, "Fresh paint, plaster greets Iran's angry students," September 20, 1999, *Reuters.*

137. "Iran's reformers decry secret death sentences," September 13, 1999, *Reuters.*

138. "Iran court commutes death sentence for rioter," November 23, 1999, *Reuters.*

139. "Shot protestor prosecuted and convicted after his death: Ezzatollah Ebrahimnejad," July 22, 2001, *iranrights.org.*

140. "Baz khani vaghya 18 tir 1378," July 8, 2008, *asre.nou.net.*

141. "Iran court hands out jail terms to protesters," September 16, 1999, *Reuters.*

142. "Jailed Iran students begin hunger strike," January 12, 2000, *Reuters.*

143. "Student anger at police acquittal," July 11, 2000, *bbc.com.*

144. "MPs slam acquittal of suspected camp-raiders," July 18, 2001, *irna.ir.*

145. "Iran arrests 98 policemen for student hostel raid," August 11, 1999, *Reuters.*

146. "Student anger at police acquittal," July 11, 2000, *bbc.com.*

147. "15 reported acquitted of raid on hostels," July 16, 2001, *altimes.com.*

148. "MPs slam acquittal," July 18, 2001, *irna.ir.*

149. "Entegahd yek faal daneshjooie dar hozoor rahbar jomhuri eslami," July 30, 2013, *hra-news.org.*

150. "Reformist student leader arrested in Iran," December 17, 2000, *Agence France-Presse.*

151. Kaveh Ehsani, "Our letter to Khatami was a farewell," July 15, 2003, *merip.org.*

152. Nazila Fathi, "Radical left challenging authority in Iran," January 7, 2008, *nytimes.com.*

153. "Tehran protesters call for Khamenei's head," June 13, 2003, *theguardian.com.*

154. "Student protest turns into demonstration against hard-line clerics," June 10, 2003, *Associated Press.*

155. Neil MacFarquhar, "Students roil Iranian capital in 3rd night of protests," June 13, 2003, *nytimes.com.*

156. "Tehran protesters," June 13, 2003, *theguardian.com.*

157. Ehsani, July 15, 2003, *merip.org.*

158. Ali Akbar Dareini, "Protests subside in Tehran while authorities arrest anti-government activists," June 15, 2003, *Associated Press.*

159. "Some 166 Iranian MPs voice outrage at the brutal treatment of students," June 22, 2003, *payvand.com.*

160. "Roundup: MPs state Tehran sit-in to protest detention of students," June 28, 2003, *Deutsche Presse-Agentur.*

161. MacFarquhar, June 13, 2003, *nytimes.com.*

162. "Iran to try next week some of those detainees in recent unrest," June 29, 2003, *payvand.com.*

163. Ibid.

164. Ibid.

165. "Cleric urges death for protester," June 20, 2003, *bbc.com.*

166. "State prosecutor orders release of Iranian student leaders," August 6, 2003, *Agence France-Presse.*

167. Dan De Luce, "Student protesters warn leaders to allow free speech or risk confrontation," June 30, 2003, *theguardian.com.*

168. "Tazahorat bozorg daneshjooyan ba shoar azadi va barabari bar gozar shod," December 6, 2006, *akhbar-rooz.com.*

7. The Rise and Demise of the Green Movement

1. Michael Slackman, "Hard-line force extends grip over a splintered Iran," July 21, 2009, *nytimes.com.*

2. "Iran's Revolutionary Guard: Showing who's the boss," August 27, 2009, *economist.com.*

3. Neil MacFarquhar, "Ahmadinejad reaps benefits of stacking agencies with allies," June 25, 2009, *nytimes.com.*

4. "Koodeta dar iran! Khamenie: shekast ahmadi nejad shekast man ast," June 13, 2009, *gooya.com.*

5. "Tajzadeh: kesani bayad az mellat ozr bekhahand ke iran ra be in vaziat asfnak va var shekasteh keshandeh and," August 5, 2013, *kaleme.com.*

6. The thirty-five members of the central council could not endorse any candidates because none received the two-thirds majority needed for an endorsement. "Nategh: jameah rouhaniyat az kesi hemayat nekard," May 24, 2009, *fardanews.com*.

7. "Chera jameah rouhaniat mobarez az namzadi Mahmoud ahmadi nejad dar sal 88 hemayat kard?" August 23, 2015, *khabaonline.ir*.

8. "NAU launches proceedings on missing $1 b," March 4, 2009, *Iran Daily*.

9. "New role for web in Iranian politics," June 11, 2009, *Associated Press*.

10. Anna Johnson and Brian Murphy, "Iran presidential challenger's office attacked," June 12, 2009, *Associated Press*.

11. Robert Dreyfuss, "Not a revolution—yet," July 4, 2009, *Agence Global*.

12. Roger Cohen. "Iran: The Tragedy and the Future." *New York Review of Books* 56 (13), August 13, 2009.

13. "Matne kamel monazereh mousavi va ahmadi nejad," June 4, 2009, *aftabnews.ir*.

14. Ibid.

15. Ibid.

16. "Anti-Ahmadinejad human chain stretches across Tehran," June 8, 2009, *Associated Press*.

17. Robert F. Worth and Nazila Fathi, "Huge campaign rallies snarl Tehran," June 8, 2009, *nytimes.com*.

18. Philip Sherwell and Colin Freeman, "Iran's Revolutionary Guards cash in after a year of suppressing dissent," June 12, 2010, *telegraph.co.uk*.

19. "Poll results prompt Iran protests," June 14, 2009, *aljazeera.com*.

20. George Mcleod, "A feeling of revolution in the air," June 11, 2009, *theglobeandmail.com*.

21. Omid Memarian, "Iran: Ahmadinejad victory sparks protests and claim of fraud," June 13, 2009, *iran-press-service.com*.

22. Personal communication with Hadi Kahalzadeh, student activist, May 20, 2014.

23. Robert Dreyfus, "The nation: Iran's rigged election," June 15, 2009, *npr.org*.

24. "Hoshdar yek namayandeh majles dar bareh takhallofat entekhabati," April 27, 2013, *kaleme.com*.

25. "Owj giri bi tarafi entekhabati," April 12, 2013, *kaleme.com*.

26. "Hoshdar haye mousavi va karroubi be maghamat: ehtemal dekhalat haye sazman yafte be goosh mirasad," June 11, 2013, *kaleme.com*.

27. Anna Johnson and Brian Murphy, "Rivals in Iran vote issue competing victory claims," June 12, 2009, *Associated Press*.

28. "Mizan mosharekat dar 10 dowreh entekhabat riasat jomhuri cheghadr bood?" June 13, 2013, *khabaronline.ir*.

29. "Rivals both claim victory in Iran election," June 12, 2009, *Associated Press*.

30. Reza Shoja, "How the greens took on the reds on the streets of Tehran," June 12, 2009, *jpost.com*.

31. "Demanding to be counted," June 18, 2009, *economist.com*.

32. Personal interview, *New York Times* reporter Nazila Fathi, January 12, 2012.

33. Anna Johnson and Brian Murphy, "Iran presidential challenger's office attacked," June 12, 2009, *Associated Press.*
34. "Matne kamel nameh mir hossein mousavi be showraye negahban," June 23, 2009, *bbc.com/Persian.*
35. "Disputed Iran election prompts rioting," June 13, 2009, *cbsnews.com.*
36. Anna Johnson and Brian Murphy, "Iran's Ahmadinejad moves into big lead in election," June 12, 2009, *ap.org.*
37. Ali Akbar Dareini and Anna Johnson, "Tehran tense after disrupted election results," June 13, 2009, *ap.org.*
38. Parisa Hafezi and Zahra Hosseini, "Ahmadinejad leads Iran vote, challenger defiant," June 13, 2009, *reuters.com.*
39. Neil MacFarquhar, "In Iran, an iron cleric, now blinking," June 16, 2009, *nytimes.com.*
40. Roger Cohen, "Iran on a razor's edge," June 15, 2009, *nytimes.com.*
41. "Mousavi supporters protest Ahmadinejad's victory," June 13, 2009, *States News Service.*
42. Ian Black, "Ahmadinejad wins surprise Iran landslide victory," June 13, 2009, *theguardian.com.*
43. Corey Flintoff, "Ahmadinejad declared winner in Iran election," June 13, 2009, *npr.org.*
44. Robert Tait, "The dust revolution—how Mahmoud Ahmadinejad's jibe backfired," June 18, 2009, *theguardian.com.*
45. "Ahmadinejad wins Iran presidential election," June 13, 2009, *bbc.com /Persian.*
46. Omid Memarian, "Iran: Ahmadinejad victory sparks protests and claims of fraud," June 13, 2009, *iran-press-service.com.*
47. MacFarquhar, June 15, 2009, *nytimes.com.*
48. Ali Akbar Dareini and Anna Johnson, "Tehran tense after disrupted election results," June 13, 2009, *Associated Press.*
49. Robert F. Worth and Nazila Fathi, "Unrest deepens as critics are detained," June 14, 2009, *nytimes.com.*
50. "Tebghe nazar sanjie dowlat entekahbat be dowre dovvom keshideh mi shaved," November 22, 2009, *bbc.com/Persian.*
51. "Shakoori Raad: sadegh larijani ham be mousavi tabrik gofte bood," December 8, 2010, *bbc.com/Persian.*
52. "Nezamian haami rahbar, mottahm be mohandesi entekhabat," May 15, 2013, *dw.com/fa-ir.*
53. Al Akbar Darreini and Anna Johnson, "Iran declares win for Ahmadinejad in disputed vote," June 13, 2009, *Associated Press.*
54. "Eateraz gharb be sar koob tazahor konandegan, edameh naa arami," June 15, 2009, *bbc.com/Persian.*
55. Robert F. Worth and Nazila Fathi, "Protests flare in Tehran as opposition disputes vote," June 13, 2009, *nytimes.com.*
56. Nazila Fathi, "Iran's top leader dashes hopes for a compromise," June 17, 2009, *nytimes.com.*

57. "Daftar tahim vahdat: haft daneshjoo koshteh shodeh and," June 17, 2009, *bbc.com/Persian.*
58. "Enteshar asami 112 tan az janbakhtegan havades baad az entekhabat," June 12, 2012, *rahesabz.net.*
59. Nazila Fathi, "Dispatches from an Unfinished Uprising: The Role of Technology in the 2009 Iranian Protest Movement," Harvard University, Joan Shorenstein Center, Discussion Paper Series D-75, 2012: 10.
60. Nazila Fathi, June 19, 2009, *nytimes.com.*
61. Robert Fisk, "Iran's day of destiny," June 16, 2009, *independent.co.uk.*
62. Ibid.
63. Robert Tait, June 18, 2009, *theguardian.com.*
64. "Wave of sit-ins at universities," June 23, 2009, *roozonline.com.*
65. Saman Rasoulpour, "Students beaten with daggers and machetes," June 18, 2009, *roozonline.com.*
66. Ibid.
67. "Wave of sit-ins," June 23, 2009, *roozonline.com.*
68. "Gozaresh hamle be amval omoomi va daneshjooyan dar majles matrah shod," June 17, 2009, *bbc.com/Persian.*
69. Saeed Kamali Dehgan, George Mcleod, and Ian Black, "Iran in turmoil: Supreme leader to speak out as silent, angry protests continue," June 19, 2009, *theguardian.com.*
70. "Shots fired at huge Iran protest," June 15, 2009, *bbc.com.*
71. Catherine Miller, "Suspicions behind Iran poll doubts," June 20, 2009, *bbc.com.*
72. Nazila Fathi, "Iran agrees to partial recount of disputed ballots," June 17, 2009, *nytimes.com.*
73. Bill Keller and Michael Slackman, "Leader emerges with stronger hand," June 14, 2009, *nytimes.com.*
74. Nazila Fathi and Sharon Otterman, "Iranian police clash with protesters," June 21, 2009, *nytimes.com.*
75. "Ozve showraye ngahban: etteham taghallob dar entekhaba 88 tohmat bozorg be nezam bood," January 2, 2015, *irna.ir.*
76. Robin Wright, "The evolution of Iran's revolution," June 21, 2009, *latimes.com.*
77. "Mousavi tells protesters to mourn for clash victims," June 18, 2009, *Associated Press.*
78. Neil MacFarquhar, "Shadowy Iranian vigilantes vow bolder action," June 18, 2009, *nytimes.com.*
79. Ian Black, Robert Tait, and Mark Tran, "Iran protests: Regime crack down on opposition as further unrest looms," June 17, 2009, *theguardian.com.*
80. "Iran prosecutor warns of death penalty for violence," June 18, 2009, *reuters.com.*
81. "West seeks Iran disintegration," June 22, 2009, *bbc.com.*
82. Farnaz Fassihi, "Inside the Iranian crackdown," July 11, 2009, *wsj.com.*
83. Ibid.
84. Ibid.

85. Tait, June 18, 2009, *theguardian.com.*
86. Nazila Fathi and Alan Cowell, "Protesters gather again, as Iran panel offers talks," June 19, 2009, *nytimes.com.*
87. Parisa Hafezi, "Thousands mourn Iranians killed in protests," June 18, 2009, *reuters.com.*
88. Nazila Fathi and Alan Cowell, "Ruling cleric warns Iranian protesters," June 20, 2009, *nytimes.com.*
89. Ibid.
90. "Dar sandoogh haye ray maaloom shaved ke mardom che mikhahand ne dar kaf khiaban ha," June 19, 2009, *leader.ir.*
91. "Letter from Tehran: With the Marchers," June 29, 2009, *newyorker.com.*
92. "Arrest of Rafsanjani kin show Iran clerics split," June 21, 2009, *Associated Press.*
93. "Iranian forces disperse protesters with batons, tear gas," July 10, 2009, *cnn.com.*
94. Iasson Athanasiads, "In shift, Iran's protesters demand new republic," July 31, 2009, *csmonitor.com.*
95. "Bayanieh shomareh panj mir hossein mousavi," June 20, 2009, *kaleme.com.*
96. Nazila Fathi and Michael Slackman, "Tehran tense after clashes that killed at least 13," June 22, 2009, *nytimes.com.*
97. "Moaven vazir kharjeh: dar jaryan eaterazat 88 ta 100 hezar nafar iran rat ark kardand," December 29, 2013, *dw.com/fa-ir.*
98. Damien McElroy, "Money floods out of Iran as election crisis continues," June 25, 2009, *telegraph.co.uk.*
99. Michael Slackman, "Iran Council certifies disputed election results," June 30, 2009, *nytimes.com.*
100. "Arrests of Rafsanjani Kin," June 21, 2009, *Associated Press.*
101. Ibid.
102. Fathi and Otterman, June 21, 2009, *nytimes.com.*
103. "Iran: Events of 2009," World-Report/2010, *hrw.org.*
104. "Arrests of Rafsanjani Kin," June 21, 2009, *Associated Press.*
105. Fathi and Otterman, June 21, 2009, *nytimes.com.*
106. "Anjoman senfi rooznameh negaran iran polomp shod," August 5, 2009, *roozonline.com.*
107. "Matne kamel ranjnameh hamzeh karami be dad setan kolle keshvar," August 24, 2011, *rahesabz.net.*
108. "Campaign to free bahman ahmadi amuee: spotlight on Iranian prisoners of conscience," May 3, 2011, *iranhumanrights.org.*
109. "See sal mahroumiyat az rouznameh nigari baraye yek rouznameh negar irani," October 26, 2010, *bbc.com/Persian.*
110. "Journalist behind bars since 2009 suffers heart attack in prison," February 27, 2015, *iranhumanrights.org.*
111. "Iran: Isa Saharkhiz imprisoned journalist," autumn 2011, *amnestyusa.org.*
112. "Iran election annulment ruled out," June 23, 2009, *bbc.com.*
113. Paris Hafezi and Fredrik Dahl, "Iran Guards threaten crackdown," June 22, 2009, *reuters.com.*

114. Borzou Dargahi, "Family, friends mourn Neda, Iranian woman who died on video," June 23, 2009, *latimes.com*.

115. Zahra Hosseinian and Fredrik Dahl, "Iran says courts will teach protesters lesson," June 23, 2009, *reuters.com*.

116. Nazila Fathi and Alan Cowell, "Fresh clashes in Tehran as cleric says Iran will not yield," June 25, 2009, *nytimes.com*.

117. Mark Tran and Robert Tait, "Police use teargas and fire weapon as Iran protests flare again," June 22, 2009, *theguardian.com*.

118. Parisa Hafezi, "Iranian cleric says rioters should be executed, June 26, 2009, *reuters.com*.

119. "Khanevadeh shahid hossein akhtar zand pas az do sal sekoot," June 11, 2011, *rahesabz.net*.

120. "Iran: Night raids terrorize civilians," June 26, 2009, *hrw.org*.

121. "Pansad hezar toman jarimeh bank allah akbar," July 26, 2009, *peykeiran .com*.

122. "Government pressure on Qom clerics," June 24, 2009, *roozonline.com*.

123. Robin Wright, "In Iran, a hostage-taker is now hostage," August 9, 2009, *washingtonpost.com*.

124. Nasser Karimi, "Iranian police use force at graveside rally," July 30, 2009, *Associated Press*.

125. Ben Child, "Jafar Panahi loses appeal against six-year prison sentence," October 18, 2011, *theguardian.com*.

126. Saeed Kamali Dehghan, "Iranian film-maker jailed for five years for collaborating with the BBC," June 18, 2014, *theguardian.com*.

127. Robert F. Worth and Sharon Otterman, "Details emerge on prison abuse after Iran vote," July 29, 2009, *nytimes.com*.

128. Robert F. Worth, "Reports of prison abuse and death anger Iranians," July 30, 2009, *nytimes.com*.

129. Robert F. Worth and Nazila Fathi, "Conspiracy trial for 100 dissidents begins in Iran," August 1, 2009, *nytimes.com*.

130. "Iran: Show trial exposes arbitrary detention," August 4, 2009, *hrw.org*.

131. "Detainee conditions will worsen if you speak up," August 4, 2009, *roozonline.com*.

132. "From protest to prison," June 12, 2010, *amnestyusa.org*.

133. "Agents at a loss," July 1, 2009, *roozonline.com*.

134. Michael Slackman, "Iran opposition leaders call for end to crackdown," July 8, 2009, *nytimes.com*.

135. Sharon Otterman, "Iranian opposition figure's brother in detention," July 24, 2009, *nytimes.com*.

136. "Banoo rabbani; hamrahi ke yarash ra tanha nagozasht," March 27, 2010, *rahesabz.net*.

137. Leila Tabari, "Dastooor hokoomat baraye baykot khabari karroubi va mousavi," September 13, 2009, *roozonline.com*.

138. "Iran: Open Tehran trial to international observers, Amnesty International challenges," August 11, 2009, *amnesty.org*.

139. Alan Cowell, "Detainees were raped in Iran prison, says reformist," August 11, 2009, *nytimes.com*.
140. "Atrocious rape of men and women in prisons," August 11, 2009, *roozonline.com*.
141. December 10, 2009, "Iran: Election contested, repression compounded," *amnesty.org*.
142. Lindsey Hilsum, "Iran militia man: I hope God forgives me," Channel 4 News, http://www.channel4.com/news/iran-militia-man-i-hope-god-forgives-me.
143. "Supreme leader admits to crimes in Kahrizak," August 28, 2009, *roozonline.com*.
144. "Baz dashtgah kahrizak be dastour rahbar moazam enghelab taatil shod," July 28, 2009, *mehrnews.com*.
145. Robert F. Worth, "Iran charges 12 at prison over death of protesters," December 20, 2009, *nytimes.com*.
146. Farnaz Fassihi, "The doctor who defied Tehran," December 19, 2009, *wsj.com*.
147. Ibid.
148. "Five year prison terms for Mohammad Davari and Mehdi Mahmoudian," May 18, 2010, *iranhumanrights.org*.
149. "Iran: Alarming spike in executions since disputed presidential election," August 7, 2009, *amnesty.org*.
150. Michael Slackman, "Iran's death penalty is seen as a political tactic," November 23, 2009, *nytimes.com*.
151. Nazila Fathi, "Iran executes Kurdish activist who was accused of armed struggle," November 11, 2009, *nytimes.com*.
152. "Iran: Unrest following Ehsan Fattahian's execution," November 20, 2009, *kurdishrights.org*.
153. Slackman, November 23, 2009, *nytimes.com*.
154. Mitra Shojaie, "Dou hokme eaadam taied shod," December 3, 2009, *dw.com/fa-ir*.
155. "Two death sentences overturned: Reza Khademi, 12 years, and Ayoub Porkar 20 years," April 11, 2010, *iranhumanrights.org*.
156. Brian Murphy, "Iran protesters put slogans on bank notes," January 13, 2010, *Associated Press*.
157. "Ahmadinejad faces test of strength as fresh protests sweep Iran," September 19, 2009, *timesonline.com*.
158. "Daftar mir hossein mousavi: mousavi dar marasem rooze ghods sherkat mikonad," September 16, 2009, *bbc.com/Persian*.
159. "Yek farmandeh sepah pasdaran; sabz ha dar rah peymaie rooz ghods Tehran 2 melion nafar boodand amma ya savki and ya mojahed khalgh," September 29, 2009, *rahesabz.net*.
160. "Hozoor gostardeh moatarezan dar rooz ghods dar iran," September 18, 2009, *bbc.com/Persian*.
161. "Ahmadinejad faces test of strength," September 19, 2009, *timesonline.com*.

162. "Ghodrat namaie melyouni jonbesh sabz koodeta garan ra shoke kard," September 19, 2009, *rahesabz.net.*

163. Bahar Yekta, "Baz tabe gostardeh eaterazat jomeh; rooze ghods," September 19, 2009, *rahesabz.net.*

164. "Hozoor gostardeh moatarezan dar rooz ghods dar iran," September 18, 2009, *bbc.com/Persian.*

165. "Daneshjooyani ke allah akbar goftand ehzar shodand," October 8, 2009, *tabnak.ir.*

166. Nazila Fathi, "Iranian journalists flee, fearing retribution for covering protests," October 13, 2009, *nytimes.com.*

167. "Arrests of journalists since disputed June election now top 100," November 5, 2009, *en.rsf.org.*

168. "Mamnouieyat estefadeh az poushesh sabz dar daneshgah allameh tabatabaie," October 15, 2009, *peykeiran.com.*

169. Ali Akbar Dareini, "Iran supreme leader: Questioning elections a crime," October 28, 2009, *Associated Press.*

170. "Eatesab ghazaye gostardeh daneshjooyan daneshkadeh fanni daneshgah Tehran dar eateraz be edamehe baz dasht mehrdad bozorg," November 30, 2009, *hra-news.net.*

171. "Shirin Ebadi Noble Peace Prize medal seized by Iran," November 27, 2009, *bbc.com.*

172. Robert F. Worth, "Dissidents mass in Tehran to subvert an anti-U.S. rally," November 5, 2009, *nytimes.com.*

173. "Sabt dast kam 400 mored baz dasht shodeh rooz 13 aban dar zendan evin," November 6, 2009, *hra-news.net.*

174. "Baa youresh maamoorin vezarat ettelaat yeki digar az bazarian Tehran dastgir shod," December 1, 2009, *peykeiran.com.*

175. "Students Day protests sweep campuses across Iran," December 8, 2009, *pbs.org.*

176. "Ostadan daneshgah beheshti be jama daneshjooyan moatarez peyvastand," December 8, 2009, *peykeiran.com.*

177. Massoumeh Torfeh, "Protests expose Iranian regime's frailty," December 8, 2009, *theguardian.com.*

178. Tara Mahtafar, "New slogans chanted in Student's Day protests," December 8, 2009, *pbs.org.*

179. Nazila Fathi, "Iranian student protesters clash with police," December 7, 2009, *nytimes.com.*

180. Ali Akbar Daeini, "Burned ayatollah photo sparks new Iranian protest," December 13, 2009, *Associated Press.*

181. "Students Day Protests," December 8, 2009, *pbs.org.*

182. Robert F. Worth, "Violent protests in Iran carry into second day," December 9, 2009, *nytimes.com.*

183. "Dar giri dar daneshgah bou ali hamedan," December 7, 2009, *fararu.com.*

184. Torfeh, December 8, 2009, *theguardian.com.*

185. "Nameh sar goshadeh asatid daneshgah fanni tehran be rahbar jomhuri eslami," January 4, 2010, *rahesabz.net.*

186. Al Akbar Darreini, "Tehran professors denounce violence on protesters," January 4, 2010, *Associated Press.*

187. "Teadadi az shoar haye mardom dar ghom," December 21, 2009, *peykeiran .com.*

188. Ibid.

189. Ramin Mostaghim and Borzou Dargahi, "Iran protests spread in heartland," December 24, 2009, *latimes.com.*

190. Nazila Fathi, "Clashes with Police reported in Iran," December 23, 2009, *nytimes.com.*

191. "Free food and tear gas," December 28, 2009, *slate.com.*

192. "Dar rooz 9 dey che gozasht," December 30, 2013, *mashreghnews.ir.*

193. "Taied koshteh shodan 5 nafar az souye nirouhay entezami," December 27, 2009, *dw.com/fa-ir.*

194. "Nemooneie az shoarha va video haye mardom dar tazahorat ashuraye 1388 tehran," January 1, 2010, *shirin.mit.edu.*

195. "Nirouhaye nezami dar barkhi az mayadin markazi tehran mostaghar shodand," December 31, 2009, *peykeiran.com.*

196. "Nirouye entezami: khahar zadeh mir hossein mousavi terror shodeh ast," December 30, 2009, *radiofarda.com.*

197. Fereshteh Ghazi, "Khoon farzandan ma mi jooshad," December 14, 2010, *roozonline.com.*

198. Masih Alinejad, "Baa mashin az rouye shahram faraj zadeh rad shodand," February 27, 2013, *radiofarda.com.*

199. "Eateraf ahmadi moghaddam pas az chahr sal," September 3, 2013, *kaleme.com.*

200. "Sister of Nobel laureate Shirin Ebadi arrested in Iran," December 29, 2009, *bbc.com.*

201. "Iranian teacher Abdolreza Ghanbari saved from execution," August 6, 2013, *ei-ie.org.*

202. "Family unfairly sentenced to death," April 20, 2010, *iranhumanrights.org.*

203. Leila Tabar, "Dar giri Hokoomat ba aza daran dar sar ta sar keshvar," December 28, 2009, *roozonline.com.*

204. "Ashura ye 88: jan haye setadeh shodeh va hagh haye gerefteh ne shodeh," December 6, 2011, *dw.com/fa-ir.*

205. "Bazdasht bish az 400 nafar dar Esfahan," December 29, 2009, *rahesabz .net.*

206. "Azadi pesar jalal eddin taheri va bradar abdollah nouri," January 8, 2010, *bbc.com/Persian.*

207. "Ayat ollah bayat zanjani: asle velayat faghieh ne az osool din ast va ne enkarash kofr avar," January 13, 2010, *rahesabz.net.*

208. "Hamleh be dafater ayat ollah saanei va ayat ollah dastgheib," December 30, 2009, *radiofarda.com.*

209. "Chera moddaian velayat dar masjed ayat ollah dastgheib ghoran ra be atesh keshidand," May 14, 2014, *kaleme.com.*

210. "Hamleh be dafater ayat ollah saanei va ayat ollah dastgheib," December 30, 2009, *radiofarda.com.*

211. "Showraye negahban hatk hormat ashura ra mahkoom kard," December 28, 2009, *mehrnews.com*.

212. "Alam olhoda: yek mosht goosaleh boz ghaleh ba velayat mokhalefat mikonand," December 30, 2009, *peykeiran.com*.

213. "Hoshdar vezarat ettelaat va ghovveh ghazaieh iran be moatarezan," December 31, 2009, *bbc.com/Persian*.

214. Massoumeh Torfeh, "Iran's judiciary takes a military colour," January 8, 2010, *theguardian.com*.

215. "Dastour dadeh iem polis hich modara nakonad," January 5, 2010, *radiozamaneh.com*.

216. Torfeh, January 8, 2010, *theguardian.com*.

217. Parisa Hafezi, "Opposition head Mousavi: Iran in serious crisis," January 1, 2010, *reuters.com*.

218. Torfeh, January 8, 2010, *theguardian.com*.

219. "How to assess political fissures in Iran," January 13, 2010, *washington institute.org*.

220. Robert F. Worth, "Iran arrests dissidents, sites report," December 28, 2009, *nytimes.com*.

221. Iason Athanasiadis," Iran uses Internet as tool against protesters," January 4, 2010, *csmonitor.com*.

222. "Pressure mounts to dissolve Daftar Tahkim Vahdat," February 18, 2010, *roozonline.com*.

223. "Az shabakeh almani ta fergheh bahaiyat; posht saheh havades rooz ashura," January 27, 2010, *mehrnew.com*.

224. Worth, December 28, 2009, *nytimes.com*.

225. "Karroubi: shah hormat ashura ra negah mi dasht," December 28, 2009, *hra-news.net*.

226. "Death sentences and executions 2009," 2010, *amnestyusa.org*.

227. "17 Kurdish citizens face death penalty in Iran," January 14, 2010, *sunni-news.com*.

228. Ibid.

229. Muhammad Sahimi, "Capital punishment, capital fear," May 12, 2010, *pbs.org*.

230. Nazila Fathi, "Iran, with opposition protests continuing, executes more prisoners," February 1, 2010, *nytimes.com*.

231. Ibid.

232. "Jannati: zaman raafat eslami nist," January 29, 2010, *aftabnews.ir*.

233. "Arash rahmanipour and mohammad reza ali zamani, eaadam shodand," January 28, 2010, *rahesabz.net*.

234. Ibid.

235. Martin Fletcher, "Iran Summons the Faithful," December 31, 2009, *The Times* (London).

236. Parisa Hafezi and Reza Derakhshi, "Iran opposition leaders face execution: Khamenei aide," December 29, 2009, *reuters.com*.

237. "Iran: Gunmen attack opposition leader Mehdi Karroubi's car," January 8, 2010, *telegraph.co.uk*.

238. Borzou Dargahi and Ramin Mostaghim, "Iran says nuclear scientist killed in bomb blast," January 12, 2010, *latimes.com*.

239. Mohammad Reza Zarifi Nia, "Rah doshvar azadi; morouri bar tarikh jonbesh sabz (bakhsh hashtom)," February 19, 2010, *rahsabz.net*.

240. "Ekhraj ostadi ke be tashyie jenazeh raft!" January 24, 2010, *kaleme.com*.

241. "Eateraz faranse be jelo giri az khorouj simin behbahani az iran," March 8, 2010, *bbc.com/Persian*.

242. "Vezarat ettelaat faaliat sithaye nehzat azadi ra mamooa kard," December 4, 2009, *bbc.com/Persian*.

243. Nazila Fathi, "Opposition hardens line inside Iran," February 2, 2010, *nytimes.com*.

244. Robert Tait and Noushin Hoseiny, "The Iranian revolution grinds to halt on the eve of its anniversary," February 6, 2010, *theguardian.com*.

245. "Afzayesh 31 dar sadi boodjeh nirouhaye nezami dar sal 89," January 29, 2010, *kaleme.com*.

246. Fereshteh Ghazi, "Hokoomatian dar hesar, madom dar khiaban," February 12, 2010, *roozonline.com*.

247. Michael Slackman, "Arrests by Iran are a bid to quell wide protests," February 9, 2010, *nytimes.com*.

248. Slackman, February 9, 2010, *nytimes.com*.

249. "Dastgiri saleh noghreh kar khahar zadeh Zahra rahnavard," February 9, 2010, *kaleme.com*.

250. "Student facing execution for throwing rock," February 8, 2010, *iran humanrights.org*.

251. "Dad setan tehran: valiant forsat darad be hokmash eateraz konad," March 7, 2010, *bbc.com/Persian*.

252. Fereshteh Ghazi, "Activists threatened: You will be arrested if you are in Tehran," February 8, 2010, *roozonline.com*.

253. "Hoshdar magham haye amniyati be mokhalefan," February 11, 2010, *radiofarda.com*.

254. "Iran issues warning on opposition Internet use," January 16, 2010, *bbc.com*.

255. Golnaz Esfandiari, "Iran touts nuclear advances amid reports of protests, arrests," February 11, 2010, *rferl.org*.

256. "Iran marks revolution with protest crackdown," February 11, 2010, *nbcnews.com*.

257. Robert F. Worth, "Opposition in Iran meets a crossroads on strategy," February 14, 2010, *nytimes.com*.

258. "Iran marks revolution," February 11, 2010, *nbcnews.com*.

259. Thomas Erdbink and William Branigan, "Pro-government rally, protests on anniversary of Iran's revolution," February 11, 2010, *washingtonpost.com*.

260. Ibid.

261. "Wife of Mehdi Karroubi addresses Ayatollah Khamenei about the torture of her son," February 14, 2010, *iranhumanrights.org*.

262. Erdbink and Branigan, February 11, 2010, *washingtonpost.com*.

263. Worth, February 14, 2010, *nytimes.com*.

264. Fereshteh Ghazi, "Hokoomatian dar hesar, mardom dar khiaban," February 12, 2010, *roozonline.com.*

265. "Didar aazaye majles khebregan ba rahbar enghelab," February 25, 2010, *farsi.khamenei.ir.*

266. Borzou Dargahi, "Iran's supreme leader demands support of clerics," October 30, 2010, *latimes.com.*

267. "Mohseni Ejeie: hokme enhelal mosharekat va mojahedin enghelab sader shodeh ast," September 27, 2010, *bbc.com/Persian.*

268. "Vazir oloom: anhaei ke dar fetne faal boodand, hagh voroud be daneshgah nadarand," April 10, 2012, *bbc.co.uk/Persian.*

269. "Vazir oloom: anhaeike dar fetne faal boodand, hagh voroud be daneshgah nadarand," April 10, 2012, *bbc.co.uk/Persian.*

270. "Edameh bela taklifi mitra aali," April 13, 2010, *dw.de/fa-ir.*

271. "Majd Tavakol pas az chehar sal zendan be morakhasi aamad," October 22, 2013, *bbc.com/Persian.*

272. "Iran should release imprisoned activist for urgent medical treatment," January 17, 2014, *iranhumanrights.org.*

273. "Jailed activist Hoda Saber dies on hunger strike," June 12, 2011, *bbc.com.*

274. "Gross negligence, rulers wanted him dead," June 16, 2011, *iranhuman rights.org.*

275. "Iran executions send a chilling message," March 30, 2010, *amnesty.org.*

276. Ahmed Shaheed (Special UN Rapporteur), "The Situation of Human Rights in the Islamic Republic of Iran." United Nations, General Assembly, 66th session, September 23, 2011, p. 19, *sheedoniran.org.*

277. Nazila Fathi, "Iran plans to execute 6 arrested in protests," March 15, 2010, *nytimes.com.*

278. "Dou zendani siasi va chahar mottaham jarayem jensi dar iran eadaam shodand," January 24, 2011, *bbc.co.uk/Persian.*

279. Mitra Shojaie, "Dastgiri panj vakil va mamnouiat mosahebe baraye vokala," November 14, 2010, *dw.com/fa-ir.*

280. "Lacking independence, bar association remains silent as lawyers are prosecuted," August 24, 2011, *iranhumanrights.org.*

281. William Young, "Iran sentences human rights lawyers to 11 years in jail," January 10, 2011, *nytimes.com.*

282. Saeed Kamali Dehghan, "Iranian lawyer Nasrin Sotoudeh has jail sentence reduced," September 14, 2011, *theguardian.com.*

283. Young, January 10, 2011, *nytimes.com.*

284. Saeed Kamali Dehghan, "Iran jails human rights lawyer for 11 years," January 10, 2011, *theguardian.com.*

285. "Abdolfattah Soltani: Imprisoned defender of human rights," *tavaana.org.*

286. "Soltani's wife sentenced for accepting human rights award on his behalf," October 7, 2013, *iranhumanrights.org.*

287. "Lawyer arrested based on revoked sentence," April 29, 2011, *iranhuman rights.org.*

288. "Prominent lawyer sentenced to eight years in prison and ten years ban on legal practice," July 4, 2011, *iranhumanrights.org.*

289. "Iranian human rights lawyer jailed for 13 years," June 13, 2012, *theguardian .com.*

290. "Jailed human rights defender awarded the Per Anger Prize," October 25, 2011, *civilrightsdefenders.org.*

291. "Narges mohammadi, faal houghough bashar baz dasht shod," May 5, 2015, *bbc.com/Persian.*

292. "Leading Iranian human rights activist to serve ten years in prison," May 19, 2016, iran*humanrights.org.*

293. Will Young and Michael Slackman, "Across Iran, anger lies behind face of calm," June 11, 2010, *nytimes.com.*

294. "Iran's war on fun," October 2, 2011, *rferf.org.*

295. "Naa gofte hayie az komiteh paygiri omoor asib didgan havades pas az entekhabat 88," September 8, 2011, *kaleme.com.*

296. William Young, "After killing at a bazaar, Iran declares 2 days off," July 12, 2010, *nytimes.com.*

297. "Iran's fashion victims," November 7, 2011, *wsj.com.*

298. "Hokme zendan maderi ke baraye pesar dar bandash mosahebe dad," December 22, 2011, *bbc.co.uk/Persian.*

299. "Mardom enghelab kardand ta monasebat padshahi hakem nabashad," February 11, 2013, *kaleme.com.*

300. "Tarh sarihe darkhast eaadame mousavi va karroubi," February 15, 2011, *bbc.co.uk/Persian.*

301. "Iran: Mr. Hossein Mousavi and Mehdi Karroubi arrested," February 28, 2011, *bbc.com.*

302. "Telefone shakhsi mir hossein ra ham mosadereh kardehand," November 13, 2013, *kaleme.com.*

303. "Ex-president Khatami banned from leaving Iran," April 16, 2010, *bbc.com.*

304. Robert F. Worth, "Iran mutes a chorus of voices for reform," April 19, 2010, *nytimes.com.*

305. "Ekhraj Mohsen mir damadi az daneshgah tehran," May 14, 2012, *rahesabz.net.*

306. "Mohsen Armin be shesh sal habs mahkoom shod," January 11, 2012, *hra-news.net.*

307. "Ebrahim yazdi be hasht sal zendan mahkoom shod," December 27, 2011, *bbc.co.uk/Persian.*

308. "Ahmad Sadr Haj Seyyed Javadi mamnoal khorooj shod," July 7, 2012, *bbc.com/Persian.*

309. "Mehdi Khazali dar baz dasht sekteh ghalbi kardeh ast," June 29, 2014, *bbc.com/Persian.*

310. "Soraj eddin mir damadi be shesh sal habs mahkoom shod," July 27, 2014, *bbc.co.uk/Persian.*

311. "Motahhari: baad az havades sale 88 lulu ie be nam fetne garan dorost kardehand," June 3, 2014, *namehnews.ir.*

312. "Motahhari: barkhi namayandegan osoulgara az eslah talaban majles sheshom khatar nak tarand," April 24, 2014, *isna.ir.*

313. "Mahmoud Beheshti Langeroudi eatesab ghaza kard," December 3, 2015, *bbc.com/Persian.*

314. "Nameh sar goshadeh bish az hezaro chahar sad tan az farhangian va faalan madani dar bareh moalleman dar band," December 7, 2015, *hra-news.org*.

315. "Iranian Teacher's Union leader sentenced to six years in prison," February 24, 2016, *iranhumanrights.org*.

316. "Eateraz be hokm sangin zendan baraye dabir kolle kanoon moalleman," February 27, 2016, *dw.com/fa-ir*.

317. "Mehdi mousavi va fatemeh ekhtesari be zendan toolani moddat va shallagh mahkoom shodand," October 12, 2015, *radiofarda.com*.

318. Nikki Mahjoub, "Sayeh baz dasht, zendan bar sar gorouhey az honar mandan irani," December 18, 2015, *bbc.com/Persian*.

319. Saeed Kamali Dehghan, "Iranian prisoners allegedly forced to run gauntlet of armed guards," April 22, 2014, *theguadian.com*.

320. "Evin prisoners at risk after report of riot," April 17, 2014, *amnesty.org*.

321. Rick Gladstone, "Iran disputes reports of violent crackdown in prison's political detainee block," April 21, 2014, *nytimes.com*.

322. Thomas Erdbrink, "Head of Tehran's cybercrimes unit is fired over death of blogger," December 1, 2012, *nytimes.com*.

323. "Shahadat nameh 41 zendani siasi band 350: sattar beheshti shekanje shodeh bood," November 10, 2012, *kaleme.com*.

324. "Pezeshki ghanooni vojud panj kaboodi ra dar jasad sattar beheshti taied kard," November 11, 2012, *bbc.com/Persian*.

325. "Pezeshk parvandeh sattar beheshti be shesh maah habs mahkoom shod," June 1, 2016, *bbc.com/Persian*.

326. "Osanloo's family calls for investigation into his prison death," June 26, 2013, *iranhumanrights.org*.

327. "Bar gozari konsert moosighi dar mashhad be dalil vojood haram emam reza shayesteh nist," February 27, 2014, *asriran.com*.

328. "Iran: Events of 2009," World-Report/2010, *hrw.org*.

329. Ibid.

330. "Death sentences and execution," March 2010, *amnesty.org*.

331. "Iran: Events of 2009," World-Report/2010, *hrw.org*.

8. Why the Movement Failed

1. In fact, Mohammad Reza Khatami, brother of the former president and a leading reformist, expressed the view of many reformists when he acknowledged that existing conditions increasingly needed reform, as everyone in the ruling circle and the opposition admitted that the situation was not desirable. He maintained, however, that reform movements could succeed gradually only through persistent work. "Therefore, we are not interested in revolution, because even if doable, the results after a few years or decades will be the same as now" *(Seyyed mohammad reza khatami: in system bedoon taghier dar siasat nemitavand edameh masir dahad)*. October 8, 2012, *kaleme.com*.

2. "Nahad riasat johuri dar jaryan ray giri ahmadi nejad ra pirouz entekhabat sal 88 moarafi kardeh bood," July 21, 2014, *digarban.com*.

3. "Rooz jome 22 khordad 1388 dar irna che gozasht," July 21, 2014, *facebook .com*. Jomeie's report of the events of election day were posted on his personal Facebook page, https://www.facebook.com/roohallah.jomeie/posts /769465143104335.

4. Muhammad Sahimi, "New evidence of fraud in 2009 election," August 11, 2010, *pbs.org*.

5. "Ma nemi gozashtim dovvom khordadi ha rouye kar biyayand," May 31, 2014, nurizad.info/blog/25179. Mohammad Nurizad posted the link of the video of Jaafari's speech on his website: http://nurizad.info/?p=25179. The speech was also posted at https://docs.google.com/file/d/0B-kdQ_db9ehNNl JUckppX1VIboE/edit?usp=drive_web (accessed May 31, 2014). The video can also be viewed on other websites, including http://www.peykeiran.com/Content .aspx?ID=76797 and http://www.kaleme.com/1393/03/11/klm-186448/.

6. "Darz video gofte haye farmandeh sepaah dar barehe entekhabat 88 be shabakeh haye ejtemaie," June 1, 2014, *bbc.com/Persian*.

7. "Rahbar iran: feneh sale 88 chalesh bozorgi bood," December 29, 2010, *bbc .co.uk/Persian*.

8. "Rahbar iran: moddaian taghallob dar entekhabat chera ozr khahi nemikonand," July 28, 2013, *bbc.co.uk/Persian*.

9. "Ravayat ali motahari dar mored defaa ayat ollah Khamenei az edameh hasr mousavi va karroubi," June 29, 2014, *bbc.com/Persian*.

10. "Farmandeh sepahe iran: basije daneshjoo ie montazer farman ma fough nabashad," October 2, 2009, *bbc.com/Persian*.

11. "Jannati: kenar raftan afrad hezb ollahi baraye keshvar moshkel iejad mikonad," March 3, 2014, *isna.ir*.

12. "Farmandeh Artesh: dar padgan ha aks saran fene nasb bood," December 5, 2010, *bbc.com/Persian*.

13. "Famandeh sepah: eaterazat pas az entekhabat 88 az jange aragh khatarnak tar bood," December 29, 2012, *bbc.com/Persian*.

14. "Farmandeh sepahe iran," October 2, 2009, *bbc.com/Persian*.

15. "Yek magham arshad sepah moddaie shod: dafa fetne 88 sakht tar az dafa tajavoz eragh bood," December 31, 2012, *rahesabz.net*.

16. "Behtarin hedieh emam be jahan eslam farman tashkil sepah bood," June 24, 2012, *irna.ir*.

17. Bahram Rafeie, "Sepah pasdaran; tanha gorouhie ke poshte rahbar mandeh," June 27, 2012, *roozonline.com*.

18. "Enteghad tond vali faghieh dar sepah az sekoot barkhi sardaran dar havades 88," July 16, 2012, *rahesabz.net*.

19. Ibid.

20. Bahram Rafeie, "Sepah pasdaran; tanha gorouhie ke poshte rahbar mandeh," June 27, 2012, *roozonline.com*.

21. Ibid.

22. Saeed Kamali Dehghan, "Ex-Revolutionary Guard general reveals dissent within elite Iranian force," July 12, 2012, *theguardian.com*.

23. "Marge nagahani yeki digar az sardarn sepah; dah farmandeh dowran jang dar kamtar az yek sal," May 17, 2012, *rahesabz.net*.

24. Hamid Reza Zarifi Nia, "Sekoot maana dar rahbari va marg haye zangireie sardaran sepah," March 4, 2012, *rahesabz.net*.
25. "Eshtebah saketeen fetneh nabayad tekrar shaved," May 3, 2014, *farsnews .com*.
26. "Times: boht zadeh az zendegan, bimnak az mordegan," December 31, 2009, *bbc.com/Persian*.
27. Nazila Fathi, "In Tehran, thousands rally to back government," December 30, 2009, *nytimes.com*.
28. "Times: boht zadeh az zendegan, bimnak az mordegan," December 31, 2009, *bbc.com/Persian*.
29. Jonatan Marcos, "Rabeteh dowlat haye khareji baa hokoomat iran pichideh tar mishavad," December 30, 2009, *bbc.com/Persian*.
30. "Daavat nameh baraye hozour ejbari dar rah paymaie khod josh," December 30, 2009, *rahesabz.net*.
31. Monavar Khalaj, "Iran responds with pro-government rallies," December 30, 2009, *FT.com*.
32. "Daavat hamegani be hozour mardom dar rahpeymaie 22 bahman," February 10, 2016, *khabaronline.ir*.
33. "Nameh Haeri shirazi be mousavi va karroubi," April 10, 2014, *isna.ir*.
34. "Ezharat pour mohammadi dar bareh shrout afve mousavi va karroubi," February 4, 2014, *isna.ir*.
35. "Amir Arjomand: agar inhaie ke sardar jaafari goft koodeta nist, pas chist," June 3, 2014, *kaleme.com*.
36. "Farzand mehdi karroubi: pedaram nazd khodayan zamini tobe nemikonad," February 5, 2014, *radiofarda.com*.
37. "Mohakemeh am konid ba hozour rasaneh ha," February 2, 2014, *melimazhabi.com*.
38. Najmeh Bozorgmehr, "Rivals unite to reject Iran's regime," July 1, 2009, *ft.com*.
39. Ali Akbar Dareini and Anna Johnson, "Tehran tense after disrupted election results," June 13, 2009, *ap.org*.
40. Behrouz Karouni, "Panj mah pas az entekhabat; shoar haye jadeed; tond tar az gozashteh," November 18, 2009, *radiofarda.com*.
41. Miguel Marquez, "Mousavi reportedly under house arrest," June 27, 2009, *abcnews.com*.
42. "Mahhaye khoon/gozaresh tafsily naghze hoghough bashar dar sayeh entekhabat dowreh dahom da iran," June 12, 2010, *hra-news.net*.
43. "Asami 112 koshteh shodeh pas az entekhabat 88," June 15, 2012, *iran-emrooz.net*.
44. Ibid.
45. "Iran: Escalating repression of university students," December 7, 2010, *hrw.org*.
46. Ibid.
47. Fereshteh Ghazi, "Mohsen Rahmani: baad az khordad 88 moatarez shodim," June 3, 2014, *roozonline.com*.
48. "Payman morovati, faal daneshjoyie ba shellik golouleh koshteh shod," January 9, 2016, *fa.rfi.fr*.

49. "Reshteh oloom ensani az sale ayandeh dar dabirestan haye dowlati tehran eraeh nakhahad shod," December 6, 2015, *bbc.com/Persian*.
50. "Bayanieh anjoman eslami daneshgah tehran va fehrest mahdoodiat haye 8 saleh," November 7, 2013, *kaleme.com*.
51. "Sar anjam daneshgah ahmadi nejad va payan bar khord haye ghah amiz," December 20, 2013, *isna.ir*.
52. "Didar Jamie az asatid daneshgah ba rahbar enghelab," July 2, 2014, *khamenei.ir*.
53. "Namayandeh majles iran: rahbar az vazir oloom khast daneshgah aram bashad," July 2, 2014, *bbc.com/Persian*.
54. Fathi 2012:17.
55. Roger Cohen, "Iran: The tragedy and the future," August 13, 2009, *nybooks.com*.
56. Negar Mottahedh, "Zanan, talaye daran jonbesh haye taghier gara dar se khizesh tarikhi iran," March 10, 2011, *bbc.com/Persian*.
57. Robert F. Worth, Sharon Otterman, and Allan Cowell, "Violence grips Tehran amid crackdown," June 15, 2009, *nytimes.com*.
58. Marin Fletcher, "Ahmadinejad faces test of strength as fresh protests sweep Iran," September 19, 2009, *timesonline.co.uk*.
59. Ibid.
60. "Bisto panj dar sad zanan zendani siasi ba hamsaraneshan dar habs hastand," September 18, 2012, *irangreenvoice.com*.
61. "Bayanat dar didar az banovan bar gozideh keshvar," April 19, 2014, *khamenei.ir*.
62. Hossein Bastani, "Afsaneh va vagheiyat dar mored mard posht pardeh dowlat ahmadi nejad," September 16, 2012, *bbc.co.om/Persian*.
63. "Iran's baby boom decree prompts fears for women's rights," May 30, 2014, *theguardian.com*.
64. Monavar Khalj, "Iranian female students face setback," November 14, 2012, *ft.com*.
65. "Bi edalati digar, 36 daneshgah paziresh dokhtaran ra dar 77 reshteh mamnooa kardand," August 7, 2012, *himt.ir*.
66. "Hazfe 11 hezaro pansad zarfiat paziresh zanan dar daneshgah ha dar dou sale akhir," August 30, 2014, *shahrwandan.ir*.
67. Niusha Saremi, "Taatili reshteh motaleaat zanan dar daneshgah Tehran," May 21, 2013, *roozonline.com*.
68. "Iestadegi zanan dar barabar talaash hakemiyat baraye hazfe aanan," September 2, 2014, *dw.com/fa-ir*.
69. "Dar aksar shahr haye iran hozoor zan dar konsert ha mamnoa shodeh ast," August 28, 2014, *rahesabz.net*.
70. "Vazir keshvar bayad az ommat shahid parvar ozr khahie konad," July 13, 1999, *Neshat*.
71. "Eslah talaban dar hale nabshe ghab khaneh ahzab sabegh hastand," March 4, 2014, *tansnim.com*.
72. "Vakenesh moatalefe be pishnehad hasr mousavi va karroubi," June 13, 2011, *bbc.com/Persian*.
73. "Iran's Wall Street: Whom does the bazaar back?" August 3, 2009, *time.com*.

74. Ibid.
75. "Baa youresh maamoorin vezarat ettelaat yeki digar az bazarian Tehran dastgir shod," December 1, 2009, *peykeiran.com.*
76. William Young, "After killing at a bazaar, Iran declares 2 days off," July 12, 2010, *nytimes.com.*
77. "Bazarian tehran moghazeh haye khod ra bastand," October 3, 2012, *bbc .com/Persian.*
78. "Iranian police clash with protesters over currency plunge," October 3, 2012, *reuters.com.*
79. "Gozaresh tafsili kaleme az tatili emrooz bazaar va rah paymaie va na arami pas az on," October 3, 2012, *kaleme.com.*
80. "Voroud amniyati ha va basij baraye taht feshar ghrar dadan bazarian be baz goshaie," October 4, 2012, *rahesabz.net.*
81. "Nahad haye kar gari hich gah be sheddat dowran ahmadi nejad mahdood neshodeh boodand," November 21, 2013, *ilna.ir.*
82. Ibid.
83. Mansour Osanloo, "Brazil should support the struggle of Iranian trade unionists," March 22, 2014, *iranhumanrights.org.*
84. "Negahdari mehdi shandeez dar miyan zendanian aaddi band 8 zendan evin," June 25, 2013, *kaleme.com.*
85. "Asami 112 koshteh shodeh pas az entekhabat 88," June 15, 2012, *iran -emrooz.net.*
86. "Iran: New arrests of labor activists," January 30, 2012, *hrw.org.*
87. Ibid.
88. Ibid.
89. "Imprisoned labor activist dies of stroke after being denied medical care," September 15, 2015, *iranhumanrights.org.*
90. Parsa, 1989: 57.

9. Irreconcilable Conflicts and Endless Repression

1. "Na jamea, na jomhuri eslami va na eslah talaban hich kodam dar vaza khordad 76 instand," September 27, 2012, *melimazhabi.com.*
2. "Ali Khamenei taghoot zaman ast," April 27, 2012, *melimazhabi.com.*
3. "Abolfazl ghadyani: aghaye sadegh larijani! mafased baz jooyan shoma rouye shekanjeh garan savak shah ra sefid kardeh ast," December 12, 2012, *kaleme.com.*
4. "Tajzadeh: dar iran be naame velayat va rouhaniyat entekhabat farmayeshi bar gozar mi shaved," September 30, 2012, *rahesabz.net.*
5. "Estebdad valayee bashad ya saltanati dar mahiyat tafavot chandani nemi konad," April 4, 2013, *melimazhabi.com.*
6. "Tajzadeh: kesani bayad az mellat ozr khahi bekhahand ke iran ra be in vaziayat asfnak va var shekaste keshandeh and," August 5, 2013, *kaleme.com.*
7. "Seyyed mostaf tajzadeh: ma hamiye zendeh baad mokhalef man khatami va doost dashtan mokhalef mousavi hastim," November 2, 2013, *kaleme.com.*

8. "Bish az shesh mah mahroumiat az molaghat ba pedar va madaar," December 7, 2013, *kaleme.com*.

9. "Hanouz omidvaram be apartheid siasi va ghazaie dar keshvar payan dahid," November 15, 2013, *rahesabz.net*.

10. "Hanouz omidvaram be apartheid siasi va ghazaie dar keshvar payan dahid," November 15, 2013, *rahesabz.net*.

11. "Payame dabir kolle jebhe mosharekat be monasebat chahar dahomin salgard taasis," December 5, 2012, *rahesabz.net*.

12. "Shoma va arbaban tan ta kay mi tavanid be aamal jenayat karaneh edame dahid," April 26, 2012, *melimazhabi.com*.

13. "Mohammad Maleki: khomeini faribeman dad," February 18, 2014, *ir.voanews.com*.

14. "On ghol ha koja va on vadeh ha che shod," April 29, 2014, *roozonline.com*.

15. "Enghelab amad ta in mardom bar sar neveshte shan hakem shavand," January 28, 2014, *noroaznews.org*.

16. "Khatami: pedar khandeh haye eslam motahajer va terrorist parvar mi goyand dare slam jomhuri nedarirm," March 31, 2014, *kaleme.com*.

17. "Mohammad khatami dar didar be daneshjooyan: fashist ha joz baraye khod, baraye kes digari azadi nemi khahand," July 5, 2013, *rahesabz.net*.

18. "Moaven avval raies jomhuri iran: mamnouiyat resaneh ei mohammad khatami be zoodi hal mi shaved," April 4, 2015, *bbc.com/Persian*.

19. "Nabayad eslam, enghelab, va emam mosadereh shaved," August 11, 2015, *jamaran.ir*.

20. "Namayandeh majles iran: rahbar az vazir oloom khast daneshgah aram bashad," July 2, 2014, *bbc.com/Persian*.

21. "Jonbesh daneshjoie arman haye jamea ra faryad konad," September 4, 2014, *jamaran.ir*.

22. "Seyyed ali khomeini: manzoor az hokoomat eslami, dowlat talebani nist," November 30, 2013, *kaleme.com*.

23. Ibid.

24. Christopher Hitchens, "Conversation with Khomeini: The ayatollah's grandson calls for a U.S. invasion of Iran," October 6, 2003, *slate.com*.

25. "Fatemeh Karroubi be hassan rouhani: dar rastaye sowgand tan, be rafter haye sourat gerafteh ba hamsaram rasidegi konid," October 19, 2013, *sahamnews.org*.

26. "Mehdi Kaaroubi: az zaman fowte emam hameh entekhabat ha mohandesi shode ast," May 15, 2014, *dw.de/farsi*.

27. "Hadi khamenei: natavanestim be ahdaf enghelab berasim," February 1, 2014, *dw.de/fa-ir*.

28. "Seyyed hadi khamenei: barkhi fekr mi konand ghodrat va heshmat anha baghi khahad mand," November 20, 2013, *rahesabz.net*.

29. "Seyyed hadi khameneie: Din hokumati nemikhahim," November 23, 2013, *isna.ir*.

30. "Aya olama be mardom naya mookhteh boodand ke sekoot har mosalman khiyanat ast be ghoran?" January 28, 2014, *kaleme.com*.

31. "9 nasihat seyyed hossein mir damadi be masoolan nezam; 11 towsieh be rahbari," May 26, 2014, *kaleme.com*.

32. "Daie rahbari: raftar zalemaneh bishtar be enghelab zarar mi zand ta amrika va esraiel," April 26, 2015, *kaleme.com*.

33. "Mohammad nourizad: be rasti agar dar sale 57 enghelab nemi kardim, aknoon dar kodam noghteh va dar koja istadeh boodim?" January 1, 2013, *rahesabz.net*.

34. "Booseh bar paye yek bahaie koochek," July 15, 2013, *nurizad.info*.

35. "Najes shemordan na mosalman va nejasat roubi az eslam," September 21, 2012, *ir.voa.com*.

36. "Fergheh zalleh mozelleh," August 1, 2013, *nurizad.info*.

37. Ibid.

38. "Motahari: dast kam be mousavi va karroubi forsat defaa be dahid," July 28, 2013, *bbc.com/Persian*.

39. "Shekayat az motahari be dalil enteghad az habs khanegi saran mokhalefan," July 6, 2014, *bbc.com/Persian*.

40. "Motahari: jannati khodash yek hafteh mesle karroubi va mousavi zendegi konad," November 23, 2013, *bbc.com/Persian*.

41. "Hasr, ahmadi nejad, osool garaie dar goft va gooye tafsili isna ba motahari," January 15, 2014, *isna.ir*.

42. "Va kenash motahari be moslehi dar bareh moharebeh be mir hossein va karroubi," November 22, 2013, *kaleme.com*.

43. "Motahari jannati ra be tars az mohakeme alani mousavi va karroubi motaham kard," November 23, 2013, *radiofarda.com*.

44. "Sepah paasdaran shabihe yek hezb siasi shodeh ast," March 16, 2014, *digarban.com*.

45. "Motahari: ravieh hazfe mokhalefin kar ghalati ast," June 27, 2014, *isna.ir*.

46. "Motahari: barkhi namayandegan osoulgara az eslah talaban majles sheshom khatar nak tarand," April 22, 2014, *isna.ir*.

47. "Motahari: baad az havades sale 88 lou lou ie be name fetne garan dorost kardand," June 3, 2014, *namehnews.ir*.

48. "Goft va gooye tafsili ba namayandeh Tehran dar majles motahari," November 2, 2013, *farsnews.com*.

49. "Sepah pasdaran shabih yek hezb siasi shodeh ast," March 16, 2014, *digarban .com*.

50. "Eslamiyat menhaye jomhuriat ghabel tahaghogh nist," March 29, 2014, *ilna.ir*.

51. "Goft va gooye tafsili ba namayandeh Tehran dar majles motahari," November 2, 2013, *farsnews.com*.

52. "Kashfe dastgah shenoud dar daftar ali motahari," July 14, 2013, *digarban .com*.

53. "Namayandeh majles: motahari ya amel em ay 6 ast ya taht tasir servis haye jasoosi," January 7, 2014, *radiofarda.com*.

54. "Ali motahari: ghovveh ghazaieh be donbal ejad raab baraye sayer montaghedan ast," January 5, 2014, *bbc.comPersian*.

55. "Namayandegan ziad shodeh boodand, az dastam kari bar nemi amad," January 11, 2015, *ilna.ir.*

56. "Bayanieh motahari dar eateraz be ettefaghat majles: movakkelin in afrad bedanand be che kesani ray dadeh and," January 13, 2015, *rahezabz.net.*

57. "Shiveh jaded obash, sokhanrani mamnooa; ali motahari ba sourat majrouh be tehran baz gasht," March 10, 2015, *sahamnews.org.*

58. "Bar gozari kongereh anjoman eslami moalleman; takid bar rafa hasr va ejraye bi tanazol ghanoon asasi," January 30, 2015, *kaleme.com.*

59. "Gharar nebood dar johuri eslami, dien baraye siasat haye ghalat hakeman hazineh shaved," February 11, 2015, *rahesabz.net.*

60. Bendix Anderson, "Aytollah watch," September 11, 2009, *pbs.org.*

61. "From condemning killings to secret meeting," June 30, 2009, *roozonline .com.*

62. Robert F. Worth, "Death of Iranian cleric could set off new protests," December 22, 2009, *nytimes.com.*

63. "Ayatollah saanei: mardom nebayad az ehghagh hoghough hagh khod na omid shavand," July 3, 2009, *bbc.com/Persian.*

64. "Ejraye ahkam ejtemaie va eghtesadi eslam menhaye mardom natijeh ash zolm va estebdad va bi dini ast," April 1, 2014, *saanei.org.*

65. "Senior cleric calls for apology to Iranian people," June 1, 2012, *radiozamaneh.com.*

66. Anderson, September 11, 2009, *pbs.org.*

67. "Did gah ayat ollah dastgheib dar bareh ezharat jannati dar bareh mousavi va karroubi: bayad towbeh va eadeh haysiat konad," November 30, 2013, *kaleme.com.*

68. "Bayanieh ayat ollah dastghaib; natijehe in salha taraj amval mardom, din zadegi javanan, bi khasiyat shodan majles, va ghovveh ghazaieh bood," February 6, 2014, *kaleme.com.*

69. "Nameh ayat ollah dastghaib be showraye negahban: nezarat estesvabi che natijeh ie joz khafe khan faragir va fesad haye gostardeh dasht," August 26, 2015, *kaleme.com.*

70. Anderson, September 11, 2009, *pbs.org.*

71. "Iranian cleric claims leadership of clergy open to referendum," April 1, 2010, *payvand.com.*

72. "Edehie shahrvand darejeh yek va dou dorost kardeh and," February 4, 2014, *ilna.ir.*

73. "Iran: Reformist Ayatollahs Bayat Zanjani and Saanei criticize the regime," October 20, 2009, *payvand.com.*

74. "Ayat ollah bayat: rahbaran dar hasr jonbesh sabz, fough oladdeh mazloom vaghea shodand," May 7, 2014, *rahesabz.net.*

75. "This election is invalid," July 2, 2009, *roozonline.com.*

76. Julian Borger, "Senior Iranian clerics reject re-election of Mahmoud Ahmadinejad," July 5, 2009, *theguardian.com.*

77. "Aghaliati ke hich taghieri ra tahamol nemi konad dam az fetneh mi zanad," December 14, 2013, *rahesabz.net.*

78. "Majmae rouhaniyoun khastar ebtal entekhabat va tajdid aun shod," June 13, 2009, *aftabnews.ir.*
79. "Majmea rouhaniyoun mobarez: raies jomhur ba jalb nazar rahbari, masaleh hasr ra be nahve asasi hal konad," January 31, 2015, *kaleme.com.*
80. "Rahbari goftand fetneh az yek markaz khas hedayat mi shaved ke aun ra nemi shenasim," December 31, 2013, *bbc.com/Persian.*
81. "Moslehi: fetneh 88 kodetaye bein ol melali dar bar andazi nezam jomhuri eslami iran," January 2, 2014, *isna.ir.*
82. "Jorm saran fetneh hezaran bar sangin tar az sareghan mosallah va mota-javezan be onf fast," January 4, 2014, *farsnews.com.*
83. "Bayanieh vezarat kharejeh amrika mozdour boodan mousavi va karroubi ra esbat kard," February 19, 2014, *farsnews.com.*
84. "Aref eslah talab shrour nist/eslah talaban mortad siasi hastand," January 10, 2015, *aryanews.com.*
85. "Entekhaba azad ramz amaliat bar andazi bood/hamian fetneh 88 salahiyat candida tori nadarand," May 4, 2013, *farsnews.com.*
86. "Senaryo ye mak farlan va ja neshini baad az emam," December 10, 2014, *farsnews.com.*
87. "Eaterazat naa bakhshoodani; mohri ke dagh shod," December 30, 2013, *bbc.com/Persian.*
88. "Mowje jaded hamelat magham haye iran be moaterazan 88 dar astaneh rooz 9 dey," December 26, 2013, *radiofarda.com.*
89. "Mardom be ma ejazeh nemidahand az mousavi va karroubi gozasht shaved," December 30, 2013, *radiofarda.com.*
90. "Jannati: mousavi va karroubi haser nistand ezhar nedamat konand," November 22, 2013, *bbc.com/Persian.*
91. "Hoshdar dar mored tashkil otagh fekr baraye rah andazi fetneh," December 26, 2013, *dw.com/f-ir.*
92. "Farmandeh gharar gah amar, mousavi va karoubi ra tehdid be ghatl dar sourat rafa hasr kard," November 20, 2013, *rahesabz.net.*
93. "Filter fays book ta zaman vojood masadigh mojremaneh edame darad," December 2, 2013, *mehrnews.com.*
94. "Mousavi va karroubi bayad eadam shavand," December 13, 2013, *digarban.com.*
95. December 23, 2013, *khabaronline.ir.*
96. "Saran fetneh mosed fel arz hastand," December 28, 2013, *mehrnews.ir.*
97. "Amadeh am mojri eadamam mousavi va karroubi shavam," December 27, 2013, *parsine.com.*
98. "Sepah har dasti ra ke aleyhe enghelab osyan konad, ghata mi konad," December 30, 2013, *farsnews.com.*
99. "Emam jomaeh mashhad: vozaraie ke khod ra payrov rahbar mi danand ba khatami didar nekonand," April 15, 2014, *bbc.com/Persian.*
100. "Mokhalefat ba hozur hassan khomeini be laghve yek hamayesh dar borou-jerd anjamid," May 5, 2014, *bbc.com /Persian.*
101. "Khishavandan emam hameh zed enghelab hastand," October 31, 2013, *digarba.com.*

102. Ibid.

103. "Mostafa pour mohammadi: agar mousavi va karroubi aramesh ra be ham nazanad afv mi shavand," February 4, 2014, *bbc.com/Persian.*

104. "Fetneh dar dast yek eddehie vasile ie baraye kaasebi shodeh ast," November 23, 2014, *farsnews.com.*

105. "Velayat keshvar ra az fetneh nejat dad/atash zir khaestar ast," December 29, 2013, *mehrnews.com.*

106. "Habibi: atash zir khakestar 88 hanouz baghi ast," June 12, 2014, *baharnews.ir.*

107. "Ahmad khatami: fetneh be dalil laj va laj bazi haye karroubi va mousvi az beyn narafteh ast," June 20, 2014, *radiofarda.com.*

108. "Bachchehaye hezb ollah va basiji hamchenan bidar bashand," July 27, 2014, *tnews.ir.*

109. "Javad larijani: fetneh 88 donbal hokoomat ghair dini bood," December 26, 2014, *tabnak.ir.*

110. "Didar raies jomhur va aazaye heyat dowlat ba rahbar enghelab," August 27, 2014, *khamenei.ir.*

111. "Eddehie ba enkar fetne moghabel nezam istadeh and," September 10, 2014, *sobhtoos.ir.*

112. "Namayandeh rahbari dar sepah: mashrouieyat nezam be raye mardom nist," September 3, 2012, *rahesabz.net.*

113. "Namayandeh rahbar dar sepah namad sabz moatarezan 88 ra be shetor ayesheh tashbih kard," December 27, 2013, *bbc.com/Persian.*

114. "Mardom naghshi dar mashrouieyat dadan be hokoomat nadarand," April 20, 2014, *digarban.com.*

115. "Dar feghhe shia be velayat sultan ham mi gooyand," January 5, 2013, *digarban.com.*

116. "Valiye faghih, mashrouieyat khod ra az mardom mi girad ya khoda?" July 19, 2009, *bbc.co/Persian.*

117. "Mesbah yazdi: nebayad donbal khaste aksariyat bood," August 4, 2013, *kaleme.com.*

118. "Dabir showraye negahban: hatta agar dar aghalliyat bashim bayad nezam ra hefz konim," December 24, 2013, *bbc.com/Persian.*

119. "Raye mardom mashrouiyat saz nist," September 26, 2013, *digarban.com.*

120. "Eshtebah saketeen fetneh nabayad tekrar shaved," May 3, 2014, *farsnews.com.*

121. Some theologians, including former cleric Hassan Yousefi Eshkevari (also a former member of the parliament) and Ayatollah Dr. Mohsen Kadivar, disagreed with such unprecedented claims. My personal communication with both theologians.

122. "Mohammad Golpaygani: ale saud be zoodi be ale soghoot tabdil mishavad," May 2, 2015, *tasnimnews.com.*

123. "Majles khebregan dar toole rahbari gharar dard na dar arz on," April 30, 2015, *mehrnews.com.*

124. "Velayate faghieh tajalli towhid ast," December 22, 2014, *farsnews.com.*

125. Mehran Mohammadi Fesharaki, "Velayate khoda ya sherk ye khoda?"

February 15, 2015, *rahesabz.net;* and "Namayandeh ayatollah Khamenei dar sepah: velayat faghieh haman velayate khodast," February 14, 2014, *iranianuk.com.*

126. "Velayat faghieh jelvehie az khodast," September 27, 2012, *snn.ir.*
127. "Towseahe diyanat va akhlagh eslami az vazayef hokoomat ast," August 19, 2015, *isna.ir.*
128. "Tardidi ndaram valiye faghih ra emam zaman entekhab mikonad," September 7, 2012, *melimazhabi.com.*
129. "Vali motlagh faghieh hich gah eshtebah nemi konad," July 10, 2011, *digarban.com.*
130. "Mokhalefat ba velayat faghih dar hadde sherk ast," April 18, 2013, *kaleme.com.*
131. "Ayat ollah mohammad yazdi: vali motlagh faghieh hich gah eshtebah nemi konad," July 11, 2011, *aftabnews.ir.*
132. "Ayat ollah nouri hamedani: shakki nist ke enghelab nezam velayie ast," August 6, 2010, *asriran.com.*
133. "Ali mesbah yazdi: mardom be vali faghieh be chashme rabbet beyne khod va khoda mi negarand," December 27, 2012, *isna.ir.*
134. "Khatami: valie faghieh tanha rahbar siasi nist balke nayeb emam zaman ast," April 26, 2012, *entekhab.ir.*
135. "Namayandeh rahbar iran dar sepah: hokm vali faghieh ham taraz ba hokm anbiyast," November 5, 2012, *bbc.com/Persian.*
136. "Takhallof az farman vali faghieh mokhalefat be farman khoda va emam zaman ast," April 27, 2011, *aftabnews.ir.*
137. "Velayat haman khodavadand ast va velayat madaran baa hooshmand," July 30, 2013, *digarban.com.*
138. "Movahhedi Kermani: showraye negahban be vazifeh ghanooni amal kard," May 24, 2013, *isna.ir.*
139. "Etaat az vali faghieh etaat az emam zaman ast," May 7, 2014, *tasnim.com.*
140. "Mohammadi golpaygani: koochek tarin bad bini be rahbari dar hamin donya oghoobat darad," January 19, 2013, *kaleme.com.*
141. "Ayat ollah mahdavi kani dar etaat az vali behtarin jaygah ra kasb kard," November 1, 2015, *mehrnews.com.*
142. "Yeki az dalael movafaghiyat rahbar enghelab ertebat bae mam zaman dar masjed jamkaran ast," May 19, 2016, *jamkaran.ir.*
143. Khomeini 1983a, 5: 4 and 15
144. "Islamic Republic of Iran Constitution," *iranonline.com/iranhall.*

Index